MW01295495

The Fishbowl Principle

BUILDING THE ARK FOR THE 21ST CENTURY

Bruce Gendelman
Robert Miller
David Taus

authorHOUSE®

AuthorHouse™
1663 Liberty Drive
Bloomington, IN 47403
www.authorhouse.com
Phone: 1-800-839-8640

First published by AuthorHouse 12/17/2009

ISBN: 978-1-4389-8639-5 (e)
ISBN: 978-1-4389-8637-1 (sc)
ISBN: 978-1-4389-8638-8 (hc)

Printed in the United States of America
Bloomington, Indiana

This book is printed on acid-free paper.

*For human beings who seek a
peaceful and sustainable future.*

Contents

Preface

There are imminent storms on the horizon. Economists tell us of worldwide financial distress, environmentalists focus on the impact of global climate change, politicians argue over the implementation of competing ideologies, and religious leaders fight hard to have their views accepted. All the while, great numbers of people are being driven further and further apart by divergent belief systems and disparate resource availability. And despite all the promise of a more tightly woven and interconnected global community, the technologies that are designed to bring us closer together end up leaving many feeling more isolated or alienated from one another. Indeed, we are at a pivotal point in human history, where our choices today will determine whether we accelerate toward cataclysm or a future that is both peaceful and sustainable, surely one we wish for our children and ourselves. We are increasingly aware that dramatic action is called for to avert those conditions that cause large-scale human suffering, but as a global society we nonetheless struggle to marshal the needed level of commitment and focus to properly prepare for those imminent storms. Why?

There are many theories, explanations, and opinions as to why humanity has landed in the sticky predicament we find ourselves in today. The understandings that many have adopted range from the comforting to the improbable, the benign to the extreme, and the rational to the downright dangerous. Arriving at an understanding, it seems, is not difficult. What is difficult is arriving at an understanding whose enactment will, in turn, promote a stable and sustainable future for Earth and we beings who inhabit it. It is the purpose of this book to illuminate pathways to such an understanding, to help to uncover some truths as currently understood, about us and our world, and the connection between the two. All of this is done with the ultimate goal of using such an understanding to identify common ground among humans and build the foundation for further collaborative work that will help to steer us clear of danger and see humanity's safe passage into calmer waters.

The pathways to such understandings are not new, nor are they difficult or overly complicated. On the contrary, the ideas this book will attempt to create in your mind are clear and as old as humanity, and often elegantly simple. They find a home in both intellectually rigorous study and common sense intuition, and are not a radical new way of seeing the world but are an unearthing and repackaging of what has been in front of us our entire lives. The logical path or history of knowledge presented here underlie and provide a basis to explain all of what is happening in the world today—both good and bad. It is hoped that the understandings proposed here may serve as a catalyst to orient us toward a shared plan of action that will see us through the imminent storms brewing on the horizon.

Just Trying To Do This Jigsaw Puzzle (Rolling Stones)

Cognitive psychologist Howard Gardner makes the distinction between a "laser" and a "searchlight" approach to learning:

> The style of the laser profile is to focus deeply and regularly on a particular domain and to make ever deeper inroads into that domain. The style of the searchlight profile is constantly to survey the terrain, to monitor many different elements, to make sure that no corner is altogether neglected, and to try to piece together a big picture. (Gardner, 2006, p. 37)

This book embodies Gardner's searchlight profile: collecting together diffuse bits of knowledge in an effort to illuminate a cohesive whole. *The Fishbowl Principle* is a humble attempt to approach the big issues of our time by leaning on many diverse intellectual disciplines and schools of thought. It is a generalist's compilation of the soundest currently understood aspects of our lives, and uses a broad-based empirical perspective to survey the universe, humanity's place in it, and the cultural systems of thought, belief, and control we have developed over the course of our history. While a wide variety of experts and thinkers are referenced, the reader is ultimately left to assess whose voices are most convincing and the extent to which the lessons of these (and other) thinkers fit into a commonsense framework for understanding humanity and the world, and how the two relate to one another and to one's self.

Everyone who reads this book will come at the "task" with the tools and bias that they have accumulated. A student might bring his or her highlighters and make notes in the margins, an academic or professional in the far ranging fields we incorporate will evaluate the authors research and premises, a business person might wonder how a profit can be made, a computer IT expert will wonder what code is used to construct the companion web site, a religious scholar will be curious, religious clergy will be very skeptical, a psychologist may be intrigued, and a fundamentalist will refuse to read it. We know that to many, the density of our information and writing style will make reading this work a real project. To others, like the authors, this is the book we have always wanted to read. Whatever has brought you to even this point; we are grateful for your effort and hope you find value.

This book leaves ample room for, and in fact encourages, sensible intuition. More correctly, this book challenges and encourages readers to engage in some intellectual work: reconciling the understandings proposed here with their own previous understandings, summoning the courage to question whatever they deeply believe and why, and synthesizing all of what they read, learn, experience, and believe into a cohesive whole. It would be foolish to ignore the best in human thinking when engaging in such work, but it also would be foolish to ignore each of our own abilities to think. The authors of this book have passionately and seriously researched experts in the diverse areas of knowledge and in a collaborative manner for three years debated each concept and sentence and now invite you to add to, refine, and even correct this work. The intent is for this book to be a continuously improved upon "living" document, a new media evolutionary manifesto for a sustainable and peaceful world.

In uncovering some of the simple truths about our world and ourselves, we suggest each of us must take great care to cultivate a healthy and informed critical eye. Because people can be manipulated into making dubious decisions based on opaque phraseology of experts or selectively limited amounts of information, a certain freedom of—

and openness to—information is essential to progress. Such conditions hopefully result in a well-educated populace, which is essential to the functioning of a society where citizens play a role in decision-making and actions are aligned with the best interests of the future.

In day-to-day life it is difficult to find the time to reflect, and it seems to us that a large portion of the world's population automatically abdicates responsibilities to "leaders," whether political, scientific, clerical, or economic. "People do not buy the premise that their role is merely to listen passively, absorb information the experts point out, and then choose among the experts" (Moyers, 2008, p. 163). We should remember that we have the fundamental obligation to think freely and for ourselves, but we should also be very careful not to embrace a false elitism or populism, and always reserve the right to "get smarter" or change ones mind. The opinions of experts are important, and it is our responsibility as non-experts to educate ourselves in the wisdom of those who have come before. But then—and this is most important—we must have the desire to question and the means to critically assess such wisdom. Common sense is always important. So are moral values. Add education and communication and the path toward an elegantly simple understanding becomes increasingly bright. History repeatedly shows that when populations abdicate morals and common sense to leaders, disaster is often right around the corner.

In general, intellectual specialization has been allowed relatively little collaboration between the teachings of disciplines as varied as religion, science, history, and the fine arts. But these islands of thought are, of course, not necessarily in opposition to each other; in fact they overlap and affect each other in profound ways. The Greek philosophers and the Renaissance enlightened thinkers discovered the power of interdisciplinary thought. Our goal is an interdisciplinary approach with a "searchlight" down a path of constructive enterprise among concerned readers and well-respected experts. In this way, we can begin to piece together that big picture, and discover the truths that may have been right in front of us for our entire lives—truths that may just be the key to our survival. We have included various song titles and their artists along the way as topic headings, as well as relevant quotations from various bibles at the end of most chapter headings as a reminder of how connected culture is to the framework presented.

The Next Movement (The Roots)

The pages that follow seek to identify and analyze the natures of the universe, thought, soul, and spirit, all within the context of our current extraordinary place in history, so that each person can come to that moment of realization that he or she is just like everyone else. We will show that the evolutionary-adapted survivor that each of us is carries the seeds of both our destruction and our salvation. The goal of this book is to enable readers to make positive changes to their worlds based on seeking commonly shared understanding. This book explores how we arrived at this moment and why integrating our past with our present is so important in the effort to establish a stable scaffolding to support our future. By laying the conceptual foundation for a hopeful and respectful ongoing dialogue about the issues that threaten our survival, this book is intended to be a precursor to practical programs of action that can be carried out by all people, at all levels of society.

To gain the perspective from which common ground may be found and action eventually taken, we will start from the beginning (just as the great bibles of the world do)—the very beginning of time and our universe as far as the laws of physics allow us to prove, or even conjecture. Just as the writer(s) of the Old Testament understood, an explanation of how we came to be is the vital link in accepted reality. This timeline analysis is important because it sets the FACTS that all of us, those currently alive and all those who follow, share in common. It is our foundation and our history. To ignore it or to create an alternate explanation is "magical thinking"—an illusion that can only result in disagreement. In examining Earth's physical development, and consequent emergence of life, two seemingly inconsistent truths will emerge: This little planet of ours is quite precious, unique, and irreplaceable, and our existence on it is insignificant in the totality of the known—let alone unknown—universe. Understanding and accepting our place in the universe, regardless of whether this is primarily intuited through a spiritual or scientific model, is essential to understanding how the imminent storms on our horizon came about and how we may most effectively act to avoid calamity. If, as a species, we achieve the sweet spot of understanding between our bipolar tendencies, which alternate between the hubris of self-pride to the cheapening of life's value, we will be more likely to take the steps necessary to change our perspective, and thereby affect positive change for the future. Instead of getting stuck debating whether the world was created in six 24-hour days or billions of years, we will look to science and religion as a basis for understanding what their views of creation may mean in present-day terms. *We will stress that it is immaterial what one believes on this topic*; the big hurdle will be to convince you, the reader, that one should not foster hate and distrust for those who believe something you do not. Tracing life from its humble single-celled beginnings to its current state of incredible complexity and diversity will inevitably evoke aspects of evolutionary theory and common (and significant) misconceptions of this important idea. The review of how we came to be in a biological sense also reveals how human culture (religion, technology, civilization) evolved out of certain unique abilities of the human mind. Integral to the thesis of this book, the theory of evolution shows that the process of evolution applies to *everything*—not just organic life—and therefore is far less controversial than its opponents wish it to be. It also will show that the dilemmas of our age, while human-created, are not necessarily based on inherently evil qualities of human kind, but are rather unfortunate by products of deeply rooted instincts, abilities, and behaviors first seen in our distant ancestors of eastern Africa millions of years ago.

Once we have completed our physical survey of the universe and traced the beginnings of that story down to the emergence of humanity on our planet, we will examine the evolution of various cultural systems we have established and used over the millennia. These cultural devices, the means by which we try to make sense of and control our environment, span outward from the individual in widening circles: family, community, formal education, development of the arts, and the institutions of a formal economy, government, and religion. Understanding their function in our world enables the recognition that humanity's problems require solutions within and across each of these spheres. This understanding also facilitates the reshaping of our personal perception of each other, our universe, and ourselves.

We will explore the lightning-like speed by which cultural evolution has outpaced the glacial process of biological evolution, how this acceleration has caused much turmoil in humanity's very recent history. We will then focus on the dilemmas that such systems of control have wrought: overpopulation, environmental degradation, depletion of energy sources, and cultural conflict within and among nations. The final chapters of the book will illuminate reasons for hope that come with a renewed understanding of ourselves and our world, and the connection between the two, and encourage readers to take actions that help create a future of greater peace and sustainability.

Back To Life, Back To Reality (En Vogue)

This book will present each reader a potentially new way to understand the world. We understand that not all readers will be interested in all of the topics, but, similar to a broad-based liberal arts background, all of these topics will most certainly help the reader become aware of aspects of life on Earth that they may only have a vague awareness of. The process of aligning our thoughts and actions with more accepting and sustainable understandings is a monumental task, but one that is absolutely crucial.

Keeping in mind that this book is intended to raise critical questions, offer a framework for common understanding, and set the table for further dialogue to find answers and forge plans of action, readers are urged to become involved in an ongoing effort of positive change in their lives, homes, workplaces, communities, and nations. Even if only a few people read this book we will have in our minds at least attempted our effort at progress for the world we will someday leave behind.

We have established the companion Web site to this book, www.fishbowlprinciple.org, to help to bring together a community of people who have a sincere desire to steer humanity away from cataclysm and into calmer, more sustainable waters. It is a forum in which ideas can evolve, be exchanged, vetted, and put into action. There people can contribute to the further positive development of the human condition, borne of a common past and hope for a common future, where one can link together and visually see connections between concepts, actions, communities, groups, and individuals.

Readers are invited and encouraged to place yourselves and your communities in a broader fishbowl and enter this Internet-based community by which you may connect, interact, teach, learn, and improve the process. Because each motivated reader will have access, abilities, and interests that vary depending upon his or her particular background, within our Web site there are "Arknodes" where we organize and link discussions about proposed solutions so that influence can be exerted at various levels—in one's self, in one's home, in one's local community, in one's business, in one's church, in one's investment and charitable decisions, but also at the level of media, national government, and international organizations. The Ark of ideas that this book and Web site support and advocate will be built from the bottom up, with the larger institutions—the participation of which is vital—being pushed into action by this grassroots movement.

Humanity has the natural and intellectual resources to overcome the adversity we all face, but our collective success requires the willingness to undertake major operational and structural changes in our enterprise. If we were to imagine the world as a business entity, and appreciate that, as such, it is on the verge of bankruptcy, we could easily recognize that covering up its shortcomings with the gloss of marketing simply will not do and there is none but ourselves to bail us out. We, as the shareholders of this enterprise, have the right to insist upon long-term sustainable growth. Let us commit to the capital call at hand—investing in our most important enterprise with the most vital resource of all: passion. *The Fishbowl Principle* aims to open minds and hearts, to provide a common ground from which people can start or help to continue such important work, and to point readers toward widely diverse ideas so we may refocus on the business we are here to conduct: to sustainably pursue lives of meaning, love, and happiness. Storms may threaten, but if we work together from a common understanding, we have the means to survive them.

I

How We Got Here

A Selected History of the Universe

1

On The Interconnectedness of Everything

A Hard Rain's Gonna Fall (Bob Dylan)

It is the crack of dawn, and the old man is throwing himself into his work with the energy of a man a fraction his age. His body is loosely draped in frayed clothes, his hair unkempt, skin burnt, and eyes ablaze. Muttering to himself, he attends to his task with feverish resolve, pausing only to shake his head from time to time in dismay. When passersby ask him what he is doing or, more typically, poke fun at him, he issues a series of bleak prognostications. The gist of what he has to say: The world is coming to an end, and he, accordingly, is taking precautions. How did the old man know of this impending threat? God told him.

Would any of us have taken such a fool seriously? Today, if someone were to take such a stand, they would most likely be labeled psychotic, or at the very least, categorically ignored. As things turned out, however, the man was not crazy; he was righteous. Upon receiving the revelation that the world was in grave danger, he felt divinely compelled to preserve what he could. So he embarked upon his project, which was to build a gigantic structure that would serve as shelter from an imminent, cataclysmic storm.

No, Noah was not crazy at all. As the Book of Genesis explains, God was disgusted with the wickedness and evil wrought by humanity and decided to cleanse Earth and start anew. Under God's plan, Noah and his family were to be saved (along with delegates from the animal kingdom) as representative models, progenitors for the world to come. He was entrusted with the task of safeguarding not just his own life but also all life on the planet. Just how Noah knew it was necessary to build an escape vessel was of little interest to the spotted owls and ferrets that would eventually float with him to safety. The animals were

3

safe and dry as the result of their steward's efforts. But Noah's soon-to-be-drowned contemporaries questioned the basis for his prophesy; they smugly viewed him as a lunatic, screaming at the gates of the asylum that the sky was falling on the most beautiful of days. So they did not heed Noah's warning[1]—and they paid the ultimate price.

Who among us, knowing what we know now, would not have sought a berth on Noah's Ark as refuge from the mass extinction outside? With the benefit of hindsight, we would all choose survival for ourselves. But imagine meeting a wild-eyed old man on a sunny day, with no clear indication of a storm on the horizon: would any of us have listened?

When the waters around us are calm, we find it difficult to anticipate, let alone prepare, for an oncoming storm with the potential to undo everything we have built. The survivors of the 2004 tsunami in Southeast Asia can tell us stories about what it means to be devastated by an event that comes without warning. But the survivors of the 2004 tsunami are not unique. There are countless others, such as the survivors of Hurricane Katrina in 2005 (who, along with the various public safety officials, *were* cautioned—and, in fact, were admonished quite explicitly—regarding the oncoming threat to human life), who can also speak to what it means to suffer unexpected consequences from natural events (Warrick, 2006). The unhappy truth is that recorded human history is woven largely from the thread of unheeded warnings. Sometimes, though, our biggest threats have not been from nature or from the heavens. Sometimes we create our own storms. Sometimes our biggest threats have come from ourselves.

---

[1]   [1]While the Bible does not expressly describe Noah telling anyone about the impending judgment to come, Peter 2:5 refers to Noah as a "Preacher of Righteousness," implying that Noah told people to be righteous, and Hebrews 11:7 refers to Noah's obedience. Also, both Peter 3:20 and Genesis 6:3 indicate that God waited a period of time before judgment, but there is no clear indication that anyone other than Noah was warned of the coming flood.

Will You Keep on Building 'til There's No More Room Up There? (Dolly Parton)

The Book of Genesis (as well as the Qur'an) tells us that God sent the Great Flood because of his anger at the wickedness of humans. God, in effect, had hit the reset button on his creation and, after wiping the slate clean, established a covenant with Noah to do things properly. After the floodwaters receded, Noah held up his end of the bargain—he was fruitful and multiplied. But over time, the great restructuring of the human soul once again strayed from its divine blueprint. Noah's descendants brought with them both righteousness and wickedness in abundant supply.

In the eyes of God, an unacceptable level of wickedness was reached with the rise to power of Noah's great-grandson Nimrod, who instructed his tribe to build a tower high enough to veritably touch the heavens and serve as testament to Nimrod's greatness. Indeed, Nimrod's tower was intended to be high enough to rival the power of God. Having seen that drowning humanity was not enough to get them to behave, God decided this time to use confusion to humble these most willful of his creations. God handily reduced Nimrod's tower to rubble, and caused all who took part in its building to suddenly speak in diverse languages. Following the tower's fall, what the erstwhile construction crew heard from each other was nothing more than a cacophony of babble.

Whether these Biblical stories are read as the direct word of God, the interpreted word of God, or instructive tales of morality, few would deny that they contain powerful images and messages. People of the "Book" (Muslims, Christians, and Jews[2]) draw much inspiration and, depending upon their level of devotion, daily guidance from these words. Throughout modern history people have argued passionately regarding

---

[2]   The Qur'an is believed by Muslims to be God's last word to humans on what is expected of them. Islamic tradition provides that Jews and Christians, who follow the earlier versions of divine scripture passed from God prior to the arrival of Mohamed the Prophet, are to be treated with tolerance and respect because they are also "People of the Book."

their interpretations of the Bible,[3] only to find, as in the story of Babel, their words falling upon ears that do not understand.

Babel's demolition, like the Great Flood, did not purge humanity of its ability to cause wrongdoing, nor was our ability to communicate permanently lost. We have persevered in exploiting our potential for both righteousness and wickedness, and continue to collaborate with one another to achieve our goals, no matter how benevolent or nasty. But human history is of course, not one exclusively marked by collaboration. Some of our more passionate arguments have had a tendency to escalate into fierce misunderstandings with those who do not share our perspective. These misunderstandings may start as a hostile exchange of words, but when words fail, the language of violence is often employed.

While many descendants of Noah and Nimrod dedicated their lives to resolving differences, others developed belief systems quite resistant to penetration by people with different views. These idea-deaf people have constructed personal towers by which they sought to climb to the heavens with an arrogance and selfishness reminiscent of Nimrod himself. And some of Nimrod's descendant's begat children interested in building nothing, men and women who see themselves entitled to forgo communication and destroy anything and everything of value to those who threaten their view.

A case in point: The group of religiously motivated zealots who saw modern Western civilization as an affront to their God and decided, in the putative service of Allah, to destroy the World Trade Center and slay the people inside. In terms of a breakdown in communication, it does not get much worse than this. The hijackers who forced planes into the Manhattan skyline in September 2001 may have seen the modernity of the West as no less an affront to God than the blasphemy that led to the

---

[3] What is frequently referred to as "the Bible" is in reality a large number of separate books, and which books are included in the definition varies among those religions embracing thirty-nine books of the Jewish religion's sacred texts, known as the Old Testament. Not all of the books of the Old Testament are accepted by all Christians, or even all Jews, as being God's inspired word. Christians include in their definition of the Bible the twenty-seven books of the New Testament; Jews do not accept these writings as divine. For Muslims, the Qur'an is the last and only expression of God's word to be followed.

building of the Tower of Babel, but their interpretation of God's will and unwavering belief in the correctness of their vision seems unfathomable to the Western mentality. Most of us are no better able to understand the motivations of those who murder in the name of religion than we would have been able to comprehend, following God's expression of wrath at the Tower of Babel, the discordant noises coming from the mouths of our neighbors.

Acute levels of misunderstanding among humans are of course not confined to the chasm between terrorist and victim, nor even to the gaps in understanding that exist due to variations of language, religion, or national cultures. Misunderstandings—and their close relative, miscommunication—are quite commonplace in our lives. Most misunderstandings that we experience do not carry consequences on the scale of Babel, the Great Flood, or 9/11. But if we were to take the morals of these cautionary tales to heart, what would we see in our present world and in our own lives that reflects the miscommunication that resulted from Babel? What could we point to as a storm on the horizon, even on the sunniest of days? And just what is it about human nature that repeatedly pushes us toward having to learn the hard way?

Things We've Never Seen Will Seem Familiar (Grateful Dead)

The cause of humanity's struggle, and the ultimate cause for many of the dilemmas of our age, is this: Each of us suffers from a sort of myopia that predisposes us to place ourselves at the center of our worldview, and to place our present needs at the center of our time view. *Individuals tend to make decisions and act based on their own perceived short-term individual benefit, rather than their perceived long-term benefit or the benefit of others.* This statement, while exceedingly simple, is the key to developing a clear understanding of our world and ourselves and how they interconnect. It opens the doorway to accurately conceptualizing humanity's place in our rapidly accelerating universe. It embodies the most fundamental explanation for how we got to this moment in history, why our culture works the way it does, and why it is so difficult for us to change our direction. What's more, it provides a very real starting point for determining how we can overcome the obstacles we have set in our own way.

This tendency toward the personal, the local, and the short-term, which will be referred to as the Fishbowl Principle, will be explored in detail in the chapters to come. Indeed, the rest of this book's task is to explain and identify the conditions that caused this aspect of human nature to come about, delineate the consequences of such a tendency for the individual and society at large, demonstrate how many of the dilemmas of our age are manifestations of this principle, and discuss why the fruits of our myopic and short-term tendencies, in all their non-biological manifestations, are accelerating at this precise moment in time to induce humanity to overcome our biologically inherited predispositions.

I Can't Talk My Talk With You (Avril Lavigne)

One important example of the Fishbowl Principle at work is how we have grown to communicate with one another; more specifically, how we have grown to miscommunicate with those who hold different beliefs than we do. Each of us has certainly read about—and maybe even knows personally—people who claim, whether based upon religion, politics, nationalism, pride, or science, that they are the holders of the one truth. The misunderstandings borne of such irreconcilable certainty create disharmony in our environment, in our society, and in our souls.

The source of this disharmony—the certainty that flows from having an isolated system of thought, immune to any outside influence—is the Tower of Babel of our time. It is constructed of the same mortar as that in the biblical story: a myopic and potentially cataclysmic hubris. People who think in such absolutes will often go to great lengths to preserve the survival of their viewpoint over a more generally inclusive way of thinking; they will also do so in a way that favors their belief system's survival in the short term over the long term.

One practical consequence of this modern-day language barrier is our failure to fully hear dialogue regarding the most important issues of our time. The problem is not the 6,912 languages currently in use by humans—translators can easily bridge such gaps (National Virtual Translation Center, 2007). Here, there is a different kind of barrier. Choosing to avoid conversation that could potentially undo our most comfortably held beliefs is the safer and easier choice; indeed, it is in our belief systems' short-term interests that we protect them from scrutiny and challenge. As a result, people employ barriers to communication.

Also, adherents of any discipline of thought tend to speak in their own unique form of jargon, which causes the focus of various forms of groupthink to be narrow indeed. Because the words of scientists, religious leaders, politicians, artists, economists, social workers, and members of governmental bureaucracy are spoken in such different tongues, much is lost in the static of interpretation. This adds fuel to the fire of partisanship, wherein leaders revert to simplistic dogma so they may persuade their supporters more efficiently. These closed-ended communication pools work fine in fostering a sense of community. But they are inadequate to the task when crises beg for innovative solutions requiring communication across the boundaries of our self-selected groupings. When challenges transcend the confines of our subdivided fishbowls, little can be accomplished through isolated groups of people talking only among themselves and past all other groups of people. It is under these circumstances that the Fishbowl Principle prevents the cross-pollination of ideas needed for a vibrant, accepting, and sustainable society.

Those who shape public policy—the policies that will, in turn, shape our future—have an urgent need to learn how to truly listen to each other. We, the people who are impacted by these policies, have the same need, because the push for our leaders to broaden their focus must come from us. Ideas have been formed, and others are germinating, that hold significant promise to solve, or at least ameliorate, some of the biggest maladies confronting our planet's inhabitants. But unless the nature of the discussion dramatically changes, we will continue to incoherently argue past each other into continued inaction. This is detrimental to our long-term success for the very reason that we no longer live in anything remotely resembling an isolated fishbowl—like it or not, we are interconnected not only to our friends and neighbors, but to geographically remote people with whom we disagree or even dislike. At some point, those who are protecting their personal belief system from scrutiny and challenge in the short term must realize that they are doing so at the expense of their own long-term sustainability.

Ideas, like animals or plants, require a certain amount of pressure from the environment if they are to grow and mature. The healthy pressure comes not from erecting barriers to threatening communication, but rather from opening gateways to understanding them. (Understanding is not the same as agreement, but it is the antithesis of contempt prior to investigation.)[4] If we are to solve problems as grand in scope as the ones we presently face, it seems we must avoid the language of exclusion and learn how to listen better.

We're The Survivors (Bob Marley)

Humanity's tendency to favor perceived short-term benefit over long-term benefit or benefit of the group is not limited to our ideas. Actually, it is not even limited to our species. The patterns of behavior that humanity exhibits are symptomatic of a far larger trend, a trend that in our specific case has caused an acute form of nearsightedness. Understanding the Fishbowl Principle, then, would lead us to become willing to broaden our focus, to enlarge our lives, and to reorient ourselves through a better understanding of our place in the universe. Let us gain our bearings, then, by putting our immediate situation in perspective of the longer view of survival.

It is widely believed that 65.5 million years ago, a huge meteorite descended upon Earth and initiated a cataclysmic event: it caused a great extinction that ended the era of the dinosaur and allowed only very small creatures to survive, much like the shivering ferrets aboard Noah's tempest-tossed vessel (Alvarez, 1983). An austere view of this event is that catastrophe is sometimes employed as part of the natural order to keep life from multiplying wildly out of control. A more hopeful view is that life, this very flexible form of replicating matter, has historically found ways to survive in the face of incredible adversity.

---

4   Political theorist Herbert Spencer said it well: "There is a principle which is a bar against all information, which is proof against all arguments and which cannot fail to keep a man in everlasting ignorance—that principle is contempt prior to investigation."

It is also thought that a comet crashed into the Indian Ocean about 5,000 years ago, creating an enormous tsunami that washed over East Africa, the Middle East, India, and Southeast Asia (Blakeslee, 2006). These areas are thought to be the cradle of human civilization, and the tsunami presumably erased millennia of hard-earned progress and development. As bad as this was for the humans who were there and the humans waiting to be born, our species was nonetheless able to survive, and thrive.

Some members of the animal kingdom produce more offspring than can possibly survive. Green sea turtles, for example, have an attrition rate of well over 95% and experience no moral dilemma as nature decimates the extras. Our own species, in contrast, has adopted a strategy where we place all our stock in the survival of very few offspring. Most of us believe that there is no such thing as an "extra" human life: Our views in this regard have been shaped by religion, society, and biological necessity, among other sources. But whether our respective convictions are based upon a belief that humanity has been made in God's image, or that we are imbued with an immortal soul, or something else, viewing ourselves as living, flesh-and-blood creatures with innate drives to procreate and survive adds needed perspective to an understanding of the nature of our beliefs. More specifically, it provides the context required for understanding our tendency to overlook the long-term consequences of our subordination of the needs of the Earth's environment to our appetites for consumption and procreation.

The Sun is due to explode in another 4 or 5 billion years (Zeilik & Gregory, 1998); what happens after then, we do not know. That type of cosmological timekeeping is beyond the realm of our comprehension; we know what the number means, but it has no practical meaning in our lives. But on a calendar graded in more understandable chunks of time (i.e., the passage of one or more generations), we face the very real potential of existential threats of our own making. Let us consider, for example, continued unchecked population growth without means in place for addressing its global consequences. If we blithely pursue such a course, a worldwide cleansing will take place on the scale of that produced by a collision with a large meteorite—through pestilence, starvation, or other disasters borne of human-made causes (such as global climate disruption). And, harsh as this may sound, if those "final solutions" fail, we ought to be soberly mindful of our proclivity, and grossly improved ability, to resort to war to bring our population levels back into balance.

We who are lucky enough to be alive today are the survivors. We are the latest in a continuous string of organisms that have successfully managed to overcome great odds. Some might say we had a huge boost in our ability to withstand the perils of nature: being chosen by God for a special purpose. But regardless of the faith of our ancestors, decisions for short-term survival were at the forefront of their existence; day- to-day life was all about seeing one's self and one's immediate circle through to the next meal, the next day, the next season. As a species we have proven time and time again our ability to withstand incredible adversity. Today things are different. Given all our modern capabilities, many of us are able to balance thoughts of short-term survival with questions of long-term sustainability. And more than altruism requires us to strive for such balance: The survival strategies that have helped us for so long are starting to fall short when we take the long view. It is for this reason that our current point in history is unlike any other previously experienced: The tendency to favor perceived short-term benefits is no longer always the best way to survive.

This time around, the question of survival extends beyond the individual or the tribe. This time around, in an incredibly interconnected world, our concern must extend beyond the immediate to include "others." We are now aware that short-term survival strategies are often not efficacious when planning for longer-term survival, or even comfort. As an example, eating industrially produced fast food for tonight's dinner might satisfy our immediate need for survival, but we have become increasingly aware of such food's deleterious long-term effect, not only on our personal health, but also on our environment. Likewise, preemptive attacks on an enemy might cripple their ability to fight in the short term, buying us a few months or even years of safety. But we are growing increasingly aware of the unintended long-term consequences when we create opportunities for our enemies to exploit our attacks through propaganda, multiplying their ranks and passing their hatred off to the next generation. Before, our own short-term survival was all that mattered. Currently, there is a greater recognition that this is not always true.

Bruce Gendelman

The flightless cormorant of the Galapagos Islands.

And This Bird You Cannot Change (Lynyrd Skynyrd)

Consider the experience of the first flightless cormorant from the bird's point of view. Previously, its ancestors were able to fly. But, after living on the Galapagos Islands, where its species had no natural predators, the need to fly was gone, and over many, many generations, its wings were flapping uselessly. The cormorant probably lacked the ability to feel frustration, even as the idea of the muscular movements for flight remained wired into its small brain. With no predators, and its ability to procreate and hunt for food left undiminished, there was no need to take to the skies, and thus no disadvantage to never leaving the ground.

But perhaps this is only a short-term view of the situation. These land-bound birds do not know whether predators will reappear sometime in the future, or whether alterations will occur in the food supply. Each of these possibilities might indicate harsh consequences to the species' long-term future because of its inability to fly. Imagine if the flightless cormorant were made aware of the original use for its wings, and imagine even further what the cormorant might think if there suddenly arose the need for such ability. And further, imagine what the bird might *do* if it had both the knowledge of its situation *and* the ability to take remedial action.

Now, consider how humanity has changed over the years. Clearly, we have undergone numerous and bountiful changes in response to the pressures around us, and those civilizations that responded successfully to alterations in their environments provided a way of life for future generations. In this way, we, the human survivors of millennia of struggles, are quite like the flightless cormorant. But unlike the cormorant, we are aware of larger trends, of the changes our species has experienced, and of threats looming on the horizon. As a global community, though, we often find ourselves acting in ways similar to the cormorant, undisturbed by approaching danger so long as it continues to appear far away, unconcerned that we cannot take flight to escape the coming storms, content enough to be able to scuttle about and provide for our short-term needs and desires. Our task is to come to grips with the recognition of how we have overly focused on our present local interests at the expense of our global future.

The cormorant's transformation was one of physiology, while the vast majority of humanity's transformation has been intellectual and cultural. Despite such obvious differences in mechanics, the two types of changes operate very similarly—with one significant difference that we will dwell on later: the speed by which changes occur. *Homo sapiens*' storyline has included incredible psychological changes over the ages, which have given birth to a vast array of human creations that can be described generally as culture. Physical, psychological, and cultural changes become fixed and long lasting when made in *successful* response to external pressures and demands from the environment (or lack thereof, as in the case of the cormorant). In our case, we made physical changes in successful response to challenges over time: among other things, portions of the human brain grew increasingly developed because those portions helped people better communicate, coordinate their efforts, and solve problems. But we also made changes in how we acted and interacted as a species, and these cultural changes manifested themselves far more quickly than physical changes. Specific knowledge of things like how to use fire, or how to turn sticks and bones into weapons, spread throughout tribes and passed from generation to generation because they provided a highly effective response to frequently occurring challenges. Thus, they quickly became *the* way of doing things, and, as ideas or cultural norms, theystuck around. Those innovations and creations that served no important purpose disappeared, much like the cormorant's ability to fly. In the short term, such changes could be characterized as adaptive. Again, this may be only a short-term view of the situation. Like the cormorant, it is unknown whether the adaptations that have served us until now will continue to be adaptive in the future. But the storms on the horizon suggest the answer is that they will not.

We differ from the cormorant (and most other animals) in one other very important way: rather than changing our behaviors to be in harmony with the environment, we have in many ways changed our environment to support our behaviors. Likewise, rather than adapting our beliefs and actions to be in harmony with the universe, many of us have adapted our view of the universe to be in harmony with our beliefs and actions. Again, we tend to promote anything that suits our own short-term individual best interest, whether it is physical, psychological, social, or other.

As for our physical environment, an examination of the living world shows us we are not alone in bending our surroundings to adapt to our needs at the expense of other ecosystems: beavers build dams that may flood riparian habitats, and insect colonies build giant nests that may break tree limbs. As biological beings, we will take the opportunity to promote our own survival in any way possible, and this is neither surprising nor blameworthy. However, anyone who has flown in an airplane (itself an astounding example of just how far humanity has come in altering our environment) over a landscape impacted by humanscan attest that we have done much more to the planet than beavers or insects. While the distribution of resources is by no means even, we have used the technology provided by our well-developed brains and systems of cultural organization to provide food, shelter, and other comforts to unprecedented numbers of people. Because we humans, by mass and energy, represent an infinitesimal speck in the universe, we would do well to recognize, humble ourselves to, and be reverent of our extraordinary fortune in how we have thrived.

But, in our mission to promote our own survival, we have also dramatically altered the face of our planet, and we have done so to the point of causing significant harm to Earth's interconnected ecosystems. Curiously, even though our very lives depend upon the health of these ecosystems, the losses here have for quite some time stirred only tepid public outcry. From a short-term perspective, no harm seems to be caused by a single tree cut down, a dam built, a glacier melted, or even a species extinguished. But from a long-term view, we are quickly realizing that our strategies at survival are shortsighted indeed.

Because of our culture's pronounced ability to impact our environment, the human species' relationship with the world has diverged from the rest of creation. In short, because humanity—and humanity alone—has experienced an exponentially accelerated growth in recent history due to our collective success in agriculture, medicine, and technology, the Fishbowl Principle has placed our long-term sustainability in jeopardy. We will discuss this more later in this book, but for now we wish to focus first on cause, which to a large degree is the global societal failure to adequately appreciate the interconnectedness of everything. As such, our collective conceptualization of humanity's place in the world is in need of a correction. We are a part of creation, but just that: part of it, not all of it. Humans tend to be forever comforted by a feeling that we hold a central place in the universe, but we cannot allow hubris and provinciality to rule our decisions. Remember Nimrod?

Humanity is subject to the same rules and regulations to which other life forms (and even other forms of matter) are subject. Humanity, like the rest of the living world, changes in response to pressures from its environment. This, in short, means that humanity evolves. Integral to our understanding of our world and ourselves is an awareness of what the theory of evolution has to teach us about of the human story and, more specifically, the special case of the human mind. (Here we refer to evolution in its pristine form, stripped of demagoguery and

16

the ideological debate that has co-opted much discussion of what the theory does and does not stand for.) It is hoped that a comprehension of scientific facts about evolution will serve to increase our wonder and awe of ourselves as well as larger forces at work in our lives, rather than diminish the majesty of creation or Creation.

But humanity represents a special case from other life forms, because not only are we able to affect incredible changes on our environment, we are also able to understand the far-reaching effects of such changes. Because we are armed with such knowledge, the larger question remains why we have been so slow to alter such a dangerous course. A discussion of the science of adaptation provides clear insight into why we are predisposed to weigh and process our own perceived short-term survival over perceived long-term survival of the group.

The Fishbowl Principle, traceable to evolutionary theory, explains much of the maladies in the world today, and demonstrates how our proclivities spring from basic, hardwired response systems to which we are all susceptible. It also provides a greater appreciation for the scale of time in which important cultural changes have occurred, and how the pace of these changes have led to the unique era we currently inhabit. This in turn leads to a deeper understanding of just how exceptional this point in history is, just how much the forces of our own creation are accelerating to the breaking point, and just how precarious the balance of successful, sustainable living can be. Once we clearly understand why we have such strong tendencies to ignore perils outside our individual fishbowls, we can better illuminate ways to refocus our common path, since the separateness of our fishbowls is a cultural invention that has outlived its utility.

I Am He As You Are He As You Are Me And We Are All Together (The Beatles)

What powers the angels, of all of our better natures, is the search for meaning. This quest is not limited to the academic elite or the well to do; everyone, in their own way, is engaged in a search for meaning. While the fruits of such a search are bountiful, there are two core lessons that can be distilled from any earnest quest for wisdom about the human condition:

1. There is a profound interconnectedness among all things. This is more than merely a concept suited for a feel-good campfire sing-along or a college "bull" session; it is an essential fact when viewed from the disciplines of cosmology, chemistry, quantum mechanics, and biology. Since, as a matter of physics, all that exists affects all that exists and all that will exist, and all is based upon all that has occurred previously, respect needs to be paid to the almost infinitely complex web of cause and effect. The interconnectedness of the universe at every level will be demonstrated repeatedly in the pages that follow. This bit of meaning cannot be overemphasized; it applies to all disciplines, all actions, all people, and all discernible realities. We find ourselves where we are in this world not only because of the will of the god (more on defining this later) in which you happen to believe or not believe, and not only as the consequence of exploding supernovas and organic deposits from impacts on our planet by "heavenly bodies," but also as the result of numerous complex cultural adaptations aimed, at least in their origination, at species survival. All is forever interconnected—an unbroken chain.

2. It is in the quest for understanding ourselves and our universe that we find the purpose and direction to choose action over surrender, and hope over despair. This is the force that provides the underpinning of our human thirst for beauty through the arts and for an understanding of our relationship with the universe through religion and science. This is also the reason for writing this book, and the hope that despite all imminent storms on the horizon, humanity will find a way to make it through.

Within our known universe, we know of only one class of highly organized sentient life form that has pondered and attempted to answer the ultimate questions about its own existence. We have spent many thousands of years trying to unravel the mysteries of who we are and why we are here, but subjectivity, debate, uncertainty, and in many cases, persecution have often interrupted our search for meaning. We, as a species, are nothing if not relentless, however, and we have gone about developing various disciplines to help identify, make sense of, and organize answers to the mysteries of the mind, the soul, and physical matter. The specific civilizations in which these human disciplines emerged have served to color the mechanics by which the sublime has been placed within the constructs of rational thought, and provinciality has produced variations and hiccups along the way. Humanity's thirst for truth and beauty has, nonetheless, at times produced a rapid onslaught of amazing discoveries. At our core, we desire and recognize the beauty of knowledge when explained in plain terms. "We want an explanation for the existence of the world—a story that answers the deep questions of our origins and puts us in a context of rich meaning" (Giberson, 2005, p. 6).

> *And I feel to be a cog in something turning*
> *Well maybe it is just the time of year*
> *Or maybe it's the time of man*
> *I don't know who I am*
> *But you know life is for learning.*

> *Joni Mitchell (1970)*

In the search for truth about ourselves, however, the real and philosophical question arises: Could it be *impossible* for us to fully understand and accept fundamental principles regarding a system in which we play an integral role? Scientific testing must be objective to be valid; how objective can we really be when examining ourselves? Max Planck, the founder of quantum theory, pointed out that "science cannot solve the ultimate mystery of nature. And that is because, in the last analysis, we ourselves are part of the mystery that we are trying to solve" (Wilber, 1985, p. 153). This phenomenon, in which we are using our brains to study our brains, is philosophically problematic at best and irreconcilable at worst. Yet, we must find a way around this quandary, and allow for the fact that each of our searches for meaning will endure such contradictions.

One point of fact that may ease the pain here is what philosophers might call the subjectivity of reality, that is, that the idea of our experienced realities may be different from the realities experienced by our neighbors: Upon close reflection, we see just how subjective each of our separate realities really are.

The well-known Indian parable of the blind men and the elephant beautifully illustrates the point:

> The blind man who feels a leg says the elephant is like a pillar; the one who feels the tail says the elephant is like a rope; the one who feels the trunk says the elephant is like a tree branch; the one who feels the ear says the elephant is like a hand fan; the one who feels the belly says the elephant is like a wall; and the one who feels the tusk says the elephant is like a solid pipe. ("Elephant and the Blind Men," 2006)

A wise man explains to them: All of you are right. The reason every one of you is telling it differently is because each one of you touched the different part of the elephant. So, actually the elephant has all the features you mentioned. The quest for the unified field theory in physics has given us another demonstration of the subjectivity of our perceived reality. The unified field theory is, to date, an ethereal philosophy about the true nature of physical reality in which scientists have attempted to integrate the proven theories of general relativity and quantum mechanics. One offspring of experiments in this field is Heisenberg's uncertainty principle, which describes a bizarre phenomenon occurring at the subatomic level, by which the mere act of observing a particle will alter the position or movement of that particle. Consider the implications of this for a moment: If the fundamental laws of the universe are, in fact, only a matter of perspective, then what awesome hubris must be at work with those who claim a monopoly, based upon *their* perspective (political, cultural, or religious), to an understanding of its workings? The best of our scientists, philosophers, and religious leaders respectfully shrug at the shrine of that which remains unknowable. We should never let certitude eclipse our sense of awe at the wonders of the universe.

So we find that in many areas of human experience and thought, reality and truth are ultimately subjective. In any search for meaning, it is important to understand the limits of one's perspective and to acknowledge that the "truth" as perceived at any one moment may only be a piece of a larger picture. This should not be used as an excuse for diminishment of scientific knowledge, however, nor should it be used to justify moral relativism. It is not enough to shrug off the largest questions with a passive "I don't really know" without first making the effort to find out. Sometimes, neither side of an argument is the "right" one, and sometimes the struggle to determine who is right is wholly unnecessary. It is familiar to struggle to find common ground between opposing sides of a given debate, but sometimes the energy of the struggle would have been better spent in trying to understand the other person's frame of reference.

How can the environmentalist, for example, convince the unemployed worker that a wilderness area should be preserved at the expense of a new factory, when the worker's family needs food? How can the specialist in neurochemistry, with her antiseptic but scientifically validated theories of neural pathways and dopamine receptors, communicate regarding the nature of human thought and emotion with the villager who, unschooled in such heady data, does have firsthand familiarity with the rapture of spiritual experience? Meaningful progress takes place when people with divergent perspectives bridge their differences. In many instances, these differences are less imposing than they appear.

Accepting that reality, to some degree, is a subjective and therefore important step on the path toward understanding, an important clue in the search for meaning. Every individual's perspective has potential validity. Each human's view of the world was shaped by what they could see from the environment in which they were raised; we are all shaped by nature and nurture—by each of our unique inherited traits, as well as learned characteristics, affiliations, and life experiences. We can work from each unique perspective toward authentic interpersonal dialogue instead of remaining mired in disagreement. We can elevate our public debate to transcend the exchanges of sound bites that do nothing to promote compromise, or even understanding. We can live in a cooperative world where TV or radio entertainers do not feel well served by calling political opponents and high elected officials Nazis. The time is ripe for a collaborative attempt to float to calmer and more sustainable waters, as more and more people redirect their energies toward lives of individual and collective meaning. Making substantial progress toward humanity's loftiest goals requires that we row, at least most of the time, in the same direction, and this requires finding a common thread between the ideas that thus far have kept us apart.

There is a paucity of spirit in much of our day-to-day lives. There is a lack of community in our local and international spheres. There is an oscillation between fear and greed in the economy. There is often a stalemate in the ability of world leaders to shape constructive policy at home and abroad. The world is in grave trouble, but there is cause for hope. Like Noah, we should be humbled by what we see and feel compelled to participate in the long-term preservation of our species.

What follows is the first step in forging a common ground: building an elegantly simple understanding of oneself, others, our world, and the interconnection between the two. From there, we can begin to build something that will carry us safely forward, an Ark for the 21st century.

We ask those who are willing to listen to join in this renewed understanding, and from it take action to diagnose and cure what ails our small planet, with movements that transcend tribal, intellectual, and religious boundaries. We ask our neighbors to lend a hand in building the Ark with us. The task before us is enormous, but like Noah, our hopes are high, and our resolve feverish. Humanity has never been faced with challenges and threats on a scale that we currently are experiencing, but humanity has also never been as capable as we are now. There are indeed storms on the horizon, but we are already starting to build an Ark of ideas that will see us through such storms. And this Ark begins here.

> *And God saw that the wickedness of man was great in the earth, and that every imagination of the thoughts of his heart was only evil continually. And it repented the Lord that he had made man on the earth, and it grieved him at his heart. And the Lord said, "I will destroy man whom I have created from the face of the earth; both man, and beast, and the creeping thing, and the fowls of the air; for it repenteth me that I have made them."*
>
> *But Noah found grace in the eyes of the Lord. (Genesis 6: 5-8)*

2

On The Physical Universe:
Time, Matter, And The Beginning of Everything

I've found that you can come to know the universe not only by resolving the mysteries, but also by immersing yourself within them. We undertake the most exquisite and noble of tasks: to unveil this place we call home, to revel in the wonders we discover, and to hand off our knowledge to those who follow. (Greene, 2005, p. 21)

Some time ago, the universe—all that humans are able to know and all we are unable to know—exploded outward from a single point in time and space. The word "explosion" may give us the wrong idea of what actually happened, to the extent it brings to mind images of fireworks, grenades, or bombs. This particular explosion was incomprehensibly bigger than any blast on the streets of Baghdad, or even the one over Hiroshima in 1945; bigger than anything humans could ever hope or fear being created on this small planet. It was 13.72 billion years ago, give or take 120 million years or so, (Hinshaw et al., 2008) and this explosion was not merely something: It was everything. And, it was absent a Creator to explain the presence of matter and the gravity that accumulated it to the point of unleashing this unimaginable burst of energy, without a known cause for its origin. In only one trillionth of a second, the universe expanded by an unfathomable 10^{50} (1,000,000,0 00,000,000,000,000,000,000,000,000,000,000,000,000) times (Kaku, 2006). Humans did not yet walk on Earth, because Earth was more than 9 billion years away from existing, and thus the God of our limited imagination had not yet heard our prayers.

Come on The Amazing Journey And Learn All You Should Know
(The Who)

There is no better place to start than at the beginning. This chapter will explain the basic science of existence. To *really* start at the beginning (or at least as close to it as we can) requires an understanding of the building blocks of the universe, matter and energy, from the infinitesimally small to the incomprehensibly large. This is not an easy subject to tackle in any depth, particularly if one is looking for concrete evidence rather than theoretical abstractions. It is the authors' aim to present this knowledge in a non-scientific yet factually consistent manner. Our descriptions here will be grounded on that which has been observed, tested, or measured; in other words, an empirically verifiable story of the origins of the universe, free of political or cultural spin. The leaps of faith required by *a priori* philosophies to describe how and why Earth was created have their place, but that place is not the same—not less than, not greater than, but simply not the same—as what we are able to know empirically.

You may believe in the superiority of your local football team or your favorite political candidate, or that your mom makes the best cookies around, and you may believe each of these things with every fiber of your being. However, you cannot expect to use this subjective and un-testable knowledge as a foundation on which to build a framework for universal acceptance. For example, suppose your friend down the block relates a story of how he saw a giant monster crawling out of the sewer drain late last night. You will probably only believe him completely when you see the creature for yourself, or are shown a photograph or perhaps a sample of monster DNA. You may have confidence in the truth of the story based upon your familiarity and trust in your friend as a reliable fellow. And, should your friend point out evidence of the monster's passage, such as bent streetlights and slimy sidewalks, you may be convinced beyond any doubt. But unless there were no other possible explanations for the property damage on display, empirical proof would still be lacking. Reliance on empirical data has little place in the life of faith, yet, as the foundation for science, it is really all there is.

It is important to remember here that science, as a body of knowledge, is both dynamic *and* fallible. Most of us think of scientific "laws" or "facts" as unmoving and inarguable, but these teachings are not written in stone; rather, they are working theories that have not yet been proven wrong, notwithstanding protracted good faith efforts to do so. At one time it was commonly accepted among scientists as immutable fact that Earth was flat. Only when contrary empirical data emerged (Magellan circumnavigating the globe) did this "fact" change. So it is with every bit of knowledge acquired through observation and experimentation: Gravity, energy conservation, atomic theory, evolution, pathogenesis, and thousands of other scientific principles have all undergone serious revision throughout the years, and will continue to do so as we amass, test, and challenge additional data and develop and revise theories of how the universe works. This is the way of science.

Throughout modern history, major advancements in knowledge have had to break through the wall of resistance presented by those who had vested interests in maintaining as valid the then-accepted notions of reality. Prime examples are Kepler's and Galileo's descriptions of the solar system, descriptions that pushed aside Earth (and a huge chunk of human hubris) to allow the Sun to take center stage in our solar system. Each of these new realities opened pathways for the development of the next generation of revolutionary concepts, concepts that would have been unlikely to emerge in a universe saddled with the reality of less enlightened times. For instance, the Newtonian view of the universe was a quantum leap from prior scientific theory, but still presented a universe where the solar system had a central role. Einstein took Newton's universe and expanded it through dimensions of thought previously unimaginable, correlating matter, energy, and time in his theory of general relativity. It is doubtful that even an individual mind as great as Einstein's could have made such monumental leaps forward without beginning his journey in the "new" universe established by the Newtons and Galileos who came before him.

Even now, leading physicists are in the process of revising their working theories for the fundamental operating parameters of the universe. String theory, a recent development, seeks to unify the set of rules governing the very small (quantum mechanics), the very large (general relativity), and events that happen on the human scale (Newtonian mechanics). String theory is the latest revision of the collective scientific view of reality, but it is by no means complete and is itself subject to ongoing challenge. This is the way of science: Something is correct until an example is found that proves it wrong. In his landmark work *The Structure of Scientific Revolutions*, Thomas Kuhn describes how the process of science is, at its heart, an evolutionary process of revising and refining theories:

> We must recognize how very limited in both scope and precision a paradigm can be at the time of its first appearance. Paradigms gain their status because they are more successful than their competitors in solving a few problems that the group of practitioners has come to recognize as acute. To be more successful is not, however, to be either completely successful with a single problem or notably successful with any large number. The success of a paradigm . . . is at the start largely a promise of success discoverable in selected and still incomplete examples.(Kuhn, 1996, pp. 23-24)

One may ask, would not the reduction of the universe to a quantifiable set of principles, based only on what can be observed, remove all the wonder and magic out of our existence? Not by a long shot. First, the scientific approach to understanding, just like the religious or spiritual approach, is a journey and not a destination. And like its more ethereal brethren (although perhaps with more sterile prose), the scientific story describes in vivid detail just how masterful the master plan actually is. We should rid ourselves forever of the image of scientists as socially awkward white men wearing thick glasses and sterile lab coats, who seek to remove our sense of awe and mystery. The best of scientists serve to bolster rather than threaten our spiritual existence, "by deepening our understanding of the true nature of physical reality, [enabling us to] profoundly reconfigure our sense of ourselves and our experience of the universe" (Greene, 2005, p. 5).

The scientist's quest is to understand everything, but as Socrates pointed out: The more that is known, the more we seek to know. As scientists learn more and more about the physical universe, their work tends to focus on smaller and smaller pieces of the puzzle. Even so, at moments of revelation that come from breakthroughs in their specialized fields, pioneering researchers are able to appreciate where their work fits into the "whole," providing a glimpse of vast new terrains that need exploring, "a universe that is at once surprising, unfamiliar, exciting, elegant, and thoroughly unlike what anyone ever suspected" (Greene, 2005, p. 5). This willingness to repeatedly tap into the wonders of the universe, being drawn rather than intimidated by a sense of awe, is the way of science.

While the scientific realm is employed to help in our searching for nature's answers, it also is acknowledged that science does not hold a monopoly on the human endeavor to "solve" the "problem" of its existence. Scholars, artists, and nonscientific thinkers have attempted to make sense of the purpose and meaning of human existence for thousands of generations, approaching the topic from the vantage points of theology, philosophy, psychology, art, music, and poetry, to name a few. No effort at uncovering truths about the human condition and the human place in the universe takes place within a vacuum, and no discipline of study can insulate itself from other disciplines when it comes to this topic. The major steps that took place from the fundamental structures of matter and energy through the development of life forms on Earth can be traced, as can the chemical, structural, and electrical functions of thought. But measuring and tracking does not identify cause and effect, and many scientists would characterize as unattainable the task of establishing such correlation. When electrical potentials are measured between certain neurons, this can correlate with a specific attribute of the human brain, but can it really say that those tiny electrical jolts caused thoughts, feelings, and actions? Scientifically speaking, no.

Other disciplines are necessary for a complete picture. Religion derives much of its power from the collective conscious and unconscious yearnings of the soul, and psychology has made inroads to understanding the importance of such unseen forces as they apply to the human brain. Historians and anthropologists have identified overlapping causes and effects between events, which connect to other events, and are able to place them on a temporal lineage linking past events to present outcomes and future possibilities. And while valuable insight into people's behavior can be gained through analysis of the biochemical workings of the mind, the depth of understanding of individuals is immeasurably enriched if one also knows how they view themselves socially, how they interact with the environment, and how they are able to cope with their emotions and *a priori* beliefs.

So as the discussion about the story of the origins of the universe as brought to us by science moves forward, let keep these two things in mind: (1) This book will present the most current theories and facts available (and have a dynamic Web presence established to accept changes, suggestions, and improvements for future versions); and (2), this basis in science is presented as part of a framework for common understanding and it is acknowledged that many cannot rely completely on science in the search for understanding. As people work on refining knowledge, the knowledge base and story will change in sometimes slight—and possibly profound—ways. As people become more personally comfortable with this common framework, artistic, emotive, and spiritual selves should impact the outcomes.

At this point in human history, as will be discussed later in the book, mankind has achieved a technological capability that causes what can be observed to increase geometrically. Technology allows observation of things well beyond the human scale: Microscopes allow humans to see ourselves as mosaics of trillions of independent cells invisible to the human eye, and telescopes enable us to reach farther outward into space than human ancestors ever thought possible. The wealth of data that is available to us now is fundamentally different—geometrically greater—from the data available to previous generations, and science has no intention of letting up. As a result, the story that science is presenting is a theory that fully can be expected to change as more is discovered.

You Were Meant to Be Here, From The Beginning
(Emerson Lake and Palmer)

If we were able to witness the birth of our universe in progress some 13.7 billion years ago, we would see the rapid expansion that accompanies an enormous explosion. But while we cannot time travel to that event, and certainly would not survive it even if we had good seats to view it, we are able to witness not only what is left of the explosion, but can in fact look back and almost see the time of the event from our safe vantage point of today. This is because the expansion from the explosive origin of the universe is still going on today, 13.7 billion years after the fact. This theory of cosmological inflation, commonly known as the Big Bang, tells the story of an event in which all matter and energy in the entire known universe, which was squeezed into an absurdly tiny space, expanded and spread out into the current distribution of known matter and energy throughout the universe.

The tiny initial point of concentration—the "singularity"—that purportedly contained all the matter and energy in the universe is not something that can easily be grasped. However, scientists are very focused in pushing back the frontiers of physics in order to fully understand the true nature of this event. Through the use of increasingly large particle accelerators, humans have been able to approximate the conditions that existed in the universe in its first moments. While one can write or speak a sentence identifying the singularity with relative ease, it is very difficult taking in and processing the sheer scale of the events surrounding the expansion of the singularity so long ago. Despite the limitations of human brains, science is giving us the tools to approach answers in this realm.

It is indeed difficult for human brains to handle understanding such events. One may grasp the concept of weighing all the grains of sand on a given coastline with a given length, but it is very hard to make meaning out of measurements of the weight of such sand. What, to human minds, is the difference between 300 million pounds and 500 million pounds? One may grasp figures quoting populations of cities such as Beijing, Calcutta, Sao Paolo, and New York in a matter-of-fact way, but does one really feel (in their gut) the difference between 15 million and 20 million people? After a point, big numbers are just big numbers. So when the age of the universe is set at 13.7 billion years, while the reader may know in an intellectual sense that this is more time than the formation of Earth (a measly 4.6 billion years ago), both numbers are perceived as abstractions. And if one finds that difficult to wrap their mind around, a concept such as the singularity containing *all* the matter and energy in the universe would have them nodding their heads in supposed understanding, without having any real hope of actually taking in with a human brain just how big the Big Bang was.

By way of attempt, though, think of anything, anything at all: a blue whale swimming in the Pacific; the Empire State Building; a thin layer of rust on an abandoned tractor in a field in Siberia; the magma boiling and brewing beneath mountains in the South Pacific; Jupiter's Great Red Spot; the microprocessor that sits inside your computer; the vast empty space that lies between the Earth and Mars; the air molecules that are compressed and hit the reader's eardrum when you listen to your favorite music and your memory of what that sounded like; the light that took millions of years to travel to Earth from a distant star in the Big Dipper; the dopamine molecule in your brain that was released into a synaptic cleft only five microns wide when you ate your last meal; the Milky Way galaxy in its entirety; anything. The singularity included all the matter, space, and energy that makes up these things, as well as everything else that ever was, is, or will be in the universe, and all of it was condensed into a single infinitely small, infinitely dense, infinitely heavy, and infinitely hot point. Every atom that would eventually make up every star and planet in the universe was pressed into this one point, and—if one could imagine—all of space itself was compressed into this point as well. Current laws of physics can predictably describe conditions just after the Big Bang, using both the laws of quantum physics and the laws of relativity. But when faced with analyzing conditions of infinite heat or infinite density, the knowledge of man as described through science has been unable to unearth an answer. The closest phenomenon that can be compared to the singularity is whatever mysterious event occurs at the center of a black hole, a cosmological spot of such intensity that even light cannot escape its pull. Some scientists, such as a group of physicists at the University of Illinois, believe that there is a singularity at the center of every black hole.[5]

> At the center of a black hole lies the singularity, where matter is crushed to infinite density, the pull of gravity is infinitely strong, and spacetime has infinite curvature.

---

[5] This, incidentally, is why there was an opposition to the completion of the CERN particle accelerator, which is thought to be able to re-create conditions similar to the ones that existed milliseconds after the Big Bang. Some scientists were worried that CERN would create a singularity that would annihilate the earth. That we are still here is testament to the fact that it isn't true ... yet.

> Here it's no longer meaningful to speak of space and time,
> much less spacetime. Jumbled up at the singularity, space
> and time cease to exist as we know them.("Anatomy of a
> Black Hole," 2009)

But of course, every bit of matter and energy that makes up every black hole in the universe (some of which dwarf the Milky Way galaxy!) was also part of the original singularity. Regardless of how and why, the singularity could not contain itself and expanded outward, thereby creating the physical reality that is known as the universe.

This story causes some logical dissonance if it marinates long enough. There are some questions that inevitably come up when one begins to think about the singularity and the Big Bang: What was there before the Big Bang? What was in the space that wasn't occupied by the singularity, for surely the Big Bang needed somewhere to expand into? How did all the matter that went into the singularity (and eventually the universe) get there in the first place? Scientists may say that the singularity and its explosion created matter, energy, time, and space as we know them, but that still may leave us unsatisfied. Even when the rules of an empirical approach to the universe are accepted, it seems that there are some things that must be taken on faith in order to move forward.

Now, one of the most unexplored frontiers is the vast space that surrounds Earth. Scientific advancement may address some or all of these questions in the future, but these questions, while interesting in their own right, divert us. For the purposes of this book, we simply wish to demonstrate two things: There are matters in the universe that limited human brains will have great trouble fully understanding, and more important, everything in the universe—the stars, the planets, and the Earth and everything on it—came from the same infinitely small, infinitely dense, infinitely hot starting point. The atoms that make up the cells in human bodies were at one point part of the singularity, just as the atoms that make up the inside of a nuclear bomb were, and just as the atoms that make up the Crab Nebula, this is truly the ultimate common ground. Knowing here (as Socrates pointed out) that humans do not know, and understanding that the stuff of which we are made is the same stuff of which everything is made, give us incredible and profoundly simple insights into the human condition. These two facts are at the center of what it is to be human: to be connected with everything else, but unable to fully understand it. Coming to terms with this reality is part of reconciling our place in the universe.

Even though we humans are persistent in understanding the secrets of creation, there currently is no way to access the conditions at the exact moment of or before the Big Bang. The closest scientists can come to this is to describe what happened 10^{-43} seconds (that is 0.0000000000000000000000000000000000000000001 seconds) after that blessed event (Chaisson & McMillan, 1993, p. 600). It is thought that within the first measurable moments of the Big Bang, the matter contained in the singularity inflated and pushed outward to 10^{26} times its original size (WMAP Inflation Theory, 2009). As a result of matter and energy spreading out and getting some breathing room, thanks to this eye-blink expansion process, the universe cooled from its infinitely hot state. Not long after, the simplest and most fundamental of particles were formed: protons, neutrons, and electrons. These subatomic particles in turn fused to form hydrogen and helium, the simplest and most abundant elements in the universe.

By the time the universe was a couple of minutes old, it was filled with nearly uniform hot gas composed of roughly 75% hydrogen, 23% helium, and small amounts of deuterium [an isotope of hydrogen that has one neutron] and lithium. The essential point is that this gas filling the universe had extraordinary low entropy. In other words, the current order is a cosmological relic (Greene, 2005, p. 171). It was at about this time that the four known forces in the universe (gravity, electromagnetism, nuclear strong, and nuclear weak) emerged. Thus, only moments after the Big Bang, the basic building blocks and operating parameters for the physical reality were established. The universe was like a bucket of Legos dumped over the floor of a child's playroom. Everything that was to come, *everything,* would be nothing more than a reshuffling and recombining of these very basic building blocks and forces.

Have You Looked At All The Family of Stars
(Jefferson Starship)

Even though the universe has expanded in time and space beyond all comprehension, the fundamental rules of physical reality established from the Big Bang still hold, albeit at a lower energy level than they were only fractions of seconds after the Big Bang. The fact that the vast majority of the matter in the universe still takes the form of hydrogen and helium,[6] and the fact that humans still are pushed and pulled by gravity, electromagnetism, and the two nuclear forces today serves as evidence that supports the Big Bang theory.

Intelligent earthlings are very far removed from the far-away and long-gone events surrounding the Big Bang. Clearly, no one was on hand to witness the event. Why, then, is this the story that anyone should accept as the story of the universe's creation? Surely there are stories that ask you to suspend no more disbelief than this, to take no more leaps of faith than being asked to take when subscribing to the Big Bang story. Moreover, other stories of creation have not changed as they have been passed down from generation to generation, while the Big Bang story is one under constant revision, subject to new research by scientists hard at work on untangling the mysteries of the opening seconds of the universe. Perhaps its mutable nature is exactly why the Big Bang story is the one to which scientists subscribe, and here is why: As with any other scientific finding, the Big Bang is only accepted as long as no empirical evidence is presented to the contrary. Much like the theory of gravity that was revised by Isaac Newton from "things fall toward the Earth" to "anything with mass attracts anything else with mass" (which was later superseded by Einstein's theory of general relativity), the Big Bang theory has been shaped and refined by ongoing discoveries in scientific research. That is something that no other story of creation can safely claim. One of the largest and most important implications of the Big Bang theory is the idea that the universe has been expanding since the initial inflationary event 13.7 billion years ago. For those of us here on Earth, this simple fact should remind us just how big the universe is

---

6   Hydrogen and helium are the two elements that comprise stars, which are by far the most massive and most numerous collections of matter in the universe

and just how small humans are by comparison. And, by these numerical reckonings, the chance that life on Earth plays a prominent role in the greater cosmology is quite low. This may be disheartening to some, but it need not be. Beyond making us feel like specks of dust (which seems to be therapeutic), we should also think about the scale of the universe in a positive way: What an incredible and overwhelming thing the universe is! This creation is truly awe-inspiring. And if science's story is correct, then something so magnanimous is only growing more so by the second.

But just how does science know that the universe is expanding? What is the evidence? From the human perspective, things don't seem to be getting any bigger. If the theory of an expanding universe is correct, this inflation should be observable. It turns out that the inflation can be seen, but not with the human eye. Human sensory ability is limited. We are not big enough to notice the curvature of the Earth, even though it is now known (and accepted by most humans) that it is spherical, so we certainly are not able to see the expansion of our universe, a phenomenon that is much, much bigger in scale than this planet. In order to observe the expansion of the universe, then, science has to rely on some highly specialized pieces of technology that can observe things on a grand scale. From these pieces of technology and the extended range of observable data they give us, it is now provable that the universe is expanding.

The first main strand of evidence is the "Red Shift," which came from an observation made by the famous astronomer Edwin Hubble (for whom the Hubble telescope is named) that many of the galaxies he was observing through his telescope appeared red in color. Stranger still, the galaxies that were thought to be farther away appeared redder than the ones close by. This was no trick of the optical systems in the telescope, however; Hubble did see red. It could be that stars (such as the Sun) appear red because of the spectra given off from a star's nuclear fusion reaction, but this sort of immense release of heat and other energy appears white to our eyes (indicating the presence of every wavelength of electromagnetic radiation). The real reason for the red appearance of far away galaxies was much more elegant.

When you consider the electromagnetic spectrum (Figure 2.1), you'll notice that red light has a longer wavelength than violet light. It is almost as if the photons of light are being stretched out more with red light than violet light. By way of example, if one were to draw a picture

Figure 2.1. Red light has a longer wavelength than violet.

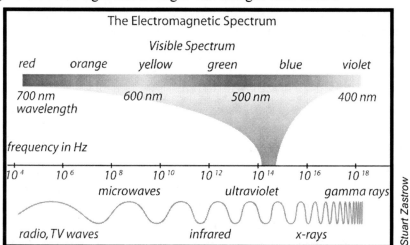

of a wave on a balloon and then blow up the balloon, the wave crests are closer together when the balloon is small (shorter wavelength). As the balloon size increases, though, the spaces between the wave crests increase (the wavelength increases). The more the balloon expands, the longer the wavelength becomes. In terms of electromagnetic waves, observers see longer wavelengths as red and shorter wavelengths as blue or violet.

Now, imagine that the Earth is taken as one fixed point and any given galaxy being observed through Hubble's telescope is taken as another point. If red is seen instead of violet, it tells us that the wavelengths of light are being stretched out. The red shift phenomenon tells us that the distance between them is increasing! In other words, "We can think of the photon [of light] as being attached to the expanding fabric of space, so its wavelength expands along with the universe. . . . The red shift is a consequence of the changing size of the universe. . . . [It] measures the amount by which the universe has expanded since the photon was emitted" (Chaisson & McMillan, 1993, p. 604).

Newton and others discovered that planets are moving things, so it could very well be that the Earth and the planets we humans are observing could just happen to be moving away from one another, like ricocheting billiard balls on a table. However, when it is proven that the red shift phenomenon happens with every observable source of light in the sky (which it does), it is safely concluded that everything out there is moving away from us here on Earth. (This does not, by the way, mean that the Earth is the center of the universe, nor does it mean that the Earth is repulsive to the rest of the universe; it turns out that the same phenomenon occurs at every point). No matter where the observer stands, the universe will always look like it is moving away from us via the red shift. Distant stars may be moving farther and farther from Earth, but Earth also is moving farther and farther away from them. The only reason one assumes Earth is not moving in this "thought experiment" is because our particular frame of reference is largely arbitrary in the context of the universe at large. It is known from the micro revelation that everything is moving farther apart from everything else and that the universe is getting bigger. From this it is inferred that at some point in the past the universe was not as big as it is today, and that it will be bigger still tomorrow. If the universe grows as time moves forward, then it also must shrink if we play the "tape" in reverse. And from this, it is extrapolated backward to conclude that this expanding universe was at one point in the past a very, very small, dense thing. This is exactly what the story of the Big Bang is telling us.

WMAP Data is the second piece of evidence that the Big Bang story is an accurate description of the origins of the physical universe and that its expanding nature involves a more recent discovery. A desire to validate and quantify the Big Bang theory of the origins led to the Wilkinson Microwave Anisotropy Probe (WMAP) satellite, whose purpose was to detect the amounts of background radiation in the sky. The events that led up to such a survey of space happened by chance: Physicists Arno Penzias and Robert Wilson, in aiming their antenna at different parts of the sky for another experiment, always picked up a degree of background static that they could not account for. They initially thought that the background noise was something on Earth interfering with their telescope's functioning, but after cleaning out the antenna and eliminating every possible source of interference that they could think of, they eventually determined that this background noise, which was everywhere, was something much more significant. The background noise was determined to be Cosmic Background Radiation (CMBR), remnants of the original burst of energy emitted by the Big Bang. Following Penzias and Wilson's accidental discovery, a team of physicists led by David Wilkinson conducted a survey of space, with the goal of further understanding the nature of CMBR and what it can tell us about the universe's origins. NASA, using the WMAP satellite, has given us an actual picture of CMBR.

While it paints a pretty picture, what use is this data to us? How does it further the understanding of the origins of the universe and, by extension, humanity's own origins? For one thing, the ability to detect (in greater detail than ever before) background microwave radiation left over from the Big Bang confirms many of the suspicions about how the universe began. The simple fact that WMAP recorded microwaves is significant. Looking back on the photo of the electromagnetic spectrum, it is noticed that microwaves (yes, the same ones that reheat leftovers and make popcorn in that box in your kitchen) are lower energy—that is, a longer wavelength—than even visible light. What is interesting about this fact is that lower-energy, longer-wavelength microwaves are much more common in CMBR than gamma rays, the form of radiation with the shortest, and most energetic, wavelength. High-energy, short-wavelength gamma rays are thought to be the form of radiation originally emitted from the Big Bang (Stecker & Puget, 1974), but according to WMAP, gamma rays are not nearly as common in space as microwaves! This indicates two things tangentially. The first is that entropy is demonstrated on a cosmological scale; the radiation present in the universe is losing energy (slowing down in the form of elongated wavelengths) such that where there were originally an abundance of gamma rays, there is now an abundance of their lower-energy cousin. The second is that the elongation of the wave might also serve as evidence for an expanding universe in the same way the red shift does: It is not the wave itself that is elongating, but the fabric of the expanding universe in which the wave is embedded.

> Scrutinizing the CMBR is crucial for our understanding of the origin and evolution of the universe, because the Big Bang theory doesn't answer all cosmological questions. The Big Bang theory does not predict how much or what types of matter and energy exist in the universe, nor how it evolved into the structures (like stars and galaxies) we see today. It does not predict a unique shape for the universe, or claim that it is infinite in extent or instead somehow bounded. It doesn't even

address how or why the Big Bang happened in the first place. The Big Bang is just a basic framework. Information encoded in the CMB allows scientists to build upon the Big Bang.

Imagine the impact of matter and energy on space after the Big Bang as a handful of rocks thrown into a pond. The rocks will make ripples in the pond. The shape of those ripples is determined by the strength and number of the rocks and the murkiness of the pond. Likewise, the CMB ripples reflect of the contents and properties of space itself.

Various cosmological models describing the shape of the universe or its mass and energy content make specific predictions about the extent of temperature fluctuations from region to region. WMAP captures the reality, and the WMAP team searches for theoretical matches to this reality. Similarly, the temperature patters offer information about the universe's age, the era of first starlight, and other parameters. Again, WMAP detects the reality, allowing the team to find a theoretical match. The team compares fingerprints of suspects (the theories) with the fingerprint left at the event (the CMB), just like a detective.

As NASA has announced in February 2003, the team has found a match. The scientists have now combined their new cosmic baby picture with an array of complementary observations to present a new cosmic consistency. The baby picture allows scientists to accomplish two main things: (1) reach back to earlier times to see what produced these patterns; and (2) look forward from the time of the picture to predict how the universe would develop, and compare this to what is seen observed by other means (with galaxies, supernovae, etc.) to get the cosmic consistency. (Big Bang and WMAP Primer, 2003)

Thus, while humans have developed a fairly refined theory of the universe's origin compared to what was once known, we are still largely ignorant of the entire story. Illustrative of this is the recent discovery that concerns itself with a very mysterious substance called dark matter. In 1998, Saul Perlmutter and a competing team led by Adam Ries built on the foundation laid by learned predecessors such as Newton and Einstein and made a major breakthrough with respect to the understanding of the Big Bang. Perlmutter proved that "the known matter in the known universe is not only expanding, but is currently expanding at an accelerating rate, and that the known matter and energy of the universe makes up only 4% of the total, with the remainder split between black matter and black energy.

Most of the 4% is hydrogen and helium; only 0.03% takes the form of heavy elements" (Perlmutter & Linder, 1999). The overwhelming bulk of the universe—the 96% that is mostly dark matter and dark energy—remains shrouded in mystery. "We simply do not know what it is" (Kaku, 2006). Thus, the knowledge of what makes up the contents of the universe only addresses the 4% that is available to scrutiny. At the moment humankind either must be content with the mystery, or suffereternally from not having all the answers.It is proven that that the expansion from the Big Bang (Figure 2.2) will continue for as long as theuniverse (or, at the very least, our local sectionof the universe) exists, and that it will do so at an increasingly accelerated pace. Thus, the red shift and WMAP tell us that several billion years down the road the universe will be larger, although it will contain the same amount of matter and, therefore, will look far lonelier to any creatures inhabiting it.

This inference, made in a universe where all things are, quite literally, moving away from one another and doing so at a faster rate with each second that goes by, brings us back to the matter of perspective. In day-to-day lives, one spends very little time worrying about matters that dwarf the human scale of perspective. More often than not, the small human problems and struggles are quite overwhelming. One's perception of reality, be it overwhelming or manageable, is based upon how time and space is conceptualized. Einstein has handily disproved the classical

Figure 2.2. The Big Bang expansion will continue for as long as the universe exists.

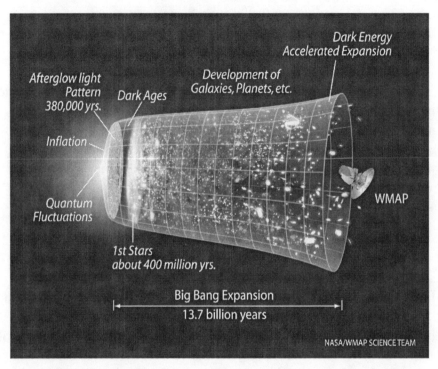

Earth-based, Newtonian view that the two are a constant, independent of the observer. This abstract cosmological truth may not affect an individual as she constantly checks her watch throughout the day, but ithas important implications for how humans frame larger questions of existence, and where they ultimately decide we fit into the natural order.

The lesson: An individual's perspective is his/her own, and while it may give them a glimpse of some larger universal truth from time to time, people are quite limited by their small place in the universe. Therefore, when the human scale of perspective is too overwhelming for us, a suggestion is to zoom out to the cosmological, to flirt with the very foundations of creation, and try to gain a little perspective on who humans are and where we fit in. Carl Sagan, in a particularly moving (and now famous) passage from his book *Pale Blue Dot*, comments on a tiny speck of light captured in a photograph by the spacecraft *Voyager* as it made its way through Saturn's outer orbit:

> Look again at that dot. That's here. That's home. That's us. On it everyone you love, everyone you know, everyone you ever heard of, every human being who ever was, lived out their lives. The aggregate of our joy and suffering, thousands of confident religions, ideologies, and economic doctrines, every hunter and forager, every hero and coward, every creator and destroyer of civilization, every king and peasant, every young couple in love, every mother and father, hopeful child, inventor and explorer, every teacher of morals, every corrupt politician, every "superstar," every "supreme leader," every saint and sinner in the history of our species lived there—on a mote of dust suspended in a sunbeam.

The Earth is a very small stage in a vast cosmic arena. Think of the rivers of blood spilled by all those generals and emperors so that, in glory and triumph, they could become the momentary masters of a fraction of a dot. Think of the endless cruelties visited by the inhabitants of one corner of this pixel on the scarcely distinguishable inhabitants of some other corner, how frequent their mis-understandings, how eager they are to kill one another, how fervent their hatreds.

Our posturings, our imagined self-importance, the delusion that we have some privileged position in the universe, are challenged by this point of pale light. Our planet is a lonely speck in the great enveloping cosmic dark. In our obscurity, in all this vastness, there is no hint that help will come from elsewhere to save us from ourselves.

The Earth is the only world known so far to harbor

life. There is nowhere else, at least in the near future, to which our species could migrate. Visit, yes. Settle, not yet. Like it or not, for the moment the Earth is where we make our stand.

It has been said that astronomy is a humbling and character-building experience. There is perhaps no better demonstration of the folly of human conceits than this distant image of our tiny world. To me, it underscores our responsibility to deal more kindly with one another, and to preserve and cherish the pale blue dot, the only home we've ever known. (Sagan, 1994, p. 7)

States of Nature (States of Nature)

The WMAP data radically altered scientific understanding of the origins of space and matter, and it helped to prove the existence of dark matter and dark energy. But it did not tell us what this stuff *is*. Maddeningly, the dark matter, which has weight, is invisible. Yet this ghost outweighs all the stars in our galaxy, the Milky Way, by a factor of 10. Then there is the mysterious force known as dark energy. Introduced by Einstein in 1917 (as a cosmological constant) (Carroll, 2001) and then later discarded (he called it his greatest blunder) (Goldsmith, 1995), dark energy is now reemerging as the driving force in the entire universe. This dark energy is now believed to create a new antigravity field, which is driving galaxies apart. If one takes the latest theory of subatomic particles and try to compute the value of this dark energy, he will find that the number is off by 10^{120}. This discrepancy is far and away the greatest gap ever found in the history of science (Kaku, 2006). Clearly, there are many more mysteries that beg to be unfolded, more things, as Shakespeare's Hamlet eloquently put it, than are dreamt of in our philosophy. Dark matter and dark energy, if nothing else, demonstrate to us that there are deep, mysterious gaps in knowledge. While science would, of course, like to paint a complete picture of the universe, there are many challenges to achieve with further inquiry, when advancements in thought and technology allow for it and agree to accept the mystery when there is nowhere left to look.

The Big Bang remains at the center of the mystery of creation. The Big Bang was the single most energy-filled event that ever was and ever will be. The universe is like a wind-up clock: All potential is stored in its tightly coiled springs, and once everything is let out of its floodgates the universe can do nothing but let its spring uncoil; 13.7 billion years later, the universe is still uncoiling. For the same reason that the first hill of a roller coaster is the tallest, it's all been downhill since the Big Bang. That single event released all the matter and energy in the universe, and sent it careening to all corners of the expanding universe we all call home. As shown through WMAP, though, things are slowing down, spreading out, and cooling off, and have been for the past 13.7 billion years. This is not to say that energy is in short supply, because a quick survey of the cosmos will reveal plenty of it. But it is to say that the concentration of energy will never be as potent or strong as it was during the Big Bang. This principle can be thought of as a natural tendency toward evenly distributed disorder, called entropy.

One experiences entropy in minuscule ways every day. A drop of ink placed in a glass of water it diffuses (which may serve as a good visual demonstration as to what is happening with the energy in the universe, if only the sides of the glass were expanding along with the ink). The engines in cars convert more fuel to heat than they do to mechanical energy, and this process grows more inefficient as the car ages. Even though we spend time cleaning our houses, inevitably, as we all have experienced, things tend toward disorder after a period of time. The molecules that make up cells in our body break down over time and stop working. Tendency toward disorder: It is inescapable. The universe is winding down. However, this is not cause for hopelessness. It is true that on a larger scale, there is nothing to be done. Earth will keep growing more and more distant from our celestial neighbors, the energy available to us will diminish over time, even the Sun will burn out in a couple billion years and incinerate the entire Earth. On the smaller, human-sized scale, though, people can and are doing many things to counter the effects of entropy. We do take time to clean our houses. We are able to perform periodic tune-ups on our car engines. And we can impose our will and energy to create more order where there once was less.

Perhaps what scientists refer to as the organizational force that caused the Big Bang is not that dissimilar from the religious notion of God's will; both suggest a force sufficient to overpower the devilishly disintegrating forces of entropy otherwise prevalent in the universe.

The Creation of Adam, Michelangelo Buonarroti, The Sistine Chapel, c 1510

Entropy is the explanation for the natural tendency of the universe toward increasing disorganization heading toward chaos. But whether one looks to Genesis (the story of creation in the Bible) or evolution (the story of creation based upon scientific observation and data collection), the organic sliver of the universe known as life on Earth suggests that in our own way, people are increasing organization over time in the face of such enormous amounts of entropy. Instead of succumbing to disorder, ours is an existence built on development. Our increasingly complex lives serve as an opposing force to the entropy of the universe. Thus, perhaps there is a balancing act going on in which humans have been entrusted, at least in our own backyard, to rebuff entropy—to creatively sculpt harmony and order from chaos and disarray. Perhaps man is supposed to perform this work *with* God.

If this is the task, then as a community, a society, and a world, we are not doing so well lately; people have been assisting, and accelerating, the process of entropy on many human-scaled fronts. Under this view, strapping a bomb on one's back to further the cause of jihad might be an abomination in the eyes of both science and religion.

Portraits Hung in Empty Halls (A Long Winter)

Clearly, there is more to the story of Earth's origins than the Big Bang itself. While it may be hard to conceive, most of the time that has elapsed since the Big Bang (the first 9-odd billion years) passed without there being an Earth at all, although there were events that provide a degree of illumination as to our origins. These events, more specifically, involve the formation of stars and planets.

The most important concept to bear in mind here is one that is often misunderstood, and that is the concept of gravity. Most of us grow up (and become grown-ups) thinking that gravity simply means *things fall toward the center of the Earth.* It stands to reason that this is true, of course: Everything that goes up on this planet must come down at some point. This is what is observed time and time again with one's own senses, and this is something that does not change no matter how many times objects from heights are dropped. It turns out, though, that this rule is employed on an everyday basis and is a special example of a more general principle that Isaac Newton hit upon as the proverbial apple famously fell from a tree and knocked him on the head. Newton realized then that nothing was special about the Earth in terms of being attractive to other objects. He posited that instead of a universe in which everything is attracted to Earth itself, every particle of matter in the universe attracts every other particle of matter. The reason things fall toward the center of Earth is that something about the Earth causes a force of attraction much greater than any other object on the Earth. Newton added two qualifications that would determine the strength of attraction. The first is that the larger (more massive) the piece of matter is, the greater the force of attraction. The second is that the closer together two pieces of matter are, the greater the force of attraction. In one decisive scientific move, Newton effectively opened the door to a more broad celestial way of thinking about the universe, and simultaneously repositioned human perspective about the world to one far greater than could possibly be imagined given the limitations of human senses.

From human frame of reference, Earth is, by far, the largest piece of matter around, and people are generally fairly close to the Earth. These two things taken in combination result in the phenomenon that is noticed: Things fall toward the Earth. However, with this new conceptualization of gravity, Newton gave us an explanation for the behavior of celestial bodies outside the Earthly sphere, as well as the strange and virtually unobservable notion that there is a force of gravity between any two things with mass on Earth. This is also true in space, and this was equally true for the atoms of hydrogen and helium that were originally emitted from the Big Bang explosion. In this way, gravity became the centerpiece and driving force for the rest of creation.

Although the Big Bang sent particles flying in every direction, hydrogen and helium atoms would occasionally move close enough together, that the force of attraction (gravity) between the separate particles would cause them to coalesce toward each other (remember that everything with mass attracts everything else with mass), forming clouds of gas known as nebulas. Within these nebulas, it was not uncommon that two atoms might pass very closely by one another. Because each one had mass, they would attract one another and stick to one another. As Newton's law of gravitation predicts, the larger the clump of atoms, the more mass that clump has, and the more force of gravity it will have on surrounding matter. Over enough time, those clumps of atoms would build up into larger and larger bodies until the collection of hydrogen and helium was so massive that the gravitational force pushing every atom toward the center of the mass would create so much pressure that the hydrogen atoms would fuse together, releasing incredible amounts of energy. This event is essentially what is behind the birth of a star, and an example of a nuclear fusion reaction. This sort of thing seems quite extraordinary, and of course it is, but it is a fairly common fate for hydrogen and helium in the universe. Billions upon billions of stars have been born since the Big Bang: Astronomers estimate there are about 100 thousand million stars in the Milky Way alone. Outside that, there are millions upon millions of other galaxies also! (European Space Agency, 2004). Stars may burn via nuclear fusion of hydrogen atoms for millions, and even billions, of years (the closest star to us, the Sun, is thought to have about 9 billion years' worth of hydrogen fuel and has already burned brightly for 4.6 billion years) (Kunzig, 2003). However, once the hydrogen supply in this mass dwindles, the star collapses and goes supernova.

Supernovae are stellar explosions. They are part of the life cycle of a star and occur when the fusion reaction that melds hydrogen and helium together either starts or stops. Supernovae are events that can be supremely destructive if they happened at close range, but they are essential to the formation of things like planets. This is because supernovae are the only cosmological events that create enough heat and pressure to form elements heavier than helium. The explosion of a star results in a further fusion of atoms into the heavier elements. This is the only way elements such as carbon, oxygen, nitrogen, iron, calcium, and the rest of the elements on the periodic table can be created. It is these heavier elements that will eventually cluster together in order to form planets such as Earth.

The creation of Earth (or any other planet, for that matter) also depends on the force of gravity in the same way a star does. In the case of planets, though, it is not hydrogen and helium particles that join together; it is the heavier elements born from supernovae. Once the heavy elements from a star are created, they collide with one another and form larger and larger clumps of matter, again due to the gravitational attraction between all the particles involved. These clumps of matter, if large enough and positioned just so around a star of sufficient gravity, will eventually amass to the point where they would be considered planets. On the planet itself, the heavier elements (such as iron and other metals) will be more attracted to one another than less massive elements (such as oxygen and nitrogen gas). While the more massive elements on this particular planet have been pulled more strongly toward the center (which resulted in solid land), the less massive elements have settled to the periphery of the planet, still drawn toward the center but not enough to pull them from their gaseous state. This process, driven by something as simple as gravity, can explain what the Bible attributes to the second day of creation: the formation of the heavens and Earth.

Need Ya to Beg My Pardon, to Tend My Garden
(Joe Walsh)

This scientific theory outlined above is the current scientific working model for how the Earth came to be. It is an example of an evolutionary theory, which describes the development of the solar system as a "series of gradual and natural steps, understandable in terms of well-established physical principles" (Chaisson & McMillan, 1993). As will become clear in later chapters, a proper understanding of the theory of evolution will be central to this book, and it will be revisited in greater detail many times over.

The primitive Earth and the development of life on it will be the topic for the next chapter. For now, tracing 9.1 billion years of history from the beginning of time to the formation of the Earth is enough for one chapter. This understanding makes some questions about humanity's own origins become even clearer. While this book's central focus is ultimately not the long ago abstract events covered by a survey of cosmology, considering the deep origins will help ground us in a discussion of things on the human scale and remind us that in the grand, grand picture, all the things on Earth share a common heritage, again regardless of one's belief system. This applies to the entirety of the planet, including the rocks that are mined for metal, the air all animals breathe, the lava that bubbles out of volcanoes, the waters of the oceans, and the raw materials that are processed into "non-natural" substances like reinforced concrete, napalm, Kevlar, Styrofoam, and DDT. Examining the chemical composition of human bodies, there is a great deal of oxygen, nitrogen, and carbon atoms. It therefore can be said, quite literally, that the matter that makes up human bodies, just like the matter that makes up everything else on the planet, is the product of stars gone supernova. In other words, we are literally made of stardust, or as Sagan said, starstuff.

Of all the millions of galaxies that condensed from matter thrown out by the Big Bang, and of all the billions of planets formed from stars gone supernova, humans have found ourselves on this Pale Blue Dot, one planet that has all the right characteristics and attributes for life to occur. It took 9.1 billion years for the Earth to form after the Big Bang; the events that occurred 4.6 billion years since on our planet will prove to be much more interesting. This is mostly due to the emergence of a special concoction of replicating molecules here on Earth that is referred to as "life," and this is the topic for the next chapter.

And God called the firmament heaven. And there was evening, and there was morning, a second day. (Genesis 1:8)

3

On the Origins of Life on Earth

A while after the Big Bang (to us, this "while" was time beyond imagining), a small planet was taking shape somewhere in the vast, ever-expanding empty space that makes up most of the known universe. The original particles that made up its first small mass most likely took billions of years and a great deal of chance to transition from a minuscule nebula of atoms into something solid of any significant size. All celestial objects, including planetsand even meteors and comets, are collections of accumulated space particles that began as microscopic collections of stardust. Given enough time and opportunity to attract (fundamental law of physics) nearby stray particles, enormous spherical masses took shape, sculpted by the force of gravity. This particular planet, which is now quite familiar to us, reached its present size and shape about 4.6 billion years ago, pulled inwards by the force of gravity toward a medium-sized star about 93 million miles away, and pushed equally outward by the force of centripetal acceleration around that star such that it achieved a comfortable and reliable orbit. The nearby star was close enough to warm some of the planet's water to liquid form, but far enough away to not boil the entire planet's water into gas. This fortuitous balance of physical conditions would later allow for collections of highly specialized and organized molecules capable of adapting to their surroundings and replicating themselves.

Through a series of completely arbitrary events and chance conditions, planet Earth developed certain physical characteristics and attributes that eventually allowed life to appear. These facts are important to understand simply to be able to show that all life has a common and provable beginning. This chapter goes through a lot of Earth science and chemistry, vital but a bit dry; so if you don't want to feel dried out and want to take our word for the fact that organic life emerged from hot specs of stardust, feel free to go to Chapter 4.

Unlike the Big Bang story, where an incredibly energetic initial event occurred and has been dissipating energy ever since, the narrative of Earth is a story of increasing energy and organization. The local microcosmic tale is one that flies in the face of entropy. The fact that the universe as a whole is inexorably winding down from its explosive beginnings does not mean that everything in that universe has to be tending toward chaos at all times. This local predicament here on Earth is one that runs against the current of the universe. On Earth there is a tradition, as the biblical tale from Genesis relays, of making order from chaos. The story of how life, and eventually humanity, emerged on planet Earth is one of development and not one of disorder.

Third Stone from the Sun (Jimi Hendrix)

The story that science spins about the origins of the Earth and its early development in many ways mirrors the scientific story of the origins of the universe. Like the Big Bang, none of us were here to witness the original formation of Earth or describe what it was like to walk that primitive land and breathe that primitive air. Instead, knowledge of the primitive Earth is gathered from data collected via empirical experimentation, measurements, and tests. Scientists who study the Earth are at an advantage of sorts over scientists who study faraway cosmological phenomena; one can interact with specimens on Earth in a way that is impossible with a supernova. Nevertheless, clues about the origins of Earth remain elusive to human biological sense organs. Humans still need technology to extend the senses' reaches in order to measure and observe things beyond this limited human capacity. If these recent technological advances had been at hand when the biblical stories about how life began were formulated, we suggest that the explanations given in those documents would be quite different. There is a vast array of instruments such as spectrometers that measure the elemental composition of certain rock samples and sensors that measure the tiny fluctuations in output of carbon dioxide and other atmospheric gases that are invisible and odorless. From this scientific information a very reliable yet developing story of the origins of Earth and life on it has been constructed.

Gravity (John Mayer)

Like the formation of stars, the formation of Earth was attributable to the force of gravity attracting scattered particles of matter into an ever-larger mass. The gravity of these particles, combined with the angular momentum they had accumulated in their circular movements around the Sun, caused increasingly larger masses of particles to slowly collect. This process resulted in the formation of the chunks of rock that would eventually become the four innermost planets: Mercury, Venus, Earth, and Mars (Lin, 2008). Even though the four terrestrial planets all formed in the same way, each of these planets has a slightly different composition of elements. In the case of the third planet out, the majority of the particles that became gravitationally bound to one another were oxygen (which makes up 46.6% of the Earth's crust), silicon (which makes up 27.7% of the Earth's crust), aluminum (which makes up 8.1% of the Earth's crust), and iron (which makes up 5.0% of the Earth's crust) (Gardner, 2007). These so called heavy elements, all born from supernovae, attracted one another through the force of gravity and, over time, accumulated into an increasingly large solid mass. This process of gravitational attraction and accumulation was probably imperceptibly slow at first, but with the passage of time and further accumulation of more and more atoms and molecules, the accumulation of matter built on its own success. It takes a very long time to get things going when it comes to cosmological events, and like the story of the larger universe, it took a long while for things to get going here on Earth to where it was an appreciable size and mass.

In the earliest stages of the Earth's formation, all elements floating in circles around the Sun most likely attracted one another in a rather haphazard and unorganized fashion, much like dust bunnies collecting under the couch. This hodgepodge of elements came together under the force of gravity, with no initial overarching pattern or organization other than the unavoidable attraction each tiny piece of matter had for its neighbors, and vice versa. Over enough time, though, and throughout the universe the more massive elements (such as iron) experienced a stronger force of attraction than the lighter elements and, as a result, tended toward the center of swirling masses. The heavier elements eventually would clump together and become the solid core in one of these locations and would become our nascent planet. The less massive elements (such as nitrogen) that did not experience such strong forces of attraction were not forsaken in this process; they simply were not pulled toward the dense and massive solid core with the same force of attraction, and instead drifted closer to the outer layers of the forming planet. These lighter elements most likely became the layer of gases that made up Earth's primitive atmosphere.

Such separation of solid and gaseous elements was made possible in large part by Earth's relative distance from the Sun. It is really the planet's—and all living beings'—good fortune that Earth is located where it is in relation to the Sun. The 93 million miles of space between the outer edge of the Sun and the Earth's atmosphere turns out to allow for a perfect range of temperatures. This temperature range keeps the planet delicately balanced between freezing solid and boiling into vapor even today, but back when the planet was forming, it allowed just the right combination of elements to gather and form both solid land and gaseous atmosphere. Venus, Earth's closest neighbor, is thought to have both solid land and atmosphere, but its atmosphere, comprised almost entirely of carbon dioxide and sulfuric acid, is not habitable for life (Chaisson & McMillan, 1993). The relatively lighter elements that make up the majority of Earth's atmosphere also make it habitable for life, as we will discuss later. On the Earth's other side is Mars, a planet with a definite solid core like Earth, but whose atmosphere is very thin, exerting only 1/150th the pressure of Earth's atmosphere (Chaisson & McMillan, 1993). It is also worth noting that because of the temperature and pressure conditions specific to Earth, the elements that happened to collect in order to make the Earth were ones that could separate into solid, liquid, and gaseous states at the temperature and pressure conditions that were developing on Earth. This, again, is not true of every planet, as is known from observations of neighboring planets such as Mars (which does not have a significant atmosphere) and Jupiter (a completely gaseous planet).

Even after this settling of elements occurred to the point where there was a discernable land and sky, the primitive Earth was not a very hospitable place and certainly not yet ready for any living beings. The earliest picture that can be painted of Earth is a hellacious one. It was thought that the earliest atmosphere was comprised, in part, of hydrogen gas (Abelson, 1966), which is at once highly combustible (think "Hindenburg exploding") and so light that the solid Earth's gravity could not hold down the gas. Hydrogen dissipated, which made way for slightly heavier given off by extreme volcanic activity to fill the skies. These heavier molecules included ammonia (NH_3), nitrogen oxide (NO_2) carbon dioxide (CO_2), nitrogen (N_2), methane (CH_4), hydrogen sulfide (H_2S), and water vapor (H_2O) (Campbell & Reece, 2005). If you or I were to stand on an imaginary bit of solid, cool land in this atmosphere, we would not be able to breathe and live to tell the tale. The closest thing that could come to experiencing the primitive atmosphere today is venturing into the fumaroles of an active volcano. In the early years of Earth, the oxygen (O_2) that we (and all land animals) depend on for cellular respiration did not yet exist in any meaningful quantity in the atmosphere. In fact, this would only come after photosynthetic cells emerged and gave off oxygen as a by-product.

Hell (Elvis Costello)

At this time, Earth itself was in the process of cooling, but surface explosions of lava were the order of the day. Earth, at this point, was too hot to sustain liquid or solid water on its surface; all the water was held as vapor in the atmosphere. Lightning strikes, caused by the difference in electrical charge between Earth and its atmosphere, were thought to be a common occurrence (Hill, 1992). Additionally, large comets and asteroids would bombard the Earth's surface on a regular basis. In its early years (say the first billion or so), Earth was a feisty planet. It was not a place that resembled this cool green and blue planet of today, and certainly it did not seem like a place upon which life could emerge and thrive. Eventually, though, the initial activity that characterized our Earth's birth and infancy mellowed. The heavy bombardment of meteors subsided around 3.8 billion years ago. As a result, Earth cooled enough to condense some of the atmospheric water vapor into liquid, which in turn formed Earth's most important resource and environmental attribute: oceans. While some theorize that liquid water was present on Earth well before this time, as evidenced by water-worn crystals called zircons that have been determined to be over 4.4 billion years old (Valley et al., 2002), oceans established their presence on Earth's surface about 800 million years after Earth formed. As ocean water contacted rumbling volcanic activity from deep within Earth's core, cool, dry land started to form in earnest. Since water (a greenhouse gas) was moving out of the atmosphere and into oceans, more sunlight was able to reach Earth's surface. This combination of surface water in liquid form, extreme volcanic activity, common lightning strikes, increasing sunlight radiation, and an atmosphere of NH_3, CO_2, and CH_4 was the crucible within which life emerged.

In any environment, even today, molecules are continually colliding with one another, bumping against one another, reacting with one another. Sometimes the molecules that meet bounce off each other and go their separate ways. Sometimes there is a release of energy like an explosion. Sometimes the molecules end up sticking together, bound by attraction of their electromagnetic charges. And sometimes these chance molecular meetings will even result in a swapping of electrons and a rearranging of nuclei (a chemical reaction), which results in a new combination of atoms that may be even more stable than the molecular arrangement before such a meeting. And for molecules, stability is the name of the game. Reaching into the recesses of your memories of high school chemistry, you might remember that atoms and molecules will continue to bond with one another and swap electrons (in other words, react) until a stable configuration of electrons is reached. This sometimes occurs in very simple ways (e.g., two hydrogen atoms binding to an oxygen atom to make water), but it can also be much more complicated (e.g., the double helix of DNA).

The encounters that any given molecule experienced in the primitive atmosphere were completely random. However, because there were so many molecules (1.33×10^{50} by one calculation) (Weisenberger, 2005) and there was so much time (1.4 billion years), the potential for every sort of interaction between molecules was quite high. Eventually, some molecular encounter had to be successful.

What is meant by "successful"? What does a successful molecule look like? A successful molecule is one that is stable (will not readily react with most other molecules that happen to bump into it) and is able to maintain its structure in the face of outside threat (survive). Eventually, "successful molecules" will refer to a molecule that would be able to replicate itself many times over (reproduce), but no simple molecules such as the ones found on primitive Earth could do that.

Among the simpler stable molecules that emerged in early Earth's atmosphere, several slightly more complex ones began to increase their numbers. These molecules, called amino acids, are the building blocks of what are now call proteins, which in turn are the building blocks for cells, which in turn are the building blocks for all living things on the planet. Amino acids appeared very early in Earth's history, possibly only a couple hundred thousand years after its initial formation. Simple prokaryotic cells were thought to have developed shortly thereafter, more than 4.4 billion years ago, but traumatic atmospheric events (such as bombardment by meteors) were thought to have completely killed off this first wave of life (Wilde, Valley, Peck, & Graham, 2001). Evidence of sulfur and iron metabolism was seen not long after the shower of celestial objects halted (Archer & Vance, 2006), which lends credence to the theory that life's story may have begun as colonies of proto-cells that metabolized chemicals such as iron and sulfur containing compounds in order to survive (Russell, Daniel, Hall, & Sherringham, 1994). From this strange beginning, the basic molecular pieces were in place so that oxygen-metabolizing life forms like us could emerge.

As far as molecules go, the design of an amino acid was a runaway success. The center, or anchor, of the molecule was very stable. At the same time, though, the molecule was very flexible. One branch of the molecule (called the "r-group") allowed for what computer enthusiasts would call "plug-and-play compatibility," that is, variations could be swapped in and out of the basic structure of the amino acid to provide several variants. And last, amino acids were structured so they could easily chain up with one another end-to-end, much like cars on a train. While it took a very long time for the right combination of hydrogen, nitrogen, oxygen, and carbon atoms to randomly find each other in the primitive atmosphere, they did, and we have evidence that the emergence of amino acids may have had a little bit of help from the environment.

In 1953, at a laboratory in the University of Chicago, Stanley Miller set up a small model of what the environment of primitive Earth might have been like. He put some water into a flask and injected the gases commonly thought to have been part of the primitive environment: hydrogen, methane, ammonia, and water. At the top of this sealed container, he placed two electrodes that provided a shower of sparks (this was meant to simulate lightning). Not knowing what might happen, he set up his closed system.

> During the run the water in the flask became noticeably
> pink after the first day, and by the end of the week the
> solution was deep red and turbid. Most of the turbidity
> was due to colloidal silica from the glass. The red color
> is due to organic compounds adsorbed on the silica. Also
> present are yellow organic compounds, of which only
> a small fraction can be extracted with ether, and which
> form a continuous streak tapering off at the bottom on
> a one-dimensional chromatogram run in butanol-acetic
> acid. These substances are being investigated further.
> (Miller, 1953, pp. 528-529)

Miller quickly determined the mysterious red and yellow compounds
to be amino acids, most prominently glycine and alanine (two of
the simplest forms of amino acid). It seems, then, that conditions on
primitive Earth may have prompted the development of amino acids,
and according to Miller's findings, the key may have been the amounts
of electric discharge provided by a shower of sparks in the experiment,
and by lightning and ultraviolet radiation in the actual primitive Earth.
Elegantly, this notion of the "spark of life" commonly is seen in human
stories and, perhaps most famously, in Shelley's *Frankenstein*. While
amino acids themselves are not considered to be alive, they are the
precursors and necessary components for life to develop, and the blaze
of life that resulted from the emergence of amino acids was most likely
started, quite literally, from one tiny spark several billion years ago.

Even after Miller's famous experiment demonstrated how amino
acids might have been generated, given the raw ingredients on primitive
Earth there is still some debate as to the source of amino acids. While
it is completely plausible that amino acids could have resulted from the
billions upon billions of chance chemical encounters, another intriguing
theory is that amino acids found their way to Earth from somewhere
outside the biosphere. In studies of asteroids that have landed on Earth,
particularly one that landed in Australia in 1969, scientists have found
an abundance of amino acids (Kvenvolden, Lawless, Pering, Peterson,
Flores, et al., 1970). Moreover, the types and amounts of amino acids
found in such space rocks mirror the results from the Miller experiment.
Other studies of comets and asteroids, much like the ones that rained
down from space during the period of heavy bombardment, have turned
up evidence of amino acids, which has led many to believe that the initial

spark of life was, quite literally, delivered to Earth from above (Pierazzo & Chyba, 1999).

While life's extraterrestrial origin is a topic worthy of scientific debate, it is enough for us to be reminded that in the grand scheme of the universe, what is on Earth is a very small part of creation. To some this may sound like fodder for science fiction movies or alien conspiracy theorists, and to others it may sound like scientific justification for the story of divine creation. Using such a theory (and, as with all scientific knowledge, it is just a theory) for philosophical ends might be too far a leap. This, like questions surrounding the Big Bang, epitomizes the idea that even at the center of the story humans are painting a search for understanding and meaning, but undoubtedly some things remain unknowable at least for an unknown period of time. This alone, should be cause for awe, wonder, curiosity, and reverence—emotions often related to personal fulfillment and for many revealed by God's work.

Carl Sagan is among those who derived a great deal of morality and spirituality from his study of the cosmos and Earth's deep history. He wrote brilliantly about the relationship of Earth to the universe, the possibility of life elsewhere, and the pragmatic and moral implications of these concepts, demonstrating that a proper scientific understanding of our origins, both proximal and distal, can do much to inform how humans eventually reconcile our place in the universe. Following is a brief extrapolation of his thoughts regarding the human role in the cosmos.

1. It is possible to estimate within a reasonable range of statistical probability the likelihood of life existing elsewhere. The factors in the calculation include the size of the universe, the range of physical conditions considered necessary to support life, and the frequency of life-destroying events such as novae, supernovae, black holes, and the like.

2. Life can exist in radically different forms than we might expect, as we have recently discovered in the depths of the Earth's oceans.

3. The fact that we have thus far been unable to communicate with extraterrestrial life does not mean it

does not exist. Other equally likely reasons why this has not occurred are because of the daunting distances between us and other potential life-sustaining locales, and because we only recently (in a relative sense) evolved sufficiently to be able to communicate over vast distances by receiving and sending radio signals. The distances our hypothetical neighbors would need to travel to get here render actual visits extremely improbable.

4. The ability of people to spread hoaxes regarding extraterrestrial visits, unsupported by true scientific evidence, reveals our vulnerability to believe that we are not alone and suggests we should be cautious of the power of those who utilize religious doctrine to further their own agenda.

5. We ought to use care in preserving our little backyard because it is precious.

6. We need to keep in perspective our relative insignificance to the workings of the cosmos. In Sagan's book *Pale Blue Dot* (1994) he emphasized how small minded are those who maintain the conceit that God's central purpose is to administer to the needs and punish the misconduct of sentient bipeds on Earth.

7. If there is approximately 70% of the universe that we do not understand at all, we should not be so arrogant as to claim to understand how even 50% of it works, and certainly should not be as pompous as to claim to understand God's mind.

8. We are programmed to be inquisitive. To suggest that God has something to fear from science cheapens not only our very nature, but also God.

Somewhere out there, perhaps millions or billions of light years away, complex arrangements of carbon, hydrogen, oxygen, and nitrogen are undergoing transformations similar to the ones known of on Earth. This sort of perspective gives us a sense of awe for how unique and precious all life really is, as we have not yet found anything like us in the rest of all creation (with our admittedly limited interstellar technology), but also a healthy respect and reverence for the enormity of our universe, and how small we are by comparison. However on a more human scale, it gives us an important framework within which we can fit the stories of science and those of God, intertwined.

A Series of Successful Molecules

Whether amino acids popped up after billions of years of molecular trial and error on Earth, on the tail of a comet (after billions of years of trial and error elsewhere in the universe), or most probably both, they made Earth their home and quickly surged in number. And clearly, the story of life on Earth does not end with amino acids. When you compare an amino acid to a simpler molecule present in the primitive atmosphere, say, ammonia or diatomic nitrogen, the amino acid has a more complex structure. However, when comparing a single amino acid to most of the molecules that make up the cells in the body, an amino acid looks incredibly simple (Figure 3.1). And indeed it is, in many ways. One lesson to be learned here is that generally speaking, simplicity means success. Mechanical and electrical engineers would undoubtedly agree with this statement, as would speech writers, marketing firms, mathematicians, poets, and chefs. On the molecular level, this is just as true. Fewer atoms and fewer bonds translate to fewer places in which a loose free radical or adverse environmental condition might interrupt a molecule's stability.

On the flip side of this formula for success, it may be advantageous for some molecules to cluster together and create larger macromolecules. Usually, it is found that macromolecules (such as proteins, made from a chain of amino acids) are able to do more than amino acids can do alone. Amino acids may be a very sharp paring knife, engineered impeccably for one discrete purpose, but macromolecules are multi-tools, wildly adaptable apparatuses that can address any number of needs.

Figure 3.1. Left: The chemical structure of an amino acid (glycene).
Right: the chemical structure of a protein (hemoglobin).

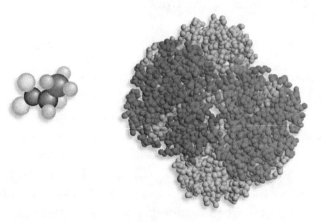

Sources: www.3dchem.com/molecules.asp?ID=40,
www.chm.bris.ac.uk/motm/hemoglobin/hemoglobh.htm

Consider all the processes that happen in the human body at any given moment: Chemical neurotransmitters flood synapses in human brains, muscles contract and relax, enzymes speed up digestion, portions of DNA code are translated and transcribed by ribosomes in every cell in the body. Neurotransmitters, muscle fibers, ribosomes, and enzymes are considered to be less than microscopic but each of these items is comprised of proteins, which are even smaller. Proteins, the multi-tool to the amino acid's paring knife, are nothing but strings of dozens to hundreds of amino acids chained together and folded in on themselves. The more complex protein has a much wider repertoire of functions than its constituent part alone. This increased functionality assuredly helps these large molecules' success, and this represents the second strategy for success: organized complexity.

The path ahead should seem clear at this point: Amino acids group together and become proteins; proteins team up with other macromolecules and form cells; cells cluster into colonies and tissues; tissues begin to specialize in their function and create more complex organisms; and after 3.2 billion years of successful clusters of molecules in varied conformations and sizes, *Homo sapiens* emerges. It is, of course, an enormous disservice to breeze past every miraculous step in this story, but this book is not the place for such a survey of natural history. It is enough to know, though, that with each imperceptible move forward, the principle supporting such moves was that organized complexity of the right kind can bring success—it is evolutionary—and it brings success much more readily than the principle of simplicity.

It is factually and undeniably true that every living thing on the planet is a success (at least to this point). If the configuration of molecules, cells, tissues, or organs were not stable or successful in some way, that molecule, cell, or organism would quickly cease to exist. If one considers each stable amino acid molecule to be a successful molecule, the sheer number of successes within each of us outnumbers the total world population several times over. Usually, the unstable molecules that are encountered (such as weapons-grade uranium or elemental sodium) have to be manufactured in laboratories. Such unstable sets of molecules do not last long in nature.

In the early years of Earth's existence, there were more unsuccessful molecules than there are now, but those unsuccessful molecules did not make it for long. All molecules were exposed to some sort of environmental stress and either broke apart, formed larger or different molecules, reacted in some way, or maintained their structure. In any sampling of molecules, you would find that some exhibit each of these four behaviors. The molecules that broke apart formed larger or different molecules, or reacted in a way that we would call "unsuccessful"; they did not maintain their structure in the face of stress. As more time went by, the number of successful molecules increased because they were stable enough to stick around for a longer period of time, and as a result the ratio of successful to unsuccessful molecules in existence increased.

This did not happen quickly in any sense; it took almost 1.5 billion years from the beginnings of Earth for amino acids to become proteins, and for proteins to combine in interesting ways with other macromolecules to create single cells, the first life on the planet. The story that science tells us, though, is that the emergence of life in this way was not intentional or a foregone conclusion. It was simply the result of billions upon billions of trials in which molecules combined in unique ways, each yielding new molecules of varying success with relation to the threats and stresses imposed by their environments. Those molecules that were more successful at maintaining their stability via both structure and function stuck around, and those molecules that were not as successful became something else. And every time a new plateau of stability was reached, increasingly complex molecules, by chance, found new ways to combine and interact, which would in turn make possible a new level of molecular complexity and functionality.

Replicating Molecules and The Emergence of Cells

At some point in the random process of combining and separating molecules, a highly stable molecule emerged with a very impressive function: the ability to make copies of itself. The advantage to such molecular changes is that the successes were cumulative. It was completely random that atoms would rearrange themselves into a configuration that was capable of replicating itself, but once the magic formula was hit upon, things on Earth changed dramatically.

The self-replicating molecule is the predecessor to DNA, deoxyribonucleic acid. This was most likely a single-stranded form of nucleic acid similar to what is now recognize as RNA. As compared to other molecules present 1.4 billion years after Earth's creation, this nucleic acid was a rather large and unwieldy molecule. Left on its own, RNA was more susceptible to environmental threat, despite its ability to make copies of itself. Of the many strands of RNA that existed, some did suffer at the hands of the environment, broken apart by solar radiation, attacked by free radicals, or reacted with by nearby molecules. However, some strands of RNA successfully encountered other molecules. Some may have provided RNA physical protection from the elements, repelling water and all the potentially nasty substances contained in it. Some may have provided a form of usable chemical energy that aided the RNA in its fairly complex process of self-replication. Some may have streamlined the replication process, making it easier, faster, or more accurate. Whenever a combination of molecules resulted in a greater stability because of organized complexity, those molecules tended to stick together. The RNA could replicate with greater ease, and its helper molecules would in turn be reproduced along with the RNA. Over enough time, the successes from this process accumulated to the point where cascades of complex molecules were working in tandem with the shared goal of being successfully stable in their environment. This was the point at which life as properly defined emerged on the planet. These first living things, most likely aquatic bacteria that converted nearby chemicals into usable energy, represented a culmination of several billion years of molecular successes.

Science has proven that all forms of life, from algae to anteaters, utilize RNA and its double-stranded cousin, DNA. As will be discussed in greater detail in the next chapter, one way to actually think of any organism on the planet, including us, is as nothing more than highly specialized and adapted DNA transport systems. Organized collections of organic molecules have grown incredibly complex; this is more than evident when you compare a human being's chemical makeup to that of a bacterium. However, for all our complexity, humans may not be any more successful at housing and passing on DNA than single-celled bacterial ancestors, whose basic design is so successful that it hasn't changed for over 3 billion years. For all human abilities, proclivities, achievements, and adaptations, human design has lost the simplicity of a bacterium's design. We humans have applauded ourselves for the ability to harness natural resources and build incredible things, like the pyramids, spacecraft, and microwave popcorn. Humans have taken pride in being able to live in almost every climate on the planet and have even reached the point where a few of us have been able to leave this planet.

These are incredible achievements and are not to be discounted, but we must remember that something else has been living quite successfully at the top of the Himalayan mountains, at the bottom of the ocean's trenches, in the middle of vast deserts, deep in the interior of the densest jungles, underneath the Antarctic ice shelf, inside fuming volcanic calderas, underneath cities' tunnels and sewers, and even within the toxic pollution dumps where we would not dare visit. Bacteria can be found all over and inside our bodies. Recent reports estimate that "the number of bacteria living within the body of the average healthy adult human is estimated to outnumber human cells 10 to 1 [by number, not weight]" (American Society for Microbiology, 2008). Moreover, we would not be able to live were it not for the bacteria in and on our bodies, such as the *E. coli* in our intestines, which we depend upon for proper digestion.

Considering bacteria in this light, we may again stand to amend the perception of where we fit into the natural order and place in the larger universe. We would do well to reconsider which form of life is really the dominant form on the planet. Upright walking mammals, of which humans are a form, have graced the planet with our presence for a little over 3 million years. Bacteria, in their many forms, have been here over 1,000 times longer, and from what is known of their incredible ability to adapt to extreme environments, they will be here long after humans are gone. Human complexity has brought incredible success, but it seems that bacteria's simplicity makes them even more successful when the bigger picture is considered. After all, when humans die, we become food for bacteria. This may be a good point to emphasize that regardless of what happens, the world and life will survive even if humans do not, but from an evolutionary standpoint, that would be a colossal failure for our enterprise as a species.

From the fiery origins of the planet, it is thought to have taken anywhere from 800 million years to 15 billion years for the first single-celled organisms to successfully survive in great numbers in this manner (Schopf, 2006). The first bacteria most likely obtained carbon from atmospheric CO_2 and obtained energy from oxidizing inorganic chemicals in their environment. Once bacteria appeared on the planet, though, the further development of the arrangement of molecules we would call living things accelerated sharply. It would no longer take billions of years for significant changes to occur. In fact, it is thought that in less than 500 million years, single-celled organisms developed the ability to obtain energy from sunlight, water, and CO_2 instead of chemicals that would have been found in primitive Earth's atmosphere. Converting energy from sunlight into usable cellular energy was only an option after the storms and dense, gaseous atmosphere characteristic of primitive Earth settled. Once the Sun started to shine through the heavy bombardment of meteors and explosive volcanic activity, life had a virtually unlimited power source from which to draw energy.

Photosynthesis (The Hot Toddies)

This process is better known as photosynthesis. Photosynthetic single-celled organisms represented the next significant plateau in the story of life on Earth. Before photosynthesis, the oxygen content in the Earth's atmosphere was quite low, far too low to allow life as we experience it to survive by breathing the air. Between 3.5 billion and 3 billion years ago, photosynthetic bacteria produced enough oxygen to increase the oxygen content of the Earth's atmosphere to close to present levels, about 18% (Buick, 2008). This increase in oxygen would allow further life forms to develop that did not depend on photosynthesis directly for energy, and it would eventually allow life to move outside Earth's waters. However, life's landfall would not happen for another 2.5 to 3 billion years, as the Precambrian era gave way to the Paleozoic era about 540 million years ago.

Like the arrival of cells themselves, the development of photosynthetic processes sped up the rate at which new, innovative changes came from the billions of molecules colliding and reacting with one another on Earth. However, as compared to the rate of change we experience in our own time, things were still happening quite slowly; 500 million years is a painfully long time to wait for chemosynthesis to give way to photosynthesis. As before, though, the rate of change life on Earth experienced was increasing as more molecular successes accumulated, and the levels of organized complexity increased.

Sexual Revolution (Roger Waters)

Bacteria, like other living things, are able to replicate themselves, thanks to the highly specialized molecule of nucleic acid they each carry. Even though we'd like to think of offspring bacteria as identical to its parent, the truth is that there is potentially quite a bit of variation. The variation is due to random processing errors when the DNA molecule is being copied. Sometimes, the DNA just is not proofread properly, and the daughter strand of DNA is slightly different from the parent strand. Since most bacteria can replicate very quickly (some as quickly as 20 minutes), this causes a great deal of randomness and variation in any given group of single-celled bacteria over enough time. It is precisely this random variation that drives the group as a whole toward increasing complexity: Some random variations will prove to be more successful than other variations in a given environment, and those successful variations are what stick around. Still, because bacteria replicate themselves individually, the amount of random variation due to proofreading errors is still quite small.

About 1.2 billion years ago, though, life stumbled upon a way to intentionally combine their DNA molecules in their offspring. This, of course, created a lot more random variation in the group of bacteria, as offspring bacteria were only half identical to their parent cells, whereas before they were fully identical, barring any proofreading errors in DNA replication. This process, which we call sexual reproduction, kick-started an explosion of changes for organic collections of molecules on the planet. After almost 3 billion years of single cells depending on random errors in replication to occur, the planet's life had stumbled onto a way to intentionally mix things up without losing the continuity provided by billions of years of accumulated organized complexity. Variety was indeed the spice of life; from the emergence of sexual reproduction, the planet saw its first authentic multicellular cooperation: cell colonies. That certain cells—all generally similar but slightly different in just the right way—could find greater stability in working cooperatively was the foundation for more complex life forms: Jellyfish, worms, crustaceans, insects, boned fish, amphibians, reptiles, birds, and mammals would all eventually follow from these simple colonies of bacteria within a short billion years. Just like the molecules billions of years ago that found a symbiosis with the replicating strand of nucleic acid, cells joined together with a common goal: mutual survival and stability.

Sexual reproduction allowed changes to come much faster than ever before. The most successful colonies of cells would begin to specialize in their functions, and those more differentiated colonies would be more successful, contributing to the overall movement of life on the planet toward complexity and organization. Starting about 580 million years ago, changes in life in response to certain environmental stresses and challenges were so rapid when compared to changes that predated this era that it saw the development of numerous diverse aquatic species, which would become the ancestors for modern life. This time period is called the "Cambrian explosion" and is the mile marker for the end of the first era of natural history on the planet. About 540 million years ago, thanks in part to the multitude of new photosynthetic species, oxygen levels in the atmosphere built up enough to allow an ozone layer to form (Berkner & Marshall, 1965). This ozone layer would block much of the harmful ultraviolet radiation coming from the Sun, preventing random proofreading errors in DNA (such proofreading errors were usually no longer beneficial to sexually reproducing life forms) and made environmental conditions conducive to life moving out of the oceans and onto land, now cooled, solid, and ripe with opportunity. Those organisms that were able to take root and breathe freely outside of the water were wildly successful, as they had far less competition for resources on land.

Each new environment that life encountered presented new challenges to life's stability. This meant that in each environment, a different set of random characteristics would be most advantageous. Just like the assortment of basic molecules billions of years previously, life in all its varied incarnations saw only the most successful survive. Those successful life forms were the ones to reproduce. The process of trial and error was still present, but it was growing more and more refined as the successful organisms remained, and the unsuccessful organisms did not.

In this way, life proceeded toward increased diversity, increased complexity, and increased organization from its humble beginnings as atoms of carbon, nitrogen, hydrogen, and oxygen bumbling into each other over 4 billion years ago. This story highlights something incredibly important: All life shares the same recent ancestry on Earth, much like all matter shares the same ultimate ancestry from the Big Bang. Living things on Earth are in a microcosm, a small model of how the universe operates, with development and organization to replace entropy in their small corner of the cosmos. Because of common molecular ancestry, all living things are remarkably similar on a molecular level. Biology will give us illustrative examples: All living things use the same molecule—adenosine triphosphate, or ATP—to power their cellular processes. All living things, at their core, replicate DNA or RNA. All living things ultimately thrive on and benefit from diversity within a given population. And despite everything we humans try to do to remove ourselves from the community of life, we are inextricably bound to all life on the planet because of these (and other) inescapable truths. The animals with whom we, as humans, share our lands are our brothers and sisters; the trees and plants are our cousins; the oceans and all the life they contain are the place of our proximal origin; the single-celled bacteria that far outnumber us are our oldest Earthly ancestors. In a time where humans find more that separates us than unites us, it is often difficult to remember these very old lessons, but they are vitally important.

It is beyond the scope of this chapter (and this book) to trace the twists and turns that living things took in order to arrive at the emergence of sentient, upright walking beings that would be considered our most immediate ancestors. Given the humble beginnings of human ancestors and the simple governing principles of how those beginnings changed, the path from the oceans 540 million years ago to the African veldt some 4.4 million years ago should not be that mysterious. Science has weaved an incredible factual story for us of our family tree, a story that has given us a place in creation, a way to connect to the rest of the natural world, and also some indication as to just how special our human condition is (or at least we so may think).

The remainder of the book will deal much more directly with humans and will zoom in on a local scale of experience, itself infinitely complex; the reader would do well to remember where you came from and how you fit into that larger context. Humans, for all our brainpower and technological achievements, are collections of organic molecules. And as will become evident in the following chapters, it may be possible to explain most of humanity—and begin to formulate some solutions to humanity's ills—using this frame of reference.

And God saw everything that He had made, and, behold, it was very good. And there was evening and there was morning, the sixth day. (Genesis 1:30)

4

On Evolution
And The Emergence of Humans

And so it came to pass that on one very small, blue-green, watery planet somewhere in the universe, life emerged slowly from nonliving matter. It took a very long time for things to stumble into correct alignment, and environmental conditions had to be just so, but they were. And now, 3.5-odd billion years after the first cells emerged, 4.6 billion years after our planet cooled, and 13.7 billion years after the bang that started it all, our little corner of the universe is brimming with life in all its glorious forms. Earth is teeming with lions and lemurs, dolphins and dandelions, echinoderms, elephants, *E. coli*, egrets, eggplant, earwigs, and more. In 1992, estimates were that there were between 1.5 million and 1.8 million identified species in existence (May, 1992), all unique and beautiful, all successes in their own way. So you might ask, "What does this have to do with a fishbowl?" "Why are these authors racing through the history of everything?" Well, the current predicaments have to do with us, people, folks, humans, and we want there to be a base understanding of what that really means. It is clear that there is great disagreement on this.

We have such a wide variety of species on the planet in large part because of the diversity of Earth's physical geography. Each of Earth's geographical environments has a specific set of characteristics that demand a particular sort of adaptation to be successful. It is ultimately the makeup of the geographical environment that will determine which characteristics and traits end up being successful. The thick fur and subcutaneous fat of a polar bear, for example, is favored in the cold of the arctic, but not in the tropics. Conversely, the absorptive roots of epiphytes are well suited to the humid conditions in the tropics, but not in a desert. Thus, as life spread around the planet following the end of the Precambrian era, the life forms that happened to be more specialized to survive or maintain stability and replicate themselves in the context of a certain environment were the successful ones. From this principle, we can explain the running speed of a cheetah, the bioluminescence of deep sea fish, the height and girth of giant redwoods, the social behavior of ants, the oils secreted by poison ivy, the hoof shape of mountain goats, the plume of a peacock's feathers, the growth patterns of lichen, and as will be evidenced, the complexity of the human mind.

We who belong to species currently in existence are successes. Not just us humans, but all of us. We who are alive today exhibit adaptations that have stood many tests and trials over untold eons. We are the inheritors of billions of years of accumulated designs that work well for survival and stability. We can see this principle at work more clearly in other species: The length of a giraffe's neck serves a clear survival purpose, as do the teeth of a shark, the echolocation abilities of a bat, or the hyphae of a mushroom. However, as will be described in this chapter, we humans also possess such adaptations, even if they are not as obvious or simple as those found in other parts of nature. Much like the menagerie that accompanied Noah onto his Ark, the myriad forms that life takes on the planet are all successful survivors, and we cannot forget to count our own species as one of those survivors. We must remember too that Noah and his family represented a species worth saving on the Ark. Noah was not just a steward of the living world; he was a member of it.

Human Song Lyrics (The Cheetah Girls)

The previous two chapters cover all but the most recent 4.4 million years in the universe's 13.7-billion-year history. This means that humanity was not even a small part of the picture for the vast majority of the universe's history in terms of time. However, as evidenced by the diagram of geologic time on Earth (Figure 4.1), most of what is of interest to us is that which is closest to us. We children of the modern era have been on the scene only very recently, when compared to the age of our home planet. Remember that because successful designs have been building upon one another to reach new plateaus of complexity and organization, the rate of productive change for living things here on Earth has been increasing. Things are accelerating, and we who represent the most recent link in that increasingly complex chain serve as evidence. The 4.4 million years of deep human history represents only 0.0007% of Earth's history and only 0.0002% of the universe's history if we are counting minutes,

Figure 4.1. Geologic time on Earth

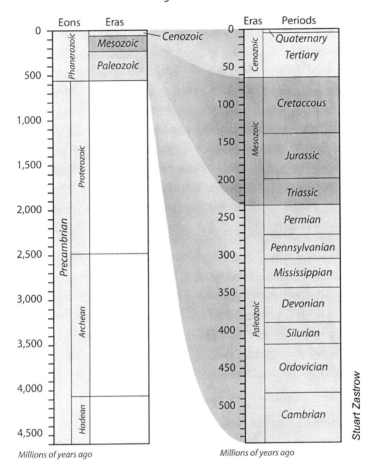

Geologic Time Scale

Millions of years ago

Millions of years ago

Stuart Zastrow

Source: http://geology.com/time/geologic-time-scale-550.gif

but the most recent 4.4 million years, formally called the Quaternary period of the Cenozoic era, is what we are most concerned with. It is where our immediate story begins. While the human history you may have studied in school covers, at most, about 10,000 years (and for good reason: The most recent 10,000 years of humanity's history are where almost all of the significant events of human history as we know it have taken place.), we do have a lot to learn from the 6 to 3.5 million-year period that encompasses our most direct (and now extinct) ancestors.

The most recent geologic period has seen more biological changes than all the other geologic periods on Earth combined, despite only being 0.0007% of the total amount of time Earth has existed. In this way, the trajectory of human history not only mirrors the history of Earth but also the history of the universe; its beginnings were laden with a long stretch of relative inactivity, where barely noticeable changes accumulated slowly and pointed toward a tipping point. Once that critical point was reached, accumulated successes (here called adaptations) began to build on one another and caused a significant and noticeable upturn in the rate of change. And so, just like the story of the universe and the story of Earth, the story of humanity's modest beginnings gives us an idea of how simple, slow, and straightforward processes can amass and eventually result in dramatic and sweeping changes. The story of our species is such a story.

About 4.4 million years ago, somewhere in a corner of northeast Ethiopia what are now the savannahs of eastern Africa, a collection of hairy milk-producing vertebrates found themselves dropping from the trees, walking on the ground on two legs instead of four, and using the opposable digits on their hands. Most important, though, they began to dramatically improve their ability to communicate with one another in social ways. The moment for humanity was close at hand; hominids[7] had arrived.

The hominid predecessors to modern humans are known about only because of fossil studies. These creatures, whose anatomy was strikingly similar to our own, provide the most solid evidence by which scientists are able to explain how humans connect to the rest of the tree of life. We are aware that this notion can be problematic to some, that some feel uneasy about a theory of gradual change over time applied to humans in the same way it is applied to simpler life forms. Those who choose a strict interpretation of certain religious texts balk at the idea that humans

---

[7] The term "hominid" refers to any member of the taxonomical family *Hominidae*, which includes the genus *Australopithecus* (to which the famous fossils of Lucy belong) and the genus *Homo* (to which we modern humans belong). While we belong to the family of hominids, it is important to remember that not all hominids can be called human. Hominids are all extinct (except, of course, for modern humans).

are in any way connected to the rest of the living world, or are subject to the same operating principles as the rest of the community of life. It seems outrageous to these people that they could share similarities with a monkey, a tree shrew, a backboned amphibian, a spinach plant, or a single-celled protozoan. This belief generally involves an emotional reaction against much of the scientific findings of the past 150 years, which strive to uncover the secrets to our very nature, just as religions do.

Through studies of fossils, as well as more recent studies comparing the DNA of humans to the DNA of other life forms, we have been able to give ourselves a sense of belonging. Because of this knowledge, we can comfortably believe that we humans, as a species, are not an anomaly here, and although we have achieved a level of cultural advancement that far surpasses any other species, we do indeed have a place in the greater natural order. This may be met with resistance and even forceful refutation in quite different ways, thanks to the successes of our culture, but the point remains that humanity is included on the list of Earth's organisms and, as such, is answerable to the same natural processes that guide chimpanzees, bighorn sheep, red-tailed hawks, nematodes, kudzu, baobab trees, porcini mushrooms, and phytoplankton, to name a few.

We should also point out here that theories of gradual change over many generations and through varying degrees of stability and success seem palatable to almost everyone when the subject of such theories is something like a bacteria strain that grows resistant to antibiotics, or an insect swarm that is no longer subdued by a certain strength of pesticide. Gradual adaptation to environmental stress is a common characteristic to all life forms; in simpler life forms, such as bacteria, adaptations are a bit easier to understand and swallow than in humans.

As we will demonstrate in this book, we virtually hairless, upright-walking mammals are not immune to gradually accumulated changes over long periods of time in our population. The history of how humans and their most recent ancestors adapted to their environment follows the same general operating guidelines as the bacteria strain orinsect swarm, and if our adaptations look different to those of tuberculosis-causing bacteria or bee colonies, it is because most of our adaptations take place from within our culture, which is vastly more developed than the culture of any other organism in existence. While there will still be those whose unwavering faith will keep them from accepting the empirical viewpoint, we can only point out that the evidence for our connection to the rest of the living world, and therefore our defined and deserved place in the natural order, is overwhelming. If we, as Trudeau points out, put our faith in branches of medicine that use these principles to counter increasingly drug-resistant strains of pathogens, employ animal studies in order to develop new therapies for humans, or rely on the principles of genetics or cell biology, then we would be hard-pressed to refute such claims of interconnectedness between humans and the rest of the living world. Recall the point made by Richard Dawkins in *The Selfish Gene* (1989): Science represents the best way we know to learn how the universe operates.

The Bass Motherland, the Place of the Drum

The story of humanity begins in Africa. Our first evidence of hominids comes from northeastern Ethiopia, where a series of 4.4-million-year-old skeletons (110 specimens from 37 individuals) were recently revealed after being discovered and heavily studied for the past 17 years (Wilford, 2009). These skeletons belonged to the genus *Ardipithecus (Ardi)*, which is older by 1.4 million years than the skeleton of Lucy, of the species *Australopithecus*. Both sets of fossils gave us clues as to the nature of their owners, which in turn did much to inform us of our own origins. "The older hominid (*Ardipithecus*) was already so different from chimps that it suggested that no modern ape is a realistic proxy for characterizing early hominid evolution" (Wilford, 2009). Studies of Ardi, the Lucy skeleton, as well as Laetoli footprints, indicated that they were bipedal, yet may not have walked with exactly the same mechanics as modern humans (Harcourt-Smith & Aiello, 2004). We can look to these creatures for answers to questions we may have about our heritage.

Like any other life form, *Ardipithecus* and *Australopithecus* were subject to challenges and stresses from the environment. And like every other life form, the random changes and resultant individual variations that occurred within a population gave the species a greater chance at success and stability. Here, it is important to comment on the environment in which our relativesfound themselves: the wooded areas and plains in eastern Africa. Due to global climactic events, what is now called the African Rift Zone was undergoing a change in its own right: The land's biomes were diversifying. Evidence proves that during the time of *Ardipithecus* the area was "a more humid woodland habitat" (Wilford, 2009), but by the time *Australopithecus* lived in the same region it had become grassy savanna, and the abundance of plants that would have been food to the area's mammals was diminishing (Reed, 1997). Those among the tree-dwelling creatures who were able to come down to the ground in search of food, especially seafood along the coastlines of lakes and rivers, would have a much better shot at survival than those who remained tree bound. In short, *Australopithecus*, if it had any hopes of survival, needed to exhibit adaptations specific to characteristics of these plains and woodlands. These specific environments turned out to be prime determinants of which characteristics and traits would be selected as successful and which would not.

Australopithecus was not the first creature to walk on two legs, but it was one of the earliest identified creatures to have this extraordinary ability (Tuttle, 1981). *Ardipithecus* pushed this known timeline back to at least 4.4 million years ago. The anatomical differences between upright-walkers and the organisms that predated them would absolutely set them apart from the rest of the crowd and pave the way for humanity's incredible success. This would free them to both move and manipulate objects at the same time, which was an enormous advantage over most other animals that could either move or manipulate objects, but not both simultaneously. Though this important adaptation marked a very serious turning point toward understanding our own story, there was more to come.

Ultimately, they did not prove to be a completely successful design. If it were, there would still be a good number of very similar creatures walking the woodlands and savannahs of the world today! Let us not delude ourselves into thinking that the set of adaptations housed in the frame of our predecessors was completely unsuccessful either; fossils identified as belonging to the genus *Australopithecus* have been found that verify that the species existed for more than 1 million years ("Long Foreground-Species Timeline," 2009). However, the line that we would like to trace back to our most direct ancestors does not connect us so cleanly to Lucy's ilk.

A vital characteristic that makes our early ancestors stand out was their enlarged skull and brain case. Skull size is the best fossil indicator of brain size, and it seems logical enough to infer that the larger the brain, the greater the ability to use that brain. A survey of the animal kingdom will corroborate this inference: The larger an animal's brain is, the more it is able to conduct higher order mental operations. Research has shown that in most instances, the larger the brain the greater the capacity to process information in a meaningful way (Reader & LaLand, 2001). A discovery made by Richard Leakey in the Olduvai Gorge in Tanzania in 1960 filled in an important piece of that puzzle (Wilford, 2007). The fossilized bones he and his parents found there have been determined to be between 1.6 and 1.9 million years old ("Evolution: Humans," no date). In this example, the skeleton that Leakey found had a brain case that was significantly larger than the brain cases of the *Australopithecus* fossils ("Section II: Hominid Evolution," no date). These two anatomical differences, coupled with evidence of flake stone tools found nearby, led Leakey to assign this particular skeleton to the genus *Homo* instead of *Australopithecus*.[8] Leakey named this skeleton *Homo habilis*, which translates roughly to "handy man." This upright-walking, opposable-thumbed, large-brained early tool user was indeed the most direct predecessor of modern humans.

Using a carved stone or bone fragment as a rudimentary tool was not a trivial matter—it was an enormous leap forward in the story of human success. Previous to the employment of rocks and bones, *Australopithecus* was forced to rely almost completely on its own body parts to do the work of survival. But *Homo habilis,* with its opposable thumbs, improved brainpower, and use of tools, was able to transcend the limitations of its physical body in a way that *Australopithecus* did not. *Homo habilis,* for lack of a better term, used its brain in new and

---

[8]   *Homo* is Latin for "man." The designation of *Homo* indicates that Leakey's skeleton was more directly related to us than the Lucy skeleton. *Australopithecus*, while closely related to humans in a more broad sense, represented an offshoot in the hominid family tree.

creative ways, which resulted in an extension of its capabilities. As a result, *Homo habilis* proved to be a much more successful species.

The use of tools provides us with our first glimpse into the power of a cultural invention. There was not any distinct or drastic anatomical change to *Homo habilis* after it started using sharpened rocks and bones to accomplish its simple goals. The shift here, instead, was one of the mind. This leap forward is extraordinary and, as will be discussed in following chapters, was the point at which the human organism lurched forward on its path of adaptation and ability, accelerating well beyond what simple biology could achieve alone. Tool use, even at this rudimentary stage, was the first sign of an emerging human quality called "culture." Culture, which is only made possible by certain developed mental capacities, is what would ultimately give us humans the ability to create bustling megalopolises, highly efficient industrial farms, air travel, microprocessors, nuclear power, international trade, hip hop, video games, universities, government, and religion. We can barely imagine a life in which we would not use tools to accomplish our goals. Forgetting for a minute how teenagers maintain that they "need" their cell phones and music players to live, we reflect that our survival depends entirely on tools. How would even the most primitive hunter or farmer get by without a knife of some kind? How would people stay warm during the winter without clothing or fire, at the very least? Our fates are bound to our tool use. This important piece of culture is first observed with *Homo habilis*, which is why we now believe that the "handy man" is our direct ancestor.

Homo habilis's successes were truly that. *Homo habilis*, like other successful species of the time, represented the culmination of random changes over thousands of generations. What distinguished *habilis* was the ability to combine its genetic advantages with intellectual innovations that allowed it to better succeed in its environment, and it was here that the physiological and anatomical adaptations we see in many other species took a back seat to newly emergent behavioral adaptations. Those individuals who were more able to walk upright, more able to use their hands for fine movements, and more capable in using tools undoubtedly survived more successfully than those who did not have these abilities, but the real secret to *Homo habilis*'s success was its ability to pass on both genes and knowledge to its offspring. Thus, after generations, *Homo habilis*'s repertoire of adaptations grew more and more refined, with biological and cultural adaptations bolstering one another. *Homo habilis*'s skull and brain size increased significantly over Lucy and her ilk. Evidence of tool use grew more sophisticated.

When the point was reached where the species walked fully upright and no longer spent time living in trees (evidence exists that both *Australopithecus* and *Homo habilis* lived a semi-arboreal life (Wood & Collard, 1999), and capacity for tool use expanded to include things more elaborate than sharpened rocks, then scientists felt the need to name this creature something different. In this fashion, *Homo erectus*, which translates roughly to "upright man," appeared on the scene about 1.2 million years ago. *Homo erectus* was even more successful than *Homo habilis,* in its ability to adapt to the African plains, and was even handier: The crude tools attributed to *Homo habilis* were far outdone by more sophisticated axes made by *erectus*. It is thought that this burst of creative tool making and use was spurred by another increase in cognitive processing power. While *Homo erectus*'s skulls do measure larger than *Homo habilis*'s, *erectus*'sgut and teeth are actually smaller. Harvard's Richard Wrangham believes that this coincident increase in brainpower had everything to do with a high-nutrient diet to support such brain activity. *H. erectus*'s brain was 50% larger than that of its predecessor, *H. habilis,* and it experienced the biggest drop in tooth size in human evolution. According to Wrangham, as quoted by Moeller-Gorman (2007) "There's no other time that satisfies expectations that we would have for changes in the body that would be accompanied by cooking."

Technology such as the use of fire ("Evolution: Humans," no date) and tools for hunting allowed *Homoerectus* to include more meat in its diet, which was thought to spur yet another push toward complexity and organization. Once technology sufficient to hunt large game animals was in place, meat became a diet staple of *Homo erectus* and its descendants. Meat, with its high energy and protein content, is able to support larger numbers of individuals per pound than plant matter. Meat also made it much more possible to support the development of a highly complex brain. This may have been the push that *Homo* needed to break through the most recent plateaus in our history. Perhaps we should think about this next time we attend a backyard barbecue: Cooking meat is ostensibly what allowed human culture to advance. Thus, the more *Homo erectus* was able to master its environment, the more it would be able to support its ever-increasing brainpower. And, of course, the more *Homo erectus* was able to do cognitively, the more it could exert its will to master its environment. It is here that the rate of accumulated adaptations seen in human ancestry took a notable upturn.

The earliest fossils of *Homo erectus* were found in Africa alongside fossils of *Homo habilis*, but *erectus* did not limit itself to only that region. Fossilized skeletons of *Homo erectus* have been found as far away as Europe and eastern Asia, which indicates that *Homo erectus* was able to migrate great distances and successfully establish itself in diverse environments. Such ability is further evidence of successful tool use thanks to increased brainpower. This sort of adaptation evokes modern human activity and highlights the fact that *Homo erectus* represented a true intermediary between modern humans and arboreal primates in the African woodlands. This was not a short-lived success, either; skulls of *Homo erectus* have been found in modern-day China that are less than 70,000 years old ("Homo erectus," no date). This means that *Homo erectus* lived for more than 1.1 million years, making them the longest lived of any hominid.

Bipedalism, opposable thumbs, and advanced mental capacities made possible by a larger brain turned out to be extremely successful adaptations for *Homo habilis*, and even more so for *Homo erectus*. Again, this had everything to do with the environment in which these creatures found themselves. The eastern woodlands and plains of Africa were more than the backdrop to the story; they were the driving force of the story. Given the type of physical environment, the climate, the natural resources readily available, the species present in the neighborhood, and the relative scarcity or abundance of food sources, the characteristics of eastern Africa were the determining factor for which adaptations would be successful (and therefore remain in succeeding generations) and which would not (and therefore phase out). Because modern humans, *Homo sapiens*, would eventually descend from the likes of *Homo erectus*, those successful adaptations became the suite of attributes common to all humans on the planet today. Thus, in the story of human origins, the savannahs of eastern Africa are often termed the Environment of Evolutionary Adaptation (EEA).

Two specific features of the EEA are worth noting here, and while both are subjects of controversy due to incomplete evidence, they are supported by enough evidence and are compelling enough to be widely accepted by the scientific community. The first feature is that between 4 and 2 million years ago, the eastern woodlands of Africa gave way to plains and open spaces, most likely due to a change in climate (deMenocal, 2004). This was thought to force primates out of the trees and onto flat ground, which set up bipedalism as an adaptive success. Using four limbs to move about is very handy when hanging from tree branches, but when walking on the ground, two legs are really all one needs to get around. The second feature of the EEA, despite this change in physical geography, was the presence of accessible water sources. It was from these water sources that early hominids were thought to have obtained much of their high-nutrient food. Commonly referred to as the "aquatic ape hypothesis," there is a growing community of scientists who believe that contact and interaction with bodies of water prompted certain distinctly human traits to arise as successful. Marc Verhaegen and colleagues summarize the position in their 2002 paper.

> The combination of comparative, dental, skeletal, fossil, biomolecular and geographical evidence suggests that hominid ancestors climbed and waded bipedally in swampy or mangrove forests and supplemented their mainly herbi–frugivorous diet with shellfish. The *australopiths* and ancestors of gorillas and chimpanzees might have lived near swampy forests and preserved their climbing abilities, whereas hominid populations that remained near or returned to the coast could have given rise to the various Homo [species]: big-brained, long-legged waders and divers who were able to take full advantage of the resources associated with coastal environments. They dispersed along the Indian Ocean and

followed rivers inland. This scenario helps to explain the long legs of humans, as well as furlessness, subcutaneous fat, infant tolerance to immersion, voluntary breath control, big brains, and the development of language and technology. (Verhaegen, Puech, & Munro, 2002, pp. 212-217)

Just as water gave rise to the first single-celled life on Earth billions of years ago, water apparently was the catalyst for more recent and complex change in hominids. This should not be surprising for a species that is about 70% water by weight and whose life and way of life hinges almost completely on the availability of water. Had we descended from creatures that spent millions of years adapting to a desert environment or a tropical environment, we would have most assuredly turned out much different. As it happened, though, we are the children of those early bipeds who came down from the trees in eastern Africa to live on the shores of lakes, rivers, and seas.

As *Homo erectus* migrated outside the EEA, the adaptations and characteristics that made it so successful generalized from the EEA to almost any environment in the biosphere, and they continued to be emphasized and refined on a global scale. As so many successful adaptations had already accumulated and built on one another, and as cultural inventions advanced, the rate of adaptive change accelerated significantly. No longer did it take thousands of generations for significant, noticeable changes to occur. Now, in hundreds or perhaps even dozens of generations, the line of *Homo* was substantially more able to use elements of its culture for successful survival. As will be discussed in the next chapter, the foundation of *Homo's* successful creation and use of culture was its highly developed brain, which allowed for complex social interactions, prediction and planning, and the development of technology. Barring several unsuccessful offshoots such as *Homo Neanderthalensis* (Neanderthals, common to modern Europe) and *Homo floresiensis* (the "hobbit" species recently found in Indonesia), the trajectory that *Homo habilis* initiated and *Homo erectus* refined ultimately resulted in the emergence of what we would officially call humans: *Homo sapiens*, or "thinking man." *Homo sapiens* appeared in Africa about 250,000 years ago (McBrearty, 1990) and, as is evidenced by our very presence, flourished in various environments and contexts and has continued to transform itself to the present day.

Two hundred and forty thousand generations of our ancestors have developed the branch of the tree of life known as *Homo erectus* into highly specialized competitors. Humans descended from primates on the savannahs of Africa and rapidly colonized Earth. This process, while very slow from one human life's perspective, was quick in geologic context and blazing fast in cosmic time. So fast, in fact, that we can safely consider ourselves to have vestiges of the Stone Age still very much intact in terms of our biological repertoire of attributes. This is why we have gone through the recounting of human ancestry: to remind ourselves that our modern minds are housed in brains that have not quite fully caught on that the Stone Age is over. However, this should not downplay our extraordinary mental abilities. Our consciousness, our ability to think about ourselves and meditate on our own thinking, is indeed quite significant. Brian Greene asks, "Was the universe a vastly different place before human consciousness evolved on planet Earth?" (2005, p. 207). The answer, on a universal scale, is a resounding no. But our small corner of the universe, our home planet, has been irrevocably changed by our presence.

Physical changes to the design of humans have been minimal over the past 250,000 years, but changes in the mind and intellect have been nothing short of explosive. Until this point, we have outlined our origins, starting from the Big Bang, working through the formation of stars, the formation of our planet, the earliest iterations of life, and the tendency toward organized complexity as a solution for stability. All the while, we have been steadily zooming in on the moment when humans appeared, where our immediate and more familiar story begins. The lessons to be learned from placing ourselves within the larger frame of cosmology and

Figure 4.3. Human cranial evolution.

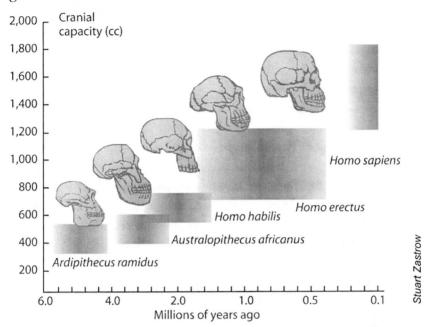

Sources: Stebbins, G. L. 1982. Darwin to DNA San Francisco: Freeman, and http://www.nytimes.com/imagepages/2009/10/02/science/02fossil_graphic.ready.html

natural history are important ones to which we will refer often, but now that we have zoomed into matters that operate on a more human scale, we are ready to address the highly complex products of the shuffling and reshuffling of matter begun 13.7 billion years ago: ourselves. Barring a little exposition on the mechanics of the process described here, the rest of the book will focus on humanity, our adaptations, our minds, our culture, where it has led us, and what we can do about it.

A Commonly Misunderstood Theory

The theory of evolution, because of certain emotional connotations it may evoke with some people, is often misunderstood to be something that it is not. As mentioned before, those who choose to adopt a strict interpretation of religious texts find it difficult to incorporate this central theory of science into their worldview, especially when it involves explanations as to how we humans arrived on the scene.

There are generally two sticking points for those who believe in the letter of the western Bible. The first is the time scale suggested by evolution and supported by studies of fossils and rocks. If the Bible is to be taken literally, then the universe is a little under 6,000 years old. None of us are old enough to corroborate this claim firsthand, but this belief is refuted repeatedly by discoveries in the natural world. Letting aside dating of geologic strata and the fossils they contain, which have been shown to be much, much older than 6,000 years, the living world contains specimens currently alive that predate the biblical time scale of creation. Scientists have discovered plants specimens, such as the creosote bush in the Mojave Desert, that have been determined to be more than 11,000 years old (Blakeslee, 1985). If that were not impressive enough, certain species of living bacteria found buried deep in layers of permafrost have been determined to be over 500,000 years old ("World's Oldest Bacteria Found," 2007). But, for a minute, let us assume for the sake of argument that the biologists who have made these discoveries are wrong. Those who believe that creation took place less than 6,000 years ago would still have to reconcile the findings of astrophysicists and astronomers, who have detected celestial bodies over 6,000 light years away. In short, the evidence that Earth is more than 6,000 years old is overwhelming.

The second issue strict interpretationists take with the theory of evolution is that it blurs the distinctions we make between ourselves and other forms of life by locating and placing humans somewhere on the phylogenetic tree of life and offers a very reasonable explanation as to how we are connected to these "lesser" life forms. This sticking point is largely due to people's incorrect assumptions about the theory itself; they believe that such connections between humans and our closest living relatives somehow demean humanity. Evolutionists would not disputethat humans are indeed special and in certain ways different from the rest of the living world: This sort of differentiation is encompassed in the theory. However, evolutionists would dispute any story of creation that does not explain the specifics as to how "God created man in his own image" (Genesis 1:27). Science's answer as to how we got here is inconsistent with stories of a highly anthropomorphized divinity literally molding the first humans from dust or clay, or conjuring humanity from nothing. Even so, that does not mean that the biblical story of creation is without merit. If we can perceive the story of our universe in a certain poetic way, one could make the argument that we (and everything else on Earth) ultimately came from the "dust" of stars, as the heavy elements that make up our bodies were originally created in supernovae. Evolution simply describes a process that fills in the intermediary steps between supernovae and *Homo sapiens*. We would hope that a more thorough description of the process of creation does not offend the religious, even if strict interpretationists find it incompatible with their belief. Religious leaders have more recently come to accept this point of view; the past two popes have issued statements that make room for evolution within the Roman Catholic doctrine (Tagliabue, 1996) (Schonborn, Horn, & Wiedenhofer, 2006). This should be indication enough that the theory is very much compatible with all religious views that allow for empirically acquired knowledge.

Faith, by its definition, does not rely upon empirical evidence, and thus scientists who study human ancestry tend to avoid arguing with people of faith because they believe that the two disciplines operate on different intellectual spheres. Consider, though, that religious scientists, nonscientific religious people, and even atheists may all actually find comfort and meaning from realizing the interconnectedness between humans and all other life forms on the planet. Some may even find a sort of profound spirituality from the notion that we humans also are part of creation, if they can avoid certain amounts of emotional resistance that prevent them from accepting the demonstrated biological connection between a human being and another form of life. This sort of spirituality is nothing short of a feeling of intense connectedness to life. Again, for the purposes of this book it is also immaterial what one's beliefs are about the origin of humans. What remains important is the basic common ground that every human is sacred. When one "sets the table" based upon this term sacred, the arguments about superiority tend to vanish.

While Charles Darwin did not prove that God does not exist, he did demonstrate that all life is related in a macro-familial sense and that the differences between any two species is due to how they have stumbled upon strategies to help them successfully adapt to their environment. This goes for all life, thought Darwin, not just the exotic, savage animals and morally neutral plants he witnessed while sailing around the world on the HMS *Beagle*. People were with him until he suggested that humans are not excluded, but it really should come as no surprise that we humans are also living things. While humans do have some peculiarities when it comes to the community of life (What other animal wears clothes? Consumes products from halfway around the world? Enslaves members of their species?), scientists since Darwin have established beyond a reasonable doubt that our biological basis for life is not that much different from the rest of the animal kingdom. It is well established that our genetic material is not far different from that of other mammals (our DNA is at least 96% identical to chimpanzee DNA, according to the National Institutes of Health, 2005), nor is it that variant from the stock of all animals, birds, reptiles, amphibians, fish, insects, plants, fungus, bacteria, or algae. Regardless of what one believes God's role is in the how and why of existence, it is a demonstrated fact that until recently, the theory of evolution has simultaneously explained the unity and diversity of life and that humans have an important place in that explanation.

Evolution (Pearl Jam)

We have gone into some detail as to what evolution is not, but before we move on, we need to spend some time defining what evolution is. In its simplest terms, *evolution is gradual, cumulative changes over long periods of time*. This simple principle is most often applied to living things, but it is important to realize that nonliving things can also evolve. In Chapter 2, our discussion of how stable molecules began to outnumber unstable molecules is really a case study in evolution. Individual molecules that "worked" continued and became more abundant, and those that did not "work" did not continue. Over enough time, the majority of individual molecules embodied a design that "worked." Or put more succinctly, "Survival of the fittest is really a special case of a more general law: survival of the stable" (Dawkins, 1989, p. 12).

Since the theory of evolution, brought to us by Charles Darwin in 1859, was developed using living things as case studies, much of the

Figure 4.4. Timeline of hominid evolution.

Source: © De Agostini / Superstock

language of the theory is life-specific. This is not a shortcoming of thetheory by any means; the living world provides the clearest examples of evolution at work and provides us with answers about ourselves previously reserved for *a priori* philosophy. Through any living thing, we can also identify and name the driving force for the process of evolution, which Darwin called "natural selection." Put simply, this means that in any population, successful traits will become more common than unsuccessful traits over time, until the majority or all the members of that population exhibit that trait. A little variation among members in a population is a prerequisite for this to occur, as is some incentive for successful traits to be selected over less successful ones (such as competitiveness over limited resources). In fact, the diversity of species and the diversity within species are the secrets of survival. Diversity within species promotes natural selection of those successful traits, and diversity between species creates certain pressures that speed up the process. Biological beings must quickly adapt, at the individual and generational levels, as a hedge against DNA extinction. As in fractal mathematics, the expressions repeat themselves at each step, whether it is in "tree branches, roots, stem, leaves and cells or within the behavior of organizations from the CEO down" (Haseltine, 2007).

Because the theory of evolution is such a central precept to the Ark that we are building, we would like to offer a more developed working definition. It is best stated stepwise:

1. All individual members of a population are different from one another in some way. This variation is, to a large extent, random.

2. If a population is able to reproduce itself, then the differences between individuals are heritable. That is, they can be passed down to offspring.

3. There are a limited number of resources in any environment, and this scarcity will put limits on who is able to survive. Moreover, the conditions found in any environment render certain traits as favorable over others.

4. Some traits allow for individuals to be more suited or adapted to their environment and, therefore, more successful at surviving in that environment.

5. If an individual's unique set of traits result in it being better adapted to its environment, then it is more likely to survive and reproduce those traits in its offspring. If an individual's traits render it less adapted to its environment, then it is more likely to die or be killed, and not pass on its traits (this is often called "survival of the fittest").

6. The successful individuals who survive to the age of propagation are the ones to pass on their traits to the next generation of individuals. Therefore, the traits that are passed on will include ones that increase an individual's chances of survival.

7. Within an environment that does not change as fast as an organism can pass on its genes, the entire population of individuals will come to exhibit the adaptations that increase chances of survival over long periods of time.

Thus, evolution attributes the survival of certain traits over others to a measure of how well those traits can promote survival in a certain context. How we turn out, even at the genetic level, has everything to do with the environment we find ourselves in. Evolution has no predetermined endpoint, and the changes that have arisen because of evolution are not intentional or premeditated. This is a very important thing to keep in mind. Humans tend to think of ourselves as the final product of the evolution of life on Earth, that all changes that matter undergone on its path to humanity were pointed purposefully toward the moment where *Homo sapiens* emerged in Africa. This simply is not the case. Evolution relies entirely on multiple iterations of trial-and-error style problem solving. Moreover, the successful solutions to any given problem depend entirely on the surrounding context in which the individual finds it. In an essay that compares naturally selected designs to human-engineered designs, Daniel Quinn clarified this point beautifully:

> Human design is always directed toward *improvement*. Evolutionary design, on the other hand, only appears to be directed toward improvement, and this confuses a lot of people. It leads them to imagine that evolution is *heading*somewhere, presumably toward the eternally final forms that God created in a single stroke. Evolutionary design in fact merely tends to eliminate the less workable and perpetuate the more workable. When we look at a seagull or a giraffe or a cheetah or a spider, we see a version of the product that's working beautifully—because all the dysfunctional versions have been eliminated from the gene pool of that species through natural selection. If conditions change, however—and we had the leisure to watch—we'd see these apparently perfect forms begin to change in subtle ways or dramatic ways as natural selection eliminates the less workable adaptations to the new conditions and perpetuates the more workable. (Quinn, 1999)

In terms of the living world, we have been able to identify the mechanism through which biological evolution occurs, and that is the field of genetics. A slightly distractible 19th-century Augustinian monk named Gregor Mendel, who spent most of his days tending to peas in the monastery garden, set forth the ground rules for heredity in 1866. Scientists were later able to connect these ground rules to

Darwin's work on evolution, natural selection, and speciation. Mendel posited the existence of genes, or some sort of unseen code that would determine a given trait, without being sure of its biochemical nature. When James Watson and Francis Crick revealed the structure of DNA in 1957, the molecular substrate of Darwin's field naturalist–based theory of evolution, driven by Mendel's laws of genetic inheritance, was revealed. We now know that DNA and RNA, the exceedingly important self-replicating molecules that chanced into being some 3.5 billion years ago, hold the key to the emergence of cellular life, and more. Because it is the encrypted code that determines how organisms are built one amino acid at a time, DNA is also the fundamental biochemical mechanism through which evolution occurs in all living things.

The Importance of Genes, and Perceived Short-Term Interest

DNA's central place in the scheme of life is no small point of fact. Anyone who has sat through a high school biology class should be able to remember that all living things contain DNA, but rarely do people think of all living things as "containers" for DNA. Thanks to certain predispositions of the human mind, we tend to think of DNA as something we just have, much like a car has steel and wires in it, and we tend to view ourselves as masters of our genetics even if we cannot actively control or change what genetics have endowed to us. We do have DNA, but we would be remiss to think that we enormous and complex organisms hold dominion over the molecule. A termite mound would not exist if it were not for termites, and likewise, we would not exist if it were not for DNA. As Richard Dawkins has successfully argued in his landmark book *The Selfish Gene*, in terms of evolution, we individuals are living in the service of our genes. Dawkins wrote:

> In sexually reproducing species, the individual is too large and too temporary a genetic unit to qualify as a significant unit of natural selection. The group of individuals is an even larger unit. Genetically speaking . . . they are not stable through evolutionary time. Populations may last a long while, but they are constantly blending with other populations and so losing their identity. An individual body seems discrete enough while it lasts, but alas, how

long is that? Each individual is unique. You cannot get evolution by selecting between entities when there is only one copy of each entity! Individuals are not stable things, they are fleeting. Chromosomes too are shuffled into oblivion, like the hands of cards soon after they are dealt. But the cards themselves survive the shuffling. The cards are the genes. They are not destroyed . . . they merely change patterns and march on. Of course they march on. That is their business. They are the replicators and we are their survival machines. When we have served our purpose we are cast aside. But genes are denizens of geological time: genes are forever. (Dawkins, 1989, p. 12)

Genes, which are defined sections of DNA that code for a specific trait in a living thing, have survived the test of time. In terms of evolution as we have defined it here, genes are the stable molecules that strike the perfect balance between simplicity and organized complexity. And like the earliest strands of RNA that probably worked symbiotically with nearby molecules to form a cell, the genes in all of our bodies work symbiotically to form us.

We commonly think about evolution on the level of the individual: the plant, the moth, the fruit fly, the lowland gorilla. Most of the time, thinking about an individual's evolution works just fine. More correctly, though, Dawkins is saying that we can do this because individuals are the carriers and protectors of the original successful units of evolution: genes. If we survive our genes survive, and this is, of course, in the best interest of the genes. Gene survival and transmission is the cornerstone of biological evolution. If evolutionary theory applies to us (which it does), our increasingly involved efforts to ensure gene survival simultaneously enhance life and advance knowledge, at best, and wreak havoc and destruction at worst.

Leaving aside for the moment the existence of a prime mover or creator in all that occurred on our mother ship, it is beyond question that organic life forms emerged from starstuff. At first, they were very simple organisms, and then they became endowed with increasing complexity and diversity in order to survive. By survival, we really mean Dawkins's version: DNA and genetic survival and continuance. Evolution is not so provincial as to care one wit about the survival of any individual member of a species.

The Fishbowl Principle

The genes that are the most stable and "lucky" to be in the right place at the right time(s)—and therefore successful—are the ones that successfully replicate themselves at all costs. Here, we can pick up on an interesting parallel in humans, one that will cut to the heart of many of the dilemmas of our age and flaws in our humanity: *Individuals will tend to make decisions and act based on perceived short-term individual benefit before perceived long-term benefit or for the benefit of others.* This simple idea, while seemingly innocuous, has implications that stretch into every corner of our lives and every topic we are taking on in this book. Indeed, this simple idea is so central to our project here that we want to name it formally, refer to it continually, and even make it the title of our book: *The Fishbowl Principle.*

The Fishbowl Principle is best understood in the context of evolution, which is why we've chosen to introduce it here. The goal of the unit of evolution on both the gene and individual level is to survive, and this almost always involves making sure that survival for ourselves, today and right now, is ensured. After all, if we do not survive today, we will not survive through next week! And if our neighbors (or—worse yet—people we've never met) survive at our expense, this does not bode well for us either. Therefore, we will make decisions that work toward our own short-term benefit first, however we perceive it. The genes that we have inherited certainly have done this . . . as much as genes are able to make decisions. We who are alive now are the recipients of the most successful genes, of course, and those genes would not have been successful if they were not looking after themselves first.Does this mean that selfishness is the law of the jungle? Does this justify advancing my own well being at the expense of my neighbor? If individual people were the functional unit of natural selection, then it might. The principle of acting out of perceived short-term self-interest superseding long-term interest and interest for the group may explain certain things about humanity, but it certainly does not excuse anything. Acting out of perceived short-term self-interest explains why fast food is so popular even though it is not very healthy, why the stock market rises and falls with rumors, why traffic jams occur, why violent crimes are committed, why products are marketed as they are, and why fundamentalists are so steadfast in their agendas. If this is not apparent now, it will be in coming chapters. For now, it is enough to say that a lot hinges on the word "perceived": In many instances, what we think is in our best interest and what is actually in our best interest are not congruent.

Sometimes, we wrongly perceive things to be a certain way (the Catholic church in Spain during the 15th century perceived non-Christians as threats and slaughtered them by the thousands), or we perceive things to be a certain way from a vantage point that does not have access to all the information (Bernie Madoff's investors unknowingly entered into a Ponzi scheme), and sometimes we do not perceive the far-reaching effects of certain actions that may come back to haunt us (cutting down rainforests to make room for cattle-grazing pastures to increase the food supply). Humanity will not always act selfishly—and, indeed, some unselfish actions end up benefiting us in the long run—but as a steadfast rule, we can safely say that people will tend to act out of their perceived short-term individual interest before anything else.

But since genes, not individuals, are really the functional unit of biological evolution, we individuals are taken off the hook in a strict interpretation of the above principle. We are not unilaterally selfish, but our genes are. Sometimes, though, our unselfishness may be thinly veiled selfishness of a different order. There are various types of self-interest that come into play, and sometimes they compete against each other. This is often the case when material self-interest ("I want more stuff") and social self-interest ("I want to belong to a community and be well liked") conflict. We individuals are integrators, placed in a role of synthesis. Our task, whether conscious or unconscious, is to aggregate all of our genes' selfish interests and trust that our existence promotes the survival of as many genes as possible, and we do this by doing what we can to promote our own survival.

This gene-centered reframing of evolution calls for a different ethic in our behavior and attitude when it comes to how we act toward each other, toward the rest of the living world, and toward the universe at large. We need to remember that we have many, many genes in common with all members of our species, not just our blood relatives. In a world where we have to depend on our neighbors for our own survival, it might just be in our best short-term and long-term interests to act in the interest of everyone. When our communities survive, the genes that we individuals carry may stand a better overall chance of survival (partially because the same genes reside in our family and our neighbors, but also because our family and neighbors can help us make it through better than we can on our own). It is therefore in our own best interest to sometimes act altruistically. Few of us would set ourselves in front of a row of tanks, as one brave soul did in Tiananmen Square in 1989, or dedicate our entire lives to pressing social causes, but we should all aspire to such ideals, and we should do so out of selfishness to our species.

We may even be able to extend the thought to the rest of the living world. We share an incredible percentage of our genome with other animals, and even with the plants around us. While we would almost always save a human from an ill fate before we save a mouse, or kill a plant before we kill a horse, we should also recognize that all living things carry the molecules that ultimately guide our bodies, and all these living things have done so quite successfully. In this light, Noah's environmental ethic of saving other animal species just may have an evolutionary basis as well.

Evolution, Human Behavior, And Sexual Selection

Even though the theory of evolution can and does apply to all forms of organized matter, we are concerned here primarily with how the theory of evolution is played out in humans. We, being living things and part of the natural order, are equally subject to the forces of natural selection as moths or giraffes or bacteria. However, our responses to evolutionary stresses and environmental pressures manifest themselves in unique and complex ways. Instead of dramatic biological changes, we see the majority of human evolutionary change in our behaviors.

The study of how Darwin's theory of evolution is played out in humans, especially as it relates to our behaviors and the aspects of our minds that make us uniquely human, is the focus of evolutionary psychology. Martin Daly and Margo Wilson summarize the study of evolutionary psychology this way:

> The evolutionary view is that the basic perceptions of self-interest shared by all normal members of a given species are products of a long history of natural and sexual selection and thus may be expected to exhibit "design" for promoting fitness (genetic posterity) in ancestral environments. The phrase "perceptions of self-interest" should be interpreted broadly. We intend that it should encompass appetites and aversions both for relatively specific pleasures and pains and for such intangibles as social status and self-esteem, and even that it should encompass processes that are not psychological in any ordinary sense of that word. Our immune systems and cell membranes, for example, operate outside our awareness, but they participate in perceiving and defending our interests nonetheless.
>
> In this view, it is often useful to analyze an individual organism into its constituent adaptations, that is, components with specific functions. A human being, for example, is a complex integrated system in which distinct tasks such as respiration, learning, digestion, visual scene analysis, killing parasitic microorganisms, and so forth are carried out by distinct bits of anatomical, biochemical, and psychological machinery. The properties of these bits of machinery are largely to be understood in terms of their separate functions, but a fuller understanding requires consideration of how they fit into the functionally integrated, higher-order agenda of the whole organism. From an evolutionary perspective, the essence of that higher-order agenda is the manufacture of additional, similar creatures, because reproductive posterity is the sole criterion by which all that complex functionality was accumulated through generations. Darwinian selection is the only source of functional design in evolution and selection is nothing more or less than the differential reproductive success of alternative attributes

(phenotypes) within populations and within each sex. It follows that selection favors any attribute that enables individuals to out reproduce others of the same sex and species, and it also follows that these reproductively efficacious attributes are the constituent adaptations referred to above. (Daly & Wilson, 1999, p.59)

One outcome of how our behaviors positively affect our survival is our increased lifespan. The human lifespan differs from the lifespan of our closest living evolutionary relatives, despite such similar genetics. "Humans seem to be something of a long-lived exception amongst their relatives. Humans live much longer than chimpanzees, for instance, whose DNA more closely resembles our own than any other in the animal kingdom. . . . This greater longevity evolved as humans, with their bigger brains, constructed social groups that provided protection from predators and other depredations" (Zimmer, 2007, p. 3). Cultural anthro-pology has provided insight into the evolutionary dynamics taking place within a group, or subset, of the entire human species. Anthropologists believe, as do we, that human responses to threats and competition for resources can be explained in ways similar to other organisms' responses, despite humans' unique behavioral adaptations and capabilities.

Success (Jay Z)

How, then, can we determine which of our highly specialized behavioral and cultural adaptations will be successful? Success in humans, like any other organism, depends on context, on environment. Any environment will favor some traits, characteristics, behaviors, and abilities over others. Ultimately, the environment will make selective combinations of abilities the optimal determinant of success. Some traits such as intellectual curiosity, bravery, confidence, and suppression of the individual ego; ability to solve problems quickly; or social acuity; as well as specific physical attributes such as fertility, more developed muscles, better eyesight, or increased lung capacity, are more generally applicable across many environments. Those are the traits that are most flexible and adaptable across environments, and those are the ones that are cultivated more frequently and actively.

Competition for food and mates has driven all life forms to change and specialize as a function of generations, environment, and time. Dawkins's gene-selection theory of evolution states that we, being containers for genes, will do anything we can to ensure that our genes get passed on to future generations. The sexes have adopted different strategies in order to accomplish this goal. Males, with their virtually unlimited number of sperm, are primarily driven by sexual urge and access to mates. The male strategy, which can be crudely summarized as "give yourself as many chances to have sex as possible," aligns itself with the law of large numbers, as their gametes are more or less expendable. The stereotypical dating tendencies of many teenage boys and philandering husbands should serve as enough evidence for this. Females, on the other hand, are born with all the viable eggs they will ever have, and their number is very small compared to the billions of sperm a male produces in his lifetime. Therefore, the female strategy is not one in which they are frivolously spreading their genes around. Instead, females tend to be much more careful how they choose their potential mates, as they have more invested in each ovum and are more aware of the responsibilities of care giving and the need to tend to offspring, both before they are born and after. Therefore, in theory at least, females will seek to find a stable, healthy, and capable mate who will serve as a provider for her offspring.

The Mating Game Lyrics (Bitter Sweet)

In most of the animal kingdom, this is much more straightforward: The peacock with the biggest plumage or the deer with the largest antlers must be the most attractive mate to females. In humans, however, our more complex social systems often make things a bit more complicated. For one thing, there is not one distinct indicator of fitness for survival in humans, as there is in peacocks or deer. There is a well-observed trade-off between financial resources, age, and the "hunk factor"—for many females an overweight sixty-six-year-old billionaire has certain competitive advantages over the handsome thirty-two-year-old used car salesman. While most species have very elaborate sexual attraction mechanisms, none are as intricate as human mating practices. Our version of peacock feathers or antlers, our markers of evolutionary fitness, often are cultural in nature. There is still a great emphasis placed on physical markers of reproductive fitness (which explains, in large part, the beauty, body, and adult film industries), but in some cases economic or intellectual fitness can be just as important as physical fitness. In the modern age, with so many cultural innovations and developments in direct competition with base biological drives, human sexuality is even more difficult to reduce to such simple terms. There are many ways for human males to advertise their fitness as potential mates, and a corresponding number of reasons why human females would choose or not choose a mate. Still, at their roots, not much has changed between the reproductive drives of most animals and humans today. Humans are still very much subject to the principles of sexual selection and competition for mates, even if it manifests itself in different ways.

Both male and female sexual strategies, however different, are pointed to the same end goal: ensured continuation of one's genes. Put simply, this means "survive and reproduce," our two most basic and simple hardwired biological imperatives. The evolutionary psychologist's task is to explain any characteristic of humanity in terms of how it helps humans successfully survive, reproduce, or both. This is as true of biological characteristics as it is of behavioral or cultural characteristics. For example, the formation of social systems such as families and tribes can be attributed to the fact that we care most about the survival of those with whom we share genes. Likewise, our valuing of human life over the life of another species can be attributed to the same principle. To expand the theory a bit, we could say that all of our social systems, while intrinsically valuable and generally celebrated to us on the individual level, are really just a by-product of our genetic survival machinery. The evolutionist's job becomes to explain how each of these cultural institutions helps genes get passed on to future generations. Evolution, in this light, is positioned to explain everything about humanity. Darwinism, then, has the capacity to become a critical intellectual lens through which we may perceive our universe, much like Marxism, neo-conservatism, Freudianism, or postmodernism might.

Reconciling Short-Term and Long-Term, Individual and Group

The Darwinian model governs the progress of life forms, regardless of any particular member's willingness to believe in the science behind it. We are hardwired to do whatever we can to survive long enough to reproduce, and to ensure that our offspring (and with them, our genes) survive. As mentioned, this most often means that we are predisposed to consider (whether consciously or subconsciously) our own perceived short-term gene survival before a group's long-term gene survival. This is what guides our thoughts, emotions, and actions, and through this, we try to influence and shape the future. This is how it goes time and time again, over and over throughout our own lives and throughout history.

The position we take in this book is that we cannot blame or fault ourselves (or each other) for decisions made in our individual short-term interest. However, in an increasingly complex and interconnected world, the rules for what best serves our individual interests are changing. The more we understand about ourselves, our world, and why we do what we do in the light of evolutionary theory, the better we can adjust to a new course in which our individual short-term interests coincide with those of our neighbors, instead of at our neighbors'—and our future's—expense. This is the essence of the Ark we are trying to build.

The broad, long-term success of the human species (and hence other species and the environment), which is our ultimate goal, may look quite different from small-scale short-term victories or defeats. Part of properly understanding our small place in the enormity of the universe is being able to make the distinction between short term and long term. We would do well to remember the time scale at which organisms evolve; evolutionary time is glacially slow when compared to the time scale of even several human lifetimes. While certain human movements throughout history have experienced brief and dazzling successes in the short term, they have not provided the foundation to our sustained viability on the planet in the way we would hope. Here, short-term successes may mean a couple of months of relative peace and prosperity, but also can be taken to mean hundreds of years of successful democratic rule. Disco's popularity was a short-term success. Medicinal leeches were a short-term success. The Roman Empire, in this light, was a short-term success. Our present way of life is certainly a short-term success, but whether it is viable in the long term remains to be seen. Our hope is to discover the secret to long-term and harmonious viability.

Certain hiccups in the ongoing human project may stand out in our minds as counterexamples to the evolutionary model. Sometimes things are phenomenally popular and successful in the short term (weeks, months, or even decades), but we should remember the scale of evolutionary time: tens or even hundreds of years of events may not determine the overall trend toward stability, organization, and evolutionary success. A one-day or one-month rally on Wall Street does not mean that a recession is over; a week of cooler than average weather does not mean that climate change has reversed. The Darwinist's task becomes how to supplant cultural hiccups with social visions that promote not only the short-term survival of the individual, but also the long-term survival of the species and the planet. The realization of our increasing interdependence on one another is a good start.

Central to the dilemma of how to proceed is the tension between the individual and the group. Anyone who has done battle on any front will agree that things that are not so good for large groups of people may be immediately beneficial for individuals, and that often the battle is worth fighting for this immediate personal benefit. This explains a great deal of wrongdoing and evil that we may experience in the world from an evolutionary standpoint. It is not that the warrior individual always intends badness to befall the masses, but fulfilling his own motivation—whatever that may be—outweighs any ill that might come of his actions to others. In this light, terrorists and thieves are very selfish individuals. What will it take to bear the burden of altruism, to swallow our instinct for immediate personal survival and think more broadly? To the strict Darwinist (or more correctly, Dawkinsist), this won't happen out of good will. Perhaps the key, then, is a scenario in which we are simultaneously betting with and against our neighbors that it is in both of our best interests to not cause undue harm to each other. We may have to suffer a little because of this gamble (or more correctly, we may not gain all that we could in terms of immediate personal advancement), but at the same time, we may have a little insurance that the worst-case scenario is much less likely.

If we humans were not endowed with highly adaptive brains, we could not calculate this. Then again, if we were stripped of our uniquely human mental capabilities, we probably would not wage war against one another. Plenty of other species fight, struggle, and compete, but humans are the only ones to wage war. We can only hope that through our social understanding of one another, we can find a way to replace war with cooperation for mutual benefit.

As individual members of the species, we view this book as a call to shape the future of our species and this small planet by stressing scientific fact, education, and moral precepts borne of respect for all genes and ideas working toward mutual survival. We do not encourage the survival of poisonous ideas—parasitic viruses, if you will—that seek the destruction of *any* particular civilization, and certainly discourage the preservation of ideas aimed at the destruction of Earth itself. Through the lens of evolution, the questions become: How can we recognize that we are operating from a perception of our own individual survival at the expense of others? And moreover, how can we self-correct when we know we are falling into this trap? The goal for us in writing this chapter, then, is to cultivate (1) an accurate and informed awareness of humanity's position in the evolutionary scheme; (2) the mechanisms for such a process; and (3) a clear sense of how our biological hardwiring intersects with the demands of the modern world to create a dissonance when we act out of individual interest for personal short-term gain. We would do well to remember that altruism, as we understand it, has a place in the natural order, albeit as a form of individual selection in a social environment. This was actually Dawkins's main point in *The Selfish Gene* (1989): Even though genes may be quite selfish, the containers of genes (individuals) may often find it advantageous to act unselfishly to preserve those genes. *Our litmus test in the marketplace of ideas, then, is to identify those that promote a long-term sustainable system from both a physical (ecological) and societal (political and economic) platform, while still maintaining the short-term individual appeal for everyone.*

Evolutionary theory, for all its elegant simplicity, still has a few rough edges when it comes to humans. Two matters confound the direct mapping of Darwin's and Dawkins's theories onto the human landscape. The first involves the issue of environment. In the traditional

101

conceptualization of evolution, individuals experience cumulative changes over long periods of time because of the stresses placed on them by the environment. This is, of course, true of humans as well. But humans have a special ability: Humans have become the first species on planet Earth to significantly alter the environment to their needs. It is true that other species may affect their environment in serious ways, but the dams built by beavers pale in comparison to the Three Gorges Dam in China, the Panama Canal, or the levees in New Orleans. In fact, humans have grown so adept at bending the environment to our whims, desires, and pleasures that we, in many cases, have eliminated the very environmental pressure that pushes biological evolution. Instead of adapting to the environment, we have engineered the environment to adapt to us. It is too early to determine the magnitude of long-term effects this process will have on the environment, but early indicators are troubling.

The second matter that confounds issues of evolution in humans is that biological evolution is not the only type of evolution at work in our world. With the emergence of the fully developed human mind, the evolution of our biological selves is being grossly outpaced by the evolution of the products of our minds, which we will refer to very generally as our "culture." Self-replicating ideas that reside in sentient hosts, termed "memes" by Dawkins (1989), will be covered in greater depth in the coming chapters. For now, though, it is enough to say that the actions of an individual or group are sometimes better explained by meme survival than gene survival, that the evolution of a tiny bit of our culture that we house in our minds takes precedence over the evolution of the genes we house in our bodies.

Case in point: Sometimes decisions are made by a group of humans to try to extinguish another group of humans. Decisions such as this are not driven by genetic differences or survival threat as much as they are driven by differences in ideology, which is an example of a meme. The bodies that are lost in such a movement demonstrate that survival of our biological selves sometimes is subordinate to the survival of the ideas we carry in our minds. Examples of this include human sacrifices that occurred in the Incan empire at Machu Picchu and sacrifices that are made by modern day suicide-homicide bombers. The message in each of these examples is that people are less important than the ideas governing them. When we see widespread action being taken in the name of an idea, we are witnessing a powerful and successful meme. The success is usually a function of one idea (e.g., the need for violence) coexisting with another powerful idea (nationalism or religion).

Business as Usual (The Blues Travelers)

Earlier generations of survivors were generally the most successful warriors. The victors and their offspring carried the traits that allowed them to successfully defeat those who threatened them. Those of us here today are the living results of generations of the most successful warriors, as well as the most successful hunters, farmers, diplomats, progenitors, and spiritual leaders. We are truly, at heart, the children of those who were the best at what they did in their communities. Even though things seem a little more complicated today, we cannot forget this. We have inherited the genes and memes that are built to last—a few of which we would be better without. And as descendents of the most successful survivors, we are the ones who get to make decisions as to what will happen next, and decide we will. Humanity has many decisions that need making, and like it or not, we must decide before things are decided for us. As we confront our possible futures, though, it is our hope that those in positions of decision-making power pay heed to the changing dynamics between our short-term wants and our long-term needs. The value of decisions about which forest should be cleared, which river dammed, and which people exterminated depends upon one's perspective. We pray that everyone's perspective involves a clear and accurate vision of humanity in the light of evolution. This becomes increasingly important as we forge ever faster into the future. Never before have we had the sort of knowledge and decision-making power we have now. Before, we were passengers on a ship who only occasionally stole glimpses of the horizon above deck; now, we are able to be the ship's captain and architect, if we so wish.

The enormous danger posed by any ideology is one of exclusivity and top-down dictates. The common ground, the foundation upon which we can build a sustainable future based on something other than fear, greed, war, and genocide, requires an understanding of who and what we are—followed by a cultural refocus away from a warrior-based course of action and toward a culture of individual and collective responsibility for sustainable survival. The principle of evolution gives us a lens with which to examine these important issues. And as products of such a splendid process, it is time to return to our core business: survival.

> *And in your (own) creation and in what He spreads abroad of animals there are signs for a people that are sure. (Qur'an 45:4)*

5

On Psychology And The Human Mind

In the grand scheme of biological evolution on earth, no single species has achieved the success that humans have. There are bacteria that live in every conceivable environment on the planet, from deep within polar ice to thermal vents at the bottom of the ocean, but these bacteria are all distinct species, each with their own highly specialized adaptations. There are certain types of insects very common to multiple regions of the world, but these insects have not been as globally successful at survival as humans have been across so many environmental contexts. Both bacteria and insects enjoy an incredible design whose secret, comparatively, is simplicity. Human design is not nearly as simple, not by a long shot, but this organized complexity is precisely why our species is so successful: No other animal has as developed a nervous system as humans have. While we have not been around as long as horseshoe crabs, cockroaches, sharks, or crocodiles (all species whose design has not changed significantly in more than 60 million years), the rate at which we have successfully adapted to the environmental stresses presented to us in our comparatively short time on Earth has been completely staggering by comparison to those relics of the Mesozoic. If you are reluctant to delve into the science of what makes up your innermost thoughts, then go on to Chapter 6; just know that others will know more than you.

The key to human success, then, has been organized complexity. This is never truer than in the case of the human brain, which has given rise to the human mind and all its creations. This brain is responsible for uncountable unique, flexible, and powerful adaptations, honed and refined since the emergence of *Homo habilis*. We can credit our opposable thumbs with the ability to manipulate objects and use tools. We can credit our bipedalism with the ability to both run and fight at the same time. These two physical adaptations have no doubt done much for humans, but the most significant adaptation that humans enjoy is the evolution of the brain.

The human brain is, at its most basic level of description, nothing more than a network of 100 billion or so neurons, surrounded by about a trillion glial cells (Bear, Connors, & Paradiso, 2001, p. 23). The mass of grey tissue we carry inside our skulls is itself not impressive, but the electrochemical signals that pass between those 100 billion neurons is what makes our brains something more than special. We can ultimately credit our mind and its complex psychology to physical developments in the brain that have been accumulating since the time of *Homo habilis*. The ratio of hominid brain size to body volume has increased significantly in the past 3.5 million years, from about 11.1 g/kg for *Australopithecus* to 16.9 g/kg for *Homo erectus* to 24.5 g/kg for modern humans (Epstein, undated). These measurements imply an increasingly higher level of cognitive processing power as hominids evolved. Simply stated, the physical changes to the biological brain have combined in such a way as to result in the highly developed human psychological mind.

More important, mental and emotional experiences can be traced to the evolution of a biological organ. Scientists are able to view the entire field of psychology as a special case of evolution: Our highly developed minds—whose incredibly complex mechanisms and interactions are unparalleled in what is known of the universe—are the ultimate adaptation (thus far). Our minds are our evolutionary niche.The human mind is a powerful tool that is often taken for granted. We are able to solve complex problems that other animals never even recognize. Humans have employed the use of tools and technology to compensate for the relative lack of strength and speed. We can keep track of information across time and distance, transmit that information fairly easily across generations and continents, and adapt that information to new situations. And, also important, we are able to handily navigate social situations, recognizing ourselves and others as independent sentient beings.

Just how our minds exploded into sentience is a matter of much speculation. One of the most popular theories is that there was a "great leap forward" (Diamond, 1993), an evolutionary period about 40,000 to 50,000 years ago where the development of the human brain outpaced almost everything else. This allowed humans to develop cultural staples such as language, which enabled us to work collaboratively and develop intellectually in a way previously unseen. Here, culture became a significant and powerful evolutionary force in its own right. Another provocative theory as to how and why our brains experienced such a large thrust forward is that the organ encountered psychotropic molecules when early hominids accidentally ingested certain plants or fungi that spurred on development, and that the hallucinogenic mushrooms ingested by early man inspired the shamanic visions that led to the birth of religion (Pollan, 2006). Religion is one of the preeminent features of human culture and will be discussed in greater detail in the coming chapters. For now, it is enough to appreciate that such cultural constructions would not be possible without a sufficiently advanced psychology to support it.

What, then, are the specific features of the human mind that have allowed humans to be successful as a species? They are worth listing here:

1. Sentience is the ability to experience a subjective reality. Humans are special in the animal kingdom in that we are aware of our own existence (and mortality), and this is a tremendous feat in and of itself that should not be taken for granted. This manifests itself more specifically in what scientists have called the *theory of mind*, which is "the ability to attribute mental states—beliefs, intents, desires, pretenses, knowledge, etc.—to oneself and others and to understand that others have beliefs, desires, and intentions that are different from one's own" (Premack & Woodruff, 1978, p. 515).

2. The establishment of complex social networks is made possible only by our well-developed theory of mind. If we did not have the capacity to understand that the contents of our mind is different from the contents of others' minds, we would not have any reason or method to establish relationships with those who share our lives with us. The scale and complexity of human relationships is awe-inspiring. We can know thousands of people well, and we have developed sophisticated methods of interactions, from fraternities and neighborhood parties to Facebook and Twitter registration. Humans are certainly not the only social organisms; entomologist E. O.

Wilson has made a career studying the social behavior of ants, whose incredible ability to coordinate actions for the colony's greater good led Wilson to dub them "super-organisms" (Wilson & Holldobler, 2008). Insects aside, it is demonstrated that in the animal kingdom, "primates [which include humans] use their knowledge about the social world in which they live to form more complex alliances with each other than do other animals" (Dunbar, 1992, p. 28). This certainly is the case with humans, even more so than with our primate relatives. Because societies are composed of individuals, the direction in which a society evolves can be examined privately, one person at a time, and publicly, by what those people tell each other. On the individual level, much of our inner monologue consists of what we tell ourselves about others and about ourselves. In one study, it was calculated that 70% of human conversations could be classified as gossip (Dunbar, 1992).

3. The importance of the development of language as a tool to communicate effectively across time and space cannot be overemphasized. In his book *Uniquely Human*, Philip Lieberman wrote, "The 'Key' to the evolution of the modern human brain is rapid vocal communication. That consequently is the key to human progress; the enhanced linguistic and cognitive ability that the human brain confers allows us to transcend the constraints of biological evolution" (1991, p. 9). Language allows us to transmit and store information accurately and handily. Without language, our knowledge of the world would be limited to what is only experienced firsthand. Because we can listen to stories told by others and read printed words our knowledge of the world is exponentially increased to things we may never encounter personally or things that happened well before we were born. Likewise, through language and stored media we can easily share events that we experience with others far away and those yet to be born.

4.   The development of technology that expands our capabilities beyond what the body alone can accomplish has resulted in our ability to affect and alter our environment in significant ways. This includes the simplest machines (levers, inclined planes, knives, and wheels), to the utilization of natural phenomena for human benefit (fire, agriculture), to the incredibly complex systems and machines we enjoy today (vaccines, internal combustion engines, microprocessors). The technological advances that humans have been responsible for are directly responsible for human civilization, perhaps more than any other single factor. The great acceleration of computer and Internet technology has hastened the acceleration of threats to human sustainability, but it also offers the tools for salvation.

5.   While the concept of culture can be hard to grasp, as it consists of "systems of symbols and meanings that even their creators contest, that lack fixed boundaries, that are constantly in flux, and that interact and compete with one another" (Findley & Rothney, 2006, p. 14), one can think of culture as the way of life of a group of people, that is passed down from one generation to the next. Culture, for the purposes in this book, includes anything that is a product of the human mind. This includes (but is not limited to) a people's religion, government, economic system, customs, traditions, music, theater, dance, visual art, social conventions, and even language and technology. The functional unit of culture, as defined by Dawkins (1989), is the "meme," which can be thought of as analogous to the gene as the functional unit of biology.

The human mind is indeed incredibly developed and highly complex. In fact, the three-odd pounds of grey-white flesh that reside in each of our heads in most ways make the most sophisticated supercomputers in the world look like middle school science fair projects. In addition, humans are endowed with a higher set of mental functions that have caused us to ask larger abstract (and often difficult) questions about ourselves and our world, such as, what factors motivate people to act? How do we view the reality of existence? What are we willing to do to get what we want? In order to effectively determine a long-term strategy of sustainable survival, it becomes important to develop an accurate, even if incomplete, model of human thought and behavior. Evolutionary theory provides a strong foundation for this project, but there are many dimensions to consider: biochemical factors, evolutionarily hardwired survival needs (food, security, sex, and shelter), genetically programmed factors (sexual predispositions, longevity), cultural factors (economic, religious, tribal, or societal status), social factors (in-group favoritism, response to authority), and individual psychological factors (depression, narcissism, addiction, and neuroses). Understanding how the human mind operates is a crucial component to building this Ark, as everyone who has ever existed is subject to the same basic psychological operating principles.

The thorough examination and continued scientific research into the attributes of the individual human mind have the potential for being among the most important evolutionary leaps in the history of the planet. All of what we humans have done here on earth has been borne out of the human mind, and in this light we try to make sense of its many creations and by-products. Humans—along with those animals whose evolutionary design has not changed since the age of the dinosaurs—have to date been some of the most successful organisms with the ability to dominate the competition. But, not endowed with the beneficial physicality of the cockroach or shark, humans have succeeded as a species, in part, by using "smarts" and social proclivities to massively change their environment. Unique amongst species, humans can even change themselves physically and mentallyfor better and for worse, to meet the perceived needs of the day. People most often make these changes in the name of their perceived need for short-term individual survival, as our evolutionary heritage would dictate. As a society, humans can look at the track record and, out of concern, take pause. Human minds have been the source of all our successes, but they have also been the reason why we now find ourselves stumbling over obstacles to a sustainable and peaceful future.

Biological Foundations

Of course, the content of the human mind is not directly available to us for empirical study. A scientist cannot open up our mind (although we can keep an open mind!) and examine its contents in the same way a mechanic can look inside when a car engine breaks down. The mind is forever private, and telepathy in any meaningful sense is science fiction. The only way to know the content of another's mind is through their language and behavior. This makes interpreting someone's mental state seem harder than it actually is. Between what someone says (or doesn't say) and does (or doesn't do), there is plenty of information available to us that will give us insights into that person's mental state. Being aware of what makes a human mind "tick" is arguably a vital link in building the Ark. Moreover, humans have evolved to be particularly sensitive to such information. Cognitive scientists like Steven Pinker (2002) believe that humans are born with an "intuitive psychology, which is used to understand other people" (p. 20). Others are endlessly fascinating to us, and many of us have quite enjoyed whiling away hours watching our fellow bipeds come and go in areas where people gather. The psychologists' discipline and structure put toward figuring out what makes people tick has yielded some interesting and important conclusions about the mind, and recent advances in technology and research have given more sources of information from which to draw the principles of psychology. Psychologists are now able to organize the investigation of human psychology into various levels of analysis. The field of psychology is undergoing a revolution and now incorporates a much greater biological perspective within its scope. In this exciting time, traditional psychological questions are being examined by a rich mixture of scientists, including evolutionary biologists, cognitive scientists, neuroscientists, and computer scientists. "We have found, as have many of our colleagues, that it is rewarding to introduce these new ideas to psychology students, who are fascinated with the workings of the human mind as it navigates a complex, social world" (Gazzaniga & Heatherton, 2003, p. 27).

Until recently, students of human behavior have taken a unilateral approach, grounded firmly in one level of analysis. The psychoanalysts painted a picture of the mind vivid with symbology and unconscious yearnings, while the behaviorists construed people as mindless machines who responded to reinforcement and punishment. As more is beginning to be understood about the mind and the brain that supports it, professionals begin to take a more integrated approach.

Whatever explanations for human behavior may finally be adopted in future millennia, the newest level of analysis employed to provide information about human psychology, as Gazzaniga and Heatherton indicate, is the biological level of analysis. This includes the disciplines of genetics, neuroanatomy, brain chemistry, and psychopharmacology. In the science of data storage and computer processing, and in the understanding of neural processes, the key to more complex processes is through understanding the ultra-small. An incredible amount of data (thoughts, memories) can be contained in a physically small area, and scientists are now able to tap into some of that data storage and transfer it using sophisticated techniques and technology culled from the life sciences and medicine. When the enormous complexity of the brain is revealed using fMRI, connectionist models, or theories in cognitive neuropsychology, the processing power of the human brain (which gives rise to the mind) makes current computer technology look like a stone abacus by comparison. Perhaps someday the thought process will be traced back to its indivisible components, and some researchers are circling in on just that, but for now professionals know enough about the brain to know that they are only guessing how they work at the level of the synapse.

At the biological level, the human mind is construed as an incredibly complex and intricate circuit board, whose wires (neurons) and transistors (synapses) are governed by physical, electrical, and chemical principles. As in all animals there are small amounts of voltage coursing through the neurons, which are responsible for the actions of the nervous systems, including the brain. The measurable energy emitted by the brain is quantitatively small in terms of watts, yet the complexities of the neural structures are enormous. "Our brains contain about 100 billion neurons, each of which sends out feelers, or axons, to link it to about a thousand others . . . thus creating an estimated $10^{70,000,000,000,000}$ possible patterns of connections (equivalent to thoughts and memories) . . . This number is so large it dwarfs the numbers of atoms in the observable universe, which is 10^{80}"(Barrow, 2002, p. 117). With such a staggering number of possibilities housed inside such a small mass of organic tissue, the human brain has demonstrated itself as one of the most adaptable entities in existence. Brains can continuously learn and adapt by creating new neural pathways. Studies of brain injuries reveal that when damage occurs to sections of the brain affecting functions such as memory and language, the brain is able to relearn the information by using other sections and creating new pathways. Bob Woodruff, ABC news anchor who suffered traumatic brain injury from a bomb in Iraq, illustrated this process in a presentation to the Aspen Institute in 2007.

> *Think of it this way: Your memory and thoughts are held within file cabinets in your house. An explosion happens and most of your files and all the papers and words on those papers are spread around on the front yard. You need to pick up those papers and pieces of papers and make them make sense. Some of those are done by using flashcards, some by making associations, and some all of a sudden flew back by themselves into the file cabinets, like the names of the states.*

The brain has evolved as an organ that can detect, store, and interpret a great deal of data, and the sum total of this data is what we experience as the mind. If one assumes that the sum of individual experiences and thoughts resides somewhere within the brain, the correct tools may allow them to be mined like any artificial data storage facility. Current technologies such as PET scans, SPECT scans, and fMRI are able to show brain activity taking place; they can illustrate differences in gender thought patterns and the neurological disorder of schizophrenia (Andreasen, 2007). Advances in technology and research have identified the brain's neurotransmitters (the chemical content of synaptic transmission), how memory is stored via long-term potentiationof certain neural circuits, and how neural networks are capable of profound recognition of imagery; and they have even begun to uncover how thought itself is initiated at the cellular level (Rosenzweig et al., 1996). There are studies that show that thought occurs before physical action (by milliseconds) and that these thoughts can be "read" and predicted by scientists (Soon et al., 2008). If one can reduce such mental experiences to a cascade of chemicals and small bits of electricity, it then follows from this that manipulating these chemical and electrical events can alter the experience of reality.

By way of example, we can reflect on how drugs affect our brains and, consequently, our minds. We know that brain chemistry greatly affects perception of reality and, hence, behavior, and it is also known that altering that brain chemistry can produce changes in the ability to allocate attention, mood, and perception of physical phenomena. For example, the receptors for the neurotransmitters serotonin and dopamine control depression and mania, among other things, which in turn can be "artificially" manipulated or altered. Psychoactive drugs like LSD, mescaline, or psilocybin affect the action of serotonin and especially dopamine (Fraser, Molinoff, & Winokur, 1994). The introduction of psychoactive drugs results in great changes to the conscious and subconscious mind.

Advances in biological psychology have helped millions who would otherwise suffer from mood disorders. Chemical and neurological functions of the brain present an alternate explanation about how our minds work and what is responsible for consciousness. The human brain is very sensitive to the chemical bath in which it marinates. Alzheimer's, schizophrenia, and other organic dysfunctions of the brain are caused by changes in the transmission of electrochemical signals, and these conditions alter reality for that individual. A psychotic person may never make the distinction between "reality" and the internal mental images that appear to be "reality." This simple truth serves to underscore two sobering facts: (1) There are as many perceptions of reality as there are individuals; and (2) All reality is constructed as a conflagration of billions of chemical reactions occurring simultaneously.

While studies of neuroscience show the basic picture of the brain "circuit boards," and this reveals a great deal about how biological brains connect to psychological minds, perhaps there needs to be more taken from the life sciences in order to understand how the human brain (and the minds they contain) operate. Much of this answer appears to lie in the study of genetics, which is the mechanism through which biological evolution occurs. The process of converting DNA's code into proteins in the body, often called the "central dogma of biology," is responsible for certain inherited traits. But there is more: Genetics are responsible for the development of the brain in the first place! Genes clearly play an important role in mental experience, but it would be a mistake to think of genes as the origin for all behavior. Most of the genetic code provides the blueprint for the "basic" construction of our bodies, which of course includes the brain. But unlike the muscles in the arms or the marrow in bones, brains are highly susceptible to changes brought about by events experienced in the outside environment. A bit of introspection will reveal to us that the external world (which includes other people's behaviors) greatly affects our own minds. Each experience we have in the world shapes our private mental universes in a completely unique and unrepeatable way. As a result, each human is biologically discrete and has his or her own thought processes that, in turn, determine all of his or her thoughts and actions. The external environment and our experiences influence each of our unique mental universes, which include family, society, and culture, but are still influenced in no small part by genetics.

The most popular theory in operation is that mental and physical traits do not descend directly from the genes themselves. DNA can be thought of as a blueprint for an incredible construction project: in this case, the construction of bodies and minds. This blueprint is quite necessary, but it is entirely probable that once the construction project is under way, things will not be built exactly to specs. Instead, it is the expression of genes that directly determines mental and physical traits, and this gene expression depends heavily on environmental influences. Cognitive psychologist Michael Gazzaniga addressed the interaction of our genetic blueprint and our individual experiences:

> What determines the kind of person you are? What factors make you more or less bold, intelligent, or able to read a map? All of these are influenced by the interactions of your genes and the environment in which you were raised. The study of how genes and environment interact to influence psychological activity is known as behavioral genetics. Behavioral genetics has also made important contributions to the biological revolution, providing information about the extent to which biology influences mind, brain, and behavior.

> Any research that suggests that abilities to perform certain behaviors are based in biology is controversial. Who wants to be told that there are limitations to what you can achieve based on something that is beyond your

control, such as sex, race, eye color, and predisposition to diseases like cancer, alcoholism, or migraines? But can genes also determine whether or not people will get divorced, how smart they are, or what career they're likely to choose? A concern of psychological scientists is the extent to which all of these characteristics are influenced by nature and nurture, by genetic makeup and the environment. Increasingly, science is indicating that genes lay the groundwork for many human traits. From this perspective, people are born essentially like undeveloped photographs: The image is already captured, but the way it eventually appears can vary based on the development process. However, the basic picture is there from the beginning. (Gazzaniga & Heatherton, 2003, p. 65)

The nature/nurture debate, and its resultant study of the interaction between genes and environment, has been fruitful ground for many scholars, but it would be too big a digression to explore this tremendous intellectual puzzle in any greater detail. For the sake of simplicity, think of genes and environment, as Gazzaniga would suggest, as a photograph; or compare genes and environment to a home cooked meal: The genes are the ingredients we start with, and the environment is the recipe we follow (or choose not to follow). Clearly, both the ingredients and what we do with them are integral to the quality of the final meal. We see here that two chefs can take the same ingredients and make completely different delicacies, and we also see here that we are limited in some ways by what we start with: There is no way to make a peanut butter sandwich out of a sirloin steak.

Making the Leap from Brain to Mind: Cognitive

Despite such well-developed biological analyses of the human mind, the notion that hard science can fully describe and quantify any individual's mental state is folly. No one can view the world exactly as another, and as much as one is able to empathize, it is not possible to fully understand another's mind, even if that person is close to you.

In some way, however small and secret,
Each of us is a little mad.
Everyone is lonely at bottom,
And cries to be understood,
But we can never entirely understand anyone else,
And each of us remains part stranger,
Even to those who love us. (Leo Ralston, no date)

Psychologists use variable-controlled experimentation to explore and describe general common mental phenomena and diagnose specific dysfunctions or talents with relation to group and cultural norms. Research psychologists can account for and predict behavior with models that explain a modest percentage of variation. This may be useful for drawing statistical conclusions about group trends, but it is not necessarily useful if your wish is to understand one individual mind as completely as possible. For this, the best shot may lie with what scientists believe humans are born with: the innate aptitude for social perception, gifted to us as the supreme adaptive evolutionary strategy. Neurophysiologists can assign numbers to other various proposed dimensions of intelligence or personality; they can even assess, with divergent levels of inaccuracy, the probability of a person committing suicide. Individuals can be labeled, grouped, and categorized into multiple subgroupings, but each person acts out within his or her own script. Hardwired predispositions and set points, hardwired into us by biology, intersect with the fluidity of the social world that we participate in. The psychological entity called the mind is the site of this intersection, and the study of the intersection of the biological foundations and conscious experience is left to the psychological level of analysis known as cognitive science.

Psychiatrists and psychologists have attempted to describe the process of human thought, character development, and behavior through a wide variety of theories: some with their origin in intuitive, reflective thought; some borne of behavioral studies; and some derived from research in the laboratory. Researchers working at the biological level of analysis have made preliminary inroads into the question of what the mind is, but much work remains. Scientists have identified areas of the brain associated with executive function, language ability, emotion, and memory, and we have determined the effects of increasing or decreasing

117

certain chemicals in the brain. Breakthroughs in knowledge such as these give us pieces of the larger puzzle of how to understand the mind, but as of yet these pieces do not add up to a complete finished solution. Creatures do not experience individual chemical reactions, after all; they experience the aggregated results as mental processes: thoughts, emotions, memories. This is the conscious experience that is most recognizable, and ultimately, these conscious cognitive processes are what concern us the most in this book. More than discoveries made in the fields of genetics or neuroscience, it is cognitive science that has been most successful at bridging the gap between the microscopic nuances of the biological brain and the more familiar conscious experience of the psychological mind. Cognitive science is the fulcrum that balances scientific discovery with real-world application (Bruer, 1997).

Some mental circuits and their resultant conscious experiences are employed more often than others and have proved more useful in evolutionary terms. The most important brain processes happen before thought is even required, such as the need to keep our diaphragms moving air in and out of our lungs and feelings of hunger or thirst. Other functions, typically ones that embody a "primordial past evolutionary advantage" (Andreasen, 2007), such as face or gender recognition, come easily and almost automatically to us. Because everyone has slightly different genes and experiences interacting with different environments, the outcome of the intersection of an individual's "hardware" (neurochemistry) and subsequent "software" (mind) will be unique. This explains the varying interests, abilities, and proclivities seen across any group of individuals at a more personal level.

The mind is more, of course, than a mere onboard operating system and storage facility for the reams of data it receives every day; it has the remarkable ability to correlate, assimilate, extrapolate, and learn. This is at the core of our hope for the Ark for the 21st century. Data is received through sensory detectors that vary by individuals and, indeed, by species: Bats navigate with ultrasonic echoes, goats see in ultraviolet as well the visible spectrum, whales utilize low frequency sound, snakes detect in infrared, and humans use language. Even if other creatures do not possess what we would call a mind, each has a unique ability that represents an evolutionary niche for that species, a survival strategy that has been refined and smoothed over time. In this sense, our use of language and our capacity for social perception to enhance our interactions and relationships is not much different from a bat's echolocation or a snake's heat-sensing abilities.

Conscious cognitive processing, which a layperson would simply call "thinking," happens with various levels of intensity and sophistication. Some individuals process and interpret data creatively, while others, for the most part, simply recall input. One of the secrets of success for those who are able to think better is practice. As trite as it sounds, the brain needs to be exercised to make you an expert thinker, just as your muscles would need to be exercised for you to become an Olympic athlete. The greater the ability to scan, store, and retrieve data, and the more practice doing so, the greater the potential to think at higher and more complex levels. This leads to a greater ability to master one's environment and successfully navigate the human social realm. This is organized complexity at its best. Complexity, however, often leaves a machine prone to breakdown, which certainly can be observed in the human mind, but complexity also can allow for self-correcting redundancies and restorative mechanisms. The mind does not seem to be an exception. Thus, this finely tooled device, this laser, if you will, has the capacity to turn in on itself with blinding power and, occasionally, cut those objects around it or even itself to ribbons.

One can think of the consciously experienced aggregation of all brain chemistry and cognitive activity as a person's internal experience or mental representation of reality, which cognitive psychologist Jean Piaget theorized is packaged into "schemata." He considered schemata to be the very building blocks of thinking (Woolfolk, 1987). Piaget thought that all people house mental representations—schemata—of reality in our minds, just as a scale model of a building would house all the attributes of the actual structure. One's schemata, which are constructed for everything from mother to food to beauty, belong to one's mind alone, even if they are models for actual things that exist outside the mind. Piaget thought, and correctly so, that what we react to and interact with is actually our mental model of the world, and not the world itself (Ginsburg & Opper, 1988). It is often the case that one's schemata is so highly congruent with reality that one doesn't have to think about the difference between the two, but this is not necessarily so in all cases. Haven't we all experienced times at which our idea of something (that is to say, our mental representation of something) turns out to be quite different from the thing itself? Likewise, we should note that any two people would build different schemata for the same thing. For example, a suburban elementary school student and a through-hiker on the Appalachian Trail will build quite different mental representations of "backpack." Neither is more correct than the other, just dependent on personal experience, coupled with what each environment demands for success. In much the same way, any two individuals will have two different schemata of justice, freedom, and God, even if they have similar upbringings and share cultures. Piaget's concept of schemata may not be so academic or benign after all; here we can see where misunderstandings begin. This notion further justifies the idea that reality as experienced is subjective. This has important ramifications when trying to "communicate" with each other.

Schemata are refined and edited with every new experience and bit of information gleaned from the five senses. Sometimes, a piece of information comes along that fits with what is constructed in one's head, and that bit is assimilated into the existing schemata (e.g., an Australian Shepherd fits cleanly into our dog schemata, even if we've never seen one). Other times, as is the case with changes in scientific thinking, new information comes to light that forces one to alter or accommodate ones schemata to this new piece of news (e.g., once one learns about the behavior of objects in outer space (and believes it), the schemata of gravitychanges from "things fall toward the earth" to "any two objects with mass attract one another"). From birth, and even before, humans and other animals begin the input and schemata-building process, learning and adapting. Animals with smaller, less complex brains develop schemata more exclusively tuned to their evolutionary survival. Humans also develop schemata that can be traced back to those biological imperatives, but the connection between schemata and human survival and reproductive viability is sometimes hard to trace and may be several steps removed.

Piaget was concerned with how we construct our schemata, and through his careful observation of his own children, he assembled a theory of cognitive development that explains such phenomena. Piaget thought of individuals, but children in particular, as scientist-like in their exploration of the world around them. He also said that our first years are a critical period of mental growth. Research shows that cognitive abilities such as language acquisition, if not developed in the first four to six years of life, will not develop fully (Pinker, 1994).[9] This is true of a wide range of cognitive functions. To many parents, the toddler who throws his dinner plate across the room is a nuisance, but to Piaget, this little scientist is building his schema of gravity. "Normal" cognitive development consists of assembling data and interpreting from experience to create a reality similar but not identical to those who share experiences. Organisms with similar environmental input—twins raised together, long-married couples, young boys in Wahabi madras, sea turtles from the same nest, or salmon hatched from the same stream—have many shared environmental inputs and experiences. With similar brain processing power, these individuals will most likely construct similar schemata, beliefs, and views of the world or reality, yet all will always have some different thoughts and behaviors that are uniquely their own.

Leaving aside religion, where faith is encouraged as a means and an end, people have a fondness for making assumptions in areas of their lives where it is unhelpful to do so, and then developing core sets of beliefs grounded on them. From such intellectual quicksand is borne health fads, bigotry, and even political and economic decisions. Common sense and everyday human experience foster the perception that "surely reality is what we think it is; reality is revealed to us by our experiences" (Greene, 2004, p. 5). However, as psychologist James Hollis wrote, "Hubris is found in our capacity to convince ourselves that we really know what is going on" (Hollis, 2001, p. 13). The disciplines of thought we have created are means of describing the "way things are." But there doesn't appear to be an absolute truth, just one's perception of what truth is. Envisioning the process of creating mental representations can be thought of as a very fine projection of a

---

[9]   Psychoanalytic theory, as a not-so-coincidental aside, also places primary importance on early childhood experience.

TV picture. Continuous inputs of electromagnetic, acoustic, and tactile information are recorded in the mind. The blue of the sky, the smell of the ocean, the recognition of a familiar face, the sound of one's baby: All of these are sequentially viewed, yet randomly stored as digital data in the vast hard drive of neural combination. Stimuli from the environment prompt the data to be recalled, correlated, and interpreted. The constantly changing individual points combine to form an image to the viewer, and this image will elicit a response in the individual mind. It will connect and associate whatever other bits of mental function happen to be paired with it, whether conscious or unconscious. The lines of cocaine on a glass table raises the adrenal hormone level in the addict; the sight and touch of a naked beautiful body of the preferred sexual orientation results in blood engorging the sexual organs; the sound of a gunshot causes the heart rate to surge in both the shooter and bystander. In the brain, the metaphorical pixels are electrochemical signals that run down neurons and through synapses and the synaptic connections that have been primed to fire more readily through experience. Viewed individually, the pixels have no significant or symbolic meaning. It is only when our brains integrate these uncountable bits of information (in mere milliseconds) that we begin to derive recognition and meaning in our minds. The neuroanatomy of our visual or auditory systems provides us the most literal examples of this process, but psychologists believe it is a similar process that governs how we form mental representations of everything, from images in our head to opinions on abstract ideas. We offer "a penny for your thoughts," when the price of admission entitles the viewer to experience a complexly textured internal drama of enormous detail, a continuous hologram of new sensory inputs, stored data from the individual's conscious and even unconscious past.

The formation of schemata is hardly a one-way process, and individual minds are not passive subjects to the whims of the environment. We are capable agents of action and play no small part in the environments of others, as well as our own. This results in a play within a play, as the viewers join in the drama, and their level of participation in turn contributes to the creation of conscious and unconscious future events. The audience is diverse, and *almost* identical mental representations are apparent to other observers of the same scenes. An individual's projection interacts with the projections of those with whom he or she comes in contact, becoming a basic starting point for relationships and societies. Jung's definition of projection is a case in point. Two people meet, "project" images onto another, and experience the poetry of love at first sight. Their psyches are receptive due to congruent personality conditions, they are aroused and open, and the projected images interact. Later, they may process more data and realize that he or she was not Mrs. or Mr. Right. Maybe it was the excitement of the initial meeting and the newness of the liaison. If this couple gets married, lives together, and deals with paying bills, sick children, job issues, cleaning the toilets, and daily familiarity, all can change at levels both chemical and consciously sublime. This is but one example of what may happen when two minds share schemata.

Romantic relationships are communications between the mental representations of individuals, with some physical contact thrown in for good measure and, if lucky, the toxically enchanting chemical soup we refer to as love. If we are remarkably lucky, that relationship evolves and strengthens over a lifetime. The romance of lifelong (or eternal) bliss, locked in each other's arms, making love to the sounds of the waves crashing on the beach, may be a fiction of the soul, but a powerful motivator for action nonetheless. As the differences between brain compositions (chemistry, psychology, and capacity) and previous learned experiences that shape current perceptions and processing functions diverge, so do the views of that mental representation and the actions of the individual living within that context.

What we conveniently think of as "reality" thus becomes a function of the individual's observing, processing, and acting out his schema. A more functional "reality," one that can be navigated and agreed upon by many people, becomes a matter of how people accept and align their mental representations in concert with others. There of course is no "real" norm, and what we think of as norms are most often given such designations because they have reached a statistical critical mass. But this is culturally and environmentally determined, as is evidenced by different standards of acceptable behavior in different world cultures. A peasant in the Third World with no formal education and no experience of other locations will have built a schema and developed norms far different from the Dalai Lama, a concert musician in Tokyo, a chimpanzee in captivity, or a physics professor in Russia, even if all are exposed at any given moment to the same sensory input. One's perspectives are unique because of their projections of the world but we must be able to communicate effectively with others regardless of their projections. If we did not, there would be no way out of this epistemological quandary, and no way of moving forward. Since we have every intention of moving forward, we need to simultaneously understand the uniqueness of our own mental worlds, and the goal of sharing our schema with our family, friends, neighbors, and fellow humans. This is the fundamental challenge of breaking out of one's individual fishbowl and expanding to ever-larger environments.

Building schema is always a work in process and is subject to continual refining. As an example, a young child hears a loud noise while trying to fall asleep. The child's first reaction may be (a primal response for survival), which employs a deeply set, protective schema of danger or threat. And why not? Good things usually did not follow sudden loud noises on the African savannah 3.5 million years ago. But because she has experienced a bit more than pain and suffering following loud noises in the past, the child then tries to analyze what is happening. Possible scenarios arise from previously formed schemata (monsters in the closet or bad men trying to break in). In reality, it is just the furnace with a broken air handler. But the child does not yet (and may never) understand about mechanical HVAC systems, so her reality is the projection of images based upon previous input (stories, fears, TV shows, archetypes) in her schema of loud noise at night. With enough time and experience in the basement of her house, she will learn to distinguish between furnaces and monsters under the bed. To the outside observer, the fear is not justified by reality, but to the child, the fantasy constructed to make sense of the unknown is her mental representations of reality. Which is correct? They both are, of course.

If our schemata remain unchecked against realities or other schemata, we experience a fishbowl effect. That is, the cognitive source of our various myopias comes to us when we do not reconcile our mental representations of reality with the real things, or with that of our neighbors. Breaking out of our individual fishbowls, which includes thinking in the long term and more globally, necessarily involves our building schemata that coincide with those of our neighbors and are accurately representative of reality. When we think about working together to build a sustainable future for all of humanity, this is a point we can never take for granted.

Hearthstone

Brightening the ordinary day—
constant—yet, never the same—
How could I possibly take for granted
that which makes life sweeter, brings comfort
and improves over time
 with ageless beauty?
No mere functionary, you give life
to sultry flames, to dance.
Casting shadows in rhythm
with private passion; they have
thrown off embers, grown, then,
into separate fires,
Multiplying the joy
of our heart's home.
You nurture and enrich all
without diminishing the steady, burning source.
I bring home wood,
And you make it magic,
Forever. (Robert Miller, 2009)

Sentience and Conscious Experience

Of all the schemata the human mind has constructed, few are as important as the mind's schema of itself. According to many cognitive scientists, humans are not alone in the ability to generate schemata; Piaget's model of mental representation can be applied to a host of life forms with well-developed nervous systems and brains. Studies, for example, demonstrate that animals can have mental representations of numbers without having the language for those numbers (Plodowski et al., 2003). However, we are seemingly alone in our ability to recognize that the schemata that we create and build are representations of the real thing, not the real thing itself, and that those representations are generated in something we call our minds. This is an enormous leap, possibly the single most important point that separates us from every other life form on the planet. It is quite an accomplishment to possess a sufficiently complex nervous system that has evolved to the point where mental representations are possible; it is even more of a miracle to possess a mind that can engage in metacognition. Indeed, "the universe in which we've emerged belongs to the unusual subset that permits complexity and consciousness to develop" (Reese, quoted in Kaku, 2006). Metacognition, or thinking about our own thinking, introduces a psychological feedback system whose complete ramifications are impossible to imagine, partly because imagining is one of the ramifications of such a system. In short, though, we who have the capacity to build a schema of our own minds, and we who are able to understand our perception of reality as subjective collection of schemata, have achieved sentience. We then are able to alter mental representations—literally change our minds—simply through thought and reflection, as well as through experience. Here emerges the conscious level of analysis that guides us through most of our regular and familiar functioning. Our schemata of our own minds are the bridge to explaining consciousness and everything that comes with it.

Underlying our capacity for metacognition is the notion that we have a mind in the first place and that the contents of one person's mind are not necessarily the same as the contents of another person's mind. As mentioned before, this notion (itself a complex schema) is formally called the theory of mind in circles of cognitive scientists. Some often take their own theories of mind for granted, but studies of younger children reveal that this is an ability that develops over time and, more correctly, with age and a certain level of neuroanatomical maturity (Astington, 1993). What should not take for granted, though, is the importance of social interactions in our lives. Humans, at our core, are highly social creatures, and sociality only takes such a central place in our lives when we realize that our neighbors' minds are different from our own. Evolution has provided that humans crave affiliation, relish in gossip, and are drawn to intimate, personal information about another. This is an excellent example of how our distinctly human traits represent a highly complex cultural twist on that which gives us an evolutionary advantage (social interactions), and is not possible without a fully developed psychology to support it. If a person were to assume that the contents of his mind are not uniquely his, or that others could know and agree upon exactly what he has in mind, that person would have very little reason to attempt to communicate with others, and therefore would lose out on forging bonds with others, learning to cooperate with others, and making alliances with others. In the African savannah, this would have meant a serious survival disadvantage; in the 21st century, with all the developed culture and technology available to us that *Australopithecus* did not have, it still does.

The emergence of human culture and human civilization follows a few giant leaps away from a predisposition for social interactions, made possible by our very sentience. We have evolved as social creatures, dependent on relationships, cooperation, and alliances, and we have our theory of mind to thank for our ability to process and engage in such relationships. Relationships spawn social networks, and social networks, in turn, spawn tribes, clans, communities, organizations, and so on. Given certain key technological innovations and tools (also made possible by our minds), clans and tribes will plant food, domesticate animals, acquire property, and form proper agricultural civilizations. And, of course, this is exactly what happened. This is our story. Our social networking gave birth to nothing short of human civilization. Civilized people, being far from perfect, needed structures in place to ensure a degree of justice and protection in their communities. In response they developed government and systems of laws to protect liberty and property. As people communicate and collaborate more and more, technological and cultural innovations skyrocket geometrically. Population also skyrockets along with technological advancement. History shows us that inevitably, a few powerful and enterprising members of civilization act out of their own individual short-term survival benefit at the expense of others less related, consolidating power and control for themselves. Trace this momentum down the line and eventually we see that some of us in the Western world find ourselves spending eight hours a day (half our waking lives!) under fluorescent lights and in front of a flashing screen, so entrenched in a complex social system that our "survival skills"— hardly hunting and gathering anymore—involve bizarre practices many degrees removed from directly feeding ourselves, sheltering ourselves, protecting ourselves. Thus, the emergence of our theory of mind some time long ago, while our ancestors still walked unclothed around eastern Africa, may be the point we could safely say that our psychological minds emerged. Perhaps more important, this is also the point that defines us as *Homo sapiens* (the "thinking man"), and the point that set us on the increasingly complex, tangled path we are still stumbling down today.

Archetypes And Unconscious Experience

Beyond our genes, beyond our hardwired circuit board of mental programming, beyond our experience, beyond even our consciousness, our minds and resultant behaviors are subject to what psychologist Carl Jung has called *archetypes.* Jungian archetypes can include myths (the fall from grace), symbols (the cornucopia as a sign of fertility), rituals (honoring the dead in some sort of ceremony), or instincts (marriage). Jung recognized pervasive patterns in human schemata, patterns that most often take the overt forms of recurring symbols in literature, in art, in history, and in each of our conscious experiences. He believed, as many cognitive scientists do, that we are not born into this world empty, but instead carry a basic set of psychological parameters that guide us in our lives. These psychological parameters were not as concrete as Pinker's (1994) suggestion of innate numerical capacity or Chomsky's (1975) suggestion of the innate capacity for language acquisition. Jung's archetypes were more symbolic than anything else, thought to exist in the mind and in the world at large. If we view each of our lives as a work of cinema, Jung might say that we see highly similar characters, and themes develop as our narratives unfold. This, according to Jung, is not because we are trying to lead similar lives, but instead we are inheritors of a certain way of successfully moving through our lives because of how we have evolved. These recurrent patterns, which Jung argues are consistent across time and culture, are seen as the symbolic key to our mind's abstract workings. Archetypes reside both in each of our own unconscious minds and as part of a more universal psychic reality, which he termed the "collective unconscious." While the concept of archetypes is nowadays more often applied quite adeptly to literature and film criticism, its origins sprang from within the field of psychology. Jung developed the concept of archetypes in order to make sense of our incredibly complex psychology.Jung, like his teacher Freud before him, acknowledged that all unconscious processes we possess, embody, and experience have their roots in our species' evolutionary adaptations. However, these symbolic residents of our unconscious minds could be discussed and conceptualized with no understanding of the biological level of analysis. Very little effort was made to map the archetypes or collective unconscious onto any discrete neurological process. Nevertheless, such symbolic structures could be addressed clinically in similar ways. Jung said that archetypes function like psychological organs, in that their presence evolved in order to help us survive successfully as organisms. Thus, the set of memes that are called archetypes, and even the concept of archetypes itself, exist and are directed toward us being successful people, survivors in the face of psychological threat. Our complex systems of thinking and social interaction demand an equally complex compensatory mechanism, and this is embodied in Jung's collective unconscious.

For the purposes of this book, it is enough to recognize that our biological brains evolved to house psychological minds with an unconscious, and that this unconscious, brimming with universally recurrent symbols, was an adaptation that allowed the human organism to be more successful in its mission to survive and pass on its DNA, and allowed the human mind to navigate an increasingly complex social world more effectively. Archetypes play a dual role in our minds: In one sense, they are governing structures that guide and shape our conscious experience, and in another sense, they are themselves memes, cultural units subject to an evolution all their own. In this second sense, we are hosts for the archetypes we carry in the same way that we are hosts for the genes that have been passed to us from our ancestors. Because they have survived, they are strong memes and hold an eminence of sorts over our minds.

While it is widely accepted that we have an unconscious dimension to our minds, and that this unconscious is somehow a survival strategy that has evolved, it still remains difficult to understand why our unconscious is, in fact, a survival mechanism for the mind. It is also difficult to make connections between the products of our unconscious and our consciously experienced reality. This, after all, is the task of much modern psychotherapy. Our concern here, however, is to identify the concepts that may help us better understand how our minds, and therefore how we, "work." Aspects of the unconscious will unfold in later parts of the book; for now, it is enough that we are made conscious of it, and how it relates to the self, the aggregation of our biology, cognition, and self-awareness. Examining the mind on the level of abstract symbology is one more valid lens through which we can come to understand ourselves. James Hollis wrote:

> Jung's view of the self is that which is mysterious, unknowable, but which expresses itself autonomously and whose effects may occasionally be made conscious. . . . Moreover it may no more be known by finite, limited consciousness than what is meant by the word God. . . . What monitors the chemical processes of the body, what occasions dream dramaturgy, what expresses purpose through symptomatology, what manifests occasionally as consciousness, is apparently derived from an order of reality transcendent to comprehension, a supraordinant reality called the Self. (Hollis, 2001, p. 29)

What Do We Do with The Products of Our Minds?

The quest by scientists to describe and anticipate human thought and action has in part been reduced to chemical reactions, and areas of the brain have been programmed to relate to certain thoughts and emotions. That the field of psychology has been tied into the process of evolution connects us to not only what life forms came before us, but also what cosmological processes resulted in the formation of our planet, galaxy, and universe. That humans are able to employ various levels of analysis to the questions of human behavior reveals just how intricate and fascinating our minds are. Despite many unanswered questions, science has amassed a body of specific knowledge about the human inner workings. However, this only seems to deliver answers to the "How?" questions, and not the "Why?" questions. When dealing with the origins of the physical universe and planet, and even the origins of life on this planet, questions of why could be explained in terms of random chance. Now, though, as our focus has traced the progression of the universe to our own sentience, questions of why seem more important. It seems that as a general rule, people would like to think of their existence as more purposeful than that of the rest of organized matter, even more purposeful than the existence of our genetic relatives on the tree of life. The highly advanced human brain and psychology has given us the ability to ask these "Why" questions, which can be considered both an incredible blessing and a terrific curse. In many ways, the culture that we have developed and its prominent features has been driven toward giving ourselves answers in our incessant search for meaning and our quest to correctly determine our place in the universe. Human exploration of these "Why?" represents the final step in the construction of the story of how we got to our present state of affairs, namely the evolution of our culture and one of its most prominent products—religion.

> *If you keep your mind on the things your bodies want to do, you will die. But if you keep your mind on the things the Spirit wants, you will live and have peace. (Romans 8:6)*

Down the Road

Been livin' in this town of old pioneers
I've been a stranger here for too many years
Three thousand miles to go
And it's time, it's been time
To head on down the road

Been spendin' all my days on rivers and streams
And I've been getting' by without many things
The great divide will agree
Rainy day, lost my way
But that's all right with me

Been wishin' someone else could carry this load
But the only home I've known I've left to the cold
Our songs might not see us through
A fleeting soul, all alone
With something to pursue

Been waitin' for the place at the end of the line
The desert has been crossed and the hills have been climbed
A few more miles to go
Say hello, let it go,
And head on down the road

(Taus, Spina, Hunt, & Esterbrooks, 2009)

6

On Religion (as Spirituality)

Then it was as if I suddenly saw the secret beauty of their hearts, the depths of their hearts where neither sin nor desire nor self-knowledge can reach, the core of their reality, the person that each one is in the eyes of that Divine.

If only they could all see themselves as they really are. If only we could see each other that way all the time. There would be no more war, no more hatred, no more cruelty, no more greed. I suppose the big problem would be that we would fall down and worship each other. (Merton, 1958, p. 157)

After 13.7 billion years of trial and error, the process of evolution resulted in a very special and peculiar arrangement of matter: the human mind, made possible by three-odd pounds of grey tissue, packed with neurons and brimming with tiny electrical impulses. Our brain, which serves as the physical housing for our mind, has proven to be one of the most successful adaptive strategies in what we currently know of the universe. While most successful arrangements of matter are strikingly simple, our brains are anything but. The vast complexity of our minds—the distinctly human abilities to store and transmit information, manipulate its environment to further its own interests, think about itself, and remain extremely flexible all the while—has proven to be the key to our overwhelming success as a species. We will now leave aside the underlying biology, the source code of our minds, and focus completely on the human mind and its products. Understanding these concepts is an important piece of building the Ark. In the telling of this story, we have zoomed in completely, covering billions of years and distances as vast as the universe itself. At the end of our selected history of the universe, our focus lands squarely on what is most familiar to us: ourselves. This is not to say that the movements of the evolutionary tides in the universe were directed toward our arrival. It is to say, though, that the way the pieces fell into place resulted in the emergence of the human mind, and with that comes all that we find so familiar: technology, civilization, and the other products of culture. The last part of the story we are to tell is the story of human culture.

Culture and Cultural Evolution

Adaptations that promote survival are not always biological. Behaviors can also promote survival. Consider the defense strategy of a deer in the forest: When it is alerted to the presence of a predator, it stays as still as possible. As it has turned out, several of its predators have visual systems that register movement much better than form, so if a deer stays as still as possible (a behavior), the chances of a predator seeing it are cut down. Over time, the deer that tended toward stillness were the ones that survived and the ones to perpetuate the deer population. Inevitably, all deer developed this behavioral adaptation, either through imitation or something more hardwired. This, paired with the natural selection of a fur color that blends in with its surroundings (a genetic adaptation), proved to be successful survival strategies for that organism.

So it is with humans, and in fact, it is even more so with humans. We are not endowed with the speed of a cheetah, the genetic simplicity of a bacterium, the wings of an eagle, the claws and teeth of a polar bear, or the venom of a snake. Instead, what we have relied on for so many millionsof years of successful survival is our behavior. We can run or fight when presented with dangerous situations, but our success has been in *how* we have run or fought. Humans have used collaboration and innovation to amplify our abilities past what our relatively hairless hominid bodies can do alone. If our bodies can't lift something, we push it up ramps or use pulleys to get the job done. If our bodies can't outfight opponents, we invent weapons to increase our clout. If our bodies can't fend off pathogens, we develop medicine to help us. Our flexible and creative minds make these behaviors possible and, moreover, provide a platform upon which we can quickly refine such behaviors, learn from previous mistakes, and transmit this knowledge to our family and friends.

We can think of the collected set of knowledge as how to survive and be successful in the world, and of this set of behaviors as the beginnings of our culture.

The definition of culture from an anthropology textbook is "information stored in human brains that is acquired by imitation, teaching, or some other form of social learning and that is capable of affecting behavior or some other aspect of the individual's phenotype" (Boyd & Silk, 2000). Already, we see the importance of social networks discussed in the previous chapter. In practice, culture could be anything common to a group of people; cooking recipes, rules for sports games, musical instruments and how to play them, architectural styles, mythologies, superstitions, knowledge of agricultural practice, courtship rituals, and spiritual beliefs all fall into the schemata of culture. The cultures into which you were born have irrevocably shaped you in both small and large ways, but we also have a reciprocal relationship with culture. Our culture does shape us, but we also have the opportunity to shape our culture.

Visionary leaders throughout history knew this well, and we would encourage all citizens of the planet to be as mindful of this point as Gandhi, Jesus of Nazareth, Alexander the Great, Montezuma, and Martin Luther King. While the mechanisms of culture can be used for selfish and destructive ends, as was the case with Genghis Khan or Hitler, the point remains: Social transmission of knowledge, customs, beliefs, values, and attitudes will shape individuals, but individuals can ultimately have a complete say as to the content of their culture. The elements of culture are hardly static. In fact, they change a great deal over fairly short periods of time. Consider fashion trends, which seem to change faster than consumers are able to keep up with them. Or consider Moore's law, which observes that the density of transistors on a computer chip doubles every two years. Thinking more broadly, consider language, which has a central role in any culture but can also be thought of as a product of culture. We would not be able to hold a conversation with English speakers from the 10th century, as the English language itself has changed considerably since then. Moreover, some of us even find it hard to translate between differing dialects of English in existence right now!

Dawkins argues in *The Selfish Gene* (1989) that the products of culture—memes—change according to the rules of evolution in a fashion very similar to how genes change along evolutionary principles. The driving force is the same: Memes will accumulate changes over time in accordance with the stresses and demands of their environments. The difference with cultural units is that we do not have to wait for a biological generation to pass in order to witness a new iteration of the object, idea, custom, or belief. Instead of using sexual reproduction as a vector for transmission, culture evolves via social interaction and learning. Cultural reproduction happens constantly, readily, and quickly. A teacher imparting a lesson to a classroom full of students, an electronics salesperson showing a prospective customer the newest features of the latest bit of consumer technology, friends gossiping over lunch, paper presentations at professional symposia, newspaper columns, television shows, books, Web sites, and Web 2.0 phenomena such as Twitter, are all examples of cultural reproduction: transmission of memes. We can see, then, that elements of culture can be transmitted with blinding efficiency and speed, and it is because of this that the objects of our culture can change and adapt at a rate that far outpaces our biology.

> For an understanding of the evolution of modern man, we must begin by throwing out the gene as the sole basis of our ideas on evolution. I am an enthusiastic Darwinian, but I think Darwinism is too big a theory to be confined to the narrow context of the gene. . . . What, after all, is so special about genes? The answer is that they are replicators. . . . I think that a new kind of replicator has recently emerged on this very planet. It is staring us in the face. It is still in its infancy, still drifting clumsily about in its primeval soup, but already it is achieving evolutionary change at a rate that leaves the old gene panting far behind.
>
> Examples of memes are tunes, ideas, catch phrases, clothes fashions, ways of making pots or of building arches. Just as genes propagate themselves in the gene pool by leaping from body to body via sperm and eggs, so memes propagate themselves in the meme pool by leaping from brain to brain. . . . If a scientist hears, or

reads about, a good idea, he passes it on to his colleagues and students. He mentions it in his articles and his lectures. If the idea catches on, it can be said to propagate itself, spreading from brain to brain. . . . When you plant a fertile meme into my mind you literally parasitize my brain, turning it into a vehicle for the meme's propagation in just the way that a virus may parasitize the genetic mechanism of a host cell.

The old gene selected evolution, by making brains, provided the soup in which the first memes arose. Once self-copying memes had arisen, their own, much faster, kinds of evolution took off. We biologists have assimilated the idea of genetic evolution so deeply that we tend to forget that it is only one of many possible kinds of evolution. (Dawkins, 1989, pp. 191-192)

When one considers how very recent technology, especially television and the Internet, has allowed ideas to be transmitted to, quite literally, millions of minds almost instantaneously, it should be apparent that memes are wildly successful in an evolutionary sense. Communication between minds on this scale is a very new thing, and the trend of globalization serves as testament to just how powerful a force it can be. This, really, is the hallmark of the so-called "information age." We, in the beginning of the 21st century, are experiencing an incredible explosion of advancement on all fronts, the likes of which the planet has never seen, and this is due almost completely to the ease with which memes are able to disseminate themselves. While the process was not always this fast and efficient, the principles have been the same for all of human history. During those many years when humans did not have computers, telephones, or even movable type available to them, they still managed to transmit memes through direct teaching and learning, storytelling, and other such exchanges around the fabled ancestral campfire. One way of looking at this is that those memes that answered the "How?" questions in primitive society eventually grew into science and technology, and those memes that answered the "Why?" questions eventually grew into religion and spirituality. Science and religion, while different in process, really are intimate relatives. Each is a child of our culture, and each, in its own way, has promoted the biological survival of its host, the human brain.

Previously we discussed the survival value of answering the how questions. This should be more directly evident: Discoveries in science and advances in technology have increased our lifespan, protected us from the elements, and provided us with food and clean water. If primitive humans were—for example—able to master the use of fire, this newfound knowledge would surely help them survive. Fire could be used to keep warm during winter months, rid animal flesh of disease-causing bacteria, melt iron into weapons and farming equipment, and provide energy for more complex machinery such as steam turbines or internal combustion engines. We will come back to technology memes later in the book, but for now, we turn to the elements of human culture that answer the why questions. The survival value of what would become religion and spirituality is not as directly evident as the survival value of emerging technology, but we would argue it exists and, in some ways, is just as important. "Some evolutionary biologists have suggested that way back a sense of meaning and rituals—religion, in other words— had a survival advantage over those who didn't. If it's true that religion enhanced survival of the species, then religion would be perpetuated, making it a universal part of our cultural heritage" (George, 2005, p. 62). Certainly, evolutionarily speaking, if religion did not somehow promote success in human societies, it would never have caught on in the first place.

Is it not that religion is itself a meme, a cultural artifact that was originally created by the human mind for adaptive purposes, but one that has in many ways taken on a life of its own? Religions, once they emerged into human cultures, have evolved and grown over time while passing through billions of individual human minds. The wide variety of religious thinking (or, more correctly, thinking attributed to religion) can be attributed to unique pressures and demands of the local environment on a culture. In this way, the religion meme evolves in a manner quite similar to the biological gene.

The cultural and evolutionary foundations for religion also might help to explain how other memes, such as aesthetic endeavors, arose. One might marvel at the cave paintings at Lascaux in France and Kakadu in Australia, or be mystified by petroglyphs, hieroglyphs, and pictograms. Cro-Magnon humans put a great deal of energy, time, and resources into creating such images, but why? Did it help them in their day-to-day struggle against mastodons and saber-toothed tigers? Did it feed their families, provide shelter, or provide protection from angry neighbors? Perhaps the need for beauty and love, as well as religious bliss, served a practical function. Taking a Darwinian evolutionary viewpoint at the issue, we note that the intelligence developed by humans—to compensate for their lack of speed, strength, and natural camouflage—gave them the unique ability to be aware of their own mortality and to question the purpose of their existence. One might contemplate that without the compensations of art, religion, and intricately networked social conceits, the emptiness of the answer—that we humans exist merely because we exist—would lead to chaos and despair on a scale too massive to allow humans to survive. The point is that for many an existential existence is simply not enough. And because over time, throughout the history of the development of the human species, many questions had no provable answers, perhaps human undertakings such as the arts and religion served the need to fill the cavernous void of our unknowing. *The Evolution of God* by Robert Wright (2009) deals more with this topic.

This chapter concerns itself with religion as a product of culture meant to enhance and promote human success. History shows that religion, once enacted in a society, entwines itself with political dynamics. The authors of this book *believe it is very important to separate religion as spirituality from religion used as a political tool.* Chapter 8 will address religion from this second, less spiritual perspective.

Religion and the Search for Meaning

In grappling with questions that may not be readily answered by empirical study and observation, even the most dedicated scientists have turned to religion to give them a sense of meaning about their lives. Scientific cosmology tells a story of a universe that is inexorably winding

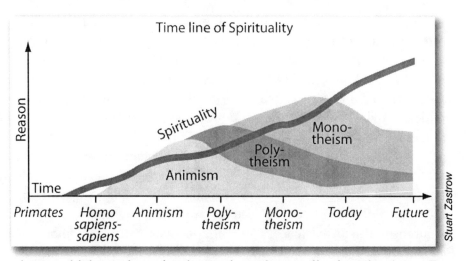

Time line of Spirituality

Reason

Spirituality

Mono-
theism

Poly-
theism

Animism

Time

Primates | Homo sapiens-sapiens | Animism | Poly-theism | Mono-theism | Today | Future

Stuart Zastrow

down, which can be quite depressing when really thought about. Even though science espouses a theory of entropy on a galactic scale, it is worth remembering that in our own comparatively minute frame of reference, we have experienced a local universe of increasing complexity and organization. We have a knack for holding chaos at bay, an ability to create order where there was previously none, to build, to develop. In short, science tells us time and time again that in one's own frame of reference we are living out a story of creation ourselves. Our minds, and everything they are capable of, embody that creation. The religion meme can be thought of as the sum total of our symbolic tendency toward creation. Jung suggested, "The traditional task of religious and mythic imagoes was to channel energy into evolutionary development" (Jung, 1977). Theologians, then, have created myth and story in order to unearth the basis of existence in this context of development, and this project is not so different from science. The Hindu cosmos concept of ever-expanding and contracting universes exemplifies a spiritual effort to define the ultimate truth, which is similar to the hypothesis of cosmological development proposed by physicist Michio Kaku and others.

Still, it is the big "Why?" questions that often still trouble most of us. We may look up at the night sky and, even with no knowledge of astronomy or cosmology, feel very insignificant. Science may offer some explanations as to our place in the universe, but it is not in the business of giving us comfort within our human scale or perspective. "By deepening our understanding of the true nature of physical reality, we profoundly reconfigure our sense of ourselves and our experience of the universe. . . . Men and women of science who have peeled back layer after layer of the cosmic onion, enigma by enigma, revealed a universe that is at once surprising, unfamiliar, exciting, elegant, and thoroughly unlike what anyone ever suspected" (Greene, 2005, p. 5).

Still, there are those who find comfort and truth from the story science has built. There are also those who need something else. The geneticist Francis Collins, who directs the Human Genome Project, wrote, "Science will certainly not shed light … on what it means to have a spiritual dimension to our existence, nor will it tell us about the character of God" (Larson, 2004). Culture, and more specifically religion, has taken on that weighty task. This has taken many forms in human history and resulted in thousands of distinct forms of human spirituality over the ages. While there are easily recognizable differences between two given forms of spirituality, it is also worth noting the similarities. Like the evolutionary tree of life, which reminds us that all life forms evolved from single-celled bacteria over billions of years, we can trace the world's religions to a common cultural ancestor: the human search for meaning in our lives. Explanations for unanswerable questions must have provided our earliest ancestors a certain comfort with their place in the universe. Perhaps it was this comfort that allowed them to gaze into the night sky and then go about their business without despairing that all their human efforts, in the end, were for nothing.

If we are religious, our search for meaning looks like a well-marked trail leading to the top of a mountain. Religion has undoubtedly given many people a sense of purpose and meaning in their lives. One of the central tenants of all religions is that they provide a path or code of morals and ethics that allow at least that culture to sustain itself. The various religions of the world, however, do not hold a monopoly on our search for meaning or morals. Religion and science are potential paths and even endpoints in the search (and both also have the potential to be wellsprings of doubt, frustration, and uncertainty), but in order to accept either system of thought, one must first be steadfast in the conviction that there is some sort of order and larger meaning to the universe, even if we do not know what it is, as well as some sort of basic truth about what is right and wrong in a society. Those minds that do not accept either story of what that order looks like, those minds that deem the universe empty of any larger meaning, still have another option and still are engaged in a search for knowledge or meaning, albeit a much more difficult one than the religious souls walking their time-honored paths. The division of philosophy that deals with the problem of existence and our search for meaning in a world apparently devoid of meaning, appropriately called existentialism, attempts a different angle of approach to these difficult questions.

Where a religious person may gaze into the night sky and see the meaningful and ordered work of God, and a scientist may gaze up into the night sky and see the meaningful and ordered set of natural principles at work, existentialists look up into the night sky and see endless chaos and emptiness. Thus, the search for meaning, for an existentialist, is a fruitless endeavor. This does not, by the way, mean that existentialists go without meaning in their lives. However, instead of looking elsewhere for meaning, the existentialists give themselves the weighty task of creating meaning for their own lives. For existentialists, this is the ultimate realization of freedom, and with it, the realization that the other side of the coin of freedom has an astonishing amount of responsibility.

The existentialists conclude that human choice is subjective, because individuals finally must make their own choices without help from such external standards as laws, ethical rules, or traditions. Because individuals make their own choices, they are free; but because they freely choose, they are completely responsible for their choices. The existentialists emphasize that freedom is necessarily accompanied by responsibility. Furthermore, since individuals are forced to choose for themselves, they have their freedom—and therefore their responsibility— thrust upon them. They are "condemned to be free."

For existentialism, responsibility is the dark side of freedom. When individuals realize that they are completely responsible for their decisions, actions, and beliefs, they are overcome by anxiety. They try to escape from this anxiety by ignoring or denying their freedom and their responsibility. But because this amounts to ignoring or denying their actual situation, they succeed only in deceiving themselves. The existentialists criticize this flight from freedom and responsibility into self-deception. They insist that individuals must accept full responsibility for their behavior, no matter how difficult. If an individual is to live meaningfully and authentically, he or she must become fully aware of the true character of the human situation and bravely accept it. (Soll, 2001)

Thus, in the face of the chaos of the universe and all the unanswerable conundrums we may encounter, existentialists remind us that it is not just in our power to create meaning for ourselves, it is imperative that we do so. The strict existentialist would insist on everyone hacking their own overland route up the mountain of meaning, struggling mightily against their own desire-ridden human nature. This tremendous and sometimes severe stance with regard to human nature and personal responsibility often gives existentialism a bad name, invoking feelings of dread, suffering, loss, and angst. But instead of being life-denying, this stance allows existentialists to cling tenaciously to their lives and consider it their highest life's work to create meaning for themselves in the face of a universe seemingly conspiring against them.

As authors, we want to weave existentialism into the fabric of this Ark because of its emphasis on absolute freedom and personal responsibility, and mostly because of the challenge it issues to those who wish to step up to it. The search for meaning as a framework for building a peaceful and sustainable future is very hard work, and like the existentialists, we sincerely hope that as many individuals as possible choose to engage in such a search. However, instead of dictating where one may look or which paths one may not walk in their search, shouldn't we encourage everyone to take the path that makes the most sense to them? If successful, the existentialist hacking his way through the dense underbrush, the religious person walking an established path, and the scientist trying to invent a contraption to carry herself to the top will all end up in the same place eventually: a meaningful life for themselves and society. It is less important to us which path one takes, and more important that one chooses to engage in the struggle, that one attempts to reconcile the big, looming, unanswerable questions.

> *I have one life and one chance to make it count for something. . . . I'm free to choose what that something is, and the something I've chosen is my faith. Now, my faith goes beyond theology and religion and requires considerable work and effort. My faith demands—this is not optional—my faith demands that I do whatever I can, wherever I am, whenever I can, for as long as I can with whatever I have to try to make a difference. (U.S. President Jimmy Carter)*

This reconciliation, this search for meaning, is the task set for each of us individually whether we recognize it or not, even when we inherit a culture that attempts to implant its memes directly into our minds, unquestioned. In the end, each of us builds our own schema. Each of us, in our own way, will make our own cave painting on the insides of our mind. One's deepest yearnings come from the desire for meaningful lives; perhaps it is helpful to see this struggle toward a meaningful life as a (uniquely human) blessing. Evolution has dictated that having children is in itself one of life's meaningful objectives, but as the poet Khalil Gibran beautifully pointed out, they are but arrows, which, once shot by the archer-parents, travel their own paths. Thus, after preparing their quiver, aimed, and fired, the empty-nester parents may find the need to resume their own search for meaning during the remainder of the flight of their own life's arrow. In addition, those people who do not have children often find their own rich paths to meaning not identified with procreation.

Some may continue to fill their yearning by having more children, but (leaving aside the issue of overpopulation, and without suggesting that good parenting is not one of the most worthwhile and fulfilling pursuits of humanity) the story of civilization suggests that having children does not quench the search for meaning, and may even make it more acute. Transmission of genes does not automatically make for easy transmission of memes. Of course, the need to survive may dominate the need to transcend, and whether because of resource scarcity, the business of life, or psychological denial, the voices in our head asking the big questions are frequently drowned out by the din of everyday existence. We may make a conscious decision to bury our heads in the sand of more mundane pursuits so as not to be confused by the more complex itches of our souls. And in an evolutionary sense, this is completely appropriate and expected, but the challenge to expand oneself is somehow an important aspect in the advancement of society.

Religion and Psychology

In addition to countering the problem of existence, religion should also be examined in the context of understanding human psychological needs and actions. Two questions that religion handily answers are, "What is the basic human condition that motivates individuals and groups?" and "Why are groups so susceptible to 'group think'?" This topic will be explored in the next chapter, but it offers a useful bit of intellectual food here. Depth (Jungian) psychologists have identified and described an important psychological concept referred to as the *Shadow.* The Jungian Shadow, which he considered to be an organ of the mind and itself an archetype, serves as foil to each of our personas, our public selves.

> Unfortunately there can be no doubt that man is, on the whole, less good than he imagines himself or wants to be. Everyone carries a Shadow, and the less it is embodied in the individual's conscious life, the blacker and denser it is. If an inferiority is conscious, one always has a chance to correct it. Furthermore, it is constantly in contact with other interests, so that it is continually subjected to modifications. But if it is repressed and isolated from consciousness, it never gets corrected. (Jung, 1938, p. 131)

The Shadow emerges, both individually and manifested through groups, as a dark anxiety management device. This tide of energies can lead us to "aggression, violence, and destruction. . . . The demands of social adaptation produce a countervailing sense of helplessness and frustration with which we cope through diversion, substitutions, and dry intoxications. Chief among these is the madness of patriotism and the seductive clamors of war" (Hollis, 2007, p. 8).

The Crusades, jihads, Nazism and their Holocaust, and the Spanish Inquisition all speak to the power of these Shadow movements. In recorded history, religion often became the vehicle of "societal progress and domination," for "war as a sanctified activity" (Armstrong, 2006, p. 45). These topics will be picked up in the next chapter; for now, we would do well to recognize that the Shadow resides in each of us and affects our minds in profound ways. Many religious themes can also be viewed in light of the Shadow.

Religion and psychology share other common ground, as Jung thought. The devout faithful and the healed neurotic do not need to know why they feel better after their respective searches for meaning and restoration to know that they, in fact, do feel better. The areas of divergence and debate are in the language of the why. Both could start off by finding common ground, perhaps, in the statement that the human animal, for whatever reason, simply cannot stand a meaningless life. Given these thoughts, we can say that we possess a psychology that is primed for spirituality; much in the same way linguist Noam Chomsky (1975) believes that our minds are primed to learn and use language. Perhaps we have a religion module soldered into our neural circuit boards.

As the contractors and builders of this Ark, we are all looking for the common thread of religion, psychology, and motivating factors for behavior. We are looking for the "dark matter" of the soul. Religious leaders preach the power of divinity and enlightenment. Jung speaks of the collective unconscious and basic archetypes underlying all human experience. We see concrete evidence of these common themes in cave drawings, archaeological digs, and ancient literature; civilizations, at times when they had no physical connection, have shared the same dreams and nightmares outside the realm of the known or physical world. Thus, we see that we not only ask similar questions, but in the broadest sense, we also have a tendency to arrive at similar answers to the big questions. The way we have ordered ourselves, both internally and socially, around such answers has become the fabric of our lives, the preeminent memes of our respective cultures. The answers to these questions have provided society with stability and evolutionary success more than they have not; otherwise, of course, such ideas would not have survived. And it could be, if Dawkins is right, that it is actually the ideas, the units of culture themselves, that are commanding their own spread in our brains. Religion needs people to spread it, and it is so successful because it convinces people that they need its answers to make for a fulfilled life.

The Intersection of Faith and Reason

Religions have made attempts at explaining the nature of reality, virtually none of which can stand up to the scrutiny of pure logic or scientific analysis. It does not make them invalid, just untestable. From the Bible's creation stories to the other thousands of identified human-created god images, the discipline of scientific proof has eliminated or demystified most, if not all, that are not broadly (if not vaguely) inclusive. Unless one wants to base his or her view of reality on *a priori* faith that directly contradicts what we know of the world through science, or on magical thinking, to be complete a discipline needs to have a set of principles or rules that are consistently applied to all events, objects, and beings in all places. Some continue to live their lives steered by this blind faith, with varying success. Others reject such choices completely. But most people fall somewhere between pure faith and pure reason.

The relationship between faith and reason[10] has not always been a contentious one. The Greeks thought of faith and reason as very much connected; both Plato and Aristotle used rational and empirical reflections on the natural world to inform their religious views. Early Christian theologians such as St. Augustine believed that while faith and reason were in fact different, one could use reason—the observation of natural reality—to enhance the Christian faith and wonder in God (Beilby, 2002). However, Augustine put limits on just how much one could rely on reason if it contradicted the Church's teachings. Almost 900 years later, Thomas Aquinas described a twofold truth, where "nature is a sketch in outline of the world of Grace" (Cushman, 1918, p. 381). In

---

[10] For more on this topic, see www.iep.utm.edu/f/faith-re.htm

other words, something could be true in the light of reason but something contradictory could also be true in the light of faith. This undoubtedly served political ends, smoothing over some rough interactions between the 13th-century Church and emerging knowledge that might threaten its supremacy. Being a man of the Church, Aquinas reserved precedence for revealed theology (a religious understanding of the universe), which concerned itself with the knowledge of God and which Aquinas called the most noble of the sciences. Even in medieval times, then, when the Roman Catholic Church was arguably at the apex of its political power and influence, some of its foremost thinkers still made room for reason inside the confines of faith . . . as long as reason never posed a challenge to the word of the Church.

Enlightenment thinkers such as Galileo, armed with advanced technology and mathematics, were able to measure and quantify the previously immeasurable and unquantifiable, which offered a viable alternative to matters that the Church wished people to attribute to God, to take on faith. Galileo's work overturned much of Aristotle's view of the physical universe (one in which faith and reason were happily coexistent) and in so doing drew a very distinct line in the sand between the empirical (reason) and the spiritual (faith). Rene Descartes, in a pivotal move, broke with the centuries-old opinion that faith had precedence over reason when the two conflicted, and claimed that anything that can be doubted must be thrown out from one's personal philosophy. His famous irrefutable phrase *"Cogito ergo sum"*("I think, therefore I am") placed reason at the center of the picture, and he went on to state that one could actually use reason to attain faith (Garber, 1998/2003). Descartes, in an unprecedented move, presented a rational argument for the existence of God, one that depended on logic as opposed to unconditional acceptance and, therefore, embodied the intellectual revolution of the Enlightenment against blind acceptance. To Descartes and those who followed him, reason trumped faith. This set the stage for empiricist challenges to faith, notably Isaac Newton, Charles Darwin, William James (the founder of modern psychology), Bill Maher ("social scientist" and entertainer), and many other scientists of the modern age, including Richard Dawkins.

Cristiano Banti's 1857 painting of Galileo facing the Roman Inquisition.

There are those who tend toward faith, who believe (in the absence of all empirical data) that the "soul" or essence of thought of that individual survives and transcends the body. This has appeal and assuredly gives some of us comfort when confronted with our own mortality but, like string theory, has not leant itself to experimental proof. At present, both require a leap of . . . well . . . faith. We suggest that while faith in the absence of evidence does often provide individuals with a fulfillment and rapture that improves their lives, it is hard to build a sustainable and practical future for ourselves as a diverse community on leaps of faith, if for no other reason than the huge multiplicity of faiths. Like in a sound business plan, we suggest the future should be based upon individual action aggregating into a group objective with a common goal. If my individual action is (hypothetically) based on the assumption that in the next life, I can have infinite sex with seventy-two virgins and all I have to do is blow up my suffering body—along with as many enemies as I can find—then we have a society built on the faith that there is an afterlife, and that it will be better than this one. This is a society that would ultimately have a short shelf life and be based on morals that do not provide respect, peace, and love.

There are also those who tend toward pure reason, those who measure and calculate and believe that the entirety of creation can be reduced to formulas and equations. These folks seek explanations for everything, thirst for knowledge that is verifiable and testable, and find their truth in the dissection and examination of the world around them. This mode of operation has undoubtedly brought amazing advancement to humanity, but it is a project that will forever be incomplete and that does not easily account for the phenomenon of synergy: the whole being greater than the sum of its parts. Cognitive scientists attempt to map the brain with hopes of discovering the mind, but the brain-mind gap will remain elusive and unknowable for the foreseeable future. This is where pure reason has hit its limit, and faith can be called to step in, for those so inclined.

It seems to many that the great divide between the religious pursuit and the scientific pursuit is irreconcilable. To overstate the point in order to make it, those who find comfort only in faith cannot be swayed by any amount of logical argument, while those who exclusively adhere to scientific thinking live in constant doubt. And those who hold these extreme views seem destined to never meet.

We would like to put forth something more moderate and hopeful here. *We can truly conceptualize the purview of both science and religion to be similar: to give us, as individuals, meaning in our lives such that our individual and group chances for success in life are increased.* We would propose that if we were to find a way to allow the two intimately related traditions of science and religion to work in harmony, we would be that much closer to truth. There have long been clashes in subjective realities involving those who depend on belief based on faith versus those who insist that their beliefs be based on reason. Of course, the world of belief without scientific proof is the separate sphere of religion, just as the world of the spirit cannot adequately be penetrated in a helpful way by science. The time for a declaration of truce between these warring sides is overdue.

There have been countless scientists in history who carried a strong religious conviction with them their entire lives. Among them is Isaac Newton. Newton, who died more than 280 years ago, is known for laying much of the groundwork for modern physics, astronomy, math, and optics. But in a 2007 exhibit in Jerusalem, he appears as a scholar of deep faith who also found time to write on Jewish law—even penning a few phrases in careful Hebrew lettersand combing the Old Testament's Book of Daniel for clues about the world's end.

Carl Jung was representative of an integrated view of religion and reason. He was frustrated by priests who would try to cure men's souls without first diving into the unconscious of modern man to learn what the modern soul is all about. Jung believed that creation was an ongoing process rather than an accomplished fact. The Book of Revelation had great meaning to Jung. He noted how the Calvinists had fought to have it removed from the Bible because it was viewed as dark and dangerously obscure. But to Jung, it is the part of the Bible that suggests the revelation of God did not end with the coming of Christ and that religion in its best sense is a process of continuing revelation—being open to the teachings of life through a greater awareness of the inner and outer universe. In Jung's construct, God did not change but the God-image, which was alive within the center of our being (the Self), did change and needed to be observed to be understood.

Likewise, there have been great spiritual leaders who remained open to the scientific process. Carl Sagan told a wonderful story to illustrate this point:

> *I have been very privileged in my life to meet many if not all the leaders of the world's major religions. I always asked them the same question, namely: "If science were to absolutely prove that a basic tenet of your religion was false, what would you do?" All of the world's religious leaders except one danced around the question. Many said, man couldn't possibly know, science is not an absolute, etc. Only the Dalai Lama was truthful. He said, "Why, Dr. Sagan, the answer is simple; of course I would change religions." (Sagan, 1994)*

Science and religion can be viewed to have domains that are completely compatible and goals that are overlapping. Both would agree that there are forces at work in the universe that we are able to objectively describe and understand, and others that we cannot. To attempt to describe these mysterious forces, scientists run tests; philosophers philosophize; and religious people take note that the Lord works in mysterious ways. Just as one must persevere in efforts to find solutions to the more earthly dilemmas of our age, there must also continue a quest for larger meaning—to nourish all of our souls. It matters less how each individual goes about that task, and more that individuals choose to search for meaning in some way. However, focusing on the search for meaning to the detriment or exclusion of quality of life on earth is both contrary to the sacred nature of life espoused by all major organized religions and contrary to the basic operating principles governing the community of life on our planet. Let us remember that both religion and science need our minds in order to survive, and that destroying our minds will also destroy both religion and science.

God Answers The Big Questions

If we put aside strict questions of epistemology (the branch of philosophy that studies the nature of knowledge, in particular its foundations, scope, and validity), is there a common ground in these different paths toward meaning? If so, what is the common ground? Where can those of rational mind and those of faithful mind find an agreement? According to Batson and his colleagues, religion is what a person does to answer the basic existential questions of life (Batson, Schoenrade, & Ventis, 1993). Such questions include: Why am I here? What does life mean in general? What does my particular life amount to? What happens when I die?

Perhaps the beginnings of an answer lie in the concept so central to the world's major Western religions: God. To many religions, especially the major Western religions of Judaism, Christianity, and Islamism, the concept of God lies at the center of answers to questions like this. But trying to pin down what people mean when they speak of God is a difficult task. One way to define God is by describing what powers he or she has. The Western monotheistic religions describe teachings via writings that have a historical timestamp dating from more than 5,000 years ago, which describe God as an all-knowing master of the universe, controlling destiny and judging our thoughts and acts. Typical Christian descriptions of God describe a figure that is omnipotent, omniscient, and wholly benevolent. Those humans who follow his dictates will prosper, and conversely, those who do not will suffer.

God does not need to be defined in this way, and there are deeply religious people who would describe any effort to define God as arbitrarily, even blasphemously, limiting. Jung wrote, God "is the name by which I designate all things which cross my willful path violently and recklessly, all things which upset my subjective views, plans, and intentions and change the course of my life for better or worse" (Quoted in Heller, 2006). When asked whether he believed in God, Jung answered, "I don't need to believe; I know" (Quoted in Hayman, 2002). He refused to believe without evidence and personally found proof of God not by having blind faith in what someone else told him to believe, not in what others wrote down as being the word of God, but in how God revealed himself in those faculties of the human psyche not confined to space and time—the ability to see around corners through dreams and visions of the past and future. Jung reasoned that if the psyche has a past and future outside the space-time boundaries of the individual, then death did not necessarily mean an end of the individual. Religion espouses the same concepts but in a different language. Other thinkers conceptualized God differently. Einstein, for example, viewed God as the ultimate description of the fundamental forces in nature. If we wish to operate on a less abstract plane, it may be argued that the existence of God, as something separate from known or even knowable matter and energy, is demonstrated by humankind's yearning for love (and love here is to be distinguished from erotic desire). Look at the true fabric of our day-to-day existence, the gossamer by which relationships are strung together or unravel. What is the physics of friendship? What is the biology of the arts? What is the evidence masquerading as proof behind our most profound philosophical truths? What evolutionary goal do the tears unleashed during a Beethoven concerto fulfill? Is this not evidence of the immeasurable echoes of the soul? Is there not something quite godlike in the human products of love?

Perhaps, in this light, we should seek a path to God by revisiting the concept "Love thy neighbor as thyself." This was the fundamental lesson of Jesus, yet it predates Jesus and Judaism. It is also attributable to the Chinese philosopher Confucius.

Confucius was horrified by the constant warfare. He felt "Till you have learned to serve men, how can you serve spirits?" . . . Confucius wanted people to become fully conscious of what they were doing. He felt that old religions interpreted tradition and focused on heaven: People had to perform sacrifices simply to gain the favor of the gods, but he concentrated on this world. His goal was to become a "gentleman," a mature profound person, and this was done by becoming a *junzi*. He had to work himself in the same way as a sculptor shaped a rough stone and made it a thing of beauty. A true *junzi* was always trying to go beyond what he was and become a thing of what he was supposed to be. If he did this he would save the world. (Armstrong, 2006, pp. 205-206)

But we believe that to know God through loving our neighbors and to work toward becoming a *junzi* is very much dependent on doing a good job of loving oneself and, thus, knowing oneself. If individuals are consumed with insecurity, hate, ignorance, fear, hunger, abuse, addiction, or any other psychological imbalance, they cannot do a very good job of loving themselves and will, thus, have very little to prevent them from projecting that trait on others. This inner work, we believe, is the essential first step that everyone can take in order to gain access to the Ark that will see us through the stormy waters ahead. The transcendentalist American thinker Henry David Thoreau would have agreed completely: "Be the Lewis and Clarks . . . of your own streams and oceans; explore your highest latitudes . . . be a Columbus to whole new continents of thought. . . . Explore thyself" (Quoted in Clough & Wilson, 1964, p. 113).

While it is tempting to philosophize about the existence of God, who and what we think God is, or whether God is, is irrelevant to the point that follows: The *belief* in God, each of our God schema, is extremely relevant—and it is so powerful that even if there were scientific proof that God did not exist, the belief in God would survive. Belief and human actions governed by belief can be seen as positive or negative by those with other viewpoints, and each of our perceptions of God have a lot to do with how positive or negative our actions may be. In this writing, we do not presuppose the existence of any deity independent of the human mind, nor do we take up debates here on the nature of God. As for how it relates to a practical program of action to deal with the problems of society affecting believers and nonbelievers alike, it matters little whether God actually exists. What matters a great deal is whether a schema of God resides in each of our minds, and if so, what that schema looks like, and how that schema affects our thoughts, opinions, and actions. More than coming to know the nature of God in a philosophical sense, we are concerned with the implications of a belief system on the state of the world. We rejoice when someone attributes positive things to a higher power, but worry greatly when prejudice, discrimination, harm, or malicious acts occur in the name of one's deity. When this happens, we feel that there has been a severe disconnect between religion's intentions and the wrongdoer's perception of religion. The religion meme, when twisted in this way, could stand to be culled from the meme pool.

Our relation to God probably has to undergo a certain important change: Instead of propitiating praise to an unpredictable king or the child's prayer to a loving father, the responsible living and fulfilling of the divine will in us will be our form of worship and commerce with God. God's goodness means grace and light, and the dark side is the terrible temptation of power. We have already received so much knowledge that we can destroy our own planet. Let us hope that God's good spirit will guide us in our decisions, because whether God's creation will continue will depend upon our decisions. Nothing shows more drastically how much of divine power has come within our reach than this possibility.

Placing Religion into Our Culture And What to Do About Fundamentalism

We have portrayed religion as a path to spiritual enlightenment and a life full of meaning, which at its core, it is meant to be. However, religion has not been without its problems when it is opened up to other elements of culture and the dark parts of the human psyche. Herein lays the problem with religion: Some individuals (hopefully a vocal minority) are so convinced of their moral correctness by their perception of faith that they will go so far as to commit "evil" acts in the name of God. Robert Wright

(2009) explains how religious, particularly fundamentalist, movements can gain traction.

> This ancient sociopolitical environment is a lot like the modern environment as shaped by globalization. Then as now international trade and attendant economic advance had brought shape social change and sharp social cleavages, delimiting affluent cosmopolitans from poorer and more insular people. Then as now, some of those in the latter category were ambivalent, at best, about foreign influence, economic and cultural, and were correspondingly resentful of the elites who fed on it. And then like now, some in the later category extended their dislike of the foreign theology, growing cold toward religious traditions that signified the alien. This dynamic to some degrees helped produce fundamentalist Christians, fundamentalist Jews, and fundamentalist Muslims. And apparently it helped produce the god they worship. (p. 146)

When we have a faction of a major world religion—fundamentalist Muslims—that has as one of its basic tenets that holy war, or jihad, on nonbelievers is God ordained, we have a real survival problem for certain members of the species. The Wahabi madrasses in Pakistan are a shining example. Reportedly, they start teaching five-year-old boys a strict constructionist view of the teachings of Mohamed that require conversion or death to those who do not believe, obedience, and compliance. Textbooks supplied by Iran to Hamas and Hezbollah teach that Jews must die because they are filth. By age 12, how can such a boy play with a Jew? At age 25, how can such a man become a painter of romantic landscapes, or teach irrigation techniques to impoverished squatters in Brazil, or write position papers for a think tank on access to medical care? How can such a man marry a woman and treat her with respect and as an equal and raise children to believe in the rights of others? There is little intellectual maneuvering room for convincing religious leaders or individuals indoctrinated within the group that there are other views worthy of respect, when the prevailing wisdom within each group is that another view should result in murder.

Take, for instance, a sector of fundamentalist Christianity that proselytizes and attempts to convert nonbelievers and impose their religious and educational beliefs on U.S. politics. We have a subset of a religion, Orthodox Judaism, that teaches its children that they are the chosen ones, have the real understanding of God, and must be separate from not only the *goyim* (non-Jews), but also from fellow Jews who do not share their hard-line belief systems. Fundamentalism by its nature is opposed to opening up our minds to acceptance and tolerance. After all, "living with doubt, being willing to dump one's hypothesis, and being open to contradictions lies at the heart of both science and mature religious faith" (Hollis, 2007, p. 146). Hollis wrote the following about fundamentalism:

> None of us are more dangerous than the righteous who critically believe they are right, for they are the least capable of knowing the harm they bring with them into this world. . . . In Eastern theological tradition, the problem of evil and the problem of contraries is a delusion of the ego. It is ego's imperial fantasies that are at the root problem as it separates itself from the flow of life and seeks to colonize the cosmos. Overthrowing the delusions of the ego is the project of Buddhism and Hinduism. In the Western theological tradition, whether Christian, Jewish, or Muslim, the Other is pathologized as the Evil One who tempts us into "sin.". . .
>
> Fundamentalism in all its forms merely compounds this problem by haranguing the ego for more and more control. . . . Central to religious insight, to religious experience, and to psychological awareness is the conscious recognition and acknowledgment of one's limits, to know that we don't know. From this insight comes less diminishment than a radical reframing of the ego. We are awed by the immensity of the cosmos, and the unfathomable mystery of our own souls. Awe is the benchmark of religious experience and psychological insight. (Think of Job as the prototype of the humbled consciousness.) Only humbled consciousness, with pride's penance, will prove psychologically and spiritually enlarging. . . . The

157

sociopath is limited to the early perception that the Other is here to hurt him, so he can only hurt the Other in return. His wound is his history; his pathology is his constricted imagination. So too the bigot. So too the fundamentalist, of any stripe. Each suffers an anxiety disorder with a reflexive treatment plan devoted to ridding him of ambiguity. . . . Each is locked into the stunted imagination of his or her complexes, and owned by the anxiety-management plan that he has evolved. The Shadow of the unlived life grows greater as our pathology spills into the world to harm others who are the recipients of our projections, transferred history, and anxiety-management systems. (2007, p. 20)

So, how can we move forward? How can we preserve everything good and right about religion, but cut away that part of the religion meme that has turned sour? Perhaps we can conceptualize and popularize the call for a truce amongst religions. Perhaps we can provide for cultural cross-education of our children.[11] We are aware that this is far easier said than done, but we still have to say something. We know the task is enormous, but consider the current alternative of jeopardizing the survival of life. This task will be the litmus test for future generations. If this gulf cannot be bridged, or the fundamentalists marginalized and isolated, a peaceful and sustainable future is not possible. We can all (and this means *everyone*) start by recognizing our own perception of truth and our religious beliefs as a matter of great subjectivity, no matter how convinced we are of our own correctness. Common sense and everyday human experience foster the perception that "surely reality is what we think it is; reality is revealed to us by our experiences" (Greene, 2005, p. 5). But, as psychologist James Hollis states, "hubris is found in our capacity to convince ourselves that we really know what is going on" (2001, p. 13). Just as the story of scientific creation humbles us to the vastness of the universe, the story of religion should humble us to the small piece of creation we are able to see and understand. Really, according to both these stories, we do not know what is going on any more than a worker ant knows what is going on in a forest miles away. What we may know is

---

[11] For instance, see www.seedsofpeace.org

our local truth, but we should be wary of generalizing that truth out of its environmental context. Religious truths, like anything else that evolves, are only successful insofar as they remain in the environments in which they originally grew. Historically, the version of locally accepted truth comes from that doctrine deemed best suited to helping its followers manage fear and anxiety and place positive controls on societal activities. An example of a locally accepted truth of this kind was the Incan belief in the Moon and Sun as gods (Bauer & Standish, 2001). These gods determined the course of all life on Earth (this, of course, is largely true in the fact that without them as they are, life as we know it would not exist). Human sacrifices (of virginal children) were an entirely suitable means of currying favor from the gods (Cobo, 1990, p. 111). We may look askance at such practices today, but we would encourage keeping as open a mind as possible, even toward such morally objectionable practices. With what authority do we have the right to condemn anyone else's cultural practices? They can do the same to us (and they often do). Societies without circumcision rituals would certainly look at such practices as barbaric; symbolically eating the body and blood of Christ might seem primitive to the uninitiated. Even infanticide, which most of us denounce completely, is still not only accepted but also practiced by certain indigenous peoples in the Arctic Circle (Post, 1988). While our personal perspectives generally rebuke suicide bombers acting from religious ideals, and fundamentalist parents who refuse to administer medicine to their dying children, let us accept that, in general, judging other religions for being strange creates a slippery slope.

This is illustrated by examples of local truths that have fallen by the wayside. Included in this category is the notion, long prevalent in many parts of the United States, that a white woman bearing the child of a black man was an affront to God, or the Incan belief in the Moon and Sun as gods that determined the course of all life on Earth. Today, a black man married to a white woman can enter most churches (even in the Deep South) without fear. And similarly, with more modern and enlightened thinking, we can now see that the Incans' practice of sacrificing virgins to induce the favor of their gods may not have been as effective a means to control their destiny as their advanced agricultural techniques.

We are not so naïve as to suggest that people change their belief structure. We simply want to point out that there is important information available from studying history, including the history of religion and the history of science. This history suggests that reliance upon religious doctrine as the sole arbiter of societal policy and individual conduct results in exclusionary practices and laws, different from person to person and group to group (hence carrying great potential for being arbitrary). This reliance may not be consistent with the "best practices" of individual fulfillment and societal survival. Recognition that religions of all variety are very recent, earthbound, human-created mythologies can help with the process. Many, of course, will refuse to even entertain the concept, which is fine. Our goal is not to offend but to demonstrate that power of the story overwhelms and transcends the type of logic that we exercise on an everyday basis. Perhaps that is the point, that faith transcends everyday life and at a depth and dimension that is akin to hearing an exquisite Brahms violin concerto or viewing Michelangelo's "David" in person. For some of us, looking out into the starry night and understanding the mathematical vastness out there is sufficient to make our skin tingle. For others, more is needed to give life meaning and direction: Perhaps it is the Qur'an's transcendent story of our role in the heavens and earth that connects the dots, as the ancients connected the stars to make pictures.

Long-term survival requires that humans learn to take a different stance with respect to their religious certainty. It seems reasonable to ask religiously minded people and their organized institutions to call a truce. Step back and look at the big picture: We are all the same species. We have virtually identical combined genetic histories. We have become the dominant species on earth and now pose the real danger of destroying it. This is when certain belief structures, ones that guide us toward actions that promote only our own individual survival at the expense of the group or our collective future, cease to be adaptive. We created the great "truths" for our religions about 5,000 years ago, which is, as the German expression says, *eigenaugenblick* (in an eye blink). We have altered the landscape, have consumed resources, have forced other species into extinction, are heating the atmosphere, have created and spread potent carcinogens, have perfected the practice of death and war, and have created nuclear weapons that truly can destroy civilization and life. How do we claim to be certain about anything, let alone whether God really wants us to cause massive extinction of his creations? We need a new set of rules, rules that can coexist with all the historical religious doctrines, dogma, and practice. We need to reach deeper for an individual and societal understanding of the basic facts of our existence and underlying psychological motives that drive us. We all have inner complexes, and we project the Shadow on other(s), but we cannot let that govern our path. "What is not made conscious will continue to haunt our lives—and the world" (Erlich, 1968).

Many of the basic major human religious tenets are very similar: a supreme organizing force (which some would call God), a search for the true path, a set of laws to learn and live by. Some religions have developed by forcing themselves into the minds of oppressed people, but others have developed by encouraging rigorous (and endless) debate about the major questions and meaning. The Talmudic study in Judaism, for example, creates this "legal" forum within its ranks for intellectual jousting and advancement by discussion, rather than jousting by the sword. In a religion where the premise is "We always reserve the right to get smarter," the forum for advancement is positive. In a religion where it is dictated that "This is God's will, and if you don't accept it you shall perish," the stage is set for power abuse and misery. Fundamentalism, exclusionary by nature, "ignores centuries of scholarship and scientific advancement" (Shelburne, 2008), and we believe it to be dangerous to the future of humankind.

We believe that fundamentalism needs to be identified and called out for its exclusionary practices in accepting knowledge. The key to finding common ground is not just maintaining a disposition of tolerance, but acceptance. Everything is open to interpretation. If not, we would not have created nor felt the need for mullahs, priests, rabbis, or monks. Rather, we would simply read the Qur'an, New Testament, Old Testament, or whatever our source document might be, and be done with it. The Bible suggests that God wanted humans to assist in creation—the world was not considered complete until humans arrived. Who, one might ask, was lonely? Was it Adam? God? Or both? An omniscient God would have known Adam and Eve would eat the forbidden fruit—

thus even within biblical logic, original "sin" in the name of acquiring knowledge is part of God's plan.

Perhaps in our era, thought will emerge to provide enlargement to the great mass of humanity, who willingly (yet perhaps unconsciously) go about each waking day within the restricted mental representations of their local norm. Those who accept the teachings *about* their God as the supreme and final word on the teachings *of* their God and, hence, their existence; those who accept their God as a personal guide for the righteous exercise of their daily lives; those who believe it their holy duty to bring jihad to the infidels or the truth to the poor natives, or moral correctness on birth control teaching; those who accept that only their view of God is the correct one, may be able to learn more about themselves and their God through an opening of their minds and hearts, and an accepting of truly infinite possibilities.

Moving Forward: Where We Are

We have now finished our selected history of the universe, starting with the moment of creation and connecting that to our current state on our small, blue-green, watery planet in the opening moments of the 21st century. The few pages or words dedicated to this task here would never do it complete justice; there are not enough pieces of paper in the universe to fully account for everything that has happened. But what has been outlined here is enough to give us a foundation of knowledge about where we came from and how we got here. Matter was created in an enormous explosive event, and as matter was flung outwards, ever expanding and dissipating, it collected into large stars. These masses of hydrogen and helium ignited, fusing atoms together to create all the elements we find in the universe, and when those various elements attracted each other through forces of gravity, planets and solar systems were formed. Our particular planet, out of the billions in the known universe, happened to play host to a small miracle: the random shuffling and combination of molecules that would eventually become life. Through processes of biological evolution, life grew in its complexity and organization, until billions of years later humans with brains capable of housing complex psychologies arrived. The human mind then became the dominant agent of change on our planet and, through its creation of cultural units such as religion, science, and technology, resulted in the civilization and state of the planet we have inherited today.

What a Long, Strange Trip It's Been (The Grateful Dead)

The next chapters will use this platform to describe the conditions under which we operate today. More specifically, each chapter will identify one element of our modern society that we believe is a "system of control," some cultural institution that has been used to advance the short-term survival of some individuals, often at the expense of many others. In the descriptions to follow, we hope to build a more complete understanding not only of what the systems of control constitute, but also how they can be explained by our deep past and by the principles that have been governing our paths from the very beginning.

> *There is no other god besides me, a righteous God and a Savior; there is no one besides me. Turn to me and be saved, all the ends of the earth! For I am God, and there is no other. By myself I have sworn, from my mouth has gone forth in righteousness a word that shall not return: "to me every knee shall bow, every tongue shall swear." (Isaiah 45:21-3)*

Connection Perspective

I Am
In Control
And Powerful.
I Know where I shall go
And what happens at each bend.
Not even the great tree, lying across my boiling stream, will slow
me down;
Over, under, and, if need be, through ... I am in Control.
Thus said the river.

I hold you in my palm.
I direct your comings and goings.
If you turn, it is I who turned you;
If you gain speed, it is I who raised you from my shallows.
Thus said the riverbed.

I, pebble by pebble; soil by soil,
Shaped you; I eroded your sides, and created your depth.
Thus said the river.

I filled the river (which shaped its bed),
With showers in summer and melting snow in spring—
I must be God, said the cloud. (Robert Miller, 2007)

II

Where We Are

Systems of Control

7

The Fishbowl Principle

In Section I of this book, we reviewed the processes by which our universe unfolded to a point where at least one small, sweet spot began welcoming life. We have explored the way life has promoted itself; and we have seen how one species among many on Earth developed a mind and what we refer to as a soul, with a unique level of self-awareness and introspection that causes it to revere the mysteries of its origin. We are now at the point in our story we will refer to, comparatively, as "today."

In the following chapters, our focus turns to where we are now. We will delve into several of the most important cultural systems we have developed over the years and how they have led to our best and worst contributions to the world. We will start with a snapshot of what things look like now and then investigate, with greater specificity, how several of our most powerful systems of control—religion, government, economics, and education—have brought us to this point. The summary of our present condition put forth here includes the bad news discussed in the first chapter regarding what ails our planet, but also the good news: People of all eras have emerged with an increased understanding of placing priority on long-term decision making that benefits the whole, a recognition of the need to take action, and a willingness to make sacrifices to improve the lot of the many. Are there enough of these people today? And more important, will enough of us listen to them and join in the challenge of their work?

While we find it vitally important to establish personal relationships with the rest of the living world, Earth, and the universe itself, and thereby gain a better understanding of our place in creation, our real concerns, focuses, and motivations sprout from what is right in front of us, what is going on in the present moment. We are predisposed toward the here and now, yes, but it is also that we are faced with enormous challenges, the likes of which have not been seen before. While we certainly should use the stories of natural and human history to advise our present course, we see very little utility in dwelling on the past, especially if it means repeating past mistakes.

We are not looking backward. Our gaze is instead pointed directly at our feet, so we do not trip over obstacles in front of us, and on the horizon, so we may have an idea of where we are going. Time is not holding us; it merely carries us forward in its currents. And all of us, like leaves in a river, are floating forward with it. While we are able to steer and maneuver around rocks and branches, and occasionally are caught in eddies for a while, we would be foolhardy to try to swim backward.

But our project here is to do more than be carried down time's river into the rough seas, unprotected. We are here to build an Ark, a vessel in which we can safely and swiftly travel through stretches of rapids and around obstacles that would otherwise mean the end of our journey. Understanding how we have gotten to this point is integral to the construction of such a vessel, but the real work is just starting. We can now imagine ourselves standing next to the unfinished frame of an enormous watercraft, still surrounded by scaffolding, on solid ground. It is by no means a finished, seaworthy vessel, but you can recognize the outline of a boat. Some might wonder why we are building a boat when there is no water nearby. And some, perhaps a small few, might ask what they can do to help. We know there are those who imagine themselves working calmly and methodically, but with an urgent sense of purpose. We're not like the grey-haired, leathery-skinned, wild-eyed old man whose boat preserved life during the last Great Flood, but in many ways it is helpful to relate to him and empathize with the enormity of the task set before him.

In our short-term, immediate scale of perspective, there is little sign of impending cataclysm. We sleep in soft beds; flip switches and turn knobs for light, heat, and water; travel thousands of miles sitting down and not breaking a sweat; have access to food from all corners of the globe right around the corner from our homes; and interact with incredible amounts of information with a few simple keystrokes. For the privileged among us, the problems of the world border on philosophical abstraction. We read our newspapers and listen as our televisions report unimaginable horrors—natural disasters, genocide, wars, abject poverty, corruption, economic crises, crime, environmental degradation, oppression—but how much do our immediate lives change? We still have food in our stores, we still have running water and electricity in our homes, our trash still is taken away every week, our mail still gets delivered. The sky is not falling: Indeed, it is a beautiful day by most measures, and we are glad to be alive in a time where so much is possible and so little is required of us to obtain it.

This is true for now, but for how long? So much in our lives depends on political stability, and there are many forces that can intervene to topple it. It takes an enormous amount of energy to maintain societal stability, and if we lose vigilance, it can very easily succumb to entropy and fall into disarray. In coming chapters of the book, we will explore the dilemmas of our age. We do this not to dwell on the bad, but to be ever mindful of what may happen if we ignore the storms brewing on the horizon and fail to build our Ark.Should we second-guess ourselves here in this effort toward a better future? Many see clouds rolling in on the horizon, but they do not seem like much that needs to be worried about. Besides, humanity has adapted successfully to everything that has been thrown at it. We are the survivors, children of leaders and warriors, and the most successful species on the planet. Why go through so much trouble to build this enormous boat when the ground around us is dry?

We view this as another way of not having to react to calamity or further degradation of what we already have. If we live completely in the present, as yogis instruct us, then some of us have every reason to believe that things are fine, because at the present moment, in some of our lives, they are. However, if we take time to empathize with others who share our planet, it becomes clear that the clouds rolling will bring more than just a passing thundershower. We could wait for the storm, and the lucky and privileged among us might even make it through for a bit. But unlike Noah's Ark, which carried only one breeding pair of every species, our Ark has enough room for every human that wants to come onboard, and offers shelter for all other species that cannot be sustained on a planet in peril. We have set the foundation for our vessel in our deep history, and now that we have an idea of how we got here, it is time to turn our attention to today.

Bruce Gendelman

"A Failed Culture: Machu Picchu"

And An Island Never Cries (Simon and Garfunkel)

There are many modern-day Noahs warning us and preparing for rising waters, but far too many of us are like Noah's neighbors. In an age where we have made incredible technological strides in communication, we are surprisingly hindered by an inability to understand and be understood by our fellows, and we continue to experience the consequences of a modern-day Tower of Babel. The warnings being made with increasing fervor, along with various proposals for building Arks that may float us to safety, are coming from experts across many disciplines. Religious leaders discuss our present challenges in moral terms, speaking of a crisis of the soul and a culture of selfishness. Economists describe worldwide financial distress and resource scarcity caused by overpopulation (Erlich, 1968), and discuss means for improving access to food, water, health care, and credit. Climatologists speak of changing weather patterns, while environmentalists focus on the indirect, but almost unimaginably severe, impact global climate change will have on humanity, through disruptions in the food supply (Shelburne, 2008), decreased levels of natural resources (Millennium Ecosystem Assessment, 2005), and diminished biodiversity (World Wildlife Fund, 2008). Engineers promote alternative energy solutions to the dependence on oil and its volatile sources of supply. Politicians argue over where and how to fight the dangers of nuclear proliferation and militant religious fundamentalism. The warnings splattered over newspaper headlines and television broadcasts are plentiful.

Even amid all these warnings, the by-products of human activity still amass toward a tipping point. Population is growing at an exponential rate, which results in a corresponding rise in the consumption of the planet's finite store of natural resources. We applaud ourselves for our culture's ability to alter our environment more than most other organisms do, but we rarely stop to realize the price that will eventually have to be paid for such drastic environmental renovations. Through complex social networks, we engineer lifestyles that insulate us from relatively chaotic natural order and allow us to maintain a semblance of control over individual destinies, while turning a deaf ear to those who say it cannot last forever. Most of our goals are hardly malicious, but it has become increasingly apparent that the means used to achieve them are having unintended harmful and far-reaching consequences. Efforts to thrive as a species have been highly successful, but many are now realizing that they have come at a dear price: In many parts of the worlds, humans have adopted a lifestyle that cannot be sustained for much longer without causing significant damage, if not catastrophe.

The consequences of our appetites have become particularly apparent in recent decades, with the "haves" struggling mightily to keep up with inflating or deflating standards that impact their way of living, while the "have nots" are trying (and some with considerable success) to get to the point of the "haves." This international economic competition has in many ways had a polarizing effect: It has resulted in a dramatic rise in the number of people living with abundance, but it has been accompanied by increasing numbers of people living in extreme poverty (Duangkamon Chotikapanich, Rao, Griffiths, & Valencia, 2007). Economist, former Harvard president, and economic adviser to U.S. President Barack Obama, Lawrence Summers noted that this phenomenon is seen not only in the Third World, but also in the working class and the upper class in the United States (Summers, 2008). The struggle to produce the energy required for economic growth places increasing demands on Earth's resources, which in turn has far-reaching human costs—taxing not only our pocketbooks but also the very quality of our lives. Our increasingly high standards of living are fueled by a similarly increasing level of consumption. We have now reached the point where our activity has affected the very functioning of Earth's natural processes (Goudie, 2000), which in turn is creating a vicious cycle with dire consequences for most living things, including us.

Cast Away

We hike as far as we can into the thicket
there is unexpected, almost frightening raw beauty
easing the pain of broken branches across our face
there are a few impenetrable spots but we know what's there
heading back to camp we regroup
we had already walked the edges
all sides the same, more or less
big ocean stretching out
and what is beyond our gaze is useless to us
trapped on this beautiful island
with only our own efforts keeping us alive
no, not true, the island has richness to yield
we look up at the night sky and want so badly
to be taken care of, to be loved,
to not be alone on this island
we think what we think, say what we say
listen to what we think we hear
and go back to clearing debris from our camp
and foraging for food. (Robert Miller, 2009)

Humans have not always stood idly by in the face of adversity. Religion, science, government, industry, and the arts have all helped civilizations navigate past many seemingly intractable obstacles. But more recently, it seems, the greater the need for action, the more we have become paralyzed. Why is it that we and our most cherished institutions are struggling to meet humanity's biggest challenges, even when faced with consequences as dire as climate change; collapse of economic systems; genocide; annihilation from terrorism, resource scarcity, or health epidemics; or societal decay borne from our deteriorating ability to agree upon shared values?

Much of the impediment to solving these pressing problems comes from the often-myopic view that is most often taken toward them. This tunnel vision is manifested in three inabilities. The first is the inability to view problems through an interdisciplinary lens. Those claiming solutions too often approach things with an absolutist singularity that, through its exclusivity, creates disharmony instead of progress. The second inability is to prevent short-term interests from depleting resources at the expense of long-term needs, resulting in fewer legacies for our progeny. The third inability is in seeing beyond boundaries of local geography and culture. This tribal myopia prevents all of us from accepting that we are, in a very real way, connected to each other and all other species in our environment, and to the environment itself, on a global scale. To find a consensual solution to common problems, a common language must be used, common ground identified, and basic operating premises agreed upon. Our actions often suggest a belief, at least at the unconscious level, that each person, city, nation, and religion operates independently. But isolation is an illusion. The 6.5 billion human inhabitants of this planet (leaving aside the members of the 30 million–plus other species) (Wilson & Perlman, 2000), and the myriad of groupings into which we have subdivided, are interconnected in many, many ways.

People should recognize our inherent myopic tendencies, but we should not fault ourselves for having them. After all, we are all were born with them preloaded into the deep structures of our brains, and they were reinforced time and time again by the environment in which we were raised. These predispositions have to be adaptive in some way. Put another way, if our myopia did us more harm than good, then it probably would have either killed us off long ago, or we would have evolved (or would be on the road to evolving) into beings with broader perspectives. Since we are still here, we can speculate that at least until very, very recently, we have possessed these qualities for an excellent reason: Our preferences for local and short-term perspectives over more global and long-term ones are hardwired biological imperatives designed to promote our individual survival. This, throughout natural history, has helped us to live to see tomorrow. But here is the thing: Now that our culture has run amok over our biology and there are enormous and fast-changing societal transformations to take into account, we would do well to reconsider just how adaptive our instinctual tendencies are when we view the survival or well-being of humanity from a global perspective.

I Can See for Miles (The Who)

This tension between the human-sized individual way of looking at things and the humanity-sized worldwide perspective is evident in many of the issues we face today. Given a limited amount of money in our pockets, most of us would rather pay rent and buy food for our families and ourselves than invest in the long-term development of infrastructure and agriculture on another continent. Our immediate individual or family survival is almost always more important to us than the potential to save dozens, or even hundreds, of anonymous lives in lands we have only heard about, even if the calculations that favor hundreds of lives over one are clear-cut at the global level. Likewise, it is extraordinarily difficult to convince a mother to not have more children so a stranger's child may be fed tomorrow, just as it is difficult to convince religious leaders to abandon the call for their followers to propagate in order to produce a larger flock. When viewed at the immediately personal level or perspective, these types of preferences are easily understandable even if they contravene larger global needs.

Yet readjusting our proclivities toward long-term over short-term reality, and global perspective over individual perspective, is vital to the type of problem solving that our species has ahead of us. And notwithstanding our deeply programmed tendencies to act selfishly and egocentrically (and here, those words are meant to be value-neutral), long-term thinking for the benefit of the group is an attainable goal.

This is largely due to the fact that as our world is becoming more interconnected, and the more we depend on one another's work for our own survival, the global perspective increasingly becomes the same as our personal perspective. Achieving this type of vision requires the acknowledgment that we all truly depend on one another in many ways, and the identification of common ground in our perspectives.

The first step in the process of broadening our focus is to gain an understanding of the fundamental nature of the myopic tendencies that pervade decision-making in the public and private spheres. This myopia, outlined above, prevents us from seeing the forest for the trees, because this view or focus for common ground is mostly an unrealistic and naïve ideal in a complex and dangerous world. So what needs to change in order for this common ground to be recognized?

The reason political pandering by our leaders emphasizes quick fixes for long-term crises rather than long-range planning based on budgeted sacrifices, is that we, as voting citizens, are not evolutionarily programmed to react with the same passion to long-term dangers as we are to short-term problems. Many Americans are frustrated and angry, believing "they have been squeezed out of politics by a system dangerously spiraling out of control, a system made up of lobbyists, political action committees, special interest organizations, and the media . . . [such that] we risk losing something precious to the meaning of the American experience . . . that the very meaning of the public good is disappearing in a sea of self-seeking" (Moyers, 2008, p. 163). But the political pandering continues because, at reelection time, the panderers find that it usually works. The politicians are hardly immune from the trappings of human nature; they have just learned how to use those trappings to their benefit. The politicians need to eat too. It is our job, not just theirs, to make sure that societal benefits are being served as well, and perspective is everything in how one approaches an analysis of politics.

Thus, problems that require long-term and global perspectives, such as energy policy in the Third World and its effect upon the environment, or in the United States with issues such as Social Security and budget deficits, are, for reasons of political expediency, put at the back end of the lists of priorities of our policy makers. There is a natural inclination to want to heat our homes in the cheapest way possible and to recoil against politicians who even mention the possibility of raising our taxes. Yet we must summon the courage and perspective, first within ourselves, and then in our leaders, to make decisions regarding life on this planet in a fundamentally different way. Aside from the futility inherent in attempts to overcome nature with human law, our policy solutions need to be geared toward long-term group outcomes that can nonetheless directly benefit our short-term needs, such that short-term needs no longer cause us to place the future of large numbers of humanity in peril. A cost benefit analysis can be conceived for any decision that models the total costs against the current short-term benefits.

While it is fairly certain that many, if not most, humans will continue to embrace separate nation-states, religions, economies, and cultures, the optimistic vision embraces the broadening of our collective vision, past our immediate horizons, and allows for us to make the choices necessary to solve such problems as pollution, poverty, and pestilence. Human culture has outgrown many of our tribal needs (even if human biology has not), and as such we should have it within us to change our tribal ways. In the past 50 years, political leaders have declared wars on ideologies as much as on each other: The wars on communism, poverty, drugs, terrorism, and energy dependence are not like the traditional turf wars among nation-states. The battle for the change humanity desperately needs today must be waged on a footing comprised of even less solid ground than these others: The battle of our lives must be fought against certain aspects of human nature.

Or Would You Rather Be a Fish? (Bing Crosby)

Think of it this way: We are swimming in an imaginary fishbowl, one that is sealed off from others and the very real ocean of the universe. There was a time when this fishbowl was all we wanted, and while each of us, pressed up against the glass, had a very limited and distorted view of the world beyond, we deemed the status quo to be sufficient. Then, thanks to time and human ingenuity, the walls of our fishbowls began to crack, and we were able to break free and swim beyond the confines of our individual limitations. Even though we embraced much of the freedom that came from this emancipation, we have a vestigial tendency to operate and respond as if we are still in our fishbowls. *Homo sapiens* have not evolved biologically at the same pace that the products of our culture have, and it is our culture and its products that are responsible for both the creationof and the breaking of our individual fishbowls. As a result, we still see much of our problems through the narrow and cloudy focus of times long past.

Each religion, each nation, each discipline of thought seems to be stuck in its own container, with a false sense of physical isolation—but a tragically real sense of being unable to effectively communicate with others. But then, how could we expect to communicate when we are swimming in separate bowls? The cosmic joke is on us: We have not *really* been swimming in separate bowls, even if we thought we were. Everything is connected to everything else, and as such, the currents and waves outside our human perception have always affected our personal, immediate scales of perspective. The difference between then and now is that in the past, interactions and effects were much more limited by cultural constraints than they are today. The trucks driven in Russia, the oil spilled in the Pacific, and the coal-burning power plants in China all affect the ice sheet in Antarctica, which in turn affects the fishing in Japan, which in turn affects economic relations between countries, which in turn contributes to political tensions . . . and so on. As chaos theorist and meteorologist Edward Lorenz famously wrote, "If a single flap of a butterfly's wings can be instrumental in generating a tornado, so also can all the previous and subsequent flaps of its wings, as can the flaps of the wings of millions of other butterflies, not to mention the activities of innumerable more powerful creatures, including our own species" (1995, p. 181).

We need to shatter the constraints we have placed on our perspective, overcome the hardwired tendencies we have inherited toward the immediate and personal, and learn how to swim in a sustainable way with our fellow inhabitants in the larger vessel we call Earth. This does not just mean species such as humans learning to coexist with polar bears, nor does it only mean people such as Palestinians and Israelis learning to live peacefully in the same world. This also means a new and transformative sharing of ideas among accountants and artists, evangelists and biologists, Republicans and Democrats, anthropologists and lawyers, Sunnis and Shiites, plumbers and presidents.

There is urgency in completing our escape from our fishbowls. Compounding the major threats we face is an acceleration of cultural phenomena and a resultant spike in the rate at which serious consequences are unfolding. Whether it is the financial devastation from a global economic tsunami, the environmental devastation from a melting polar icecap, or the reputational devastation from a false rumor carried over the Internet, the storms once thought to be on the horizon are imminent and threaten us with increasing rapidity, intensity, and consequence. Yet, our brains do not register the very real threats we face over the span of months or years in the same way a stampeding elephant headed our way would influence our behavior. And so we stand transfixed and vulnerable.

I Will Choose Free Will (Al Rush)

Storms are on the horizon, but are we at a point in the history of the planet where only another catastrophic cleansing will do? There are subscribers to such a philosophy. This is not limited to doomsday cults; visions of a final judgment and end of days come from the most sacred stories of many cultures, including the Book of Revelation, Hindu references to Kali, the Rangarok of Norse mythology, and many native American beliefs in the coming of a new age. While most people on the planet would just as soon sustain and nurture our world, there are those who think it is preordained that we must suffer an apocalyptic event in the near future, and that this is an event to be anticipated and embraced with joy.[12] Such believers are not concerned about the coming annihilation of their physical body or world, because they believe that their god will deliver them to rapture while the rest of us, who believe in the wrong god (or do not correctly believe in the correct god), will be left behind— in the most horrible sense of that phrase. If this is so, and if God is going to perform these terrible acts, nothing that our preachers, politicians, or scientists do will matter for the rest of us.

---

[12]   Notable here is the fundamentalist, evangelical version of the end of days.

But then again, don't the same books that give some a welcome view of the apocalypse speak to the sanctity of life? *"This is what the Lord says—he who made you, who formed you in the womb, and who will help you"* (Isaiah 44:2). What of the most basic biological imperative: our divine instinct to survive and perpetuate our species? What if we believed that we actually have a say in whether we destroy the world or save it? If we are rendered helpless, do not the same books tell us that we will be defended? *"For you have been a defense for the helpless, a defense for the needy in his distress, a refuge from the storm, a shade from the heat"* (Isaiah 25:4). Are we any less entitled to reach for the lifeboat than Noah's sinful contemporaries (who, as the story goes, were given time to become righteous before the rains came)?[13] There is certainly a less fatalistic course of action to pursue, just in case the world is not going to be destroyed by its maker in the immediate future.

The hopeful vision we hold out is this: As more and more signs of a different kind of oncoming storm have cropped up, thousands of modern-day Noahs are scrambling to build their own versions of an Ark (based on their expertise, their morality, or their gut feeling) to save those wishing to be spared from the storms brewing on the horizon. These concerned people are currently speaking out about problems of tremendous importance, but whether by oversaturation or by problems in communication, we as a species do not seem to be really hearing what they are saying. Meeting the needs of our time requires synthesis, an Ark for our age built of more flexible and durable stuff than wood and pitch. It must be constructed from an interdisciplinary dialogue, in which we take action based upon the best thinking of physicists, religious scholars, biologists, economists, poets, political scientists, and ordinary citizens. These actions must be led and implemented by dynamic, honest, clear thinking men and women. Those seeking a peaceful and sustainable future do not suffer from the lack of will or the lack of ideas; we suffer from the dissemination of a "democratic" clearing house for ideas and action: a modern day town square where anyone can stand on their soapbox and shout at the top of their lungs for others to hear them; a forum for

---

[13]   Peter 2:5 refers to Noah as a "Preacher of Righteousness," implying Noah told people to be righteous, and both Peter 3:20 and Genesis 6:3 indicate that God waited a period of time before judgment.

ideas, discussion, and linkage; a worldwide forum for ideas to be shared, discussed, cast aside or implemented. The cream will always rise to the top, but that assumes a free flow of information and the freedom to act on it. It is precisely this reason that entrenched and institutionalized "control systems" like governments and religions most often try to block the flow of information that threatens their ideological roots.

The companion Web site to this book attempts to provide such a forum for connection. Any individual, entity, organization, or group can enter a node on the Ark at www.fishbowlprinciple.org. This node is their mission, their idea, and their invitation for like-minded people to join them. As connections are made one can visually see how interconnected they are. We know that not all "crowds" have wisdom, but some of the best thinking of this Internet age has occurred from this emerging disciple of open innovation. "But, a look at recent cases and new research suggests that open-innovation models succeed only when carefully designed for a particular task and when the incentives are tailored to attract the most effective collaborators" (Lohr, 2009).We need to do more than listen to prognostications. We need to join forces, to lend each other a hand in the construction of the Ark that will protect us from maelstroms and guide us into calmer waters. We need to break the cycle of poor communication that began with the Tower of Babel. We need to assume and embrace the responsibility that comes with our freedom, and we humbly offer this book as a means to provide the common framework upon which a civil, meaningful, and progressive debate can be facilitated.

Doin' It (LL Cool J)

More than any other time in history, mankind faces a crossroads. One path leads to despair and utter hopelessness. The other, to total extinction. Let us pray we have the wisdom to choose correctly. (Woody Allen, 1980)

There are many indications that we have arrived at a critical point, demanding a fundamental change in direction of how we choose to live if we want to improve our odds for species survival beyond the limited time we can comprehend. While we do not carry signs saying the end of the world is near, and we are mortally ignorant of what tomorrow or the next 10 or 1,000 years will bring, we are convinced we can influence our future trajectory with action borne of hope. The same process of cultural evolution that has amplified our ability to destroy ourselves also allows positive change to occur more swiftly and effectively than in prior generations. Because the human mind is the host in which viral ideas grow, it follows that our recently developed ability to transmit information with breathtaking rapidity may, if carefully harnessed, prove to be more a blessing than a curse. What we need to do is channel the growing recognition that many old ways are not working and that we need not only new solutions, but more important, new ways to find solutions—a more unified, rational approach to the most intransigent difficulties of our time.

The author Daniel Quinn makes a distinction between a vision and a program: "Vision is the flowing river. Programs are sticks set in the riverbed to impede its flow" (1996, p. 49). Programs are reactive measures intended to modify existing visions. A vision, on the other hand, is a prescriptive philosophy so encompassing as to be the riverbed itself. Quinn further suggests that our cultural river is flowing toward catastrophe and argues that the better approach "is to change the direction of the flow, away from catastrophe. With the river moving in a new direction, people wouldn't have to devise programs to impede its flow, and all the programs presently in place would be left standing in the mud, unneeded and useless" (p. 52).

Despite the short-term, immediate effectiveness of many programs at work in the world, there are not any quick fixes to the global problems of terrorism, tribal hatred, resource scarcity, or climate change. In this book, we are advocating less for programs that serve as stopgap measures (although some of these are important as well) and instead promote a vision of life on this planet that can be widely accepted and can encompass basic inalienable human rights for all of the worlds citizens, individual responsibility, common ground amongst our diversity, and a thirst for peaceful sustainability. We live in a world of practical and sometimes difficult choices, one that can hold seemingly contradictory truths at the same time. A nation cannot ensure its own peace without being able to at least project a credible ability and willingness to wage war. One cannot simultaneously have large governmental spending and low taxes without incurring the consequences of massive debt. One cannot continuously dump pollutants, even into something as vast as the ocean, and not expect them to build up over time and cause harm. Prices of real estate can go down as well as up. As is the case with any difficult choices, the solutions to the problems of our time require some sort of tradeoff or sacrifice. Not only is there is no free lunch, the cost of pretending there might be one is getting more expensive every day.

Questions that demand answers loom: Do we opt to play the role of critters clinging to safety on a sinking ship, or do we, as individuals, as societies, as cultures, as a species, take on the responsibility to become captains of our own destiny? Do we heed the warnings of the wild-eyed boat builder, or laugh at his fanatic efforts? Do we choose to rely on programs that are often founded in our own myopia, or attempt to implement a new vision, and in so doing, entirely change the direction of our future? How will we as a society bring about the dramatic, needed changes of behavior and policy? How do we overcome the proclivity of politicians to focus almost exclusively on solving short-term problems for immediate political gratification? How do we overcome religious leaders who too often focus on what makes their particular sect different, or emphasize policies designed to promote their belief system's perpetuation, as opposed to helping their followers fulfill their innate yearning for a universal unifying force that spreads love unconditionally? Can we figure out a way to survive without offending God or the cosmos (notwithstanding those people who believe their version of God wishes us dead)?

The emergence from our respective fishbowls will not only enrich us with access to viewpoints different from our own, but such diversity in ideas will also give us strength and security, and allow freedom from the chains of propaganda. A citizen's exposure to a wide variety of information coming from many sources immunizes him or her from the insidious weapon of selective education. In George Orwell's classic dystopian novel *1984*, his character O'Brien demonstrates his awareness of this. O'Brien, speaking on behalf of Big Brother, says, "We shall squeeze you empty, and then we shall fill you with ourselves" (Orwell, 1949, p. 256). He got it right, and we see this technique used with consistent resolve in autocratic nations and too many religions. "People without memory are at the mercy of their rulers because there is nothing against which to measure what they are told today" (Moyers, 2008, p. 127).

In addition to changing our narrow approach to competing ideas, we need to change our limited approach to our relationship with the world's natural resources. We must realize that Earth's resources do not exist solely for our use. Put another way, we can no longer be content with changing our environment in order to survive—it is *we* who must change; we must change the way we interact with our environment, so we may live in harmony with our planet and our fellows. To survive, hordes of locusts consume all natural resources in their paths. The scale of human capabilities and population is too large and powerful for Earth to sustain this type of behavior from us. Those who are not struggling on a daily basis merely to survive can no longer think exclusively about what we want to take from Earth today; we need to lift our eyes from the ground and gaze to the horizon.

To accomplish our greatest goals, we must all act humbly and carefully, with a full and accurate understanding of our place in the universe, because it seems that those with variant world creation views are resistant listening to one another with open minds and hearts.

Empty Pages (Steve Winwood)

The world's religions reflect wisdom that, depending upon the particular religion and one's particular beliefs, is either the direct word of God, the divinely delivered truth transmitted through human or godly agents, or the recorded wisdom and knowledge of the times. Whether written in the time of Moses (some 5,000 years ago), Jesus (some 2,000 years ago), or Mohamed (about 1,300 years ago), they codified existential issues and described rules for humanity's conduct. Each religion was designed with a basic text and also with a system whereby subsequent theological leaders could interpret what the text meant and how to apply it to situations that would arise over time, so the religions would be able to speak to practical problems faced by their followers through generations to come. This subjectivity of doctrinal interpretation is why we have rabbis, popes, imams, ministers, ayatollahs, clerics, and monks, to name a few.

More recently, other popular documents came into existence with different sets of rules. One of them, which has been widely admired over its relatively brief existence, is the U.S. Constitution. It described rights of humans (regrettably, initially only some humans) that were granted to them by God, but did not serve to describe that God. It recognized that, as a document written by men (and it was not written by women), it was fallible and, therefore, established a self-correcting mechanism by which this so-called "living" document could be revised. Thus, it eventually came to include all the country's citizens in its sweeping reach, and while even at its inception it was, for its time, very inclusive, few would argue that its "life" has improved since its writing. Again we see that the reality in which the Constitution was written was different from the reality in which later generations would live. The Constitution's success has come largely because it is a doctrine designed with a built-in ability to become altered—not easily, but rather only with great effort—to accommodate the needs of subsequent realities not foreseen at its inception.

The United States of America, a country built upon the foundation of this Constitution, attracted people from far and wide seeking physical, spiritual, or economic freedom. The United States was inhabited by diverse nationalities, religions, and cultures, which includes the indigenous peoples of North America who met the Europeans when they arrived (and then were largely decimated in a genocidal manner), as well as those brought to these shores in bondage. While not all new arrivals were welcomed over the years, at its best the United States has been described as a melting pot. As the symbol implies, the national character forged from the diverse ingredients that went into it found strength in its complexity and diversity.[14] But the heat under the U.S. pot was not the tribal cultures of religious or national origin—this could not have unified people who came from different places and followed different religious practices. No, the country was built on ideas, and the core ideas on which it was built came from the Constitution.

---

[14]   This is a theme we also find in the study of biology. We will pick up on this thread, and what human culture can learn from the community of life, later in the book.

Just as the Old and New Testaments and the Qur'an were not designed to be scientific treatises, the Constitution was specifically designed not to be a religious document. Religious and nonreligious people alike, when they are able to work together toward common goals, do so because they are unified by common ideals; disruptions and disharmony result when groups are threatened by others with competing ideals. In history, there has never been one set of ideals embraced by all humans at any one time, and this leads to two important questions. First, can a core set of common ideals be identified that can withstand the test of time? And if so, can these core ideals be captured in a doctrine embraced by a sufficiently large group of people so that principles of conduct and public policy solutions can be implemented on a scale previously unheard of?

The authors are of the mind that the answer is yes (it was a close vote), but it will require unprecedented concerted effort by many to achieve such a goal. We are pragmatic and understand the magnitude of the obstacles ahead, but we are also optimists. Keep in mind that the alternative to the strong metal forged in a melting pot is the separation of the ingredients into disparate and weaker units. We do not have to sacrifice our individuality, cultural identity, nationality, or religion to become a global community. We do not have to swim in the same direction as everyone else simply because we have escaped from our fishbowl. We (humbly and yet boldly) have written this book and created its Web site as a means by which we as individuals can offer our voices for a potential path and to provide a forum to catalyze a change for the better in humanity at all levels of society. While we have our own biases and make specific and explicit suggestions as to what can be done from these biases, our main purpose is to promote a conversation among the readers of this book based upon a broad view of issues common to the human condition. The dialogue that ensues, the exchange of ideas and relationships forged therein, may very well become the Ark we have been hoping for, one that can see us through the storm and carry us into calmer waters.

How do you draw people from their fishbowls and onto the Ark? We seek to harness the power of religion in terms of its ability to move people's hearts; the power of science in terms of its ability to move people's minds and offer technological innovation; the power of economics in terms of its ability to connect policy with self-interest; the power of philosophical, psychological, and moral precepts to harmonize divergent thoughts and passions regarding what is good; and the power of government to coerce behavior for the public's benefit—even where this may vary from any one individual's religious, scientific, or economic viewpoint.

Bruce Gendelman

Blue-footed Boobie, Galapagos

This project is an ambitious one, but the dilemmas of our age are of the highest urgency. Changing minds, as the precursor to changing hearts, is the precursor to summoning the collective will and energy required to work toward a more sustainable, secure future for all humanity. Many prominent and humble people and organizations around the globe are hard at work securing a sustainable future for humanity. This work is primarily a synthesis; an effort at identifying a message that may transcend cultural, religious, and political boundaries, and appeal to a wide audience. We invite debate, ideas, and criticism central to this project and will provide the cultivation for a fresh perspective on what it means to be human. Integral to this perspective is a reframing of each person's role in society and humanity's place in the natural order, which includes not only our role as organic, sentient beings here on Earth, but also how we fit into the larger story of the universe and cosmos.

> *We are stardust*
> *Billion-year-old carbon*
> *We are golden*
> *Caught in the devil's bargain*
> *And we've got to get ourselves*
> *Back to the garden (Mitchell, 1970)*

Further Down the Road (Taj Mahal)

The previous chapters of this book have given us a story about how we got here. We should hold this rich perspective of our place in the universe close, or debate the facts and evidence for those that disagree, as we move forward with the construction of our Ark. In the next chapters, we will explore where we currently are as a species. More specifically, we will examine the systems of control that have pushed us down the path we are currently walking, systems that we created ourselves. Our goal here is not to dismantle these systems of control; indeed, they are some of the most stable and powerful cultural institutions that humankind has ever produced, and we believe that it would place us in great danger if society dismantled them. Instead, we seek to identify and describe these cultural artifacts. We do so with the hope that we will be better able to understand the inner workings of these systems so we will be able to work with them effectively, tweak them when opportunities present themselves, and overhaul them when necessary. Thinking more broadly about these systems of control, and reframing them in terms of a reconfigured schema of human nature and of our place in the world, is the next step toward securing a sustainable future for everyone.

8

On Evolutionary Religion

There are power dynamics at work in any social relationships. Managers instruct employees, teachers evaluate students, parents limit the freedoms of their children, and religious leaders preach and try to enforce what is and is not socially acceptable. Even in the most egalitarian of relationships, such as friendship or even marriage, there exists a constant push and pull of power, a dialectic equilibrium of decision-making. In any relationship, though, it is unfortunately up to the person in power to determine how that power will be spent or used. And, because we are creatures with biological drives and survival aspirations, any social advantages we have will often be used to promote our own short-term survival over anything else.

Inevitably, given a population of individuals with varying proclivities and abilities and a finite amount of resources, some individuals will be more successful than others at accumulating and using those resources. This can be traced back to the principle of natural selection: Variations will cause some individuals to be more suited to survive in a particular environment, and those individuals will be the ones who survive long enough to produce the next generation of individuals. Who among us would not choose to be the sheep with the biggest horns, the elephant seal with the most mass, or the tree with the highest branches? Genetically speaking, these are not attributes we are able to choose; we are born with them. This lack of choice is unfortunate, but genetic determinism is not the whole story.

In humans, much of our success or failure does not hinge on biological differences but on cultural differences like education, social status, wealth, access to technology, or quality of alliances with others. Those cultural differences might unfortunately relate to biological differences in some cases, but biology is not ultimately what is responsible for the relative success of any individual. This is as true on the schoolyard playground as it is in the UN General Assembly. Because there are so many people and such limited resources, and because the elements of culture are able to evolve at a rate that far outpaces our biology, those who have mastered the more modern means of survival have accumulated wealth and power in amounts that have led to a world in which those means of survival are concentrated in the hands of a very small percentage of the population.

Jared Diamond, in his book *Guns, Germs, and Steel* (1997), traces the success of certain cultures back to the physical geography of the land in which those cultures evolved. But whatever the ultimate cause, we have seen that in order to protect and safeguard their good fortune, the powerful few have instituted what we have labeled "systems of control," cultural structures to ensure that their success is maintained, even if it comes at the expense of countless others. This section of the book will highlight some of the more powerful systems of control at work in the world today, describing their origins, explaining how they are maintained, and offering some points on how we can work toward the best interests of everyone, not just those who happen to control resources, wealth, and power. The first system of control we will examine is religion.

Religion as a System of Control

In the last chapter, the statement was made that it matters little to our world whether God actually exists. What matters a great deal is whether a schema—a mental representation—of God resides in each of our minds, what that schema looks like, and how that schema affects our thoughts, opinions, and actions. More than coming to know the nature of God in a philosophical sense, the concern is with the implications of a belief system on the state of the world. The previous chapter on religion was concerned with how spiritual enlightenment can be seen as an adaptive evolutionary strategy in humans; this chapter is concerned with more worldly topics. It will not examine the internal psychological experience of religion, but rather the way in which religion has shaped social culture throughout history and in the world today. This chapter is about how humans have organized with and against each other under the banner of religion.

Almost by definition, for any religion to be successful, it must convince people that it holds central answers to important conditions of human existence, such as the nature of that existence, the role of the individual, rules of behavior, what binds us to each other, and what force created us all and decides our fate. Religion's allure for individuals is a certain comfort in questions of existence, a fulfilled search for meaning, a set of morals and ethics to follow, and a community in which they can belong and feel welcome, loved, and protected. One reason for Christianity's initial success was the acceptance and "brotherly love" of the outcasts of Roman society (Wright 2009). The social aspects to religion cannot be overlooked and may be more responsible for many people's affiliation with their religion than any existential relief or spiritual gains they might experience. Whatever the connections, the power of religions is so great that people throughout history have been willing to sacrifice their very lives for the sake of it.

Those who have been able to capture an audience with their own particular brand of religious message or philosophy have generally experienced incredible personal success and enjoyed substantial amounts of power and wealth. While it is true that many of the primary figures in religious traditions (most notably, Jesus of Nazareth) were in no way powerful, wealthy, or privileged, we must keep in mind that the originators of the message were often not, historically speaking, the founders of the religion that eventually stemmed from teachings attributed to them. Christianity did not exist when Jesus walked on earth; it was only after his death that Jesus's followers spread his teachings far and wide. What followed was undoubtedly tied to wealth, power, and control: The Church (and the Pope who presided over it) was the primary political force in Europe for well over a thousand years following the establishment of Christianity. Countries whose leaders ascribed their beliefs to slightly differing teachings within Christianity became enemies, which aligned political divisions with religious schism (think of the civil unrest that has plagued Ireland). Even to this day, the Roman Catholic Church is one of the most powerful political entities in the world. Jesus, as historians understand him, would probably not have ever predicted the political path the Church would take.

A more recent example in the United States was Joseph Smith, killed before his particular brand of direct-revelation Christianity could bring him wealth (although he already had accumulated a great amount of power over those who believed in his professed spirituality). It was his successor, Brigham Young, who reaped the material benefits of the new religion of Mormonism once he and his flock settled in the American West (Krakauer, 2004). Others, who call themselves religious leaders, have been more directly motivated by personal gain and power, as has been the case with many cult leaders.

Conversely, some political leaders found religion a very effective means by which they could claim and maintain their power. Chinese emperors ruled by what was called the "Mandate of Heaven" (Perry, 2001), meaning that their rule was ordained by the heavens and would last as long as the heavens willed it. A similar concept was found in medieval Europe, where monarchs and aristocracy claimed the "divine right of kings" (Figgis, 1896), attributing their power and fitness to rule to the will of God. Despite the spiritual good intentions of a given religion, religious teachings are often twisted or forsaken completely in the interest of political gain, accumulation of wealth, or control. There have been many cases throughout history where "religious" doctrine was issued from a leader with the sole purpose of increasing wealth, power, or control. The Crusades, European colonization of the New World, and many modern-day terrorist attacks all invoke aspects of religion to justify themselves. This, to our dismay, has become commonplace, almost expected. Power can corrupt, it seems, no matter how pious one may claim to be. Even in the face of such incontrovertible historical evidence, we need to keep in mind that religion may be used as the vehicle for the ascension of some individuals to power, wealth, and control, but that does not speak to religion itself. Rather, it speaks to the dubious creativity of those individuals who are able to take humanity's thirst for meaning in life and turn it into a tool of manipulation and control.

We suggest that it is vital to transform the mindsets of humanity to understand the history of religious thought and the role that religion has played in society. Taking note of the time frame in which religious development has occurred provides additional perspective on its role. As before, we think it best to start at the beginning. This time, though, the beginning is only 6,000 to 7,000 years in our past.

Fishin' for Religion (Arrested Development)

Humans existed for ages without the influence of the Western and Eastern religions we recognize today; the religious practices of all major existing organized religions are very recent inventions when compared to the total time man has walked the planet. Humans who lived through this so-called "prehistory" were probably not devoid of spirituality, though, and evidence exists that cultural and spiritual practices occurred before religion as we know it became a proper fixture in human society. They also weren't significantly different from us genetically.

The strongest evidence for cultural practices has been found in ritual burial sites that are more than 100,000 years old (Lieberman, 1991), but these elaborate burials did not necessarily indicate the presence of a proper religion as much as a tribal culture. The relatively small size of a tribe in prehistory guaranteed that everyone knew everyone else personally, preventing the need for larger cultural structures that would otherwise tie the community together, which is one major function of religion. Furthermore, the need to prescribe rules of behavior and cultural norms (other important functions of religion) might not have been as necessary in small enough social groups. Indiscretions and violations of social norms did not require a legal system; in such intimate social networks they could be dealt with on a case-by-case basis. Religions as we know them developed in earnest as tribes of humans expanded into ever-larger groupings. Only when the size of a functional community reached the point where it was impossible to know everyone personally did cultural institutions such as rules of behavior and cultural norms need to be codified.

According to *The Great Transformations: The Beginning of Our Religious Traditions,* the first people to exhibit a formal religion were the Aryans, a racially diverse collection of people who shared various cultural aspects. The Aryans lived a simple and relatively unambitious life from about 4500 BCE, and spread outward from southern Russia (the Caucasian steppes) in about 3000 BCE. The unambitious nature of the

Aryan way of life may very well have been what gave rise to religious practices. Because they had no aspirations to gain territory or conquer neighbors, the Aryans lived a life of peace and security, with plenty of time to engage in activities not directly necessary for survival.

> Like other ancient peoples, the Aryans experienced an invisible force within themselves and in everything that they saw, heard, and touched. Storms, winds, trees, and rivers were not impersonal, mindless phenomena. The Aryans felt an affinity with them, and revered them as divine. Humans, deities, animals, plants, and the forces of nature were all manifestations of the same divine spirit. . . . It animated, sustained, and bound them all together. (Armstrong, 2006)

From this basic characterization, the Aryans developed personas for the various forces at work in their world, and this developed into a pantheon of deities.

As tribe size increased and their range of movement overlapped with other growing tribes, conflicts occurred at the boundaries of contact between groups with different beliefs. In particular, as the smaller tribe populations expanded, either due to their success and prosperity or, conversely, because they were not successful and needed different resources, they would encroach upon neighboring tribes. Unfamiliar belief structures and cultural practices between tribes led to natural human suspicion and distrust. As time and contacts continued, each group would adopt its "rules of engagement," specific ideas that first and foremost protected their own interests. While sometimes this would lead to the establishment of trade and cooperation, most of the time this would result in aggressive behaviors toward the strange neighbors who did things differently. The morality and righteousness of brutality and murder was then sanctified; short-term individual gain once again won out over long-term group benefit. Beliefs such as "We are the chosen people amongst all the people of the earth" proliferated. Because resources were limited, groups fought over them, not only for the right to exist but also to expand lands for their tribes. Victors and the vanquished both suffered in loss of life and treasure and attitudes were hardened toward neighbors, and the cycle perpetuated itself over years and generations.

Neighboring cultures began to diverge sharply in many ways; differences grew into misunderstandings, which grew into mistrust, opposition, and prejudice. Violence became an important means of convincing people that their ways were wrong, or at least unwelcome. Misunderstandings and erroneous assumptions surfaced when neighbors began to mistrust each other. That cultural practices were becoming less similar did not help the degree of trust; the strangers who did things differently across the way were becoming less appealing as friends and allies.

There were always the options of engaging in mutual agreements to not attack or attempts to achieve relative stability; however, because of cultural differences that tribes must have thought strange at best and evil at worst, these did not seem likely or wise options. As a result, an operating premise for most—if not all—rules of engagement became that "they" are strange and different from "us" and are not to be trusted, and furthermore, "we" have priority over "them." After all, who would you rather survive and prosper: your family, or those groups that you believe want to destroy you (or who at a minimum would to capture your women and take your food)? If threat to survival is perceived as real and immediate, our hardwired responses aimed at survival would be sure to kick in. We, as individuals, are survival machines, and here we can see that Dawkins (1989) was correct: Our evolutionary programming does not operate on the group level as much as it operates on the individual level. So even from the loftiest goals of prehistoric cultural doctrine, wars and genocide have sprung and continue to occur—all based in the misunderstood differences in cultural practices like religion.

As religious populations migrated and gained in size, some of the core values of the original followers began to diverge. This most likely occurred because control, wealth, and power became entangled with the aspects of a culture that experienced success at the expense of another culture. It became increasingly important to those in power to organize the social workings of the groups, as their actions, borne out of personal short-term interest, became more of a threat to surrounding tribes. They did this by establishing rules of conduct within the group and installing checks to ensure that nobody overstepped their bounds or made sufficient cultural advances that would challenge authority and power. This development provided a given culture an evolutionary advantage:

The organized complexity of well-developed social structures and alliances kept order and stability, and kept a population unified enough to stave off outside threats in an increasingly hostile world. Neighboring tribes, perhaps previously not perceived as threats, were construed as competitors for resources—food, land, and potential mates. But there were also power struggles within tribes, and we must keep in mind that those who fell into leadership roles and experienced the successes of personal control, wealth, and power most likely did what they could to preserve their own lofty position, even at the expense of their fellow tribesmen. We see, then, that the most basic desires for survival in any individual, combined with misunderstandings in divergent cultural practices, can result in heinous acts toward others, both within and between basic social groups, and especially those who are different. This began at an early age in human civilization and continues to this very day.

The Axial Age, and Subsequent Fallout

The frequently stated main purpose of religion has been to attempt to define why life matters. This is not at all problematic (unless we have the all too common situation where the answer is that "those" people's lives don't matter, life on Earth doesn't matter because what is really important is the external afterlife, or humans matter less than the religion itself). When, religious zealots, in order to fulfill the work of their God, apply coercion, sometimes violently, real trouble and misery occur. While we would like to attribute such zeal to an earnest desire to see as many people experience rapture and spiritual enlightenment as possible, it seems the unfortunate motivation for many religious leaders is sometimes a bit more worldly. And still, whether motivated by enlightenment, wealth, or power, there have been periods in our history that have seen explosive developments and changes to religious culture. Perhaps the most important of these periods occurred between 2,800 and 2,000 years ago.

During the Axial Age, religious leaders became imbued with the power of political leaders (and, often, military leaders). Matters of the spirit, as well as doctrine that dictated correct action and gave structure to society, were held in such high regard that those who taught such philosophies held increasing power over the minds and hearts of the population. It was also during this axial period that writing and literacy became more commonplace among the cultural elite. Evidence of human writing or record keeping dates back to before 3000 BCE, but such depictions were largely pictographs or systems developed to keep a tally of property. The Phoenician alphabet, which is thought to be the precursor to the Arabic, Hebrew, and Greek alphabets, first appeared around 1200 BCE (Coulmas, 1989). Such a (appropriately called) phonetic alphabet, where written symbols represent sounds of words as opposed to complete ideas, allowed stories, laws, and other cultural artifacts to be encoded with a far greater ease than before. However, only the literate could exchange and manipulate these cultural artifacts. Before technological advances allowed writing to be so widespread, everyone in a community was better able to participate fully in the oral traditions and customs that made up their religion. With the emergence of a literate upper class and an illiterate lower class, religious authority began to fall along socioeconomic lines and therefore became more entangled in issues of wealth and power.

In Europe, the monarchs and emperors served also as religious leaders for their countries and, subordinate only to the Pope spoke with authority about God's intent. In India, the Brahmins (priests, rulers, and teachers who represented the highest social classes) were the literate authorities on religious matters, while merchants and artisans occupied a lower caste and simple laborers occupied a lower caste still. In both cases, the upper classes that held social power were very few in number when compared to the general population: It is estimated that about 90% of the population in medieval Europe were peasants (Applebaum, 1992), and only 4% of the people in modern India belonged to the Brahmin caste ("Brahmins," no date). Here, religious piety was directly connected to social class, and those in charge specified that one could move up or down in the system only in the next life. If religious piety meant a more powerful and wealthy place in society, and that meant a greater chance at survival, we can see very clearly how the religion meme connects to our evolutionary needs. Beyond giving us answers in our unending search for meaning, religion positioned individuals as highly successful social beings in their communities.

Challenges to Religious Rule

Organized religions, as institutions, have at times supported the enrichment of human knowledge, but at other times they have served as barriers to progress. Indeed, millions have died for resisting or questioning the "truth" as defined by the authorities of the time. The Crusades, jihads, and the Spanish Inquisition are all examples of religion being used as a political tool that resulted in enormous bloodshed. Still, there were always those who would challenge the supremacy and infallibility of religion and, in doing so, called class and social power structures into question. Those religious leaders who wished to maintain their control had found a very convenient explanation and justification for their place in society, one that needed no evidence outside their word and only the continued relative ignorance of a much larger lower class. Therefore, threats to the presiding religious viewpoint, which commonly took the form of advances in science and technology, also represented political threats, threats to power.

Discoveries in science and technology usually promised an empowerment of everyone, not just those in power, and as such it was in the leadership's best self-interest to squelch or censor scientific advances. An extreme case of this was in China where civilization had developed technology well before the West. The emperors, seeing such developments as a means by which competing factions could empower themselves and possibly overthrow their autocratic rule, made efforts to limit kind and degree of technological progress made by its best scientists and engineers (Diamond, 1997). Because China's government had been unified and centralized since 221 BCE, at the start of the Qin Dynasty, one decision by those in power would prove to be quite pervasive for the entire country and population, which was immense. Diamond suggests that China's historical failure to keep up with technological advancements after leading the world in scientific innovation for 1,400 years stemmed from decisions of the ruling class that were based on local politics and personal short-term interest. It was certainly no Mandate of Heaven that kept the Chinese emperors in power.

In Europe, where power was not as centralized as it was in China, scientists and engineers enjoyed a bit more tolerance from religious leaders, but only to a point. The European tradition of empiricism, and natural philosophy cultivated in ancient Greece, provided a foundation for scientific work to advance, but those in power (most often members of the Church) would make every effort to hinder scientific findings that ran counter to the predominant religious teachings of the day. Advancements and discoveries such as Copernicus's work on the nature of the cosmos and Galileo's furthering of his heliocentric theory, or Darwin's explanation as to how we came to be, certainly posed threats to religions that narrowly defined such matters. The foundational texts demanded strict interpretations or else the basic truths and infallible word of God would seem to be in question, and the very religion would crumble. Galileo's work posed a grave threat to the basic tenets of Catholicism as practiced by the Church leaders of the time, and the Church forced him to recant his findings. It was not because the Church categorically was not interested in scientific discovery even though it would pose a threat to certain foundational spiritual tenets the Church maintained, but the real issue was a fear that the Church's authority could be called into question. A religion that is rigidly interpreted is bound to face conflicts with new thoughts and facts introduced by adherents who do not suspend their inquisitive nature in the name of faith. Practices such as this by governing bodies are not limited to antiquity or to medieval history. Even now, we see evidence of religious institutions resisting scientific discovery. Darwin's theory of evolution, which is not only the cornerstone of all of biology but a foundational process in all matters of the universe, has only recently been approached by those who hold Catholicism's highest office, and still causes controversy when it is taught in high school science classrooms (Miller, 2008). In addition there are legions of "Creationists" who firmly believe that the Earth was created by God on the second day about 6,000 years ago, and that all evidence to the contrary is just "not what it appears to be" (Gendelman, personal conversation with a Baptist minister, September 2009).

Reconciling Religion and Politics

Depending on one's vantage point, religions have either directly received divine truth, have interpreted such truth through an intermediary, or have made guesses and assumptions about the nature of reality, but by their very nature, whether gospel or dogma, such information is not designed to withstand efforts at objective validation. That is why the mechanism that propels the devout religious observer is referred to as "faith." The Bible's creation stories have provided inspiration that has enabled countless human souls to improve their lives. While the discipline of scientific proof has demystified various religious explanations of our origins, it has done no damage to the fervency with which faith-based people hold to their view of Genesis. It is not our project here to debunk these strict interpretationists, as long as what they hold to be true is not harmful to anyone. For many people, however, questions will always exist about the extent to which biblical writings were intended to be scientifically or even historically accurate. We as authors align our thinking more with this lot and believe that in many situations the cultivation of a healthy skepticism can benefit anyone. In the end, though, global society must strive to find public agreement on some level among the fundamentalists, the healthy skeptics, and even the atheists.

The validity of any analysis of past, present, and future events through science, religion, or philosophy depends upon the application of agreed-upon facts to the theories being advanced, and the integrity of the endeavor falls apart to the extent that it relies on guesswork, falsehoods, or illogical reasoning. Political decision based in science can rely on logic and sound reasoning, but religious leadership is often subject to the whims and fancies of whoever may be in charge. Religious scholars who believe their teachings constitute the direct word of God claim that the benefits they derive from their faith prove the correctness of their creed. But can there be two religious leaders preaching different messages that are simultaneously correct? Logically speaking, it's impossible, yet it happens every day, many times over.

There are powerful examples throughout history of people who embrace a spiritual life, or at least one based on faith, achieving miraculous transformations of mind and even, at times, body. If this were the only motivation for religious leaders, and if religion had stayed out of politics, we think that much of the trouble we experience in the world today would not have been. The difficulty of accepting the words of such leaders, however, is that the faithful are themselves only human, mere mortals, influenced by the subjective vicissitudes of the psyche.

Proof of this fallibility is revealed by the simple fact that groups of the faithful have proclaimed with conviction through the ages, and still do so forcefully today, that other groups, who bear equally forceful witness to the power of their faith, are completely wrong. We all want to believe in our own correctness, of course, but reality does not reveal as convincing a story. Instead of worrying about whose beliefs are right, we suggest that it is more important to worry about whose beliefs are doing the most good. If reality as we experience it is subjective, then there is rarely a part of reality more subjective than our *a priori* belief systems.

Stories from more modern history have set out to disentangle religion from politics. The United States was founded by religious refugees, and although they were men of Christian faith, they were also determined to leave religion out of their nascent government as much as they could. Both types of opponents have distorted the principle of separation of church and state: by those who want to destroy that separation, as well as by those who have no tolerance for people of faith. But there is no inherent need for the voices amongst different religions, or between people of faith and science, to drown each other out, so long as everyone can agree that all perspectives are subjective, that all is open to interpretation, and most important, that those who claim to be religious are so because of a desire to further their spiritual path, not to gain wealth, power, and control. Now is the time to search for answers in the sacred place where spiritual belief and empirical knowledge intersect, a place where morality, forgiveness, intelligence, and compassion reside. It is a humbling task, one that should be pursued with a great sense of earnestness and respect, but also one that is embodied both by religion and religion's opponents.

The Social Functions of Religion

Karl Marx's famous line from his manifesto on the plight of humankind decreed "religion is the opiate of the masses" (Marx, 1843). This conclusion was based on his observation and belief that organized religion created doctrine and dogma that supplanted an individual's need or interest to understand the world and its relationships in an original or individual way. Regardless of whether religion encourages or discourages individual spiritual growth, we find that the extent to which religion has been used as the *stimulant* of the masses is of far greater concern. Throughout recent recorded history, religion has been used to draw borders between groups of people, identify friend from foe, and drive mass social movements pitting one group of people against another. The question then becomes, Why have we groups of humans, often in the name of a loving and wise God, committed such hideous acts? In order to fully answer that question, we need an understanding of religion as it relates to social functioning and plays into the relative success or failure of a group of people.

It should not go unsaid that religions offer many positive characteristics for the human condition. "Religious people played a role in the abolition of slavery, in the independence movement in India, and the civil rights movement in India" (Sagan, 2007, p. 206). There are numerous accounts of Christian orphanages that housed Jewish children during the Holocaust. Even in less extraordinary times, religiously motivated souls contribute a lot of good to the world. Religions are major providers of education and charity; organizations such as the Christian Children's Fund do immeasurable good in the lives of many disadvantaged souls in the world; and while their motivation may stem from religious beliefs, their actions are simply good, free of religious bias. The churches in many inner-city communities in the United States are the moral center for families, providing a practical alternative to the streets and a spiritual alternative to hopelessness. The concept of charity is built into many of the world's religions. Islamism, for example, holds charity (*zakah*) as one of its five central pillars of faith. The Jewish concept of *tzedakah* is no different, nor is the conceptualization of charity as Buddhist perfection. Many religions, as prescriptions for personal and social harmony, stress introspection, love, and compassion for fellow humans. Organized religions provide a sense of affiliation and community for people, some of whom would not otherwise belong to any social groups. Religions also prescribe rules of conduct that instill a positive moral compass in their followers and offer a path toward a righteous life. These are only some of the positive aspects of religion as it functions in our social world, and they should not be forgotten.

Religion can be used as an organizing tool, a force that binds people together. The reasons people might choose to attend their place of worship stems from the desire to be part of a positive community of friends and neighbors. Certainly in the early years of human civilization there was no difference between one's religious community and their neighborhood. In the Middle Ages and even through portions of the Enlightenment, churches were the largest and most central structures in any European town. Nowadays, while it is common to find that the people who live close to us do not attend the same place of worship as we may, our own places of worship still provide that sense of community and support for us. Those of us who live in a pluralistic society like the United States should recognize that religion may not blend into our secular lives the way it would in other countries where religion is much more standardized, and for this we should remember that we are the exception in this case (albeit a very large exception). Yet, even we Americans can appreciate how much of our social lives is organized around religion, from youth groups, to brotherhoods and sisterhoods, to the friends we may make when we attend our chosen place of worship.

Much of the social organizing accomplished by religion has positive effects on people's lives. However, religious beliefs as directed by the Shadows of religious leaders (Jung, 1938) have the power to stimulate individuals and groups within to kill, subjugate, conquer, dominate, convert, convince, or isolate other human beings. These leaders attribute their means and ends to a doctrine or a deity, but the more worldly reason for their actions is that *they* are not *us*. Any suicide bomber, worth his or her "salt," will tell you with absolute conviction what is required by God and the rewards that they expect in their life to come, but cannot get beyond their absolutist position and admit that such horrific means cannot justify such selfish ends in this world. Every religion has a few basic founding assumptions. Many of these tenets are based on the thoughts and writings of their founders—and are often described as being divinely determined. Frequently the writings (sometimes written hundreds of years after the events) describe dreams or visions where God made himself known and ordered or enlightened the founder with knowledge and a special message to inform and organize the tribe. Individual reflection morphed into a mass reflex. The messages are organized and institutionalized by the religious leaders of the time, and their conscious biases as well as their Shadows become part of the movement. Because these original messages are "God ordained," an institution of believers devotes considerable resources to making sure God's wishes are carried out. The Crusaders, the Jonestown mass suicide victims, and the 9/11 hijackers were all performing what they were convinced was God's will, as privately revealed to the select participants.

Why has religion been so successful at organizing groups of people? The structure a religion provides in terms of establishing social norms and customs that benefit the group as a whole is a clear example of an adaptive survival strategy for the group. The divine founding scriptures of the world's religions were, when introduced, unifying forces for very large numbers of people and served to promote great intergroup harmony, until they became bases for focusing on the otherness of those following a different religion. Furthermore, memberships in organized religions and religious institutions were in many cases the only way someone of lower class could become educated and attain a higher status in their respective societies. This was true in medieval Europe, but is also true in impoverished communities in the modern world. And finally, the promises of enlightenment, understanding, or a ticket to a better afterlife have been a very powerful motivating force for many individuals throughout history, and one that organized religions are able to lean on without much cost or evidence from this life. Because religion's promises involve things that cannot be seen or measured, as well as things that we will allegedly get to enjoy once we die, the product being sold to religious followers is unlimited and completely free, and their appetite for it is insatiable.

Religious movements, which are the ultimate examples of social organization around religion, have in many cases become the dominant themes and movements in societies. Only recently was religion disentangled from government; until the founding of the United States in the late eighteenth century, almost all societies depended on some sort of religion to bind them together. Some religious movements are so powerful that millions have died at the hands of those who enforce what they extol as God's will. Those who dared resist or question the version of truth in vogue at particular times in history usually ended up dead or exiled. Secular leaders have often used religious thought to motivate others into mass political and even military action, and even in so-called secular societies, leaders appeal to religion for moral guidance and sometimes justification that their political platforms are the correct way to see things.

Where Religion Has Led Us Astray And What We Can Do About It

Make the lie big, make it simple, keep saying it, and eventually they will believe it. (Adolf Hitler)

We can imagine with a great deal of reality the predicament of three young boys growing up some time in the late 20th century: Amir was born in a village where no one believed in Jesus Christ as the son of God. Amir, his friends, and his family will not be saved—at least that is what Nicholas's parents believed. Nicholas felt pity for Amir, who would not be given a place in his heaven. Isaac was born Jewish; he grew up believing that he was one of the "chosen" people. Isaac's parents had carefully explained to him that this did not imply he was superior to non-Jews, but rather that his people were to lead others to the truth about God. Yet it was hard for Isaac not to feel that if his people were special in the eyes of the Lord, that this made them somehow . . . better. Amir would not wish to have Nicholas or Isaac live in his parents' home country because Nicholas, being Christian, would be considered an infidel, and Isaac is so vile to the elders in Amir's world that he does not even deserve to live. Let us assume that each of these boys attended the same school, sat next to each other in classes, shared lunches, and played together at recess. And yet, because of the cultures they have been born into, they felt quite estranged from one another.

Each of these hypothetical children and their parents believe unconditionally and unquestioningly that their religion is the only true path. Each of these children was raised to believe in an all-wise and all-merciful God, who has condemned the others (by virtue of their birth into a family of the wrong faith) to lives devoid of grace—because of their ignorance of the one and only truth. Each of these children can point to sacred writings, and while there may even be some agreement between them on which books are considered holy, the points at which they disagree drive them further and further apart. The more objective truth is that the three Western monotheisms of Judaism, Christianity, and

Islamism have more in common with one another than they do not, and certainly each religion's hopes and dreams for humanity are similar, but because the religions are so embedded into such different cultures, the differences between religions are what people notice and remember.

Again, this is as true on the schoolyard playground as it is at the UN General Assembly. Ronald Reagan referred to the former Soviet Union as an "evil empire" (Reagan, 1983). Hugo Chavez spoke of George Bush as the devil ("Chavez: Bush 'Devil'," 2006). Mahmoud Ahmadinejad spoke of Israel as a country that must be "wiped off the map" (Fathi, 2005). While such words are usually chosen because of the political impact they have with their countrymen as opposed to foreign listeners, the statements reveal much about the mindset of both speakers and intended audiences. It can safely be said that statements such as these carry religious overtones, but are not in reality connected to religion itself. Here, as in many other cases, religion is being used as a tool of persuasion to accomplish political ends or, worse yet, for leaders to gain wealth, power, or control. Political power, after all, is derived from there being symmetry between what a leader is saying and what their subjects want to hear, and those in power have become quite adept at using religion to align their speech with their audience's desires.

Religion cannot be used universally in this way, though. Imagine if the president of the United States had a vision in which God told him that he had to make peace with Osama Bin Laden on whatever terms were necessary, even if it meant removing all U.S. military from Islamic countries and severing all U.S. ties with Israel. Imagine if the president was certain that he was not delusional and that what he had received was the word of God. Would the coalition of Christian and Jewish activists who had provided a portion of his political support agree that this man of faith should direct U.S. policy as ordained by God? Probably not, in the case of the United States, but in other countries and in other times absolute rulers will do as they wish.

The power of government. Adolph Hitler

Historic genocides have occurred based upon these psychological factors. Masses or societies of otherwise good people have been manipulated by the Shadows of individuals who sought great power to act out of selfish short-term interest, whether expressed as religious or other culturally defining fervor. Hitler was a prime and recent historical example of the Shadow (with religious themes) being imposed upon a willing populace. His leadership model was clearly not to treat all people as one, or to love his neighbors as himself. Hitler used the Shadow images of the Jews (and homosexuals, gypsies, the disabled, and others) as the root of all his country's troubles in order to co-opt a willing populace to conquer the world and create racial purity and a super race, or, at the very least, to earn himself a seat of power in his home country. "What is shadowy in our psychic life is projected onto others, whomever we can blame, denigrate, attack, or accuse precisely those motives that we have denied" (Hollis, 2007,p. 205).

The Spanish Inquisitions, the Crusades, the genocide in Darfur, the Sunni and Shiite rift in 1300, the 9/11 terrorist attacks, and the Cambodian genocide led by Pol Pot, are all examples of movements and actions initiated by a person or a small group of individuals to destroy fundamental ideals. It is immaterial whether these actions were based upon laudable goals. Whether the aim is to make the world safer by creating a democratic outpost in the barbaric Muslim world, creating a superior race of people, avenging the death of one's martyr, taking back land that we need for crops to feed our children, or making the birthplace of our savior the rightful home to our religion, the result is terrible conflict, death, and misery.

The framers of the U.S. Declaration of Independence and the Constitution understood this fundamental concept of human pathology and crafted it into a flexible form of government based on laws, not men. It was agreed that power is corrupting and that people with power cannot always be trusted. In order to ensure that power would not be concentrated too much in one person's hands, two precautions were taken. The first was that religion was extracted from the workings of government. The second was that checks and balances in all aspects of governing were installed. The founders of the United States (all white males) allowed for individuals' representation in government (as long as they were white males), as well as for groups of individuals to have the ultimate power through majority rule, all while respecting their inviolate self rights. They envisioned a mechanism for change and allowed for important ideas to become accepted and eventually made into policy. They allowed for flexibility and reserved the right to get smarter. People, governments, and religions that are fundamentalized or institutionalized are rarely so open to change and, hence, dangerous. "Religions are never perfect. Great traditions have a tendency to abandon the innovative openness of their originating moments. The need to safeguard their precious heritages can gradually seal them off from the rest of the world" (Haught, 2005, p. 45).

We are not saying that the American solution is ultimately the complete answer; clearly, there are many criticisms that can be brought up about the U.S. governmental system. However, we suggest looking toward the ideals outlined in the U.S. Constitution and Declaration of Independence as ways to disentangle political aspirations from religious moralities and to check abuses of individual power, and then to resist all efforts to re-introduce religious believes into the governmental control system.

The New Axial Age?

Those who speak the language of religion have reached an impasse in their debate with those who do not. There are times when these opposing camps are less militantly inclined and are willing to talk to each other. When they do so and are acting on their best behavior, the abrasive level of dialogue ratchets down to that of a polite misunderstanding. The rules of engagement are well defined and abysmally unproductive. Sometimes, people engaging in policy (whether politicians, philanthropists, religious leaders, or scientists) will speak to each other in the language of faith, and sometimes they will speak to each other in the language of pragmatic and established fact. But it is as if they were speaking at times in German and at times in Swahili—those who do not speak these languages are left at best perplexed and at worst feeling disenfranchised. Disenfranchised people can be dangerous. Of course, leaders engaged in policy who are perplexed about the needs and demands of the governed are engaged in stirring a volatile stew. So long as secular-minded people attempt to shape policy without understanding and speaking the language of faith, nothing will be accomplished. Humanity's need for faith and the consequent power of religion is far too ingrained and primal to ignore.

We need to turn our attention away from coercion and toward root causes, and seek to neutralize the ideological conflict emanating from competing political and religious dogma. We have a tendency to demonize people who threaten us so that they are perceived more unlike us than is actually the case. (It is a well-kept secret that Republicans and Democrats share strikingly similar DNA!) And, as for religion, while it is clear that religion itself may not at times be the source of conflict, it is an unfortunate fact that, for reasons having more to do with human attributes than religious affiliations, people within the same religions—or almost the same religions—all too often attempt to destroy each other in the *name* of their so-called religious philosophy. Religion at its best is a path to understanding and, perhaps, salvation; at its worst, it merges with politics and becomes one of the most potent methods for manipulating the innocent and supporting the behavior of warriors and charlatans.

The Aryans of the Caucasian steppes built a peaceful society upon the concepts of loyalty, truth, and respect. They also believed there could be no progress, materially or spiritually, without self-sacrifice (Armstrong, 2006). Confucius taught that in order to establish oneself, one should try to establish others. Just as the new religions developed in the Axial Age and were founded upon the concepts of justice, compassion, and love, perhaps we can reinvent those concepts but with a deeper understanding of the psychological makeup of the human mind, a more holistic perspective on human culture and its various contributing forces, and the scientific explanation of the mysteries that confront us. Jung notes that "therapy can bring us insight. Then . . . courage to face what must be faced . . . and then endurance to stick it out until we arrive at the place intended for us from the beginning" (Quoted in Hollis, 2007, p. 199).

Even though our world is quickly becoming more interconnected and globalization pushes us closer and closer to every other human on the planet, we see various cultures and religions as residing in their own fishbowls, isolated in varying degrees from their neighbors who ascribe themselves to a different cultural or religious system. As long as we remain within our segregated fishbowls, we deprive ourselves of the environmental pressure necessary for our own evolution.

Changing Minds, Changing Behaviors

Religion's strongest asset as a system of control is that it leverages humanity's greatest existential fears and hopes against us in order to maintain structure and order. It appears that those motivated by religion are generally motivated by intangible and unobservable rewards: the promise of enlightenment, the end of human suffering, the immortality of the soul, perhaps a post death existence full of rapture and pleasure, and even an attainment of peace and meaning on this mortal plane. The carrot that historically successful religions dangle in front of their disciples is inexhaustible and infinitely tantalizing, promising things that can't be refuted (at least during that time period) or will never run out. Some religious leaders who have secured some degree of authority from which they can espouse their particular brand of salvation or enlightenment have learned to use this unlimited and irrefutable currency to further their own ends, no matter how benevolent or malevolent. Religious leaders are fed by the knowledge that their particular philosophy, the meme that resides in their minds, is replicating successfully, but they also can be fed by power and control.

That society would evolve to allow for such power dynamics is not surprising. There needs to be some sort of structure in any social group of any size that maintains order if that group is to be successful. Part of the evolutionary adaptive function of religion is that it prescribes very clear rules of behavior for individuals so that the group can function successfully. But religion will only work to the extent that people willingly ascribe themselves largely to the teachings of that religion. If one renounces the tenets of the religion that is governing their behaviors, they become free from that religion's bounds and are far less likely to live according to that specific religious doctrine. There is no ceremony that needs to be performed or paperwork that needs to be filed when someone renounces a set of religious teachings; all that needs to happen is a change of mind. This fact represents quite a threat to the sense of authority of religious leaders and makes it vital to indoctrinate children early for a religion to be sustained. Religions often create strict rules and taboos that formulate the cultural constraints.

Perhaps in our era, thought will emerge to provide enlightenment to the great mass of humanity unconsciously swimming within the confining fishbowl of our respective local norms. Those who accept the teachings about their God as the supreme and final word would do well to take notice if the fishbowl were opened into a lake, and even more so if they discovered, for the first time, that there was such a thing as an ocean. Those who accept that it is their holy duty to bring jihad to the infidels, those who accept only their view of God as correct, may be able to learn more about themselves and their God through an opening of possibilities. The course we set must sail through these rough waters. Our goal is to have you harness that power and use it in the name of peace, justice, and humanity, the core Confucian and Axial Age values.

We also suggest that in order to emphasize those values we can offer three guidelines for everyone on the planet, regardless of religion:

1. Do not think others should believe in your God.
2. Realize that all in the world starts within you.
3. Know that everyone has a duty to become established by seeking the truth, while respecting others.

So, while Marx was right that religion can act as an opiate—a depressant on individual imagination, creativity, and responsibility—he did not accurately describe a big part of the picture. Religion has been the major stimulant at the heart of human conflict as demonstrated by the following quote from the Old Testament. We challenge you to entertain certain possibilities that might be at odds with the letter of your religious laws so that religion can be disentangled from the politics of wealth, power, and control and become the stimulus to social and cultural righteousness.

> *As for the towns of these peoples that the Lord your God is giving you as an inheritance, you must not let anything remain alive. You shall annihilate them—the Hittites and the Amorites, the Canaanites and the Perizzites, the Hivites and the Jebusites—just as the Lord your God has commanded, so that they may not teach you to do all the abhorrent things that they do for their gods, and you sin against the Lord your God. (Deuteronomy 20:16-18)*

9

On Evolutionary Government

Government is not reason. Government is not eloquence.
It is force. And, like fire, it is a dangerous servant and a
fearful master. (George Washington)

It is vitally important that we understand the basic functions and legitimacy of government, because this is the vehicle through which public policy is most often implemented. Government, ideally, is a machine designed and maintained to facilitate the ability of its constituents to engage in the pursuit of happiness. At its worst (and many unfortunately function this way), government is one of the biggest barriers to the economic, social, or spiritual freedom of its citizens.

Selfish (N Sync)

As long as people have lived in social groups larger than the family unit there has been a need to organize those groups. Given the Fishbowl Principle, people have needed to find ways to temper their immediate hardwired selfish interests with the knowledge of potential long-term benefits that come with belonging to a group. The political philosopher Thomas Hobbes (1651) believed that without some sort of social organization, people would revert to what he called the "state of nature," a savage disposition in which selfish interest would be the rule of the day and would ultimately mean the downfall of everyone. Hobbes wrote that in order to avoid this primal person-against-person struggle, some agreement must be reached between people and an organizing structure. Namely, individuals would need to give up some degree of personal liberty and temper their own short-term interests for the sake of long-term preservation and social sustainability.

> The final cause, end, or design of men (who naturally love liberty, and dominion over others) in the introduction of that restraint upon themselves, in which we see them live in Commonwealths, is the foresight of their own preservation, and of a more contented life thereby; that is to say, of getting themselves out from that miserable condition of war which is necessarily consequent, as hath been shown, to the natural passions of men when there is no visible power to keep them in awe, and tie them by fear of punishment to the performance of their covenants. (Hobbes, 1651)

Hobbes was making a bridge between the two things that seem to be at odds in the Fishbowl Principle; he was saying that it is actually in people's best individual short-term interests to take the long view and sacrifice some independence, personal liberty, and autonomy for the sake of social stability. This is at the heart of what government is and why it is necessary: Its role is simply to balance individual short-term needs of its subjects against the needs of the larger group of constituents as a whole, which in turn secures a long-term future for each individual. Hobbes (and John Locke, Jean-Jacques Rousseau, and others who followed) called this idea the "social contract."

Hobbes's position was that the social contract would be most effective in a government that was controlled by a monarch, but as we know, that is hardly the only way to organize politically. Over the ages, humans have developed a wide variety of governmental systems, including hereditary-based monarchies (usually the leaders of these governments base their claim to power on rights bestowed by God), military dictatorships, parliamentary systems, communist regimes, tribal leadership, fascist regimes, Sharia law–based government (in which religious leaders have a direct role in shaping policy and dispensing judicial decisions), federalist democracies, and many hybrids and variants. All of these systems serve as a means to organize and establish certain social rules and power structures that are either expressly or implicitly agreed to (or enforced through coercion and force) by the governed. A government's purpose is to see to it that order is maintained and its citizens are given a degree of security. This can express itself through the use of military or police force, economic policy, social programming such as public health initiatives or public education, or protection of commonly shared resources. All successful governments do this for their citizenry in exchange for the sacrifice of certain rights and resources (such as money in the form of taxation). The social contract, then, is at the heart of our understanding of government.

A well-rounded understanding of how governments operate, where national interests should end and global interests predominate, also requires to some extent that we be students of history and anthropology. This is why we have spent so much time and effort constructing our own human story in the previous chapters of this book. Science confirms, and we hope that religion preaches, that we are all humans made of the same stuff. We are vastly more similar than we are different. We hope that all humans would believe that we should be, as brothers and sisters of the same species, entitled to the same inalienable rights, and that borders between countries should not change this fact. But we need to be honest with ourselves: Our tribal origins and our present cultural, political, and economic systems do not accept this philosophy when issues of survival are on the line.

This is so because some of our thinking predates the circumstances in which we now live. Our evolutionarily hardwired predisposition for the promotion of perceived individual short-term interest (as manifested by the male attributes of aggressiveness, valuing strength, and domination) is an inheritance from millions of years ago, and while it still has relevancy in our present time, it has to be tempered with an awareness of our more recent explosive cultural advancements. It behooves us to determine whether we are thinking and speaking our own thoughts when we discuss these issues, or those of our parents, our parents' parents' grandparents (or their religious leaders), or even our hominid ancestors who roamed the African savannahs long ago. We should understand our place in history enough to know that the answers of old may no longer hold relevance or utility for us, but that there is still much to learn from those who have gone before (even if it is the knowledge of how not to do things). While we can never (and should never) escape the intellectual environment and memes into which we have been simmering since our individual births or the birth of our species, we should make every effort

215

to realize that the world we live in now operates under very unique parameters and conditions, for which there is little historical precedent, and that the old ways can only take us so far.

The Government Meme

Government itself is a meme in the same way that religion is a meme, and it therefore stands to reason that once a form of government is created, its function is the perpetuation of itself, regardless of what the stated purpose is. Governments, like any other evolved systems, are entities established with a primary objective of protecting their own survival, and thus they are no different from people in their proclivity to take action in furtherance of their perceived short-term self-interest. Thus, in a sense, governments must adapt to their cultural environments in the same way that biological beings have to adapt to their natural environments if either wishes to survive successfully. One of the biggest differences, of course, is in composition. Organisms are made from amino acids, carbohydrates, and other organic molecules; governments are made from ideas of morality and justice (hopefully) but can also be based on other sinister values. The living creature works from a plan of genetic directions, obeying the dictates of chromosomes as it adjusts to its environment, while a government, a cultural unit, is typically founded on the unique perspective of a specific territory and the people populating it. Sometimes it is guided by tradition, and other times by revolutionary principle, but in either case government responds and adapts to the environmental stresses it encounters. As this non-carbon–based unit of evolution grows and develops within its cultural surroundings (economic, cultural, political, environmental, and diplomatic), it takes on a "life" of its own. That is, the direction of a government begins to be pushed more by the government itself and the people who control it, and perhaps less by the people who dreamed it up in the first place and the people subjected to its power. The government meme, like any other successful meme, is at the center of the picture, and we the people are simply there to carry it forward in time.

Like any entity subject to the principles of evolution, nations are collections of successful survival strategies, refined over multiple iterations of trial and error. At the core of each noble nation is the hope to protect its people and their enjoyment of land, property, and freedom, but also to ensure its own continuation. Government has proven to be an incredible social adaptation in human history, and governments that work have used invaluable survival strategies. This is especially true of societies with large populations, where the survival needs of many individuals compete with one another, and the possibilities of doing harm to another by trying to advance one's own social standing are high. And as we know, choosing to further our own cause, even at the expense of others, is something everyone can count on. In fact, the anonymity that we enjoy in populous societies may even increase our likelihood of acting selfishly. After all, who are we less likely to be concerned about and more likely to treat in an unprincipled manner: those people we know and have shared our lives with, or those we have never met? We would like complete freedom to pursue our own interests unhindered, but we know it is good that limits are placed on us in this manner. In fact, the survival of government itself depends on such limits and restrictions. This sort of structure really does give its people the freedom that they desire, as well as the ability to store and transmit the government meme to further generations.

Government And Power

What is government itself but the greatest of all reflections on human nature? If men were angels, no government would be necessary. (James Madison)

Government, simply put, is institutionalized power that can be held legitimately or through force on a largely unwilling populace. In the best-case scenario, all members of a society reach a mutual agreement on what entails "right" conduct, and if someone steps out of line, all that is needed is a friendly reminder from the rest of the group. At its worst, those in charge decide what entails right conduct and use threats of violence to enforce their vision and maintain their control. Still, in any example of government, we have a tension between competing parties simultaneously wishing to maximize their own position. If we think of separate parties having to face this choice simultaneously, we can see that the best overall option is for all parties to make a mutual agreement to minimize their own selfish choices, with the knowledge and trust that everyone else with whom we share a culture is doing the same. This is the goal of government leaders and even between governments through diplomacy and, in a sense, is what government is supposed to be all about: making sure individuals act unselfishly enough to maintain stability on a society-wide scale.

Government's power, when put into practice, can be expressed through communication, passive force, and overt force. Each of these may be applied outwardly (between societies) or internally (within societies). The expression of power through communication is achieved internally in an open society through the public debate of its government's members, and in a more dictatorial scenario, through control of the media. Externally, power is applied through communication via diplomacy aimed at the leaders of other nations and propaganda aimed at their citizens. Passive force is expressed internally by legislation and the judicial process, and is expressed internally and externally with economic regulations that manipulate conduct through secondary reinforcements such as subsidies, tax breaks, tariffs, and treaties. Overt force is expressed internally through police power and externally through military action. We can think of power applied through passive or overt forces as operating under a behaviorist paradigm: Humans, like any other organism, will change their behavior according to differential schedules of rewards and punishments. Power expressed through communication is meant to address people's underlying beliefs and thoughts, which in turn will cause them to change their behavior. This tactic is similar to that of religion as a system of control: change minds in order to change behavior. The use

Bruce Gendelman

"Power"

of force and other behavioral techniques is successful at their goals of modifying behavior, but only as successful as they are able to deliver rewards and punishments. It is useful to understand why societies with different viewpoints hold their beliefs, and also to understand whether a given set of actions is likely to win hearts and minds or achieve the opposite result. While government, as a meme, would like to replicate itself with 100% fidelity in the best-case scenario, the reality is that sometimes the costs of persuading its citizens is just too high, and the government itself must evolve if it wishes to survive. Government constitutes a social contract, and we can think of it as an autonomous entity, but we also need to remember that governments are made up of independently functioning individuals, just as our body is made up of independently functioning cells. And just like our body's cells, each individual who makes up a given government will tend to make decisions that benefit themselves as individuals.

One of the most common and effective methods in which governments work toward their own success is through their vested interest in developing nationalistic themes as a means to promote cohesiveness in their subjects. This is the exertion of force via communication embodied, the glue that enhances "buy-in" from the citizenry, and the thing that, in effect, fastens power to those at the helm. When individuals fail to primarily identify with their government's nationalistic theme, tradeoffs must occur, and that government must work harder to incorporate itself into individuals' self-schemata. For example, if I think of myself first as a Sunni and only secondarily as a Saudi, my Saudi government must make concessions or I will not cede to it the power it wants over me. If I identify myself first as a Jew (or Mormon, Southern Baptist, Hawaiian, Republican, gay, black, or animal rights activist) and only secondarily as an American, my leaders may have to wave enticements other than the red, white, and blue to get me to buy into the American dream. In the ideal case, we find a personal affiliation with our governments on our own. However, because governments by their very nature exert their power in order to prevent us from attaining certain selfish desires, the ideal case is almost never the actual case. Therefore, we find in our world that governments must work very hard to bring their citizenry into the fold. In other words, having a government does not automatically mean that you have a nation.

What Defines Nations?

It is worth briefly exploring what sets governments apart from one another, what makes them unique. On the most concrete level, governments (and countries by extension) are defined by their political borders. Many of us look at a world map and see two adjacent swaths of land painted different colors, and we accept that this represents an agreed-upon line, where one government operates on one side of the line, and another government operates on the other. Putting aside the fact that many political borders correspond to physical geography (such as rivers or mountain ranges), national boundaries are largely constructed by historical incident and social convention, based on victories in tribal disputes and sometimes even by mere accident. Because tensions arise from agreement over where these lines should fall, once they have been drawn or redrawn, they become quite real. And we, the inheritors of such tribal disputes, become conditioned to cling to the idea of "our country" with intense national pride.

Humans developed as tribal cultures, and purely as a matter of survival individuals owed unwavering loyalty to their tribe. Today we hold onto these notions in the name of what we call nationalism or patriotism, and fail to account for the fact that through globalization—with global instant communication, a global economy, global environmental impact, and global political issues—we can think of ourselves as one very large tribe, but governed much more locally. Many thousands of years of governmental evolution have brought us more than 200 national and tens of thousands of local entities, all with different forms and rules. Earth currently has kingdoms, parliamentary democracies, republics (representative, people's, and cooperative), monarchies, dictatorships (civilian and military), commonwealths, grand duchies, confederations, principalities, states (united and one papal), unions, sultanates, emirates, tribes, and at least one Jamahiriya. And within each of these nations, we find remnants of that tribal survival instinct: nationalism.

Nationalism at its heart has proven dangerous, but how we love our invisible little boundaries. We have seen time and time again the effects of such subjective moral reasoning in international relations and throughout history. When Hitler was promoting a policy of hatred toward Jews in Germany, but not yet known to be engaged in genocide and in pursuing the policy of *lebensraum* (living space) by invading much of Europe and Russia, was it in the national interest of England to oppose him preemptively? The story, as it unfolded, yielded no as an answer. Then, was it in Britain's national interest to get involved only when its own borders and people were threatened? History tells us yes. More generally, is it an appropriate national interest for a nation to promote its political beliefs on other nations for their own perceived good?

Governments and nations are entities that are far more abstract and complicated than individuals, so it is often difficult to determine what the best course of action would be in terms of furthering national interest. A nation's government often chooses its allies and enemies according to how those allies and enemies will further that nation's agenda. This, however, can operate at several different levels, and those levels can sometimes be at odds with one another. For example, the United States supports Israel with more foreign aid, per capita, than any other country in the world (Tarnoff & Nowels, 2004) for ideological and moral reasons, in spite of the fact that its economic interests in securing good relations with oil-producing enemies of Israel might suggest a different course of action. In almost all cases nations will act to further the policies that will satisfy their more basic needs first, and worry about higher order needs later. This is akin to individuals satisfying their basic physiological needs before others; the psychologist Abraham Maslow implies this in his famous hierarchy of needs. Maslow's theory (1943, pp. 370-396) essentially says we must ensure the basic needs of food and shelter before we can have any hope at working on higher order personal needs, such as the promotion of morals or self-actualization. Nations and governments work in a similar way. Issues that impact a nation's base quality of life will get first priority, even if that nation's leaders try to reframe the issue as a moral one. This is the likely reason why we see a vested U.S. interest in countries such as Saudi Arabia: They have something that dramatically affects our base quality of life.

Has the morality of our human culture evolved beyond the survival instincts present in the rest of the species living in the world, where the fittest take what they need to survive and prosper? We have not yet found an adequate cultural solution to the biological imperatives that govern us all, but it may be instructive to rework our idea of religious, tribal, racial, gender, or national borders with the knowledge that these political boundaries by and large are culturally constructed. In reality, we are all connected, and increasingly so. Ideally, yet naively, this realization should be enough to do away with detrimental thinking, to coax us out of our fishbowls and into the much larger ocean that covers our world.

Another important defining feature of governments is an agreed-upon central idea that becomes a foundational text or teaching. When government and religious domains overlapped, religious texts also doubled as governmental treatises. Indeed, most religious texts were penned with government in mind, and we can see this clearly if we care to browse the *Tao Te Ching*, the Old Testament, the Hindu *Vedas*, Martin Luther's *95 Theses*, or any number of other religious texts. Some of the most famous secular writings in human history also have been instructions for government. The Code of Hammurabi, perhaps the best archaeological evidence we have of legal systems in early civilizations, is itself a set of laws that were meant to sustain Babylonian society by protecting the rights of citizens and preserving the power of their rulers.

Plato's *Republic*, even now a foundational text to students of political science and law, is an account of how government was set up in ancient Greece. And in the modern United States, the Declaration of Independence and Constitution are among the greatest national treasures.

Of course, countries still exist in which religious texts double as political precedent. While we want to believe that the intent of any religious text is inherently good, we are also aware that they are open to personal interpretation, and those interpretations cover more varied ground than interpretations of legal texts. As was discussed in the previous chapter, it is very hard to find common ground on matters of faith, and because of this the most successful and stable free nations employ a cogent and unambiguous secular text as their founding documents. Some nations that still rely on religious texts are stable and successful by some measures, but this is mostly because of the stringent autocratic style of rule in such countries.

A final, more controversial, defining feature of governments is some sort of commonality between its citizens. As we have discussed, tribal societies shared religion and culture, and because of smaller populations and clear observable differences between neighboring cultures, there was little confusion about which group an individual belonged to. It was astonishingly simple, so much so that nobody had to think twice about it: You belonged to the group you were born into. As such, at one point there may have been genetics that all members of a nation shared, which would handily tie nationalistic tendencies to evolutionary kin-selection theories for most of human history. In other words, promoting the success of one's social group and promoting the success of one's genes were the same for the vast majority of our time on earth.

Indeed, as we might imagine, genes diffused as human culture grew in its ability to organize and mobilize larger groups of people. Genetic differences between neighboring cultures became more homogenized, and genetic differences within each tribal group increased. In our modern world, we would be hard-pressed to identify any genetic differences that correspond to political borders, and as such the potential commonalities to which we refer are largely cultural and ideological.

The Evolved Government

In beginning to unearth the roots of our current governmental structures, we hope to shed a little more light on what makes government and politics work. And in doing this, we hope to empower ourselves to be at once critical and constructive of the governments that impact our individual lives. This sort of understanding is not accessible only to academics, lifetime politicians, or lobbyists; we firmly believe that everyone can understand the fundamental driving forces of government because those forces are the same ones that drive us.

Like anything else related to living beings that exists on earth, be it genetic or cultural, governments evolved over time. Those forms of government that were not able to sustain themselves faded from the world scene, while those that thrived became larger, more widespread, and more pervasive. Students of history would point out that no single form of government has been so successful to last intact for more than a couple hundred years at most, and we can attribute this to the ever-changing cultural environment to which governments must adapt. There have been very rigid forms of governments that have worked in the short term, and others that mandate strict adherence to fundamentalist religious views that have lasted longer, but ultimately fundamental human desires that affect culture governments must ultimately be flexible and adaptable or will be overthrown in the long term. This flexibility seems to be increasingly true today, when culture changes and evolves at an ever-accelerating rate. This is precisely why fundamentalists feel so threatened by Western influences in their countries.

As with any other replicating unit (gene or meme), governments are continually biased toward themselves and will always act to promote their own short-term survival before anything else (as determined by the memes of those individuals and groups that truly hold the power or pockets of power from time to time). This perspective may sound dour and pessimistic, but we believe that given our evolutionary heritage, it is a realistic and practical premise we all need to understand when we think about governments. Surely, if one were to pursue a course of action that threatens any government, they would find themselves fighting directly against a well-established and fortified system of control, desperately paddling upstream in already choppy waters. This is true whether it is a democratic movement in China or Iran, or civil rights protestors in the United States in the 1960s. History shows us that controlling ideas or memes can be changed over time, perhaps generations, but ideas are continually shaped by people and events and some one or some group is always behind those changes. Another outcome of this self-serving bias, is that in order to rally their citizens under one banner, governments tend to use ideas (or propaganda) to focus on differences rather than similarities, invoking "the Others," the metaphorical tribe on the other side of the river, or as George Orwell's brilliant polemic and social satire *1984* portrays, the eternal, ever-threatening but never-seen enemies of the protagonist's home state of Oceania. These political sleights of hand do work but when unveiled, they begin to fall short of their intended goal. It is far easier to unite people against a common enemy than it is to unite them around a shared interest, but it is exactly these shared interests that we must tease out of our individual needs if we hope to move forward.

In this light, we would like to start with a very optimistic idea, one that is well understood by policy makers worldwide. Namely, it is that an educated populace will make the best decisions most of the time. There are three qualifiers here: that the populace is, in fact, educated (the topic for Chapter 11); that the populace is large enough that the summation of people's needs and interests realistically reflects the people themselves; and that there is a free flow of information. These ideas are the kernel of democracy. We know that in the natural world, diversity makes for stability and strength, and we feel that this is no different when it comes to decision-making power in the political arena. Even then, though, the simple majority may not be trusted (and certainly was not trusted by the U.S. framers). Variations on democratic governance, such as a representative democracy and the need for supermajority votes, have evolved as more modern forms of government, in order to balance competing interests and to keep change from happening too radically or too fast.

This Government Needs a Tune Up (The Beastie Boys)

Because the United States represents the first modern successful implementation of a secular democracy in history, and because the United States commands such power on the world stage at present, we feel that our home country is an important case study deserving of our attention. We should neither undervalue nor overvalue the importance of how the U.S. government functions on the world stage. Over the past 200 years, those who value basic human rights have emulated our model. We have at times been flattered through imitation; at other times, our government has imposed its system on other countries by coercive means ranging from economic leverage to outright military force. The U.S. system works well for its citizens and can be adapted to other environments and work similarly well, but it appears that the U.S. system will only work when the environment into which it is placed is similar to that of the culture of the United States. Trying to implement a variation of the U.S. government in foreign cultural environments that look much different from ours can be like dropping a polar bear in the desert: It has simply not evolved to be successful in that environment. More often than not our nationalistic pride and our tribal myopia prevent us from seeing this, but we would do well to remember that our perceptions of reality are quite subjective, and that we need to allow for multiple perspectives in this new ocean we have been emptied into. Recent international efforts to instill democracy in foreign countries such as Vietnam, Iraq, and Afghanistan serve as evidence of the latest in a long line of largely unsuccessful attempts to create an American-style democracy in the heart of countries defined by artificial borders, not borne of common cultural homogeneity, perceived shared political objectives, or national loyalty. Whatever positive objective we may have wished to achieve, clearly our means have not met the test of the facts on the ground.

There are aspects of the U.S. government that have worked wonderfully, possibly better than any other government in human history. The structure of government for the United States was designed to place power in the electorate, establish basic liberties, and protect the citizenry (originally white male landowners) from the potential for abuse of power by their government. The Declaration of Independence itself states:

Governments are instituted among men, deriving their just powers from the consent of the governed. That whenever any form of government becomes destructive to these ends, it is the right of the people to alter or to abolish it, and to institute new government, laying its foundation on such principles and organizing its powers in such form, as to them shall seem most likely to effect their safety and happiness.

The founders of the United States (themselves revolutionaries from the British point of view) were acutely concerned with placing too much power in the hands of any individual, or even group of individuals. When it came to what they deemed to be "inalienable rights," they wanted to be assured that these rights would be protected from periodic emotional disruptions of the populace, and on the subject of personal freedoms they were willing to die for, they not only wanted to be protected from centralized power, but also from the passing whims of even a majority of their neighbors. As a result, the framers of the Constitution created a highly flexible system in which change over time (evolution) was not only anticipated, it was prepared for. The rule of law rather than the rule of man is at the core of the success of our government.

Recognizing the importance of allowing for change over time was an enormous leap from the absolute monarchy from which the United States sprang. It took a great deal of consensus and humility, but these were key steps toward stability. The founders of our country were very careful to not place too much power in the hands of any one person or governmental entity; they knew as we do now, that power will corrupt. Instead, their system of checks and balances ensured that different divisions of government were accountable to one another and oversaw one another's work. While this often proves frustrating, it provides for stability and the system has stood the test of time.

Moreover, the founders correctly viewed fast change as being potentially very dangerous, and they encouraged such changes to come about at rates that were relatively slow and, therefore, more manageable. The mechanism that was installed to incite such changes was two-fold: judicial review and the ability of citizens to vote to replace elected representatives and to modify the Constitution. Judicial review ensured that laws, once thought to be immutable cultural monoliths, could be molded and shaped to the needs of the day. The founders of the United States, therefore, did not rely on any group of absolute principles, other than the principle that Charles Darwin named 83 years after the Declaration of Independence was issued: Everything changes in response to its environment. Another strength of the U.S. government is that it has found a way to manage incredibly large and diverse populations and areas by subdividing responsibilities and jurisdictions at different levels of society, all the way from local governments to the federal government. The tension between federal and local control, again, is sometimes frustrating to certain individuals in positions of decision-making power, but it ultimately provides stability to the government as a whole. The balance between local interest and national (or even international) interest is not as clear as it once was. From its inception, the U.S. system of government jealously protected the rights of states from intrusion of an overly powerful federal government. A final strength of the U.S. government that we would like to mention here is its advocacy for a free and unbiased media. The First Amendment guarantees freedom of the press, and its presence in our founding documents has ensured that the government's business is not legally conducted in secret and that the government is ultimately held accountable to its citizenry. Recently, however certain media outlets have been given the freedom from regulation to be platforms for one-sided viewpoints, and to be used to further agendas exactly opposite from those originally intended.

> Our Founders' faith in the viability of representative democracy rested on their trust in the wisdom of a well-informed citizenry, their ingenious design for checks and balances, and their belief that the rule of reason is the natural sovereign of a free people. The Founders took great care to protect the openness of the marketplace of ideas so that knowledge could flow freely. Thus they not only protected freedom of assembly, they made a special point—in the First Amendment—of protecting the freedom of the printing press. (Gore, 2007)

Robert Caro's 1990 book on U.S. President Lyndon B. Johnson described in detail how Johnson forever changed the rules in his campaign for U.S. Senator, using radio as the device for "informing" voters *en masse* of the simplest message that could be packaged and purchased like toothpaste. Interest groups have amassed disproportionate power through organizational structures in which money buys access, and they are the dominant influence today in representative democracy. A counter to this was the successful candidacy of U.S. President Barack Obama, which proved that a vigorous grassroots movement could be created by using Internet technology and broad mass appeal. It seems as though history shows that above all else true democracy requires a healthy, unbiased, free, and functioning media. When individuals only hear the "facts" and arguments from one viewpoint, a false sense of reality is created. These non-discerning audiences are subject to biased reporting (otherwise called propaganda) that is designed to influence opinions rather than report on the facts.

There are also aspects to the U.S. government that have not worked, and continue to not work, despite over 200 years of opportunities for evolution. Many of the government's shortcomings stem from the friction between its self-serving pursuits and those of the people who use its power for their own selfish ends, as evidenced by some government officials being susceptible to corruption to some degree or another. Leaders whose campaigns were supported by special interest groups may often find themselves continually answerable to those groups whose interests do not necessarily run in alignment with the societal long term "best interests." We are able to conceptualize a government as its own entity, a self-sustaining, replicating unit, but we also must keep in mind that a government is comprised of individual people, themselves self-sustaining, replicating units with needs of their own. And although the government meme is contained and transmitted from mind to mind, those persons must bow to the perceived needs of the individual if the two come into conflict. After all, if people don't survive, the ideas of government that they carry with them will not survive either, which is exactly at the root of the case made by those want to maintain power at any cost (genocide being the ultimate meme purifying example).

The U.S. government has proven to be thus far successful in the face of imperfection, adversity, and shortcomings. It is a meme that is evolutionarily stable in its current cultural environment because of its flexibility and evolution in law and in placing power in laws before people. However, the government meme is not invulnerable in all nations and at all times, even in the United States. We can conjure images of the lawless state after Hurricane Katrina to remind us that government can break down very quickly in trying times. In the process of evolution, certain things may be tried and discarded or other things refined. After more than 200 years of checks and balances and majorities making slow changes, the U.S. government has evolved beyond the inclusion of only white males and allows and encourages participation of all non-felon citizens who are eighteen years or older in its representative democracy. To this day, the U.S. model stands as one of the most enduring exemplars of a government that works.

Government, Violence, and War

For all our successes, our clout, and our rich history on the world stage, the U.S. government is currently experiencing challenges to its status as the world's leader and dramatic transformations on the domestic front as we face several serious trials as a country and as a world community. The government meme needs to adapt to the evolution of other world trends, such as globalizing technology, economic shifts, climate change, and overpopulation. In this time of rapid worldwide transformation, the emerging importance of tribal and borderless systems of government cannot be safely ignored. It is not that any government will remove itself if it is not respectful of its citizens and citizens of the world, because governments, as we define them, would never willfully remove themselves. Rather, it is that the things that define nations (physical borders, shared national interest, foundational texts or teachings, commonalities among citizenry) have never been so pliable, so widely distributable, and so easily accessible. Before, our communities were limited by physical location: our neighborhood, our towns, and our cities. Now, in the age of information, our communities can transcend physical space quite easily. We may find kinship with people halfway around the world, while at the same time we may not share an interest in the same religious or political theories as our neighbors. Culture is changing, and government needs to keep up with that change if it is to be successful.

Before in human history, war amounted to soldier classes, with various degrees of armaments, attacking each other. This is tragic but not nearly as tragic as what is possible in the age of advanced military technology. This at once increases our capability for destruction far beyond anything the human organism is built to manage on its own and makes possible widespread calamity, particularly if those who hold the religious beliefs that the eternal afterlife is the ultimate goal obtain nuclear weapons. There are tremendous limitations in the effectiveness of the outcome or aftermath of war in the age of nuclear weapons and terrorism. We have invested in wars that cannot be won in the traditional sense, wars that are waged not against fixed and finite foes but against abstract concepts and problems driven by the darker sides of human nature. We do not suggest that there is one approach to fomenting peace between governments, or that war is never an option. We do suggest, however, that war is always a terrible option and that it will inevitably create unintended and unforeseen consequences and thus must always be viewed as a last resort. As an example, American leaders have said we are engaged in a war against terrorism. But terrorism is tactics used by groups who lack standing armies yet wish to exert power through force. If we were to be more thoughtful about the battle we would recognize that we cannot eliminate terrorism as a tactic and that as long as that is our goal, we will always be on the defense. Thus, if we really want to "take the fight to them," we will first and foremost recognize that terrorism is a symptom of a war of ideas. Once this is acknowledged, the next step is to learn the lessons of history, which demonstrate that force may achieve many ends, but never has it proven to be an effective way to change *how people think*. And this, really, is the purpose of the Ark we are attempting to build: to ask people to reflect and learn about what it means to be a person and what responsibility one has to others.

A good starting point in influencing governments is to adopt the operating premise that governments will inevitably act out of self-preservation first. We challenge you to find finding ways to define and promote the basic rights, freedoms, and responsibilities that all humans are entitled to within those parameters. We can then start to identify global public policy initiatives that can be implemented to move toward these ideals in an effort to bring our species in fold with a sustainable and commonly agreed-upon moral future. In order to accept the basic

231

rights of all humans, governments will need to be convinced or changed from within, that accepting these is in fact an adaptive measure, one that will ensure their own survival and stability.

All Around The World The Same Song (C.K. Williams)

It is apparent that governments have evolved into an incredibly complex and diverse system designed to achieve various types of control over every inch of land and every person living on Earth. The diversity of geographical and cultural conditions currently in existence on the planet highlights the difficulty in achieving global solutions, but we believe that in an age of globalization, problems must be addressed on this level. We again invoke lessons from evolutionary biology and suggest that diversity of opinion and background, coupled with strategies that are positive memes such as creative energy and courageous sustained will, are the means by which we can break the glass of our respective fishbowls and identify the common ground on which a sustainable and stable future can develop.

Efforts at governmental cooperation are as old as civilization, but never before have had we had the means and reason to attempt to work toward solutions on a unified global scale. Those efforts that have been met with success have been built on common objectives that would take the survival and stability needs of all participating parties into account. The history of humankind has seen many attempts made at unifying diverse tribes. These attempts are usually local or geographically related (the EU), based on a common ancestry or religious belief (Catholicism around the world), or done by brute force (the Golden Horde). In each case, attempts were made to align and unify through shared culture. The obvious failure of the "business plan" of our species when it comes to government is that there is a lack of standardization. There is no single set of declared rules of conduct that apply globally. While it may have been true that global forms of government or standardized laws at what rights each person has were not necessary in the past, in many ways it is no longer true. The world of humans is a complicated mixture of groups of people, who are likely to disagree more often than not. "An international society, however, exists only when states in an international system have common interests and common values, conceive themselves to be bound by a common set of rules, share in the working of common institutions, and have a common culture" (Huntington, 1996). We have documents that establish widely accepted doctrines of behavior, to be sure: The Ten Commandments address individual behavior, and the Geneva Convention addresses permissible conduct in war, as examples, but we do not have a universally accepted Ten Commandments for how governments and the nations that house them should treat each other or their people. Is it time to develop one? Part of the project here is to outline a value system upon which all nations can agree, but before we concern ourselves with abstract ideas such as morality, we should take some time to explore the more concrete and tangible roots of conflict and of control. Remember Maslow's needs hierarchy for us to be able to deal with higher order political theory: we would need to ensure that the basic needs of nations and their people are met and that resources are equitably distributed to the people of the world. A set of principles and theories already exists for how to accomplish this, as well as an entire academic discipline: economics. Economics, at any level, is also a study of resource allocation, which is another way of implementing power and control. This will be our topic for the next chapter.

10

On Evolutionary Economy and Energy

Working largely independently of government and on a day-to-day basis, economics are systems of control that influence how people, businesses, and countries behave with respect to the flow of goods and services within the system of rules established by government. In order to be effective in developing solutions, it is important to have at least a basic understanding of this complex mechanism. If you have such an academic or practical knowledge feel free to move on to Chapter 11 where you will learn about learning.

Economics is the discipline that analyzes how decisions about hiring, firing, borrowing, spending, saving, buying, selling, investing, trading, and printing money interact with each other. During the past 75 years, the discipline of economics has benefited from mathematical modeling and empirical research, including the psychological underpinnings of economic decision making, and has divided into two main fields: macroeconomics (the study of large economic systems) and microeconomics (the study of individual decision making). Economic issues intersect with the lives of everyone, regardless of their belief systems, and affect people on a daily basis. Economic policy is an extremely powerful meme and provides great hope for overcoming the Fishbowl Principle because it is one area where we already have a good bit of experience in adjusting our short-term wants for long-term needs, and because it is a system of control in which people tend to assume they are acting at least partly by choice, as opposed to direct government intervention.

A common economic strategy to overcoming the difficult odds of surviving is for people to band together, forming interpersonal alliances and pooling resources to increase the chances of success. This strategy should sound familiar, as simple molecules floating in primitive Earth's atmosphere used a similar strategy. Those molecules that successfully bonded together in a mutually beneficial way survived and were the predecessors of cells and higher organisms. It should also sound familiar because it is exactly what social animals do when presented with a challenge or stress, and as we have seen, humans are the most social of animals. Humans have evolved to value cooperation and collaboration as survival strategies, and it should be no different with economic survival. Those individuals who band together into a more stable economic diverse organism usually (but not always) have advantages over those who fend for themselves. This sort of behavior is the foundation for "higher order" artificial entities such as corporations, partnerships, joint ventures, mutual funds, hedge funds, cooperative housing, labor unions, and the (aptly named) nuclear family.

Take This Job And Shove It (Johnny Paycheck)

Each person on the planet is a consumer. It is our biological nature to consume, and in this culture, we are able to consume only to the extent we accumulate money or credit. This system is based on the principles that people are motivated to contribute to themselves and hence society. Because governments obtain the funds they use to operate by, in general, taxing workers, these workers become invested in their government's policies (and because they are subject to the rules imposed on by the government). Workers are the producers in our society, and the responsibility of supporting non-producers falls onto their shoulders. The simple fact that humans are pressured by culture into contributing time, talent, and energy to the economic system to receive compensation is itself a system of control. Other than the very lucky and the very unlucky, we have no choice but to work.

Humans today are similar to primitive humans and to animals in striving to acquire what we need to survive. But with the development of the meme of working in exchange for money, our culture put a new twist on the story of adaptation. Distant ancestors and fellow animals adapted physical and behavioral traits in order to find and secure food or territory; to become productive workers humans have adapted intellectually and culturally. The ability to contribute to the economy is, in many ways, the key survival strategy. It replaces original survival strategies, which involved learning direct coping mechanisms for interacting with and obtaining needs from the environment. Now there is a layered and extremely indirect system in which each aspect of survival is highly subdivided into minute tasks, the vast majority of which are performed by others. After the most basic food and shelter needs have been fulfilled, most humans tend to move on to accumulating additional resources. Accumulating a surplus reservoir of money usually requires extraordinary amounts of labor, a highly specialized skill, a high degree of discipline through savings and non-consumption, good luck, or a combination of these factors.

Families are unique in the sense that they combine aspects of biological and cultural bonding, and it is for this reason that society values the family as one of its strongest and most revered institutions. Family groups have hierarchies, with established divisions of labor. In almost all societies, until very recently in human evolution and history, the male provided while the female focused on household tasks and caretaking for children. These gender norms have changed significantly in the Western world in the past 40 years, but are still prevalent in many parts of the world.

Whether they choose to form cooperative economic bonds or not, a great many people (the majority of humans on Earth today) spend their entire lives in a subsistence mode of operation. Those fortunate enough to accumulate excess wealth will move on to things they want but do not necessarily need to survive. As cultures and societies develop, the consumption choices increase, and as wealth increases, the amount of consumption also usually increases. There is subjectivity involved in defining what constitutes a luxury, and the definition varies from culture to culture.

I'm All Right, Jack, Keep Your Hands Off My Stack
(Pink Floyd)

The free market is not altruistic. Its guiding principle is something like "If you are able to accumulate wealth, then you should." This holds even though there are people who could feed themselves and their children for years with the amount of money a celebrity spends on one night of merrymaking. For those with significant financial means, the largest yacht, grandest parties, most precious jewels, rarest works of art, most luxurious travel, biggest and most numerous homes can be the objects of competition. It is interesting to ponder the evolutionary adaptive utility of such pursuits. The answers probably lie more in the realm of psychology than economics or biology. It is no accident that historically one of the paths chosen by people wishing to devote themselves to spiritual pursuit is to divest themselves of the trappings of material wealth. For much of the world, luxury is an abstract concept. Those able to indulge in luxuries, those most successfully adapted to their economic environment, offer best non-institutional avenues to help heal the world. Philanthropically oriented endeavors of the well-to-do represent some of the most effective methods by which the fishbowls or the suffering are made better by providing connections with humanity that advance the causes of peaceful sustainability in the world.

> *Fame or integrity: which is more important?*
> *Money or happiness: which is more valuable?*
> *Success or failure: which is more destructive?*
>
> *If you look to others for fulfillment,*
> *you will never truly be fulfilled.*
> *If your happiness depends on money,*
> *you will never be happy with yourself.*
>
> *Be content with what you have;*
> *rejoice in the way things are.*
> *When you realize there is nothing lacking,*
> *the whole world belongs to you.*

(*Tao Te Ching*. Chapter 44. Steven Mitchell translation)

I Said, Oh Oh, Domino (Van Morrison)

The macroeconomist's task is to use and measure broad national-based monetary and fiscal policies designed to impact small (microeconomic) interactions in a desired way, decided by government and almost always controversial. Sometimes, it is decided that the desired way is to promote spending and investment, and thus to implement policies that increase the flow of money into the system. Sometimes, it is decided that the desired way is to reduce or prevent inflation, and thus to cut back on the money supply so that prices do not keep rising, even though this will usually be at the expense of some people's jobs. But what makes macroeconomics really complicated in a global economy is that countries are making their own sets of economic policy decisions, sometimes in concert with—and sometimes in reaction and opposition to—decisions being made by other governments. At its base all governments to one degree or another are in economic competition with all others.

Most macroeconomic study focuses on ways to manipulate fiscal and monetary policy to achieve that sweet spot of growth, stability, and productivity: the balancing act where inflation and deflation are avoided, while providing incentives for utility and resources for those unable to provide for themselves. Economic theory derives insight from the study of ecology, with its focus on how organisms in an environment interact with each other and with their environment. In both ecological and economic systems, every action by one unit (a biological organism or an economic transaction) affects, to a greater or lesser degree, every other unit in the system (biological environment or economy), as well as the overall functioning of the system. As an organic system, an economy is incredibly complex and is always morphing, slipping and sliding, growing, and dying. When taken at its largest level, this thing called "the economy" is like a huge, complex, multi-headed organism, highly evolved, always looking to feed itself with resources and to purge itself of waste. Economists, the scientists who study this leviathan, dissect it in order to understand it so they can better predict and alter its behavior.

Harvard Professor of Economics Gregory Mankiw (2008) describes the process in making individual decisions at the margins; he conceptualizes people as autonomous decision-making machines who will do whatever they can to make choices in which they receive more than what they lose. And ultimately, it is the individual's actions that dictate the path of any economic system. Adam Smith identified the basic "invisible hand" in commerce as the underlying concept that each person acts in his or her self-interest, which then provides for the goods and services that are most desired.

Economic decision-making and growth evolve. When given the opportunity, people will tend to act to benefit themselves in the short term before they act to benefit others in the long term. People, of course, do not make their choices in isolation from one another. It is just the opposite, in fact: every choice one makes affects the potential choices of the interrelated people and vice versa. It is thus the sum total of many "selfish" acts that causes the flow of products and services from person to person, business to business, and country to country. The aggregation of these interactions is referred to as a market, and the mechanism by which markets operate is central to economic theory.

Leaving aside for the moment centrally planned economies, it is this aggregation of choices that makes a free-market economy an efficient means by which to distribute goods and services. It encourages specialists to emerge with particular skill sets, which in turn allows for variety in the choices available to consumers. It also regulates the prices and quantities of things sold in the market, guided by the invisible hand of aggregate consumer choices (assuming there is true competition). Until now, it has been assumed that these transactions were taking place in an entirely free market, but that does not actually exist.

The ability of a country's economy to produce and deliver goods and services directly affects the standard of living of its citizens; the average income of a nation's workers rises as its economy's overall productivity grows. Thus, there is a tribal quality to the desire of people in any country to want their government to promote their economy to the exclusion of others. Protectionism is what happens when the invisible hand arm-wrestles with our tribal instincts to benefit local businesspeople. It is a controversial policy because it instinctively makes sense at the local level, but often backfires and harms the people it was designed to protect.

There are many other instances where governments step in and manipulate the free market based on policy choices. Sometimes there is a strong desire or need for oversight, as in the case of antipollution legislation enacted to prevent water and air supplies from being inundated with toxic substances. Another instance where even so-called free-market governments manipulate the economy is with regard to control of the money supply. Keep in mind that money is an abstraction: It consists of paper or coins that *represent* value and that are not themselves intrinsically valuable. The mints where money is made are controlled by each nation's government, which decides how much of the stuff to produce. Once again, like any other commodity, when supply goes up, value goes down. Thus, when a government prints large quantities of money, the value of the money falls in relation to other economies (unless its valuation is readjusted based upon an objective standard of wealth or production). This in turn causes prices to increase, because now more of the same money is needed to buy the same goods and services. A government may also vary the interest rate on loans it makes to banks to increase or decrease the flow of money, and it can affect interest rates indirectly by its decisions regarding how much money it borrows from other countries. Again, like any other commodity, abundance of supply usually leads to reduction of price, and vice versa. Thus, if a country is borrowing a lot of money, it is reducing the supply of money available for people (or businesses or countries) who want to borrow, and interest rates go up to allocate the resource.

The entire system has an organic nature that makes it in aggregate hard to control and predict. The divisions of labor within an economy reflect the biological benefits of diversity in any ecological system, and here the system is human culture. Specialization of labor also creates a great deal of interdependence, as those who know how to make their own blouse may also have the knowledge and access to milk their own cow, but they are highly unlikely to have the ability to make their own car, and they are even less likely able to drill for the fuel to run it. Because humans are hardwired and primed for social interaction, it is no surprise that one of our most pervasive and enduring memes has evolved in order to require us to trade with one another and depend on one another.

One can also see the evolutionary components of protectionist trade policies, in that economic isolation stems from our natural tendency to worry about our own fishbowls and treat other fishbowls as different, competitive, and threatening. Sometimes, some of the occupants of the other fishbowls are all three, but the fish are virtually identical genetically, and the cultural differences are generally decreasing due to globalization. Perhaps one should be mindful of this the next time he buys bananas grown in Central America, shoes made in Southeast Asia, or a "Made in the U.S." automobile constructed with electrical components assembled in India and a chassis made from metal mined in Russia. We live and consume in a global economy. Due to the acceleration of globalization, the specialization of labor, the development of rapid transportation, and the breathtaking speed at which electronic information, including money, flows to virtually all parts of the world, interdependence of this system is inextricably linked to our standard of living and even for our ultimate survival as a species.

But if You Try Sometime, You Just Might Find
(Rolling Stones)

It is worth taking a moment to review the history of economic systems that have been used to determine or influence how goods and services are allocated. History has demonstrated that some work better than others, but the ideal is elusive because the fortunes of any economic system will in large part be dictated by factors such as political stability; geographic access to trade through ports or bordering countries; population size; proximity of hostile neighbors; and availability of education, technology, and natural resources. But the degree of success or failure of any form of governmental or economic system is ultimately going to be determined by the ability of the system itself to effectively respond on an ongoing basis to the specific stresses and demands of the place and culture in which it exists. The economic systems still in effect have therefore continued to evolve alongside the human species and our culture.

In prehistoric times, economic systems were far simpler than they are today. The primary factor was the scarcity of resources. The labor pool was far less specialized, there were fewer people involved in each system, resource availability was far less extensive, the opportunity to trade with other societies was much more limited, and opportunities to accumulate wealth were determined to a greater extent than now by luck of ancestry. Moreover, what we would now call religious values often mandated a tribal or group approach to survival as opposed to an approach where individual benefit was most valued. Work, for most of human history, was directly tied to the necessities of life.

It was during the industrial revolution of the 1700s and 1800s that work became more removed from the means of survival. Food became more plentiful due to the industrialization of agriculture, which had a direct effect on population growth. One of the most numerous and "natural" checks on population growth is the horrible death from starvation. With the exponential surge in population came a corresponding surge in the capacity for production, which created a need for a more specialized and diverse labor pool. With such changes came new twists on the old problem of how to distribute resources. This problem persists to the present and has only increased in its complexity, as the world has grown more interconnected.

In recent history, there have been two predominant schools of thought when it comes to deciding how to best allocate resources in a large population: capitalism or socialism. The popularity of these philosophies over time has been affected by political vicissitudes, and both systems have advantages and disadvantages. Some of the debate regarding them is academic, in that purely socialist forms of government are very rare, and there has never been a government where the market was completely free (i.e., all economic decisions being determined by the market without any intervention or influence by the government). The purest national systems of socialism have been failures. Karl Marx advocated a socialist, centrally planned system that made all means of production a function of the collective good. History reveals that this system, as implemented by Lenin, Stalin, Mao, Castro, and others, created a perversion of basic human motivations that ultimately led to great inefficiencies, abuses of power, and widespread individual misery for those same masses that Marx was trying to liberate. The most attractive feature of socialist forms of economy is their intent to provide a safety net such that few are allowed to go without the necessities of life including education.

Criticisms about this economic system revolve around practical as well as moral issues. Some complain that these systems reward laziness, requiring the industrious to support those who work little (or not at all) as a matter of choice. Criticisms based on practical grounds speak of the inefficiency of socialism: In complex economies, single individuals or small groups of decision makers will not be able to know what to produce, how much to produce, and at what price they should be sold to provide for the highest and best use of a nation's resources, regardless of the intentions of the leadership. In the Soviet Union, socialism was efficient in supplying dachas for the ruling class, and tanks and nuclear warheads for the Party, but inefficient in providing food and housing for most.

The success of capitalism indicates that the process by which a free market caters to the self-interest of consumers making individual decisions about what they want to buy and rewarding workers for quality and productivity, is what makes an economic system most efficient in creating and allocating resources. But there is a caveat to all of this. China, with its socialist government engaged in centrally planning much of its economic policy, has recently been wildly successful in generating economic growth by allowing significant free-market activities to function under the umbrella of the communist government. There is another form of hands-on market; the centrally planned economies of dictatorships that provide concentrated power by those in control. History suggests that these forms of government inevitably lead to corruption in the hands of those making the decisions.

The Rich Stay Healthy, The Sick Stay Poor (U2)

Purely free, unregulated economic flow has been shown to lead to unintended ends through concentrations of wealth and, with it, power and abuse. In past human history (e.g., in the times of pharaohs, kings, and other dictators), that is just how things were: The powerful few called the shots and controlled the less wealthy masses by economic or overt force. It was not a free market or a centrally controlled market as much as it was the king's market and no one else's. Concentration of wealth and governmental suppression tends to lead to destabilized governments and revolution of the impoverished masses (czarist Russia, Marie Antoinette's France). There is a country that had its origin as a territory subject to the economic whims of the King of England that was launched from such suppression: the United States.

There has been a gradual shift over the past couple hundred years away from the autocratic model as the predominant governmental system. Since the age of Enlightenment, varying degrees of power have been relinquished to white men (and more recently, nonwhite men and all women). Economies evolve to work within the framework established by government, and as governments experimented with democracy, their economies became freer. But history has demonstrated that hands-off systems will invariably lead to abuses by some of those in control of the markets and, as in the days of ruling monarchs, result in gross inequities.

Without regulation between the economic sector and the political sector, those in control of most of the money can also buy influence over governmental policy in order to accomplish their selfish ends through unchecked lobbying, political contributions, and outright bribery. History and current events also support the premise that free-market economies that attempt to be "pure" are unsustainable in the long run. Even Alan Greenspan, who as chairman of the Federal Reserve promoted an Ayn Rand–view of the world governed by free-market perfection, admitted on October 23, 2008 in testimony to Congress that he had made a fundamental mistake in following this view. Humans do generally act in their own self-interest, and this does not mean that they always act reasonably or honestly. Concentration of wealth in free-market economies often leads to inefficiencies in supply or pricing because of the stifling of competition.

In the theoretical hands-off free-market system, markets are left to be governed solely by the interplay between two primal human emotions: greed and fear. There should be a distinction made between greed and self-interest. Both are human characteristics and can be thought of as matters of degree. Self-interest can be explained quite adeptly by evolutionary theory; we, like any other organism, will protect and defend our right to exist and pass on our genes. Self-interest speaks to preservation, saving, and building wealth, while unchecked greed can produce an insatiable gluttony that knows no bounds of respect for surrounding life forms. Self-interest, if appropriately managed, will result in sustainability; unchecked greed will result in harm and destruction. Of course, this concept of consumption falls along a continuum and is relative to local norms and values.

A Little Bit of This, A Little Bit of That
(Carolyn Dawn Johnson)

Modified free-market systems, that is, economic systems that are mostly hands-off but have some degree of hands-on oversight, support order by attempting to control the effects of greed and are regulated enough to prevent the exploitation of others to the point of causing suffering, but not at the expense of providing opportunities for advancement and meeting people's self-interest. The U.S. economic system and its history have been marked by swings in the pendulum between a laissez-faire approach and paternalistic policies. Many proponents of capitalism have a libertarian streak that causes them to advocate that the cure (government) causes more harm than the disease (unchecked greed). The debate over where the balance is has been capably argued by both sides, and it appears that the most recurring consensus of the experts is that the balancing must be carefully undertaken and frequently adjusted based upon the health of the economy at any given time. Experience has also demonstrated that regulations frequently have unintended consequences, because, among other reasons, humans are notoriously clever and tend to work their way around regulations (example: the U.S. Tax Code and the industry of lawyers, accountants, and lobbyists that exist to manipulate, monitor, and advise on the system).

Because it seems that governmental policy makers worldwide have learned through experience that neither completely hands-off nor completely hands-on economic systems work well for most people, most current economic systems are based upon government-modified free-market economics. Tariffs, regulations, government purchasing, treaties, taxes, lobbyists, stimulus packages, war-time spending, and resource allocation decisions all push and pull at the invisible hand. While there is plenty of room for open economic competition, there may be constraints placed on how far individuals and businesses will be permitted to go in their competition to reduce their ability to control large segments of economic power. Likewise, the government may decide to establish a floor below which point it will not allow its citizens to fall, and at which point it agrees to step in to provide for its people's most basic economic needs. Ideally, a healthy economic system depends on the best ideas winning the day, which in turn requires free-flowing and predictable information. Notwithstanding the best efforts of hands-on capitalists, libertarians, Marxists, fascists, and so on, we have not yet hit upon the perfect economic system, but those in existence today will continue to be shaped by the forces of cultural evolution. The challenge to the systems that presently represent the best we have (in terms of efficiency and fairness) will be to operate as hands-off to allow individuals to be self-reliant, while at the same time allowing government to curb abuse and concentrations of power and address those economic emergencies that periodically pop up at the local, national, and global levels. These systems will also continue to struggle with finding the right balance in placing enough (but not too much) hands-on controls and oversights, to prevent resources from being "inequitably" exploited by those with economic power, while not so much as to unduly burden the free market. When economic policy is overly confining, it restricts the ability of the markets to create wealth from enterprise, innovation, and risk. When economic policy is so loose it allows for a free-for-all, economics becomes more than a system of control; it becomes a system of resource and power concentration

One Life, You Got to Do What You Should (U2)

There is great complexity in this age when we find the economies of separate nations interacting, and with additional layers of complexity added because each nation has its own unique operating model for its economy. Each of these models is constantly modified based upon their respective government's reaction to recent and current events. Each government's economic productivity, monetary, and trade policies affect all others, and also affect the value of each other's currency. Not all currency valuation is determined by the free market, however, and as part of their jockeying for competitive advantage in the global economy, nations sometimes will artificially inflate or deflate the value of their currency to influence the ability of their local businesses to sell products internationally.

If there ever is consensus on objectives, economics can effectively model potential solutions (subject, of course, to the rules changing—which they always do). Solutions that are based upon individual psychological behavior (survival, greed, fear) and policy rewards (profit) and penalties (tax) in influencing supply and demand are available and can offer us a great deal of insight as to how to manage what we have available to us in the most effective way possible. Societies have allowed one way or another, individuals or groups, to set the solution agenda. In the United States, there is a constitution that provides for checks and balances and places the ultimate power in the voting populace (assuming the military continues to accept to and abide by the rule of law).

A sustainable future requires that the economy provide answers though the sum of each individual's (micro) transactions that form, when aggregated, macro movements that are then shaped and overlaid by governmental manipulations. The world's economies historically have wobbled from bubble to bust, from panic to fear. Since the WWII era, these cycles in the developed world have been both moderated and exacerbated by governmental policies, but with a general upward trend line in growth and productivity, along with increases in population and technology. It has become the hallmark of Western civilization that economic and financial progress is available for its citizens and their children. Yet all is not well with the realizations of dreams and aspirations of the people. There is often a loss of confidence in the ability of mere men to control the future financial well being. The future of governments, and war and peace, hang in the balance.

I Don't Believe in Excess—Success Is to Give (U2)

Economies function best when individuals who are motivated to survive and prosper are permitted to do so, but not to the point of exploiting others. Technological advances, combined with improvements in economic science, may allow us to continue to refine our systems toward a more sustainable economy and future. Fundamental to successfully completing this task will be our ability to reduce our consumption of dwindling natural resources through conservation, improved food technology, greener energy technology, and most important, reductions in the rate of growth of world population. These goals can be achieved only if there is a large enough group of people with the requisite knowledge and technical proficiency, which requires taking enough of these marvelous human brains from this and the following generations, and educating them.

> *Judas did not say this because he cared for the poor people. But he used to steal. He carried the disciples' money bag and he used to take money out of the bag for himself. (John 12: 6)*

Rest From Work

I.
And she bends
Her hands are hard with dirt and sun
She's far from done

And he sweats
The golden clouds push into his skin
She's there with him

She's feeling tired / He will confide
They sit a bit / and unwind
She'll stay a while / He'll take his time
And let the day / drift into night

II.
On summer days
Our toes dig into earth
and green
The golden gleam

We just may
Capture time
and stretch it out for days
We just may

We're feeling tired / we will confide
We sit a bit / and unwind
We'll stay a while / We'll take our time
And let the day / drift into night

III.
And he waits
The stories flow and colors shine
He's doing fine

And he paints
Turns summer dreams to memory
The golden gleam

He's feeling tired / He will confide
He sits a bit / and unwinds
He'll stay a while / He'll take his time
And let the day / drift into night

(Lee & Taus, 2008)

11

On Evolutionary Education

What Is Education?

Whether we are aware of it or not, we are always learning. Our education, in the most general sense of the word, is very broad and deep and happens to us every moment of our lives. When most of us speak of education, though, we often mean formal education. It is important to keep in mind that schooling (which will be discussed in greater detail) is of course just the tip of the iceberg when it comes to our education. The world around us presents us with stimuli and elicits responses and changes in our brains that shape our thoughts and cause us to change our behaviors, and this happens constantly from the moment we are born. Education, then, really is a natural and continually occurring process to which every human is subject. If you don't think you need to learn anything because you know almost everything, skip this chapter and go to Chapter 12 where we explain a few important facts about sex.

Thinking back to our discussion of human cognition in Chapter 5, we are all conditioned by our social and physical environments and have no trouble learning, building, and modifying our schemata through experience with the world around us. We can think of education, then, as any instance in which our schemata are changed or used, when we assimilate pieces of information into our existing schemata, or when we accommodate our schemata to new pieces of information. In this light it should be clear that we are—very literally—always learning. It stands to reason that the more educated people are (that is, the more one has been taught), the better prepared they are to become masters of their own domain, to successfully navigate the various pitfalls and trappings of their environment. Knowledge really is power, and this is not just knowledge of specific things. It is valuable for the bushman to know that this plant is okay to eat and that plant is poisonous, but this is only part of the picture when it comes to learning. The bushman must also know how to test whether a new plant he has never seen is poisonous. In other words, the ability to adapt and cope successfully with new situations is a valuable part of knowledge, what some might call wisdom. This is a competence that education researchers call "habits of mind," methods of thinking that effectively solve problems. What we build into our schemata is undoubtedly important, but of equal importance is *how* we build our schemata, and we do this by cultivating our habits of mind. In some ways, the learning and refining of our habits of mind are more important than the acquisition of discrete knowledge. If we can cultivate adaptive cognitive strategies to help ourselves cope with problems, we are able to solve both old problems and new. However, if we rely only on a discrete set of facts to solve problems, we will have trouble with new problems we encounter that do not completely apply to that specific set of knowledge. "The goal of education, therefore, should be to support others and ourselves in liberating, developing, and habituating these habits of mind more fully. Taken together, they are a force directing us toward increasingly authentic, congruent, ethical behavior, the touchstones of integrity" (Costa & Kallick, 2008, p. 40).

Learning is simply a result of life experience. We are of the mind that education (in the broader sense) does not need any additional motivation if it is authentic and relevant to one's life. Football players sit for hours watching videos of opposing teams, investors scour the stock reports daily, musicians absorb new albums from their favorite artists, and teenagers gossip endlessly about the new kid in school. These are all situations in which people are learning, and doing so with no need for extrinsic motivators. The learning is itself motivating. We can imagine learning being like this in prehistoric times. Perfecting hunting techniques, determining which plants were edible, and refining weaving or smelting techniques were intrinsically motivating. Survival depended on this knowledge. As our culture grew more complex and our daily work grew more removed from the means of our survival, what we learned in the course of our day required more extrinsic motivation.

Today, there are plenty of contexts in which we seem to require a little more extrinsic motivation to learn. Schools are among those contexts. As places where education is often presented in very formal and prescribed ways, schools, or more specifically, their administrators, worry about what motivates people to learn because they often find themselves having to persuade people to learn. Students regularly do not see the connection between what they are learning in school and how it will benefit them personally in the short term.

We see this condition as an exception, not a rule. People will seek out opportunities to learn about things they are interested in and things that will help them. We all have had the experience of being so immersed in something that we tried to learn everything about it. The most unmotivated and poorly performing students in school surely have expert understanding about something that interests them, which could range from basketball to video games to who has a crush on whom. Those of us who are lucky find ways to make careers out of our expert knowledge, but even if we do not, we should be aware that learning in the broader sense is not usually something that needs to be enforced, coaxed, or bribed in anyone's mind.

Still, the special case of school, one that occupies—at a planned minimum—12 years of our Western lives, has informed us that certain conditions help us learn more effectively. Education's National Research Council (2000, pp. 60-61) has identified factors that increase our motivation to learn:

1. Challenges and problems must be at the proper level of difficulty to be and remain motivating.
2. Social opportunities allow for learning from peers and others.
3. Learners are more motivated when they can see the usefulness of what they are learning and when they can use that information to do something that has an impact on others—especially in their local community.

For things that we learn naturally, these motivating factors are more or less built in. It is only in more manufactured and institutionalized learning environments that education and the motivation to become educated become estranged from one another. For most things in our life, though, we are intrinsically motivated to learn more. And learn we do, from everything around us, from a very early age.

Education as a System of Control: Religion and Family

How we learn is uncontroversial in a moral sense. The process of learning does not change with the material being learned, but value judgments can be added when we stop to consider just what is being learned. The content of our knowledge has the potential of being very controversial. Boy Scouts and members of a street gang, for example, employ the same mental processes as they build their schemata about the world around them, but the content of their respective inputs yields quite different educational outcomes. Boy Scouts may tend to act altruistically toward strangers they encounter on the street, while gang members may tend to act aggressively or criminally given a similar situation. In both cases, though, education is taking place, and the learner is internalizing both discrete knowledge and a value system that may guide actions and beliefs.

We recognize here that both the environment in which we become educated and the teachers who taught us matter a great deal. All of us are irrevocably shaped by our education, and much of our education can be attributed to dumb luck. We have no choice as to what sort of family structure, social class, or environment we are born into. As such, we only rarely have a say as to which "schools of thought" we may be exposed to. Some are born into situations in which they are exposed to wide ranges of ideas and thoughts and are given the space to exercise free and critical thinking. Others are born into situations where far fewer ideas are made available, and those ideas that are represented by teachers are done so in very absolutist sense. Some of us find ourselves in intellectually stimulating environments from very young ages, while a great many grow up in environments that are intellectually dead. Most of us fall somewhere in between. While the first extremes represent the ideals in free and informed thought, the second represent a totalitarian (or fundamentalist religious) system of control that creeps its way directly into the deepest cognitive structures of our minds, atrophying and freezing our curiosity and trapping our minds in place. We, of course, hold with the ideals of free and enlightened thinking, but what we are most interested in exploring here is how our life's education can control us and limit our thinking. We want to explore education as a system of control that we can unlock, to liberate ourselves from oppressive or dictatorial systems of thought.

Even though some of us are born with genes that enable us to more readily process information, education is an environmental phenomenon. That is, our experience is what teaches us, and the educators in our lives potentially hold an amazing amount of power over us. But two of the greatest sources of learning in our lives are religion and family.

As is true of any meme, one of the paramount functions of a religion is to make certain that the religion itself continues. Therefore, religious education is particularly fervent in many cultures, and its importance and central role in human culture ensures this. The practices and the teachings of any religion will readily become institutionalized within a culture and provide an environmental starting point for everyone who enters into that culture. Religion, then, becomes one of our most defining characteristics, alongside our gender, age, sexual orientation, and ethnic heritage.

Our quest for spiritual meaning does not begin in a vacuum. As much as some would like to believe, we do not have a free and unbiased choice of which spiritual path we can pursue as youngsters. Aside from the extremely rare case of abandoned infants being raised by wolves, every human comes into the world with exposure to a culture of some kind and, therefore, has exposure to some sort of spirituality or religion. We are born into certain traditions, and in the modern world we have the teachings of the spiritual traditions of our caregivers available to us for study and contemplation. "Any predisposition to religious belief can be powerfully influenced by the indigenous culture, wherever you happen to grow up. And especially if the children are exposed early to a particular set of doctrine and music and art and ritual, then it is as natural as breathing, which is why religions make such a large effort to attack the very young" (Sagan, 2007, p. 152). Indeed, the religion meme's best chance of implanting itself in a new, impressionable mind comes during the critical period of that mind's development. It is much easier to steer a youngster than an adult in certain religious directions. Even so, given the broadening of horizons that comes with adulthood, some of us may find more spiritual latitude in our later years.

> In the history of the world, there were probably tens, maybe hundreds of thousands [of religions] if you think back to the hunter gatherer ancestors. . . . It's a vast array of things that people believed. Different religions believe different things. There is a grab bag of religious alternatives . . . and related questions about sacrament, religious mutilation and scarification, baptism, monastic orders, ascetic expectations, the presence of an afterlife, days to eat fish, days not to eat at all, how many afterlives you have coming to you, justice in this world or the next world or no world at all, reincarnation, human sacrifice, temple prostitution, jihads, and so forth. (Sagan, 2007, p. 150)

Considering the numerous possibilities of religious systems one can be born into, it is not surprising to see just how many outcomes religion can have on its cultural hosts and the subsequent effect it has on the minds of individuals. While this is certainly true when we compare one religion to another, it is also true when we consider different factions within one religion.

As has been addressed in previous chapters, the religion meme exacts a powerful influence on the minds that harbor it. This is especially true when religion mixes with political interests and when religious views are rigid. Political leaders throughout the ages have exploited religion because of its power to organize, motivate, and control people. In many of such cases, we find that the spiritual component of religion is lost somewhere along the way, and the social force of the meme is what remains. Whether in the context of politics or not, religious teachings, and one's religious education, have elicited incredible responses in their students. Some students of religion have done unequivocal good in the world, spreading spiritual messages of acceptance, love, and charity far and wide. There are servants of God who have dedicated their lives to helping the poor and disadvantaged. Other students of religion or spiritual disciples have accomplished incredible feats that stretch the limits of human capability, forgoing food and water for days or even weeks, not speaking for extended periods of time, living in social isolation from all people for years, or not engaging in the human drive for sex. And still other students of religion have taken their teachings to be justification for committing heinous crimes against other humans, wreaking destruction upon their neighbors, and oppressing those who do not agree with their viewpoints.

Most religious teachings advocate values that benefit all who would adopt them. Remember that one explanation for the emergence of religion is that it helped organize and manage tribes of recently civilized humans. At this time in human history, religion, government, and culture were really one in the same, and as such, it makes sense that one's "religious" education was something very pervasive and important in one's everyday life. Nowadays, religion still can have that same stronghold on our minds, but because matters of spirituality have in many nations been separated from matters of politics, its influence is not direct and necessary. As a result, we witness some fairly unbelievable behaviors that result from religious teachings. Certain sects of Jain monks own nothing more than a bowl and the clothes on their back, and they walk barefoot from place to place, never settling anywhere (Vallely, 2002); fundamentalist Mormons engage in polygamy (Quinn, 1998), and will even marry and impregnate young teenage girls (Kent, 2006); Hindu scholars spend countless hours memorizing sacred texts whose pages number in the hundreds of thousands, and have transmitted their scriptures orally for over 3,000 years (Fuller, 2001); kamikaze pilots in World War II sacrificed their lives for their country, their emperor, and their own perception of honor; and certain fundamentalist Muslims willingly commit suicide and homicide in the name of their God. That religious teachings can elicit such extreme responses in their students serves testament to the fact that one's religious education holds a great deal of influence over the individual mind and can fairly easily override commonly held values and morals, including our hardwired biological response for self-preservation. This is indeed astounding from an evolutionary standpoint. The religion meme's influence on its host can be so strong that people choose to sacrifice their physical selves and lives for the sake of their religious ideals. In this extreme case, we see just how powerful a force our culture is when compared to our biology.

Religion has the power to transform lives for both the better and the worse, and it has done both with great success.

Our first exposure to religion usually comes from our family. In fact, the family is the primary conduit for most of our education, especially early in life. This cannot be taken for granted even though it may seem obvious: We, as young children, can thank our parents or caregivers for the vast majority of how we perceive and interact with the world. This is not a matter of convenience; it is not that our caregivers just happen to be there when we are developing our identities. Rather, we go through a critical period early in life during which certain lessons must take hold if they have any hope of sticking. In other words, we need to be exposed to certain things during our formativeyears if we ever have hope of learning them. An example of this is language. If someone is not exposed to language for the first several years of their life, they will not develop a full capacity for language later in life (Lenneberg, 1967). In fact, there is a correlation between the amount parents read (use language) to their child in the first three years and the child's verbal and cognitive ability, and school success later in life (Raikes, Pan, Luze, Tamis-LeMonda, Brooks-Gunn, et al., 2006).[15]

Three factors may account for this critical period of learning that we owe to our parents. The first has its basis in our neuroanatomy: We are born with incompletely connected nervous systems (Johnson, 1997), but while most or all of the cells might be in place, the connections between them have not been completely formed. Throughout the course of our childhood, our brain literally rewires itself, making an explosion of synaptic connections from birth to age two (Geitman et al., 2000), and then rearranging those connections again at the onset of puberty (Bruer, 1999). The formation of these synapses in the brain is really what makes developmental advances in the mind possible.

The second factor is our evolved predilection for social interaction. We are social creatures, and it therefore stands to reason that anything that would encourage the formation of social bonds (such as the need to learn so much from one's family) would be selected as an adaptive

---

[15] Television, as it turns out, is not a successful substitute for talking directly to your child.

trait. We already have discussed how the transmission of culture from mind to mind is one of the hallmarks of humanity; this transmission is most common and most potent from parent to child. Our caregiver (traditionally our mother) is usually the person we interact with most during early childhood, a time period in our lives that has been shown to be extremely critical for our cognitive development.

The third factor, which really stems from the second, is our disproportionately long childhood. We seem to have been primed to indulge in the parent-child social relationship for quite a long time; the human childhood (a period during which we are dependent on our parents) is much, much longer than the childhood of any other animal, including our closest living primate relatives. But psychologists believe that there is a very good evolutionary reason for this disproportionately long period of dependency (Bjorklund, 2007). This is thought to facilitate the transmission of culture from parent to child and is why human culture is vastly more intricate and complex than the culture of any other animal (Biological Sciences Curriculum Studies, 2003).

Thus, our families matter a great deal, and in more ways than genetics. Researchers do not discount the role of genes in determining our cognitive abilities (Plomin et al., 2006), but acknowledge that what we learn from our caregivers environmentally accounts for about half the story of our general cognitive ability (Plomin et al., 1997). Our family environment, the most significant environment of our early childhood, will predispose us to various conditions, some of which will promote healthy and full development of our cognitive processes. But our families also have a great deal to do with the development of the content of our thoughts: Our value systems, morality, and opinions on controversial issues often closely resemble those of our parents or caregivers. A relationship between family influence and political party affiliation has been demonstrated (Jennings & Niemi, 1968), as has a correlation between the level of formal education attained between parents and children (Cattenao et al., 2007), and similarities between parents and children in terms of their attitudes toward social issues (Martin et al, 1986). In all these cases, we can say that such correlations were caused, in part, by what children learned from their parents environmentally. There is no Christianity gene, libertarian gene, theater-loving gene, or

English-speaking gene; these are all learned traits. Cases of adoptees raised apart from their biological parents have confirmed this: Children born to individuals who speak Chinese but are raised in the United States from a very early age will speak flawless English and not know any Chinese. We would fully expect children—especially younger children—to be similar to the adults who raised them in terms of broad cognitive trends.

What is most interesting about these correlations, though, is that when it comes to moral traits, how we are taught (especially at a young age) is more important than what we are taught. Children, it seems, learn much more from their parents incidentally and indirectly, from watching them and emulating them. Again, our sensitivity to social interaction proves to be our most potent channel of education when it comes to our families.

As we grow older, though, we grow apart from our parents in many ways. Young children depend much more heavily on their parents to meet their basic needs; older children who are able to clothe themselves, feed themselves, and eventually financially support themselves find that they become less influenced by their parents. We differ from our animal relatives in this regard. Social insects are thought to have a more complex familial social system than humans, but humans far surpass insects and all other animals when it comes to the creation of a nonfamily social system. Other teachers enter our lives as we develop into adults: Peer groups and the media hold increasingly important roles in our education as we move through our teenage years. As many parents can attest, values and cultural identifications are aligned more with our peers than our parents even before we reach adulthood—just ask any teenager (or reflect for a second on your own teenage years), and the evidence for this will be overwhelming.

School is another influence in our lives beyond our families and our religions and assumes primary responsibility for our formal education, for literally teaching us a discrete set of facts that will ensure we participate in and perpetuate the culture into which we were born. This institution has long-lasting effects on us in terms of what we know as well as how we eventually will develop into adults.

We Don't Need No Thought Control (Pink Floyd)

Those of us who have already put in our time in school can safely say that as adults few of us would willingly continue to engage in something so difficult, tedious, and time-consuming that we are not being paid for and see no immediate reason for doing. But, we expect our children to do exactly this because we cleave to one thing we do know about our culture: How we perform in school has a lot to do with which opportunities are available to us as adults.

In purely economic terms, one's level of school achievement is directly proportional to the amount of money one can potentially earn as an adult (with obvious—yet exceedingly rare—exceptions). That is, the better we do in school and the further we go with our education, the better off we probably will be as adults. School, then, can be seen as a warm-up of sorts for the working world. Alfie Kohn points out that even our choice of words about schooling reveals the connection we make between school success and job success:

> Importing the nomenclature of the workplace is something most of us do without thinking—which is in itself a good reason to reflect on the practice. Every time we talk about "homework" or "seat work" or "work habits," every time we describe the improvement in, or assessment of, a student's "work" in class, every time we urge children to "get to work" or even refer to "classroom management," we are using a metaphor with profound implications for the nature of schooling. In effect, we are equating what children do to figure things out with what adults do in offices and factories to earn money. (Kohn, 1997)

It could be that most of us, having bought into the ideas behind the data set presented here, see no other way to properly answer the question of why schooling is important. Many of us are resigned to believe that we, as individual citizens struggling to carve out a comfortable life for ourselves and working toward our individual short-term interests, cannot do much about how the system is set up, and feel disempowered. As a result, we experience a de facto buy-in to the educational system. A few of us wish it were different, even fewer of us try to make it different, but we quickly realize that the task of overhauling school operations in our society is a mountain that must be moved slowly, if it is to be moved at all. At this, we lose patience and acquiesce to the more personal and immediate short-term realities of the situation. Those of us who are aware that varying levels of school performance direct us toward corresponding socioeconomic strata play the game as best we can. We have lived under this system, and we do not see it changing in time to spare our children.

Because the children we hear complaining about school are often our own, we are incredibly invested in seeing them succeed in this world and would never think of allowing them to turn their backs on their best and most obvious chances to access opportunities as adults. Even if the children doing the complaining are not our genetic offspring, chances are we have invested in more than a few memes that they may be carrying and would like to see them succeed. When we consider accumulating wealth as a way of quantifying fitness for survival in the modern world, we could think about this familiar scenario in evolutionary terms as well: The opportunity to make more money represents a degree of evolutionary success in human societies, and in this present culture those who have access to such money-making opportunities hold fitness advantages over those who do not. Because our own children represent our biggest evolutionary investment, we would of course give them every opportunity to achieve competitive success and do what we can to help them secure a stable life full of resources. The best way to do this, as most of us are aware, is to encourage our kids to do well in school, regardless of what that actually entails. School success gives people flexibility and options in their cultural environment, and flexibility is the evolutionary name of the game.

It is vitally important to note that the vast majority of our reasons for encouraging a child to endure 12 or more years of formal education are extrinsic to the child's immediate life circumstances. Very rare is the case where we would say that children should engage with the educational system because they might learn something intrinsically valuable about themselves. This does happen, of course, and many of us can (hopefully) conjure up memories of that "Aha!" moment that took us by surprise and guided our life's trajectory as we sat in a classroom sometime long ago. Those moments are really what education is and should be about. Schools are designed, ideally, to foster as many of those moments as possible, but schools miss that mark repeatedly when their designs are enacted in a culture that places demands, expectations, and benchmarks for economic progress on them.

This is the reason the rest of this chapter is not actually about education, despite the glaring contradiction to its title. Instead, the remainder of this chapter is about schooling, as schooling and the so-called educational system in place are really the system of control at work when we consider where public policy meets the reality of equipping the world's children to build a peaceful and sustainable future.

I've Never Let My School Interfere With My Education (Mark Twain)

As we wrote at the beginning of this chapter, learning is something that we enjoy constantly and across every context in our lives. We also learn in school, but we need to be very aware that school does not hold the copyright to education. School represents an intentional and overt means of education, but we do not need to go to school to learn. Specifically, we do not need school to become educated in things that are immediate and necessary for our living and survival, or for things that motivate us intrinsically. Barring certain tragic cases of cognitive disability, none of us needs school to learn how to dress ourselves, feed ourselves, hold conversations with others, or even engage in simple intellectual tasks that are directly related to how well we are able to make it through the day.

We do not need to go to school to know how to walk down the street and buy food at the local store, or to discern edible food from inedible objects. What is schooling good for, then? We make the argument here that schooling (formal education) accomplishes two things. The first is that it provides specific knowledge about the world in matters that our senses and direct experience cannot acquire. The education we receive in school is for subjects that we would not otherwise access in our daily life, such as the accumulated knowledge of science, the history of humankind, or the rules of calculus. We do need to go to school, though, to understand more abstract and distal explanations of reality, such as the topics covered in the opening chapters of this book: cosmology, chemistry, evolution, anthropology, and the like. Also included here, to a degree, are the arts: literature, music, theater, visual art, and dance.

Let us remember our discussion of theory of mind from Chapter 5: We have evolved the ability to differentiate between human minds and in doing so developed the ability to acquire and transmit third-party information—information about people, places, and things that are not immediately present. Third-party information is the currency of school knowledge. School is where we learn *about* things and also hopefully help to form the means to discern methods for problem solving. School should be good at transmitting knowledge(that the curriculum drafters allow)across distance and timethat our biological shells alone could not span. In this way, schooling feeds directly into one of the most important evolutionary niches we humans occupy: the housing and transmission of memes. School is, at its most basic, a machine that promotes the social transmission of knowledge from one mind to another.

The mixing of the bits of knowledge that we pick up in school may not be immediately relevant to our short-term survival. While it may fulfill needs of higher order, our comprehension of the periodic table of elements, appreciation of Shakespeare, or understanding of the emergence of *Homo erectus* in Africa several million years ago, will not directly help us feed ourselves, shelter ourselves, find us mates, or ensure the continuation of our genes. And if we are not sheltered, clothed, fed, and otherwise socially satisfied, we will not care much about the items that may inform our larger worldview. No amount of intellectual meaning will compensate for satisfying our basic needs. Schools would do well to remember this, as many students walk into school every morning without their basic needs having been met.

The second thing schooling is good for (and this is more pertinent to it being a system of control) is that it prepares people to be able workers under the current economic system. Larry Cuban of Stanford University noted an interesting trend in the history of formal education: Schools and school reform would always shadow a larger economic need.

At two separate points in the past, the end of the nineteenth century and then again at the end of the twentieth century, business-led coalitions forged political alliances among public officials, union leaders, educators, and community activists to draft public schools into preparing students for skilled jobs. In those two instances, training students for the ever-changing workplace has overwhelmed the literacy, civic, and moral goals that have historically guided public education. Consequently, age-graded schools have become an arm of the national economy. "Good jobs," President George W. Bush said, "begin with good schools." In getting students ready for an information-based workplace, American schools now concentrate on rigorously preparing all students for college, thus perpetuating one ideological version of a "good" school. (Cuban, 2003, p. 5)

We see the push to prepare every student for college as a noble thing, a force that will bring equal access to opportunity. Just as the educational system in the early part of the 20th century trained youngsters for a vocation during the rise of industry, our academic educational system is aimed toward training today's youngsters to integrate themselves into the 21st-century, information-based working world.

Because membership in our culture is inescapable, what students are learning in terms of job skills actually doubles as survival skills from a cultural point of view. That is, we use what we learn in school to acquire and secure our means of survival. In indigenous societies where there is no formal schooling, survival skills of youngsters are literally that: how to build shelters, how to hunt effectively, knowing which berries are and are not edible, how to use elements from the environment to fashion goods. In our more complex society, where labor is divided and highly specialized, and we are separated by several degrees from the things that actually keep us alive, our survival skills take on different, increasingly specialized forms. All of our survival skills, though, are directed toward making money in some way, because money is what translates roughly to our ability to survive in this culture. As a result, our knowledge of the periodic table or our appreciation of Shakespeare could very well translate into our set of survival skills when we are thrust into the world of work.

The more schooling students undertake, the more survival skills they supposedly acquire, and the better suited they are to succeed in the world at large. This is reflected in the U.S. Census Bureau's data comparing formal education level achievement and income. Children do not need to be told this outright, nor do they even need to be persuaded that school success places them into the economy at increasingly higher levels. They need only to observe the way things are, to take note that the more economically successful adults in the world tend to have had more schooling, and the rest takes care of itself. This sort of learning does not require external motivators; it is in this way that the schooling meme perpetuates itself. In the situation where the student is unwilling and unproductive according to the school's measures, the long-term consequence is generally one in which that child falls a couple rungs down the socioeconomic ladder. But, because humans, and especially young humans, are not always aware of consequences too far in the future, this is not always readily apparent to them as they choose to watch TV instead of doing their homework. Isolated examples of individuals who have been highly successful in our culture without the benefit of schooling, such as athletes and entertainers, do much to confound the issue in some minds. However, the correlations do exist.

The Purpose of Formal Schooling

Now that we have disentangled education from schooling, and pointed to schooling as the real system of control at work in our culture, we can start to tease apart the specific purposes of schooling. As hinted at above, we would be hard-pressed to consider the majority of our public schools places in which a great deal of self-actualization occurs. There are no doubt cases and points in time in which students make great philosophical leaps forward because of their coursework, but by and large (and this, we believe, is truer of the public educational system), school is not the venue for such thinking. If students are asked repeatedly to demonstrate their understanding of a certain set of knowledge in a very specific way—in the form of highly structured essays, for example—we probably would not see anything other than stock answers in very prescribed formats.

Successful students in this system really have demonstrated only that they are very good at doing exactly what they are told. Higher-level educational systems such as elite high schools, colleges, graduate schools, medical, and law schools, have recognized that advancement in the fields demands intellectual rigor, flexibility, creativity, cooperation, and an abundance of hard work.

Schooling And Social Class

As suggested earlier, school is also a tool of the economy and government(s), designed to distribute people into the prevailing economic system at different levels. Students' success rates in school determines what sorts of jobs will be available to them when they are ready to enter the job market. Therefore, in order to maintain an evenly distributed job market, we depend on schools to sort people into that market at various levels. Schools do that by assigning grades and tracking students into ability-based groups, and ultimately setting a benchmark that is either met (graduation with a diploma) or not met (dropping out). This is also true of postsecondary educational institutions. Consider this observation by Daniel Quinn:

> Schools are doing just what you actually want them to do, which is to produce workers who have no choice but to enter your economic system, presorted into various grades. High school graduates are generally destined for blue-collar jobs. They may be as intelligent and talented as college graduates, but they haven't demonstrated this by surviving a further four years of studies—studies that, for the most part, are no more useful in life than the studies of the previous twelve. Nonetheless, a college degree wins admittance to white-collar jobs that are generally off-limits to high school graduates.

> What blue-collar and white-collar workers actually retain of their schooling doesn't much matter— in either their working lives or their private lives. Very, very few of them will ever be called upon to divide one fractional number by another, parse a sentence, dissect a frog,

critique a poem, prove a theorem, discuss the economic policies of Jean Baptiste Colbert, define the difference between Spenserian and Shakespearean sonnets, or explain why the oceans bulge on opposite sides of the world under the influence of tidal forces. Thus, if they graduate without being able to do these things, it really doesn't matter in the slightest. . . .

Culture's deception here is that schools exist to serve the needs of the people. In fact, they exist to serve the needs of your economy. The schools turn out graduates who can't live without jobs but who have no job skills, and this suits your economic needs perfectly. What you're seeing at work in your schools isn't a system defect, it's a system requirement, and they meet that requirement with close to 100% efficiency. (1997, pp. 144-145)

This can be construed as a pessimistic and malicious viewpoint of schooling, particularly public schooling in the United States, and it may be, but we think it is undeniable. School is itself a meme, a cultural unit whose main goal is the perpetuation of itself, and because it is so inextricably tied to the economic system it serves, in all countries under all governments (also a very powerful meme), we find that our minds and the minds of our children become ready receptacles to carry on this little bit of culture. In some ways, school is the perfect context in which to implant memes. School is how we learn about other things, yes, but school is also where we learn about our socioeconomically stratified culture.

Schools in the United States are hardly uniform in quality, resources, and educational experience for their students; this sad fact made clear by Jonathan Kozol (1992) and others further reinforces the role of schools as cultural status symbols and tools meant to maintain stratification between differing social classes. As Kozol has demonstrated, the stratification comes within schools (the valedictorian versus the drop-out), but also comes between schools (the well-equipped private school located in the suburbs versus the underfunded, under-resourced public school in the middle of the city). Even the reputation of a school—how the population perceives it—makes a difference. Most of us would agree that a graduate of Harvard, Yale, or Princeton would be more competitive in the job market than someone who earned the same degree at a college of lesser reputation. And tracing backward, we would find that acceptance rates to any postsecondary place of learning skew significantly toward those who have been fortunate enough to have had access to wealth, educational resources, and intellectually enriching activities as younger students. "Substantial gaps in college access still exist by income level. Low-income high school graduates in the top academic quartile attended college only at the same rate as high-income high school graduates in the bottom quartile of achievement" (Long & Reilly, 2007, p. 40). Former Harvard President Lawrence Summers points out that "three fourths of the students at selective colleges come from the top income quartile and only 9 percent from the bottom two quartiles combined" (Lehechka & Delblanco, 2008). A private school education, often considered to be a superior schooling experience to public education, usually places applicants on distinct tracks toward universities of corresponding reputations. Thus, the lessons imparted to us by our experience with school, starting at a very young age, run deeper than the subjects we are taught; the entire institution of schooling in this country reinforces many unspoken realities about our culture.

There are those, though, who see schooling as an opportunity to overcome certain cultural barriers, even if school itself represents a barrier. Theorists and visionaries such as Paolo Freire (1970), who advocates "education as a practice of freedom," envision schools as the cultural vector through which sweeping social change is carried out. Freire and others believe that schooling is a system of control, but it does not necessarily have to be if enough people choose to seek a better way. Instead of using the educational system's machinery to perpetuate the status quo, Freire and those who think similarly believe that those who seek a better world can use the educational system's machinery for change.

In many ways, changes to the educational system represent the best chance at long-term change for society. Today's students will be tomorrow's leaders, and the lessons they learn (both actively and incidentally) in school are the memes that will be carried forth into the future. We want to stress that a true meritocracy in all educational systems would best serve the future. The ideal would be that the best and the brightest, not just as tested by one standard like the SAT, would be based on all measures of all intelligence. There are great numbers of very poorly educated citizens in almost every country, even very wealthy ones like the United States. We believe this to be a moral failure of society and needs to be redressed to make progress toward our ultimate evolutionary goal.

Education And Memes

As mentioned, school itself is a meme. It is a construction of our culture that is designed to, among other things, perpetuate our culture through the efficient transmission of information from one brain to another. In understanding this, we hopefully see that school is a particularly important meme, because it is the system through which the other memes that build our society flow. Practically every scientist, engineer, and inventor who has contributed some inspiration and perspiration to the human cause is indebted to a teacher or a school. Schools have allowed us to accumulate past knowledge and build on it, to stand on the shoulders of giants and literally reach for the stars. This accumulation, this building on what has come before, is the most important feature of the school meme. Because we have teachers, books, and electronic media, our educations do not start from scratch and we do not have to reinvent the wheel with every individual student.

Every student's mind becomes a potential host for these accumulated ideas (as does this book). Some hosts might allow the memes imbued to them to trickle out of their minds and become lost; others may store the memes they inherit and pass them on verbatim; and others still (a far fewer number) might use their accumulated set of memes to construct a path toward a new idea altogether. In the past, this third case has resulted in such wonders as psychoanalytic theory, the incandescent light bulb, calculus, impressionism, Keynesian economics, antibiotics, and countless other memes that define our cultural world. And we, the present students of the world, play host to those ideas. Ideas will assuredly accumulate in our lifetimes and spawn the next generation of ideas, built on the foundation of millions of ideas that came before it. This collaborative approach is the evolutionary advantage of humanity, the gift of our social culture, and the wellspring from which our worst problems and greatest solutions have risen.

Revisiting Dawkins's (1989) idea that the unit of selection in any evolutionary process is not the individual but the replicator (the meme or the gene), we can infer that our culture survives only because it is a successful host for so many memes. This is analogous to the idea that the individual's physical survival is in the best interest of all the genes it carries. Culture is really the organism of memes, and the teacher-to-student relationship that exists in schools is the cultural equivalent of biological parent-child relationships. Teachers transmit memes to students as parents transmit genes to children, and as such, one's students can be thought of as one's cultural children. School is the medium through which this transmission occurs. Therefore, school as an institution of teaching and learning (meme transmission) holds as central a role in the perpetuation of our culture as the act of sex holds in the perpetuation of the human organism. This may be why so much effort is being made to standardize the education we receive in school—the job of our schools is to perpetuate our culture in the minds of future generations, as is. This also may explain why it is so hard to reform schools—changes to the structure of schools introduce cultural "mutations" that potentially threaten the stability of the meme pool. It needs to be stressed that obviously not all schools are alike or even serve the same underlying purpose. A Montessori school on the upper West Side of New York City teaching 5-year-olds does not educate the same or even serve the same meme as the Madrass teaching a 5-year-old in Pakistan.

Schools are at the root of all our systems of control, and as such have proven to be incredibly stable and static, like any good unit of evolutionary replication should be. It is quite fascinating to see the intersection between the control systems of education, government, and religion. In failed countries in particular, the early indoctrination of ideology seems to be the primary motivator behind curricula.

Looking Ahead: Where We Are Going
(Dilemmas of Our Age)

We have now identified and described the most important cultural systems of control at work in the world today: family, religion, government, economics, and education. Each of these cultural units, in their own way, exists with the purpose of preserving the culture in which it grew, because if the host culture is preserved, it will live to see tomorrow. However, as we have begun to hint at, these systems of control have wreaked havoc on other aspects of our culture, and things have gotten to the point where the damage caused could very well be our undoing. The next section of the book will concern itself with the unfortunate by-products of so much cultural evolution, which we will recognize as some of the foremost dilemmas of our age. So, before you start the next section, take a break. Think about your life and the many roles you have and the connections in your life. You may be a parent, have a job, belong to a church, volunteer at the animal shelter, be an alumnus of a university, enter triathlons, and only buy organic foods. Go to www.fishbowlprinciple.org and enter the ARKNODE, put in your connections as they relate to your worldview, and by the time you finish this book you will see how many more connections you have to a peaceful and sustainable future.

We will begin the next section with the idea that cultural evolution far outpaces biological evolution because the elements of culture are able to accumulate much more rapidly than the elements of physical life. While this idea may seem academic at best and fairly straightforward, it actually is the root of all the dilemmas of our age.

III

Where We Are Going

Dilemmas of Our Age

12

On Acceleration And The Dilemmas of Our Age

We have presented the case for making connections between seemingly irrelevant cosmological events that happened billions of years ago; chemical and biological events that happened millions of years ago; cultural events that happened thousands of years ago; and religious, governmental, economic, and educational events that are happening now. And the events described—all the events and things that ever were and that are—are interconnected. More specifically, in a very real way all events (past and future) rest upon on all of the events that came before them.

Had we not possessed the biological adaptations in our brains that made it possible and advantageous to process complex social information, we would not have developed cultural institutions like government. And those brain conditions would not be possible if amino acids and nucleic acids hadn't emerged from the primordial soup millions of years ago. And so on. If we wanted to, we could ostensibly trace everything back to a single point, a single beginning and a shared origin. Whether one calls that single point the Big Bang or God or the fundamental organizing law or principle in the universe is, of course, a personal choice, but for our purposes, they are one and the same, and the name is immaterial. What we are focused on here is the construction of a picture of our world that takes into account just how interconnected everything is, the knowledge that our present state of affairs depends on what came before it, and the comfort of understanding where we fit into that incredible picture.

As was stated at the end of Chapter 11, the story of how things got to be the way they are is a story of accumulation over time. Evolution, as it has been described here and applied to atoms and molecules, biological beings, cultural institutions, and memes, is simply a description of slow accumulation over time. Things have been accumulating, progressively, and steadily from the very beginning. Whether we choose to look at the 13.7-billion-year history of the universe, the 4.6-billion-year history of Earth, the 4.4-million-year history of bipedal hominids, the 13,000-year history of human civilization, or the 6,000-odd-year-old period of recorded human history, we should note that things have been slowly and steadily accumulating within each time frame (along with some reversals like the black plague) and gaining momentum all the while. This may seem counterintuitive in a universe that has been described as entropic, losing energy from the moment of its inception, but ours is a story that flies in the face of these larger patterns. Ours is a story of accumulated development, and as such, ours is a project that is constructive by its very nature. This becomes more apparent the closer in time we get to the present moment.

It is tempting to assume that the beginning stages of each of these time frames were periods during which nothing really happened. After Earth was formed, we tend to think of the first couple billion or so years as empty of activity. It is true that most of the action (from our human perspective) has taken place only very, very recently on Earth's 4.6-billion-year timeline, but it would be a big mistake to think that nothing happened for the first 2 or 3 billion years. Many things happened, in fact. Whatever it was that took place occurred much more slowly than events do now, and changes may have been imperceptible to human observation (had we been there to observe them), but things were most definitely happening. It is important to understand that the rate at which stuff happened at first was much slower than the rate at which stuff happened later on. We see this pattern at every frame of reference: Slow changes accumulated over time and gained momentum during this accumulation. In other words, evolution takes place on all scales of perspective.

"Einstein, Sagan, Jung, and Garcia"
by Daniel Dens

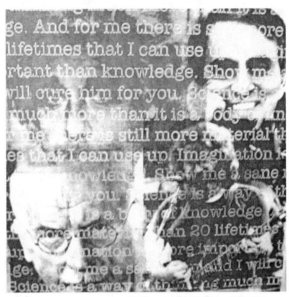

Collection of Bruce Gendelman

This is never as true as on the human scale of perspective. As an example, let's consider the quantity of food available to individuals throughout the course of human history. In pre-civilized times (meaning the time before humans were able to settle down and build civilizations—over 6,000 years ago), people lived on what they could find on any given day, by either gathering plants or hunting animals. People lived, quite literally, hand-to-mouth. There was no food surplus (Cowie, 2006). Later, after humans developed agricultural techniques, food surpluses became possible. We have evidence of grain storage technology from many ancient cultures (Currid & Navon, 1989).

As agricultural techniques and technology progressed, so did food surpluses. Throughout history, the specialization of labor and the development of increasingly efficient agricultural techniques progressively improved the odds for building up food surpluses, even to the point where civilizations often could insulate themselves from famine. Today, technological and economic innovations have produced efficient trade networks, enormous industrial farms, and improved means of food preservation and transportation, which have created an incredible surplus of food for most of the First World countries. Slow changes, virtually imperceptible from the perspective of a human lifetime, have led us to how things are, and looking back, we realize that things are quite different. What would a medieval serf think if he were to walk into a 21st-century supermarket? How about a Paleolithic farmer? A prehistoric hunter-gatherer? By comparing the state of food at each of these cultural checkpoints, we see that the amount of food produced by humans has increased, and the level of technological advancement that humans have employed to increase the availability of food has also increased. In both instances, changes came slowly at first but picked up momentum as more successful strategies accumulated.

We label this general process *acceleration*. Acceleration is one of the central themes of this book, because it serves as a cogent explanation for why the times in which we live are fundamentally different from every other time in the history of this planet, and why the problems we face as a species today are so serious. The term "acceleration" has different meanings in very diverse contexts, and we would like to apply the definition of the word as in classic mechanics (change in speed over time) to the speed at which our culture evolves. Newton might have developed the concept around apples falling due to the force of gravity, but acceleration is no less true when we are talking about meme evolution.

As we have already discussed, our human thought creations (memes) evolve far more rapidly than our biological components (genes) do. The result of these varying rates of evolution is that the phenomenon of acceleration in our culture is many more times pronounced than in our physiology. Both genes and memes are subject to the principle of accumulated changes, but we can transmit memes with far greater efficiency and ease than we can transmit genes. This has caused our culture to accelerate at a pace that leaves biological evolution far behind. Our rapidly accelerating culture has enabled us to realize our wildest dreams and exact our will upon our environment in a way that has never been possible before, but it has also resulted in our causing undeniable changes to our world for both human benefit and for harm. However, because our hardwired biological feedback mechanisms that normally put constraints and limits on acceleration have not accumulated as quickly, and the rate of change in our biology has no chance in keeping up with the rate of change in our culture, we are at a point where we are no longer able to keep up with ourselves. And as is the case with most sorts of rapid change, our culture has developed a tendency for unintended (or at least unanticipated) consequences. These elements of our culture have kept moving faster and faster, threatening to spin wildly out of control, and have brought us to the point in our story where all those slow, seemingly insignificant things that happened in the first stages of our history have achieved a critical mass, pushing us past what we are belatedly learning to be thresholds of safe operation. And like a train about to jump the tracks, it is difficult to predict the exact point or speed at which we actually become derailed.

Whether it is the development of new technologies, or the evolution of sentient life, all processes that involve an accumulation of things or effects over time will accelerate; that is, they will follow an exponential model (if they are not limited by external factors).

Where are We Runnin (Lenny Kravitz)

What would you say the graph in Figure 12.1 represents? Because all things that accumulate changes over time follow this exponential trend, this could be a graph of any number of things: the amount of amino acids present over the first 3 billion years of Earth's history, the population growth of a bacteria colony in your bathroom, the accumulated interest on an investment, world human population throughout history, or really any measure that is somehow related to human population (rates of deforestation, production of specific goods, water usage, or adoption of technology).

Anything that adheres to an exponential growth model will pass through three distinct phases (labeled on the graph) in their existence. A long initial stretch of relatively little activity and very slow acceleration characterizes the first phase. When things have accumulated to a critical mass, acceleration begins to increase, and we see a noticeable upturn in the amount of whatever it is we are observing

Figure 12.1. Where are we in this graph?

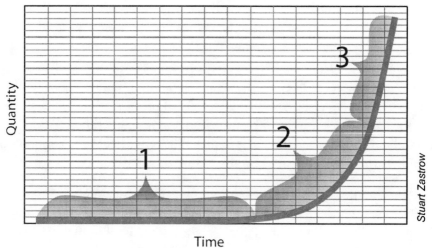

Stuart Zastrow

(marked by Phase 2 on the graph). This is the turning point, where acceleration has reached the point that results in significant increases.

Pure exponential growth is actually a rare thing. In most systems, acceleration is mediated by some sort of factor in a negative feedback fashion: The growth of a bacteria colony is limited by the size of its environment, or the rate of production of motor vehicles is controlled by the demand of the market and the supply of raw materials. This is what moderated the population predictions made by Malthus (1798), which included wars, famines, and disease. However, in a purely mathematical model, exponential growth is not limited by these real-world constraints and will continue to spike at higher rates of acceleration (Phase 3 on the graph) until it approaches infinity. There are cases where we have removed some of the past constraints that have kept us from spiking endlessly upward on the graph and there are other cases where the constraints on acceleration are so weak that they are effectively nonexistent. As we will argue, it is the lack of effective mediating factors in our culture that makes our acceleration possible and allows for example an unsustainable population growth that becomes a very dangerous condition.

So where are we, right now, on this graph? It depends on which phenomenon we are talking about. If we take the evolution of life on Earth, we can easily map the various geologic eras onto the graph and place ourselves accordingly. The long stretch of relative inactivity that characterized the Precambrian era (the first 4 billion or so years of Earth's 4.6-billion-year history) can be thought of as Phase 1 on the graph: Changes, advances, and acceleration were very slow indeed. Then, at the dawn of the Paleozoic era, matters pertaining to the success of life on Earth accumulated to a critical point, and as a result, acceleration of life increased noticeably. We therefore would put ourselves somewhere at the very end of Phase 2 or even in Phase 3 on the graph. However, if we take a different example—say, the evolution of artificial intelligence— we would not place ourselves in a place so steep on the graph because we are really just getting started with whatever may become possible with this meme. Despite these differences, each example's trajectory is typical of phenomena that follow exponential growth patterns: Very long initial stretches of very slow changes amass to a point where those changes build on one another and increase their frequency and potency.

This trend is true of human history as well. Significant historical events happen with much greater frequency as time moves closer to the present day. Chiseling cuneiform onto clay tablets was first seen in Mesopotamia about 5,000 years ago (Kramer, 1988). Around 3,500 years ago, the Egyptians developed a hieroglyphic system of writing and painted their written symbols onto papyrus (Bryan & Smith, 1974). The Phoenicians developed an alphabet about 3,200 years ago (Coulmas, 1989) and engraved its letters on stone and wrote on papyrus, animal skins, and wax tablets. The Greeks expanded on the Phoenician alphabet, adding vowels somewhere between 2,700 and 2,400 years ago, which they wrote on wax using styluses (Coulmas, 1989). Alphabets grew more and more refined, as did methods of writing and writing technology. Paper was developed in China 2,100 years ago, but the technology did not make it out of China for a couple hundred years (Hunter, 1943). The fountain pen was instituted in Egypt about 1,100 years ago (Vallely, 2006).

Movable type in the form of Gutenberg's printing press emerged about 550 years ago, and this invention was refined and specialized to the point where mass production of print material was made possible during the industrial revolution a little over 200 years ago. It was during this time that the typewriter was invented, which was, of course, the precursor to the electronic word processor. With the widespread proliferation of computers and the invention of the Internet, the history of writing has seen significant and accelerating changes over the past 50 years. Piggybacking on the development of language and writing technology is the proliferation of ideas, which ultimately is the source of cultural acceleration. This is the hallmark of the information age and an excellent example of acceleration at work in human culture.

While writing is a technology that has helped humanity, there are other bits of culture that have evolved at an accelerating pace that have harmed humanity. Our weapons technology, our production of toxic chemicals and waste products, and our ability to strip Earth of its natural resources are a few memes that have accelerated to the point of serious harm. It is precisely the acceleration of our culture and its products that has taken us to where we are today. Because we are aware of acceleration on many fronts, we are most assuredly not currently located in the first phase of the exponential growth model. We are experiencing an upturn in the rate of change of our culture, and our environment and ourselves.

Now, since we have the technology at our fingertips to carry out wholesale annihilation of our species rather efficiently, the question looms of how our accelerated culture will affect itself in both the short-term and long-term. The answer will come from the subjective perspective of generations to come, the custodians who inherit the future of our species. Presently, we are on guard duty, and before our watch is over we need to keep our eyes on multiple threats. These are as complex as intensified hurricanes borne of human-created climate change or threats to the food supply by diversion of forests or rivers, and as simple as ambitious, militaristic political regimes with nuclear-tipped ballistic missiles capable of reaching across the continents. If those who care about such things slumber as these threats accelerate, the future of humankind may be drastically altered and the acceleration will be reset.

Our experience with the rapidly moving world around us serves as testament to the fact that the time for long, slow changes has gone. We are also living in a world that has grown more aware of the limited nature of resources available to us; resources whose increasingly short supply threatens to put some serious constraints on our culture's acceleration. So, depending on the events or resources being measured, we are literally "all over the graph." However, in this world of greatly accelerated interconnections and interrelations, all events are correlated. We are, on so many fronts and for so many reasons, at the moment of transition where the slope of our culture points sharply upward and things "progress" at a much faster pace than ever before.

We are not at all worried about acceleration toward infinity. Infinity is not a possibility in our very real universe. At some point, our culture's acceleration will be curtailed by factors beyond our short-term control, but *this is precisely what we are worried about.* We are worried about what might happen when our culture, which has gained an incredible amount of momentum, slams head-on into the various environmental constraints to its acceleration.

Acceleration And Technology

As has been abundantly mentioned, the elements of our culture (memes) evolve and accelerate much more quickly than the elements of our biology (genes). In order for genes to change, we must patiently wait for a biological generation to pass, and even then there is no guarantee of a significant adaptive mutation in DNA. In order for memes to change, we do not have to wait nearly as long. Memes can leap from mind to mind in a matter of seconds as opposed to decades (although, to be sure, some memes take decades to transplant themselves into new minds). As evidence, consider the many cultural changes that have taken place in one generation: How many fashion trends, political opinions, technological innovations, scientific discoveries, or works of art have come to pass in the past 20 years? How many cultural phenomena that occurred only one year ago do we find dated or obsolete? While some of the memes that have evolved in the past 20 years are trivial, generally inconsequential, harmful, or doomed to drip out of the meme pool (lawn darts, reality television, the Heaven's Gate cult, Billy the Singing Bass), there are other memes that have changed the face of human civilization (the Internet, mobile phones, the Human Genome Project, widespread use of high fructose corn syrup). More than any other type of meme, the products of culture that drives our own acceleration as a species are our technological innovations. Technological innovation, a special subset of memes, is wholly responsible for much of our society's forward momentum. Here we take technology to be any product of our culture that is not an idea, any physical thing designed by humans to make a certain task easier. Technology can be (and at one point was) as straightforward and simple as a plow, a wheel, or even a sharpened rock. Technological evolution is the very essence of our modern First World society. We can thank advances in technology for almost everything we experience in our lives: access to food grown in faraway places, news stories made available to us as they break, the ability to communicate and travel across great distances with ease, lightweight and portable consumer electronic devices, an incomprehensible array of disposable plastic consumer products, advances in medicine, temperature regulation systems, public works, and so on. We take all this for granted most of the time, but we would do well to remember that every bit of technology that influences our lives has evolved from a countless iteration of previous technologies. Even the most ubiquitous pieces of technology we encounter on a daily basis—a screw and nut assembly, a disposable pen, a light switch, an inflatable tire—are finely tuned, highly precise, evolutionarily stable successes. Imagine how many advances in civil engineering, manufacturing, and materials development had to go into making the locks on our doors or the bottles and cans our food is packaged in. And again, as units subject to the process of evolution, our technology adapts to its specific environmental need. Just as the populations of finches on the Galapagos experienced biological adaptations to the shape of their beaks according to the relative stresses of their environments, so do microprocessors change and adapt to the varying needs of the laptop computers, GPS units, iPhones, DVD players, and video game consoles in which they will ultimately operate.

The technology we have created throughout history follows the model of exponential growth in the rate of its emergence and impact on humanity: Things started out very slowly, but as innovations accumulated and technologies were combined, acceleration increased. Just a little more history: The first major milestone in human technological evolution was the agricultural revolution, which occurred somewhere around 10,000 years ago in the Middle East. Once people were able to grow crops instead of hunt and forage, they assumed more direct control over the means of their survival. Farmers were no longer as subject to the uncertainty of food availability as their hunter-gatherer neighbors. Because they no longer needed to follow animal herds or seasonal growth cycles, early agriculturalists were able to leave their nomadic lifestyles and establish permanent communities, the progenitors to cities. Living in such close range to others had tremendous cultural advantages. Days were not filled with the single-minded pursuit of dinner, allowing other interests—hobbies—to be pursued. For perhaps the first time, human activities could be distinguished as either work or play. A non-nomadic living arrangement also allowed people to accumulate more ideas and technologies. This spawned the specialization and division of labor (preceded of course by the division in labor mandated by child birth), and with some people able to focus exclusively on their trade of choice, an explosion of technological innovations followed (one of which was written language). Food surpluses also caused populations to increase, and with more people came the need for more goods and services. Already the accumulations of culture were picking up momentum.

The next major technological leap forward was the industrial revolution, which occurred less than 300 years ago. For the industrial revolution to occur, technologies developed in the previous 9,700 years needed to amass to a critical point. Here, the development of enormous machines ushered in an era in which human culture could accomplish things people used to do by hand with vastly improved precision, efficiency, and output. The slow acceleration that had been gaining steam since farmers first planted crops between the Tigris and Euphrates rivers so long ago moved into a machine-driven period of even more explosive cultural growth. The industrial revolution enabled urbanization to occur and allowed certain resources that were previously inaccessible to humans to be harnessed and used. This laid the groundwork for the digital revolution, where emphasis shifted from the production of goods to the management of information in digital form. Thus, using these three markers of human ingenuity (the agricultural age, the industrial age, and the information age), we can see once again a model of exponential growth. The first 9,700 years following the agricultural revolution, while certainly significant, were glacially slow when compared to the more recent innovations of the past 300 years.

Technology has evolved very quickly in our lifetimes, and its evolution is still accelerating at an increasing rate. We have turned the corner on our exponential graph in a serious way. Memes, in this sense, have been much more successful replicators than genes and have far surpassed the comparatively slow biological processes to which we fleshy beings are still tethered. It took about 3.2 billion years for organic molecules to evolve into human brains, but it only took 24 years to move from the invention of the transistor (1947) to the first microprocessor computer (1971). If we are counting seconds and comparing the capabilities of the human brain to that of a computer, these estimates of time would tell us that our culture—and specifically our technology—is outpacing our biology by a factor of over 100 million.

We know that technological acceleration happens, but it is worth considering here whether the rapid acceleration of technology is a good thing or a bad thing. The answer to this question ultimately depends on the type of technology and the context in which it is used, but we still will attempt to make some general points here about the question.

It is often true that when humans and what we have created come into direct competition, technology almost always wins out. If, for example, you needed to perform a difficult arithmetic calculation, would you work the problem out in your head (a time commitment of a couple of minutes and some demand on your brain) or punch the numbers into a calculator (a mindless couple of seconds)? If you wanted to visit your mother who lives a hundred miles away, would you walk (a trip of five to ten days), ride your bicycle (a trip of one to two days), or ride in a motor vehicle (a trip of two hours)? If a mosquito bit you and a week later you began to experience nausea, vomiting, fever, and headache, would you rely on plenty of water and rest (depending on biology), or see a doctor to be treated for malaria (depending on technology)? The overwhelming answer in all of these cases, and most cases that we encounter in our lives, is that human technology will be adopted when it makes our lives easier. More to the point, humans will tend to act so as to maximize their short-term individual interest, which in many cases means accomplishing tasks by using as little energy as possible. Our brains are still considered to be the most complex piece of matter currently known to us, and we would agree that our brains can accomplish creative feats that technology cannot, but we would do well to remember that technology can accomplish things that stretch far beyond the ability of the human body. Even Noah, when building his Ark, used tools to join boards together. Our lives have been incontrovertibly altered by the evolution of technology, and that technology that does work for us will continue to evolve and improve at an accelerating rate so that we humans can meet our needs and wants in the easiest ways possible.

Technology has been so effective for us that there are cases in which technological advancements, already far outpacing our biology, actually take away the environmental pressures that cause our biological selves to adapt. Take, for example, our eyes. Most of us have a visual system that works fairly well, but a lot of us experience some decreased acuity in our vision for genetic reasons. Instead of waiting for multiple generations of humans to undergo processes of natural selection for 20/20 vision, we have sought to maximize our own short-term situations as much as technology will allow. We have adopted technological fixes (glasses, contact lenses, Lasik surgery) that preclude the need for any genetic changes. Therefore, parents continue to pass on the genetic need for glasses to their children, and as a result, poor vision does not get selected out of the gene pool. The same principle can be extrapolated to other bodily conditions that are maladaptive but have nevertheless been passed on, such as food allergies (Duke, 1998), or treatable single-gene disorders, such as phenylketonuria. The traits being passed on are benign in most cases; slight variations in vision will probably not be the make-or-break trait that decides one person's evolutionary fitness. However, this example and those like it may result in a very real impact on human biological evolution at the hands of our culture. Geneticist Steve Jones (2008) has even made the claim that the age of human evolution is over, attributing this, in part, to the fact that our technology has allowed individuals to survive in the face of environmental threats that would have previously eliminated them from the gene pool.

One thing is for sure: Our technological evolution and the culture it has supported move us further and further away from the rest of the natural world in our own minds. Our memes have such an incredible influence over our lives, in many cases more so than our genes, and this could be, in part, why our understanding of our place in the universe has strayed from one in which we have a place in creation. Our memes, especially our technology, have been so successful that in some cases, they have released a degree of evolutionary stress on our genes and effectively removed us from the normal rules of evolution under which every other living thing exists. As we are the products of our genes, it would stand to reason that a little evolutionary pressure would probably be a good thing and that disencumbering ourselves from the rules of nature may present some problems. Nobody sees it this way in the short term, of course. We cannot fault ourselves for choosing to engage in agriculture or wear glasses; we will of course do whatever we can to promote our own individual survival. However, given a new broader perspective on the effect our accelerating technology may be having on our biological selves, we should pause and reflect.

Still, most of us would not trade our technology for anything. Most of us who live in the First World today find it hard to imagine living a life without laptop computers and mobile phones. Even those of us who admit there was a time when we, as a species, got on just fine without these things would probably not have an easy time giving up light bulbs and indoor plumbing. And the remaining few of us who are able to recognize that humans survive without even these (which most First Worlders' consider to be basic necessities for living) probably would not turn down the option to use knives and wheels if given the chance. No, we would not trade our technology for anything once we have it, nor should we. Use of technology, handed down to us from *Homo habilis*, is one of the most prominent features of *Homo sapiens*. Simply stated, we would not be human without our technology.

However, we cannot help but think that there is a point at which our reliance on technology somehow impacts our humanity in a negative way. We are not talking here about technological innovations such as the atomic bomb or nerve gas (although they are most certainly dehumanizing). We are, instead, talking about the fact that we humans are no longer limited by the constraints of our weak, inexact, fleshy bodies. We are talking about the fact that most of us take for granted that a hundred miles can be traveled in well under two hours, even when the human body is not built to travel at such speeds. We are talking about expecting previously life-ending illnesses to be cured with ease and expediency, and that physical and psychological pain will disappear with a small pill. We are talking about that almost none of us know where the food we eat comes from (and no, food does not ultimately come from a grocery store). We are talking about the perceived connection we make with another person when we chat with a friend over the Internet, or the perception of community we feel when we watch television by ourselves.

Our technology, in many of these cases, fools our biology into thinking it can do more than it really is able to do, or that it is experiencing something actual when it really is not. Communication media are constructed well enough to elicit basic social responses set in each of our biological wiring, but we would argue that Internet chat is no replacement for a face-to-face conversation. Airplanes take us thousands of miles away in mere hours, but we would argue that instead of being upset by a three-hour delay, we should be thankful that we don't have to walk the entire distance. Technology has taken some aspects of our humanity and made abstractions out of them. Our biology is nevertheless triggered by this technology and responds to it in earnest, much like we respond with fear to a scary movie, but that is only because our biology has not caught up to the point where it is able to effectively discern an electronic conversation over the Internet from a face-to-face meeting.

Our point here is that the evolution of technology, while an integral part of the human experience, can be a double-edged sword. Manufactured perfume and cologne can elicit sexual responses in many, but this is no replacement for pheromones. Modern medicine can mend bones quite effectively, but this is no replacement for prudent and cautious behavior. Social networking Web sites satisfy our need for affiliation and belonging, but they are no replacement for actual human interaction. Our technology has been so successful that, in some cases, it has made our very humanity an abstraction. If we are not careful, technology could supersede our humanity entirely. This is not quite science fiction. We live in an age where artificial hearts, radar, particle accelerators, and gene therapy are a reality. While we may benefit from these, our biological housings—our bodies—are not built to accommodate them and, given the current rates of cultural and biological evolution, have no hope of catching up to them. This two-sided take on the acceleration of our culture is a lens we can use to examine and explain much of the dilemmas of our age: overpopulation, depletion of natural resources (of course we would cut down more rainforest for cattle grazing if we could), and consumption of resources (of course we would extract more oil from the ground if we could). We point out that technology has very effectively distanced ourselves from our biological heritage, and we would urge people to think twice about whether we should do something just because we can.

And yet, the acceleration of our technology might offer us as many solutions as it has created problems. As the complexity of the events that we are trying to combat increases, so does our ability to combat those events. In other words, technological problems sometimes can be addressed effectively only by technological solutions and by evolutionarily beneficial meme advancement. We will not be able to genetically increase our ability to use neural pathways in our brain fast enough to keep up with the emerging dilemmas introduced by our culture, but we can use culture's tools to collaborate on solutions. In addressing the many dilemmas of our age, we will need to network our mental computers with others who have ideas complementary to ours. We will need to utilize our capacity for social interaction to find social solutions to cultural problems. We see excellent working models of this idea in the realm of the Internet (and apply them in www.fishbowlprinciple.org): open source computing, Wikipedia, and social networking sites that have granted everyone access to information and empowered human beings to collaborate like they never have before. In this light, technology is not just a dehumanizing force in our lives; it can also be our ally in building the future.

Is Acceleration a Problem?

Acceleration itself is not good or bad. It's just how things work. We have chosen to name and discuss this principle here, at the beginning of the part of the book where we address the dilemmas of our age, because we can consider the principle of acceleration to be integral to all the dilemmas we are facing as a species right now: overpopulation, depletion of natural resources, consumption of energy, and breakdowns in communication.

One important thing to consider is that we, as a culture, are moving and changing faster than we have ever before in human history. The accumulation of a critical mass of people and the impact all of us make on our environment make this era fundamentally different from anything that has come before. The sheer speed at which things shift and change is itself potentially unsettling and is causing our civilization's accelerating train to jump the track more every day. As was hinted at in Chapter 9, fast change can be very dangerous to the stability of a thing or organization. We can think here of the model of government outlined in the U.S. Constitution. The Constitution allows for changes to be made, but those changes as wisely crafted by the founding fathers, can only occur gradually and must be broadly based. A changeable and flexible governmental system has advantageous evolutionary attributes that will not bend to social forces that demand fast or rash change, but will accommodate well-thought-out improvements (embodied in the amendments to the Constitution). This sort of constraint on acceleration has proved to be a stabilizing force for us, and one that leads to systemic longevity, a key factor in our goal of peaceful sustainability.

The U.S. government is designed to work well within certain parameters and to tolerate changes that occur at a certain rate. The human body operates in a similar fashion. Our biological evolution has given our bodies a certain set of operating parameters, and we are well built to function effectively on this human scale. We, for example, are built to travel at walking speeds, and not much faster than the speed at which we can run. Technological evolution has enabled us to travel at hundreds or even thousands of miles per hour, speeds that the human body is not built to withstand. Pilots of high-speed airplanes can attest to this, as they experience the effects of "g-forces" and other physical phenomena that people who do not travel at such speeds ever encounter. But we do not have to be traveling at supersonic speeds to understand this principle; even moving at speeds two to five times faster than a human can run results in undue stresses on our bodies.

The principle extends beyond physiology and the effects of literal speed. Exchange of information and social interaction, something humans have been quite good at historically, has also been accelerating. The result of such informational webs is what economists and businesses call globalization. Author Thomas Friedman (2005) described the world as having become flat; meaning instant access to information has made it small. The world's physical size has not changed, of course, but how we perceive distance has changed a great deal. Globalization offers an unprecedented opportunity for rapid dissemination of tools (information) by which to effect positive change. But the world has also been made small because of our mass production of people and the things that people have wrought: pollution knowing no boundaries, global warming affecting all environments, weapons capable of causing massive devastation, and philosophies spreading virally that promote the wholesale elimination of nonaligned groups. These memes no longer travel at word-of-mouth speeds; thanks to electronic media these ideas fly around the globe at unprecedented rates of speed.

Information is available to us as it never before has been, and in quantities that we're not able to adequately handle. We notice our culture's acceleration when we compare ourselves to the vestiges of civilizations that have passed before our time. More predominant in older cultures, less so in modern ones, is the notion of venerating the elderly. The magnificent and mysterious statues on Easter Island, for example, were once thought to be gods, but they actually were built as displays of local power and to commemorate that civilization's wise village elders and leaders (Diamond, 2005). This had a practical component in an age where communication was slow and literacy rare, and where, if the elders did not transmit wisdom to the next generation, it would be lost. Not for a minute do we wish to diminish the wisdom accumulated through experience in the minds of the elderly, but the simple truth is that changes happen so rapidly in modern civilization that in certain instances our world is not the same as the one in which they came of age, and some of their knowledge (and the means by which it is transmitted) may be quite dated.

Humans, like other biological entities, are built to process what is going on directly around them, what they can directly observe with their senses. This event horizon is the human scale to which our biology has been responding for millennia. However, with the effects of globalization and the rapid exchange of information, humans are privy to information about things that are not going on directly in front of them, and yet in some cases, they are expected to respond to them as if they were. We all know that it is far different to witness a murder firsthand than it is to read about one in the news. Even though our accelerated technology has made this sort of knowledge possible, how can we be expected to respond in a similar fashion? We would all have a visceral response if a couple of acres of wooded land near our homes were cleared to make way for cattle pasture. Even though we may hear about this happening on much larger scales in places very far away, it does not strike us nearly as powerfully. On our human scale, a couple of acres of cleared forest that we can use is a tremendous deal, but tens of thousands of acres of rainforest in another country that we have never visited is an abstraction.

In both these cases, we do not intuitively understand very large numbers or spaces in the same way we understand numbers or spaces that we have firsthand sensory experience with. Human activities at this accelerated scale become abstractions. What is a million acres of rainforest? Can our fleshy brains even imagine such a thing? Our knowledge of the world has expanded greatly beyond our own eyes and ears thanks to accelerating technology. However, this doesn't mean that our minds have kept up the pace. And because so much of what goes on outside our sphere of sensory perception is so abstract, we cannot react to it with the same immediacy and urgency that it really requires.

One of the most troubling effects of the acceleration of our culture, though, is both very concrete and so vast and sweeping that we have a hard time truly understanding it. We believe, however, that if we were to solve this very serious dilemma, then everything else would follow behind it. We are speaking about the rapidly accelerating human population here on planet Earth. Population, and more specifically overpopulation, will be our topic for the next chapter.

The Lord is not slow in keeping his promise, as some understand slowness. (2 Peter 3:9)

13

On Population

There's too many people on the bus to the airport,
too many holes in the crust of the earth.
The planet groans every time
it registers another birth. (Paul Simon)

Of all the cultural phenomena that are accelerating in our world today, perhaps the most important and most serious is the rapidly increasing number of people currently alive on the planet. The scope of world population is incredibly difficult to grasp. This is mostly because, as we discussed in Chapter 2, numbers like 6.7 billion are far too large for our brains to effectively comprehend. It is also because our human scale of perspective allows us to take in only mere slivers of large populations at any given time, and even the most advanced technology gives us access only to observations of population growth on a very small scale.

Attending large events such as concerts or political rallies might provide firsthand experience with crowds of 100,000 or 200,000 people, or even a million people in rare circumstances, and those of us who have walked the streets of the world's megalopolises may have passed within eyeshot of similar numbers in a given day, but neither of these scenarios even comes close to giving us a complete picture of just how many people there are alive right now. To think about all the people in a medium-sized city is difficult enough. Trying to comprehend the number of people that occupy Manhattan Island at any given moment in time, or the teeming masses that live in cities like São Paolo, Beijing, Tokyo, Bombay, London, or Lagos, is nearly impossible. And when we try to imagine that the populations of these cities and all cities in the world exist simultaneously, we may begin to understand what we are dealing with when we talk about world population.

Figure 13.1. Population ratesportray an especially sharp increase when compared to other measures of acceleration.

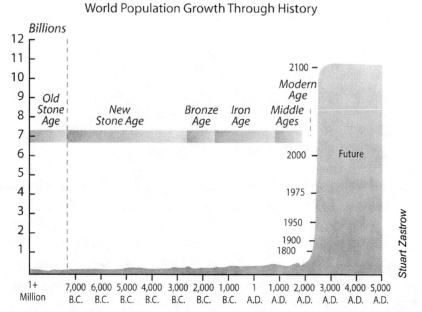

World Population Growth Through History

Source: *Population Reference Bureau & UN World Populations Projections*

Compounding the issue is the fact that population is hardly a static quantity; it is growing, and fast. World population is currently increasing at an exponential rate of 1.188% (U.S. Central Intelligence Agency, 2009). While this seems like a small rate of increase, and has indeed provided for a relatively slow growth for most of human history, we know that in our day, population growth is anything but slow. At the time of this writing, world population is somewhere between 6.7 and 6.8 billion people, but is expected to shoot up to 9 billion people by the year 2040 (U.S. Census Bureau, 2009). According to most analyses, we have reached and passed that turning point at which population's exponential growth takes a sharp upturn.

The graph in Figure 13.1 shows that world population throughout human history can serve as the prototypical example of acceleration: imperceptibly slow initial increases that accumulate to a critical point, after which a sharp and dramatic intensification in the rate of growth takes place. Note here that, as with anything that grows exponentially, the first 10,000 years of human population levels on this graph can be characterized by comparatively low levels and very slow growth, and that only recently (in the past 300 years) has the graph spiked sharply upward. Population rates, when tracked over the course of even modern human history, portray an especially sharp increase when compared to other measures of acceleration. For most of human history, population levels that could be observed were large enough to be abstractions, but small enough to not cause alarm. Humans could procreate and consume resources without worrying about whether there would be enough. However, Earth only has so much habitable land and so many usable resources that will sustain life. In recent years, we have at last encountered the constraining factors on population, the outermost limits of our watery blue cage.

The rapid growth in world population is not expected to desist in the near future. Short of a catastrophic event such as a giant asteroid striking Earth, nuclear war, or an acute climactic event that affects the entire globe, humanity has seemingly positioned itself to continue increasing its numbers as long as there is minimally usable land and minimally sufficient resources. Even in the low-growth projections, we will still see a marked increase in the number of people that are expected to be alive in the near future.

Like any trend that exhibits exponential growth, population growth is its own catalyst. That is, population accumulates and builds on itself. The more people that are alive, the more people will be born, which causes more people to be alive, which causes more people to be born, and so on. This positive feedback system would continue to feed itself and spiral upward to infinity if it were not limited by factors such as the quantity of natural resources available to support a certain amount of lives, the presence of terrible diseases and epidemics, and

Figure 13.2. World population projections through 2050.

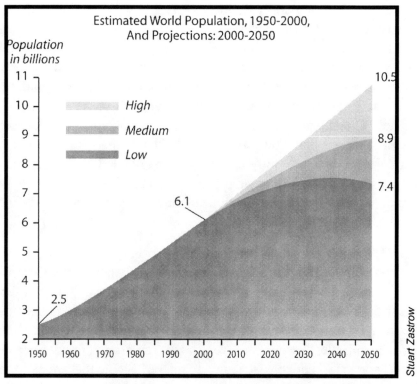

Source: UN Population Division, 2000 Revision

slight blips in the otherwise stable set of environmental conditions necessary for human life. These limiting factors, common to all life forms, will usually cause graphs of population over time to level out at a point, creating an S-shaped curve. The graph of our rapidly accelerating human population is not S-shaped (not yet, anyway) and seems to be pushing upwards to infinity at an accelerating rate of change. It could be, as some people think, that we simply are not at the point of population stability, what ecologists call "carrying capacity," but as will be discussed, it is more likely that we have found a way to remove ourselves from some of the limiting factors that keep the population rates of all other species stable. Indeed, there is no consensus among experts as to what the specific carrying capacity of Earth is for humanity, and the number, if there were one, would be subject to changes depending on several factors; it is really quite uncertain (Cohen, 1995). Among those factors is human culture itself: Collaborative work and innovation on technological fronts can increase (and has increased) the carrying capacity of our population (Boserup, 1981).

At some point, we will hit an upper limit as to how many people Earth will support. Whether the rate of change in human population levels out smoothly in an S-curve or takes a dramatic turn downward will depend a great deal on how we choose to conduct ourselves in the coming years.

Why Is Population Growth Such a Problem?

Few topics may be found that embody the level of importance and the potential for controversy as the problem of overpopulation. Of all the concrete, measurable variables that affect our society in the world today, the most important quantitative factors that must be dealt with are tied to current population trends. It is the underlying cause of many of the dilemmas of our age, and one that most pretend is simply not there. Whether policy discussions are about immigration reform, birth control, environmental issues, public health, hunger, and even warfare, our political and religious leaders tiptoe around issues of population. All of these hot-button issues of our day involve population in some way, but the publicly stated causes and effects of overpopulation have remained largely taboo. Why is this? Some reasons that appear likely are the dictates of religion on the subject (e.g., *Be fruitful and multiply*—with the "God" given mandate to keep that religion growing); the unequal status of nations (e.g., it might appear unseemly for the United States, with its relatively small per capita birthrate and high consumption rate, to advocate economic policies in countries that have much higher birth rates but smaller consumption rates). Underlying all these cultural reasons is the simple tension between the short-term individual perspective and the long-term group perspective: Decisions about governmental policy involving world population are much different from the personal choice to have children. And again, we see that our decisions founded in short-term individual interest have unintended consequences when we widen our field of perspective.

In our endlessly interconnected world, it is obvious that all the threats to species survival that population issues pose are global. As the world economies grow and information flows more freely, more people will also begin to consume like First Worlders, which takes a greater toll on our home planet. The increased impact of people already alive exacerbates all the problems that population causes. This highlights the essential nature of a solution to population being one that can have global effects. Overpopulation, while enacted on the personal level, knows no boundaries in terms of the ripples it casts into neighboring and faraway communities and countries. Having babies is the ultimate illustration of the Fishbowl Principle: individuals thinking of their very immediate urges or needs that result in more immediate people in their very close clan.

It should go without saying that the more people there are, the more mouths there are that need to be fed, the more bodies there are that need to be clothed, the more families there are that need to be housed, and the more providers there are that need to be employed. In an age where we are being made acutely aware of the finite nature of our natural resources, an increase in demand for these resources that stems from an increase in the number of people who need them can only put more strain on our industrial, scientific, and economic systems. Yet to a great degree the world economic "engine" has been built to require even increasing numbers of consumers and workers to keep the system growing. Economic and even political stability depend on it (the U.S. Social Security system, for example, needs lots of young productive workers to pay for the baby boomers' retirement). In other words we have a "Ponzi scheme" economic problem. We are already struggling to meet the needs of a great number of people in the world; adding more people to the equation will not make the tasks at hand any easier.

As can be seen in Figure 13.3, the overwhelming majority of population growth is occurring in developing nations. According to the U.S. Central Intelligence Agency (2009), nine of the ten countries with the highest birth rates in the world are in Africa (the tenth on the list is Afghanistan). At first glance, this may seem a boon: The planet and its finite resources are affected much less by the standards of living in developing nations than by First World standards. However, the rapid growth of the Third World is highly problematic, for two main reasons. *Figure 13.3.* Projected population growth through 2050 by region.

Figure 13.3 Projected population grown through 2050 by region.

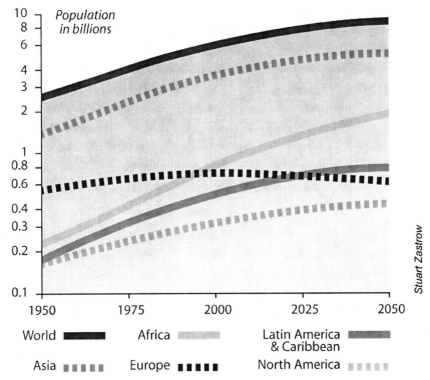

Regional Population Projections, 1950-2050

Source: *United Nations Population Division, From World Population Prospects: The 2000 Revision*

The first is that many countries in the developing world do not have sufficient technology, infrastructure, or resource supplies to support their population without help from the outside; as a result, the outside does help, and in amazing quantity. The United States, in 2006, sent $23 billion in aid to Africa, which has "helped cure diseases, educate children, and build new roads and infrastructure" ("Bush Urges Congress," 2008). An additional $15 billion has been invested in emergency AIDS relief in Africa, and 2.75 million metric tons of food (over 6 billion pounds) was sent to Africa in 2003 in order to feed 35 million hungry people ("USAID Africa Humanitarian Crisis," no date).

Not lending a hand to people in need when we in the United States are enjoying a comfortable surplus does not seem to be an option. We would be morally blameworthy if we in the developed world were made aware of the terrible plight of our brothers and sisters in the Third World and did nothing to help. In our interconnected world, our knowledge of the terrible living conditions in parts of Africa translates to a humanitarian crisis to which our individual short-term personal hardwired sensibilities feel compelled to rectify. The surplus that the First World produces and enjoys is redistributed to the Third World, and when the less fortunate survive with our help (and have babies of their own), their livelihood becomes ultimately dependent on ours. And as the populations of the Third World increase at a rate far greater than the populations of the First World, more and more people become dependent on aid.

There are plans to help the citizens of impoverished countries help themselves, such as Nobel Peace Prize recipient Muhammad Yunus's microfinance initiatives, and more of these plans have become reality as of late. But they have not yet been proven to be successful methods of eliminating poverty (Westover, 2008), and they have come after a significant increase in population that often exceeds the limits that local land and resources are able to support. This population spike in the Third World has been due to direct aid from the outside, specifically medical aid that addresses an acute need (Singer, 1975). Thus, developing nations that receive aid from the outside have put additional strain on the global production and distribution of the means of survival, and set up potentially unsustainable survival situations in parts of the world that are independently unable to support populations that currently exist.

We are not saying that sending aid to people in the Third World is a bad thing and should be stopped. We do, however, wish to point out that those who give aid do it with the best of intentions, but also do it from a deeply personal, short-term perspective. If we give a man a fish today, as the African proverb says, he will eat for a day. What, then, happens tomorrow when he has survived long enough to support an ever-growing family, who all are hungry? Continuing to send exponentially increasing amounts of aid is not a viable solution. Teaching a man how to fish so that he may eat forever by feeding himself is a much better solution, but it is not practiced as often as perhaps it should be. Helping others to help themselves does not always assuage people's personal, short-term altruistic goals and motives, nor does it address issues of acute and immediate need. And there is currently acute need; because of the First World's efforts in sending direct aid to impoverished countries, there currently exists a Third World population far greater than can be supported by locally produced resources. In terms of population growth in the developing world, we have already dug ourselves a hole and jumped in.

The second reason why the rapid population growth in developing nations is problematic is that the rest of the world is now becoming aware of, and as a result aspiring to, First World standards of living. It is enough of an impact on our planet to have population increases in the developed world, where far fewer people consume resources and produce wastes at a rate several-fold higher than people in developing countries. To combine that with the increasing taste for First World luxuries in developing nations will push global demand for resources and rates of consumption and waste production past the point of feasibility. Those of us who enjoy First World luxuries may know in a very factual, abstract way that our lifestyles are, in some ways, unsustainable[16] but we do not take it upon ourselves to make any severe course corrections to our consumptive habits. As a case in point, one of the biggest differences between the developing world and the First World is increased demand, not only for more "stuff" but also for meat. The following is from the *New York Times*:

> Growing meat (it's hard to use the word "raising" when applied to animals in factory farms) uses so many resources that it's a challenge to enumerate them all. But consider: an estimated 30 percent of the earth's ice-free land is directly or indirectly involved in livestock production, according to the United Nations Food and

---

[16]   There are many great Web sites that can estimate one's consumption habits. One of these is www.myfootprint.org, which uses a short quiz to estimate the toll one's lifestyle takes on the environment. One author, who lives in a major urban area, rides his bike religiously, composts, recycles, and lives very modestly by most American standards, was told that if everyone lived his lifestyle, we would need 4.18 earths to support everyone.

Agriculture Organization, which also estimates that livestock production generates nearly a fifth of the world's greenhouse gases—more than transportation.

To put the energy-using demand of meat production into easy-to-understand terms, Gidon Eshel, a geophysicist at the Bard Center, and Pamela A. Martin, an assistant professor of geophysics at the University of Chicago, calculated that if Americans were to reduce meat consumption by just 20 percent it would be as if we all switched from a standard sedan—a Camry, say—to the ultra-efficient Prius. Similarly, a study last year by the National Institute of Livestock and Grassland Science in Japan estimated that 2.2 pounds of beef is responsible for the equivalent amount of carbon dioxide emitted by the average European car every 155 miles, and burns enough energy to light a 100-watt bulb for nearly 20 days. (Bittman, 2008)

The care and feeding of livestock for purposes of meat production "plays a critical role in land degradation, climate change, water and biodiversity loss," (Stanford University, 2007) and the energy cost of maintaining animals on the planet strictly for human consumption is very high. "Grazing occupies 26 percent of Earth's terrestrial surface, while feed crop production requires about a third of all arable land." (Food and Agriculture Organization, 2006). The toll is taken in especially sensitive ecosystems; it was recently noted that cattle-grazing pastures were responsible for up to 80% of the deforestation in the Amazon rainforests (Greenpeace, 2008). But it is not just land that is impacted; it is the community of life itself. In the United States, for example, 70% of the grain grown does not end up directly on our dinner plates; it is used to feed cattle, chickens, and pigs (Lewis, 1994). Despite this incredible amount of food going into the mouths of livestock, we carnivorous end consumers only enjoy a fraction of that food energy. According to the U.S. Department of Agriculture (1997), in 1993 only 1 pound of edible meat was produced for every 6.2 pounds of feed ingested by livestock. Improvements in food productivity have been dramatic and are largely based on information technology and the use of more fertilizer and water, disease-resistant genetically engineered crops, shorter maturity crops, improved animal breeds, and methods that push growth (hormones, antibiotics, feed lots, feed). However, each of these advances are limited and come at a significant price to our environment and, as we are finding out, our individual health.

Meat consumption, in terms of energy costs, is horribly inefficient compared to making vegetables the centerpiece of one's diet. Generally speaking, only about 10% of the energy in any ecosystem gets passed on to the next trophic level (Campbell & Reese, 2005). This means that of all the energy converted into biological energy by plants via photosynthesis, only 10% will be passed on to the animals that eat those plants. If there are one or more intermediary animals in the trophic chain (if we eat animals or, worse yet, if we eat animals that themselves eat animals), then the efficiency of the system is decreased by a factor of 10 with each step added to the food chain. Therefore, the food energy we may obtain from 1 pound of beef requires about 10 pounds of grain!

The most efficient thing to do, both in terms of economics and ecology, is to be vegetarian, as most members of the developing world are (although more by circumstance than by choice). The research on the environmental and economic impact of farming meat is extensive, and all indicators point to the conclusion that a meat-based diet and corresponding demands of the meat industry cause significant increases in consumption of limited natural resources and increased economic strain (Bittman, 2008). Such stress is hard enough from a predominantly meat-based diet in the First World. When Third World demand for meat increases to levels seen in the First World, the Western diet's impact on both environment and economy will undoubtedly be many times more severe.

We see, hardly for the first or last time, the underlying human predisposition to favor ourselves and our own short-term immediate situation over those far away and those we have never met. This happens in subtle, almost innocuous ways, but to be sure, the decisions we make in the aisles of the grocery store, in restaurants, and in line at the local fast food chain do add up to something quite serious. In the First World, through our diet choices, we give ourselves permission to cause incredible personal impact on the world, and most of us continue this course of action even though we know that if everyone had the means to act as we do, it would be to our undoing. To confound the issue, we place ourselves in these murky moral waters as we simultaneously export our lifestyles and our memes to the rest of the globe.

> The biggest problem is the increase in total human impact, as the result of rising Third World living standards, and of Third World individuals moving to the First World and adopting First World living standards. I have met many "optimists" who argue that the world could support double its human population, and who consider only the increase in human numbers and not the average increase in per-capita impact. But I have not met anyone who seriously argues that the world could support 12 times its current impact, although an increase of that factor would result from all Third World inhabitants adopting First World living standards.

> People in the Third World aspire to First World living standards. They develop that aspiration through watching television, seeing advertisements for First World consumer products sold in their countries, and observing First World visitors to their countries. Even in the most remote villages and refugee camps today, people know about the outside world. Third World citizens are encouraged in that aspiration by First World and United Nations development agencies, which hold out to them the prospect to achieving their dream if they will only adopt the right policies, like balancing their national budgets, investing in education, infrastructure, and so on.

> But no one in First World governments is willing to acknowledge the dream's impossibility: the unsustainability of a world in which the Third World's large population were to reach and maintain current First World living standards. It is impossible for the First World to resolve that dilemma by blocking the Third World's

efforts to catch up. Even if the human population of the Third World did not exist, it would be impossible for the First World alone to maintain its present course, because it is not in a steady state but is depleting its own resources as well as those imported from the Third World. At present it is untenable politically for First World leaders to propose to their own citizens that they lower their living standards, as measured by lower resource consumption and waste production rates. What will happen when it finally dawns on all those people in the Third World that current First World standards are unreachable for them, and the First World refuses to abandon those standards for itself? Life is full of agonizing choices based on tradeoffs, but that's the cruelest tradeoff that we shall have to resolve: encouraging and helping all people to achieve a higher standard of living, without thereby undermining that standard through overstressing global resources. (Diamond, 2005, pp. 495-496)

Diamond also pointed out that if population levels were to freeze immediately and the living standards, consumption, and waste production of China were to elevate to First World levels while everyone else's standards stayed the same, it would effectively double humanity's impact on the environment. Third World countries, especially emerging economic giants such as China and India, would present an enormous threat to the health of the environment if the 2.47 billion people who live in these two countries begin to pursue lifestyles similar to those that we enjoy in the United States. In the coming years, China and India will have to find a balance between the ambitious reality of enjoying a First World lifestyle and the ecological realities associated with achieving that lifestyle. The struggle is with how to apportion the sacrifices as they view themselves as playing catch-up with the United States. This small thought experiment, better than the best-case scenario we could predict in reality, illustrates the point that the sheer quantity of people alive puts increasing stress on an already taxed system. Population growth on any front and in any standard of living will present problems to humanity, but the rapid growth of the populations in developing nations, supported by the global interactions that make such growth possible, are of special concern to all of us.

Long-Reaching Effects of Overpopulation

While it may go without saying that more people cause more difficulties and stress to limited (and quickly diminishing) resources, some do not appreciate the extent to which population places stresses on both human social systems and their environmental substrates. We would like to take the time to enumerate some of these stresses here.

Lack of fresh water: While we would like to imagine that drinkable water will flow freely every time we turn on our tap, the truth is that the world's fresh water supplies are running low as more and more people demand more and more water and the crops it irrigates. In 1999, BBC News reported that within 25 years, half the world's population could have trouble finding enough fresh water for drinking and irrigation. As of 2002, 46% of the world's population (2.6 billion people) lacked access to "improved water sanitation" and 17% of the world's population (1.1 billion people) lacked access to "improved water sources" (World Health Organization, 2004). As population increases, especially in the developing world, these numbers will only increase and freshwater supplies will correspondingly decrease. Desalinization of seawater has been proposed as a solution to the shortage of drinking water, but the process is currently prohibitively expensive for much of the world. In addition, as global warming accelerates sources of fresh water are literally evaporating.

Inadequate sanitation: A panoply of health concerns follow from inadequate clean water supplies. Combined with extremely crowded living conditions, especially in the large urban areas of the Third World, poor sanitation, uncontrolled urbanization, the inability to properly cope with waste products, and crowded living conditions are implicated in an increased rate of transfer for infectious and communicable diseases (Weiss & McMichael, 2004) such as flu, malaria, yellow fever, hepatitis, and HIV.

Fossil fuels consumption: As more people demand and consume more resources, the industrial infrastructure that provides those resources must step up its productivity. Factories, trucks, machines, heating systems, and households all use energy, and the current primary source for that energy is fossil fuel. Clearly, then, an increase in population will result in an increase in fossil fuel consumption, which causes global warming, pollution, and increased political and religious conflicts. This will be addressed in greater detail in the next chapter.

Pollution: It is not just that there are more people every day; it is that more people are reaping the benefits of the industrialized world. We are, however, also suffering from an increase in the by-products of such industrialized bounty. Most notable in the news is perhaps the air pollution that comes from the use of fossil fuels, which contributes to climate change, but pollution is certainly not limited to that. Industrial chemicals and increased amounts of livestock and factory farming models pollute groundwater and soil, and all manner of direct human activity adversely impacts the natural environment in which we live. Ours is an age where more people are urbanizing, and the increase in urban areas, which are considered to be their own biomes (Ellis & Ramankutty, 2008), yields increased levels of chemical pollution, as well as noise and light pollution.

Loss of ecosystems: People need places to live, and more people need more places to live. As a result, cities and related infrastructures expand. More people also need more food to eat, and as a result, more land is converted into farmland or grazing pasture. Natural ecosystems are destroyed every time humanity requires the land to suit its own ends. Ecosystem loss, which includes deforestation, is intrinsically undesirable, but eliminating the diversity of life and the quantity of photosynthesizing plants on the planet has direct implications for climate change and Earth's ability to support life. Deforestation specifically has a direct relationship with global warming, as well as loss of arable land and desertification.

Species extinctions: Loss of native ecosystems inevitably reduces habitats for animal life and causes extinctions (Leakey & Lewin, 1996). This is not just unfortunate for the animals that die off; it also has effects that we humans feel in no small way. Any loss of ecological diversity upsets the food webs upon which we depend for survival.

Poverty: Indeed, when there are more people vying for resources, there is less to go around. An increased distribution of resources results in more poverty. This is seen most acutely in the Third World. Poverty, in turn, leads to high rates of infant and child mortality, low infant birth weight, malnutrition, starvation, and low life expectancy, and dependency on aid on the cultural front.

Unrestrained immigration: In an attempt to flee impoverished conditions, a large concentration of people immigrate to urban centers, particularly in the developed world. While 30% of people lived in cities in 1950, 47% of people lived in cities by the beginning of the present millennium (University of Michigan, 2002). The United States and Europe have experienced an influx of immigrants on a scale unprecedented in human history, which creates demographic and political problems in both the countries of destination and countries of origin.

Interpersonal conflict: With an increase in demand for resources far outpacing an increase in supply, we see more conflict to obtain those resources. This happens on a local, as well as a global, scale. The types of conflict range from petty crimes to full-scale warfare by country against country.

The above represents a cursory overview of just how far the ripples of overpopulation carry in our human ocean. These are problems that no single fishbowl can contain and that no single fishbowl can protect us from. Taken in this light, we see that issues of overpopulation are truly the center to the dilemmas of our age. Many of the problems listed above would exist even with fewer humans alive, but overpopulation magnifies these problems to the point where they become severe and significant.

Thinking back to Chapter 3, there are two ways for something to be successful. The first is simplicity and stability in structure and function, and the second is organized complexity, which yields a host of flexible abilities. Since humanity is well past the point of simplicity, we are left with the challenge of finding organized, complex solutions to the problem of overpopulation. We will turn to potential solutions later. For now, it is instructive to turn our attention to the causes of overpopulation. We will identify both proximate and ultimate causes here, with the hope that we can begin to understand this important phenomenon at many levels of analysis.

Ultimate Causes of Population Growth: Medicine and Health Technology

What has fueled such staggering population growth in the past 300 years? One factor, as discussed in the previous chapter, is the role that technology has played in the fields of medicine and public health. Over the past 300 years, scientific inventions, innovations, and discoveries have been very successful in prolonging life, sparing the sick, and removing potentially lethal pollutants and biological agents from food and water supplies.

A little history of medicine

Among the most notable advances in medicine, we have the invention of the microscope in the 17th century and Robert Hooke's observation of cells, for the first time, in 1665. Just three years later, Francisco Redi debunked the traditional (and false) notion of spontaneous generation of complex life from decaying matter, an incorrect theory that dated back to Aristotle. What followed was a more complete and accurate germ theory of disease, one in which bacteria (and later viruses) were identified as responsible for many forms of disease. From here, we have reaped the benefits of work from figures like Edward Jenner (the progenitor of vaccination), Louis Pasteur (for whom the process of pasteurization is named), Jonas Salk (who invented the polio vaccine), and countless others who are not as celebrated but just as important for their contributions to the medical profession.

Many of us take for granted the fact that we have medical care available to us for infections, broken bones, bacteria- and virus-caused conditions, and even terminal illnesses. However, it is only very recently that conditions such as cholera, smallpox, malaria, polio, and tuberculosis have been made far less threatening to human life. Nearly all of us take for granted the fact that clean drinking water flows freely from our taps and food (hopefully) free of pathogenic bacteria is readily available in our restaurants and supermarkets. It is also only very recently in the scale of human history that we have had the knowledge and technology to stop the spread of many waterborne and food borne pathogens. Most of us take for granted that the corner store is brimming with pills, materials, and devices designed to ease our pain and discomfort. From the short-term individual perspective, these innovations in health and medicine are the stuff of divinity. These are all things that people believe to be good, of course, and our appreciation for such innovations is reflected in where we place much of our social value. We do not want to downplay the importance that these figures have on our world or the important role that they play in society. We do believe that saving lives is a good thing. But we want to point out, again, that we react to the services doctors and hospitals provide, services that ensure and prolong our very lives, from our individual-centered, person-scale of perspective. How could we not? If a family member is in need of medicine that treats a horrible disease, we will generally do whatever it takes to get them to a doctor. We cannot, in good conscience, think of the human community as if it were an ant farm, where individuals matter little, because we are acutely aware that the individuals in question are us and the ones we love. We consider it inhumane to be opposed to things like finding a cure for AIDS, treating public supplies of drinking water, or inoculating infants against potentially life-threatening diseases. It is a very, very rare case where someone chooses to sacrifice their chances at individual survival for the benefit of others, especially others they have never met, or for a higher cultural principle. With so much technology available to easily and handily extend our own health and lives, we find that not taking full advantage of our technological triumphs over nature's way is the exception, rather than the rule.

Ultimate Causes of Population Growth: Food Availability

Another factor that has led to the incredible amount of population growth we have seen throughout human history is the increased availability of food. Thanks to the products of the industrial revolution, in the past 300 years we have discovered and implemented ways to grow and harvest crops and livestock with amazing efficiency and on a scale previously unparalleled. We have subjugated wild lands to produce edible plants, diverted rivers and created freshwater lakes to irrigate arid lands, and amassed reserve stores of food that would see us through natural disasters and famines as a result. In short, we have literally changed the face of the planet, converted Earth's surface from its natural wild state to a domesticated one in order to fulfill our ever-increasing appetites.

While our increased ability to produce food has insulated us from famine and disruptions in a chaotic natural order, which would otherwise limit the number of people who need to be fed, it has also removed humanity from another of nature's systems of checks and balances that ensure population stability. The very lives of humans, like any other organism, are subject to the availability of food (Hopfenberg & Pimentel, 2001). If there are no rabbits, the foxes will starve. If there is no detritus, the worms will expire. If there are no eucalyptus leaves, the koalas will pass on. If there is no CO_2 and sunlight, the plants will not grow. And if there is no food for humans, we too will die. This is an inescapable fact. We, luckily, have adapted to be quite flexible as to what other organic matter we can consume for food; few other animals have such a range of options for what can make up their dinner. Still, there are times and places where food is in short supply, and people die as a result. This is tragic, but it is also natural. Populations of all organisms are kept in check by the availability of food sources, and humans are no different.

Thomas Malthus in his landmark *An Essay on the Principle of Population* (1798) claimed that because population's exponential growth will far outpace the linear growth of food production, humanity puts itself at serious risk for a dramatic and tragic population correction in the long run. We do know that if left unchecked population in all species grows exponentially. We also know that food cannot be produced at rates that keep pace with the population explosion in the long run (Erlich, 1968). Food supply, then, becomes a very important and very limited resource that needs to be managed if it is to be equitably distributed to as many people as possible. Our food supply, once we gained the ability to control its output for ourselves, falls under the auspices of economic theory, and we can turn to economic theory to identify and explain the relationship between food and population. We do this out of our moral sense, because we wish to see as many people fed as possible, but we also do this with hopes that in understanding one of the ultimate causes of population growth, we can find a way out of the conundrum it has created.

The Economics of Food and Population

When we are hungry, angry, lonely, or tired, we are at our most vulnerable. The psychologist Abraham Maslow (1943) outlined a hierarchy of human needs in which our physiological needs were paramount to all other needs: We, being bound to and limited by our mortal flesh, need to take care of our physical selves before anything else is possible. Therefore, the most important economic issues of our time are unsurprisingly related to food, water, shelter, and medicine, and these basic human rights in turn support population growth.

Indeed, the most primitive economies in human history centered on food: agriculture and livestock. Food, being one of the most important resources we require to meet our evolutionary imperative of survival, is rightly the centerpiece of our economic worldview. In order to cultivate a sustainable future, a future where all humans have the opportunity to lead productive, peaceful, satisfying lives, providing food for its people is a non-negotiable and necessary focus of any organizing structure of culture, such as government. Accordingly, as economist Joseph Stiglitz (2003) notes, lack of food is an indicator and exacerbates poverty, which in turn breeds a population of people who feel insecure, powerless, and angry with their government. It is under a scarcity of food and difficult economic conditions that the voices of hatred, preaching the gospel of us against them, may best be heard—this is when the search for scapegoats is most easily satisfied. Hitler knew this, and Osama bin Laden knows this. Commerce, human rights, and dignity cannot succeed well in environments that are hostile and certainly cannot exist in environments where people are denied their basic needs. And of all our basic needs, food availability (along with drinkable water) tops the list.

In addition to maintaining the availability of food, a central worldwide economic policy assumption is to strive for living environments that are secure and stable. If your family has been decimated (perhaps along with your entire village), by war, disease, or hunger, loneliness and anger are likely to overwhelm and make impossible any thoughts of universal understanding, common ground, love, or a sustainable global future. Again, Maslow's hierarchy reminds us that we have to take care of our basic needs first if we have any hope of moving forward. Thus, the availability of certain resources such as food, water, and safe shelter are prerequisites for more than mere survival; they are the foundation for societal stability on the individual and group level. When food needs are satisfied, survival is that much more ensured. And as more people find ways to survive, population increases.

The population of any society depends on an adequate food supply to support it, and food supply is ultimately dependent on economic systems. Population levels of ancient cultures (as well as animal populations) were directly impacted by the limited food supply they had available to them. This kept prehistoric societies relatively small in number when compared to current societies. Significant population increases were only possible by productivity gains in the food supply—better hunting techniques, agriculture, domestication and selective breeding of plants and animals, storage technologies, and the like—and with these productivity gains came the need for more sophisticated economic systems. In today's very crowded and complex world, population is still governed by food supply, albeit in a much more interconnected and complicated fashion. It is no surprise, then, that the least economically developed countries are largely food deficient; they rely on food produced elsewhere to supply their needs. Therefore, economic stability, as well as political stability, has everything to do with food availability, and issues of hunger can be thought of as a matter of profound political and economic interest.

Our economic, political, and technological innovations have found ways around the limits of local environment. In a less interconnected world, food supplies would be limited by the local environment's biodiversity and suitability for agriculture. This is not as true in the modern world, where food and other resources can be shipped to areas where they cannot be grown or raised. We can also thank our cultural advancements for the ability to redirect resources to environments where they were not previously found. For example, the cities of the American southwestern desert such as Las Vegas, Los Angeles, and Phoenix require resources far beyond what their local environments are able to supply (Reisner, 1986). Each of these cities is possible only because of technological advancements that divert necessary resources (most notably water) directly to them. We can take for granted that lush green golf courses are found in the American Southwest, and that New Englanders can eat tropical fruits in the dead of winter, but we should keep in mind that these resources are only available because of cultural and technological evolution. Similarly, the ability to grow or raise food in sub-Saharan Africa or the Indian subcontinent is limited by the amount and kind of yearly rainfall, the biodiversity of the area, the frequency of natural disasters, and other environmental factors. But, a population cannot be sustainably maintained if environmental resources necessary for survival are lacking, unless support from the outside is constant.

However, even in areas where resources are plentiful, some people may not have access to such resources. Even though the United States is thought of as one of the wealthiest countries in human history, there are still leagues of homeless people living in abject poverty, malnourished people, and those who are incapacitated by addictions, sharing cities with some of the wealthiest individuals in the world. Social services are put in place that attempt to grant as many people as possible access to the necessary resources for survival, but gaps in wealth and shortcomings in public policy sometimes prevent this from happening as effectively as it could. In many cases poor education and lack of opportunity strip the young of their potential. Here we see that resource availability has become much more than a question of international economics; local class issues permeate the problem on an individual level.

Taking the politically correct stance of wishing to reduce global hunger for these very good reasons is justified and good, but as stated earlier we also must be aware that such solutions constitute a program that affects positive change only in the short term. To speak more generally: If we increase the food supply, population will rise and food demand will also increase in the long term (Hopfenberg & Pimentel, 2001).

Our responses to such short-term pleas will mean that the problems we grapple with today will be much larger a couple of months or years down the road. Therefore, in order to address the problem of population from the lens of food availability, we will be forced into a very difficult reckoning between our short-term sensibilities and some particularly difficult long-term realities.

In this light, one of the biggest questions put to economics has become: How can we meet the world's food demand in a sustainable manner? For one, in many cases the land or natural resources needed to feed current population levels simply are not there. In sub-Saharan Africa, for example, crops needed to feed local populations depend just as much on soil quality as they do on politics. However, soil fertility is being depleted, which is one of the major limiting factors of how much food can be produced locally in the region (Sanchez & Leakey, 1997). This is not limited to the developing world. "During the last forty years, nearly one third of the world's arable land has been lost by erosion and continues to be lost at a rate of more than 10 million hectares per year. With the addition of a quarter of a million people each day, the world population's food demand is increasing at a time where per-capita food productivity is beginning to decline" (Pimentel et al., 1995, p. 1117). No matter how much training and infrastructure are put in place, it is nearly impossible to grow crops in the quantities necessary in certain parts of the world, and moreover, the world's ability to successfully grow crops is declining. For another, even if there is farmable land and sufficient natural resources, aid-dependent population levels may have expanded past a point at which the land can support it. There are technological advancements that have allowed for deserts to bloom (drip irrigation) that can allow for sustainable local populations. There are cultural considerations as well. Food types, eating customs, local traditions, ancestral ways of life, and the use of certain technologies may, in some cases, not be compatible with the belief system of a given group of people. Simply increasing food supply will not solve the problem, because as more people are fed, more people survive and have children, which will inevitably cause more people who need to be fed in the coming months and years. Instead, then, of thinking about increasing food supply to feed an increasing population, we would encourage a refocusing on population itself. Food and population share a reciprocal relationship, and as such we can use the economics of food to address population issues in a much more humane way than war, plague, or natural disaster. It is the moving target of population growth that results from increased food production, and the increasing impact on our limited resources by increases in the standards of living in developing nations.

Economic theory teaches us some harsh realities. It is often said that there is no such thing as a free lunch. We cannot have systems built upon perceptions and expectations, bubbles, and Ponzi schemes. We cannot borrow indefinitely from future generations to pay for our current consumption; one way or another collectively we will be forced to learn to live within our means. We must balance the humanitarian urge to feed the hungry with the knowledge that in the long term, an increase in food supply will inevitably result in an increase in population. If we do not, the future becomes a very real and immediate struggle for survival. These big human brains of ours have created innovations that liberated us from constraints all other living things are subject to; certainly, they can also plan for a brighter, sustainable, permanent enterprise for us now that our original innovations have presented us with serious long-term design flaws, an enterprise more in line with what our brains and bodies were originally designed to process.

Proximate Causes of Population Growth: Sex

While advances in both medicine and increased food availability provide a foundation for longer and more lives, the decisions that affect population do not occur at the macro level in any meaningful way. Population growth can instead be thought about as the aggregation of billions of individual decisions (however intentional) to reproduce. Passing on genes and survival of the next of kin is, after all, the end goal of biological evolution, and hard-line Darwinian thinkers would say that everything about us is somehow geared toward our surviving long enough to reproduce. In our daily conscious experience we see this commonly manifest itself in a preoccupation with sex. Sex takes center stage in our social world; it is the driving force behind much of psychotherapy, daytime television, advertising campaigns, gossip magazines, fine art, popular music, indigenous worship rites, and much more. Sex, after food, is one of the most powerful motivating forces in our lives. Beneath the countless advertisements that feature near-naked attractive people, behind the fashion and beauty industries, and some would say underlying our urge for artistic creativity (Miller, 1999) is the highly intimate and highly biologically enjoyable social act that results in the passing on of our genes. In short, we are hardwired to want to and try to have babies.

More correctly, we are hardwired to want to have sex. Sex leads to babies, of course, but there is more to sex for humans than just procreation. We have evolved in such a way as to find sex extremely pleasurable, and as a result, the act accomplishes two evolutionary adaptive goals for us: procreation and the formation of close social bonds with others. We are able, in our minds, to separate sex from reproduction, and to an extent this is a fair separation to make, but it is also true that up until very recently in human history, the only way population increased was by people having sex.[17] But whatever the underlying cause and explanation in terms of evolutionary adaptiveness, we all know that sex and the things that lead up to sex are some of the most prominent preoccupations of almost every human that has passed through puberty. This is true at the more animal, instinctive level inside all of us, but it is also true at higher intellectual, cultural, and emotional orders.

Even though population is ultimately limited by resource (food) availability in the long term, we are creatures that make decisions based on the short-term and immediate situation at hand. This is never truer than the search for a sexual partner. What, then, are some of the most important variables that affect the chances that we, as individuals, will have sex, and eventually procreate?

Sexual urges: The physical urge to have sex is such a strong motivator that we humans often find ourselves doing things that surprise us in order to increase our chances to land a partner for even one night. It is often the case that people do not make the connection between sex and procreation and are sometimes confronted with the unexpected fruits of their labor. According to the national campaign to prevent teen and unwanted pregnancy, about one third of the pregnancies that

---

[17] In recent years, medical technology has discovered how to induce pregnancies without sex actually occurring.

occur in the United States are unwanted, and that figure jumps to 45% in women aged fifteen to nineteen ("Unwanted Pregnancy," no date). Despite everything we know about the personal, social, and economic strain unwanted pregnancies and teen pregnancy can cause, despite our awareness of sexually transmitted diseases, and despite our understanding of overpopulation, people still make the choice to have sex. No amount of legislation, education, or religion has stopped this, nor will it ever. We, therefore, should take as a given that most people will have sex, even if it is not the best decision to make, and that sometimes this will lead to babies, particularly where there is a lack of knowledge or taboos surrounding the use of contraception.

The advent of various forms of birth control, but most notably oral contraception, has gone a long way toward separating sex from its after-effect: more people. This is a case where we have used our culture's accelerated rate of evolution to solve a social problem unsolvable by our biology alone. Birth control in the form of contraception enables people to separate sex from procreation, and it has been shown to be an effective regulatory measure in terms of decreasing fertility rates (United Nations Department of Economic and Social Affairs, 2003). Birth control does not seek to tame sexual urges, which we assume will never go away, but it does significantly diminish the chances that sex will lead to procreation.

Health: People will have sex no matter what, but for a pregnancy to come to term, the mother-to-be needs to be sufficiently healthy. In the First World, where people have better access to both health care and ample nutritious food, infant mortality rates are much lower than in the Third World (United Nations Department of Economic and Social Affairs, 2007) (and indeed, infant mortality rate is often used as a reliable indicator of a country's overall stability). This is due to access to both health care and quality food. Diseases and infections such as malaria are a major cause of stillbirth, abortion, and intrauterine growth retardation in the Third World (Brabin, 1991). As would be expected, though, with improvements to social inequalities and impoverished conditions in developing nations, as well as in the First World, the rates of infant mortality are dropping, and life expectancy is increasing (Marmot, 2005).

The unspoken consequence to such seemingly positive progress in the field of health is that when infant mortality decreases, population increases. This feeds on itself in the previously mentioned positive feedback fashion and creates a situation in which there are more and more people who will themselves eventually require health care, food, resources, and so on for themselves and their children to be.

Religious dictates: Religions often foster the notion that it is God's will to produce quantities of offspring. These mandates most likely date from the nascent days of the religions, where tribes sought to expand their reach as much as possible in order to ensure that their culture would survive. After all, the more minds there are to carry and pass on the religion meme, the better. It is no mistake that God's first commandment to humanity was to *"be fruitful and multiply"* (Genesis 1: 28) a commandment he repeated to Adam, Noah, Abraham, and their descendants. The historical context in which this emerged was one filled with nomadic tribes. Life was arduous, life expectancy was significantly shorter than it is today, and infant mortality rates were much higher. It was up to the leaders of tribes, who happened to double as the tribe's religious authorities, to sire many children, often with multiple partners with the expectation that some children would not make it to adulthood. The Bible indicates that the patriarchs of Western religion all had multiple wives. Abraham engaged in such behavior, fathering Isaac (who would give rise to the line of Jews) and Ishmael (who would give rise to the line of Muslims) from different women. His grandson Jacob, we are told, had thirteen children.

This reproductive strategy was undoubtedly successful for people of the biblical age, and creating young minds into which a new set of religious values can be poured will certainly help the survival of that religion. However, in our modern age and everything that comes with it, in general we have far less need to be fruitful and multiply in the service of our religions. Most no longer live in tribal ways, we have much better access to food, our medical advancement has significantly lowered the infant mortality rate and extended the average lifespan, and as such, the reproductive strategy of having dozens of offspring is simply not as warranted. Yet it is characteristic of fundamentalist religious families to be very large. In having many children and refusing contraception, fervent adherents to texts such as the Bible believe that they are doing God's work and following his most sacred commandments.

Children as insurance policies: When we enter old age and are no longer able to provide for ourselves, who will take care of us? In some developed countries, government has taken on this responsibility with programs such as Social Security and Medicare. The more wealthy and fortunate among us may be able to afford professional care in our later years, or check ourselves into a retirement home or nursing home. These are all cultural innovations that came about as families grew more distant. Today, as we read about the potential collapse of the U.S. Social Security system (Cooley & Soares, 1996) and the dissolution of the nuclear family (Williams, Sawyer, & Wahlstrom, 2005), and as retirees move away from their family's homelands, we may often forget that hundreds of thousands of years of human culture transpired with a very simple insurance policy for old age: Our children will take care of us. This simple cultural institution has proven highly stable and will, most likely, prove more stable than any governmental program.

Education: Knowledge is power, and a real knowledge of what it takes to bring a life into this world and care for it, as well as an accurate and correct understanding of contraception, can potentially have a positive effect on pregnancy rates. While sex education will not stop people from having sex and will not prevent all unwanted pregnancies, it can be an effective, cheap, and easily distributed tactic to counter poor individual decision-making that leads to unnecessary population growth. By education, we do not necessarily mean a formal class taught in an academic setting. We can think much more broadly about education than that. There is a cursory sex education curriculum in place in most schools in the United States, and its effectiveness varies widely (Kirby, Short, Collins, Rugg, Kolby, et al., 1994). A specific curriculum dealing with family planning has yet to be developed that would be accepted on a global basis, partly because of religious and tribal resistance.

When we speak broadly about education and in its traditional sense, we find that formal education of any kind has an inverse relationship with birth rate. A study by the Centers for Disease Control in 1997 found that a woman's level of formal education is the best predictor of how many children she would have, with less educated women more likely to have more children than women who have completed more schooling (Matthews & Ventura, 1997). While we understand that this correlation does not mean that education level directly causes changes in birth rates, there is a meaningful connection between the two, a connection that most likely speaks to the cultural interference in a woman's life between motherhood and professional success. We also find such results disturbing; education in any form is an important prerequisite to a more meaningful, sustainable existence. As discussed in Chapter 11, a great deal of one's education comes from one's caregivers early in life, and we believe it is tragic to think that an increasing number of caregivers are themselves very poorly or narrowly educated. U.S. Secretary of State and former senator from New York Hillary Clinton emphasized the importance of education as a means to a sustainable and equitable society—specifically, the education of girls. In a February 9, 1999 keynote address to the Cairo Five Plus Forum at The Hague, she said:

> We are called upon to make investments in the human and economic development of people, particularly girls and women. To understand that when we educate a woman, we educate a family and when we educate a family, we educate an entire society. We lower the risk with an educated woman that her infant will die and we increase the chances she will be able to feed, clothe, and educate her children.

The education of girls is an act of social justice that has very real implications for issues surrounding population. There is a correlation between lack of formal education and higher birth rates in the West, but we also should not forget that in the developing world, women who often do not have the chance to go to school exhibit birth rates far above those in the West. Sub-Saharan Africa experiences a population growth rate of over 3%, which is more than double the worldwide rate.

In many African countries the status of women is low. They often cannot own land or find work outside the home, and do not have equal access to education. High infant and child mortality, a mostly rural, subsistence economy, and the low status of women combine to reinforce a traditional preference for large families. Yet, while decisions to have many children may be understandable on an individual family basis, the effect on a country as a whole is devastating (ReVelle & ReVelle, 1992). Thus, efforts to educate and thereby empower girls can have a very real effect on limiting population growth, especially in places where population growth is most rampant.

Final Thoughts on Population

Individual decisions and circumstances govern population growth, and the summation of those individual cases will result in larger trends in population change over the long term. We can identify factors that might influence an individual's decision to procreate, but ultimately we can never hope to control anyone's sexual practices. If we were to examine ultimate causes of population growth we may begin to make inroads into how to affect change on this difficult and complex problem, with the knowledge that any solution must trickle down to the individual level.

In all species, including humans, populations are kept in check by limitations from the environment. We know, however, that population growth follows an exponential model when there is enough food to support such growth—which means that the more people there are, the more upward pressure there will be on having more people. This creates an increased need for more food, and fewer resources per person (land, water, biomass) upon which to produce it. These self-correcting systems are very simple, but effective.

As members of the living world, that is our history, and that is also our destiny. The difference between human and foxes, though, is that we have been able to produce our own food via agriculture and animal domestication, thereby removing some of the more immediate constraints from the negative feedback system that has kept our population in check. Because of the many cultural products of our clever brains, we can control our natural environment, build cities, push agricultural yield, and deplete the oceans of fish. From our individual short-term perspective, we have been wildly successful and very fit for survival. However, because our consumption has accelerated much faster than that of our fellow plant and animal species, and because our desire to produce our own food has wrought destruction on our environment, we are approaching the upper limits on what Earth itself can provide. And there is no way out of this negative feedback mechanism. At some point, if current trends continue, there will be a cataclysmic tipping point of the collapse of the supply, with a devastating result: There will just not be enough food for the number of people alive.

One way or another, the world population will again come into a sustainable balance. It is the core purpose of this book to challenge us all to recognize this danger before it is upon us (and if it is upon us, before it gets any worse), to heed a warning, to plead for us to look beyond our own fishbowls and think more globally about issues of scarcity as if our lives depended on them. While the massive loss of human life brought about by our self-correcting mechanisms is viewed as grossly unethical when done consciously, when such deaths occur as an inadvertent consequence of choices we have made (i.e., unchecked famine), this is deemed tragic, but for some reason less evil. Either way, a correction is coming. If we do not end up self-correcting, either in benign ways or malicious ways, the balance of nature will do it for us. Unlike the sea turtle, it is not in our survival strategy to let 95% of our populations perish; we who are currently living in the shadow of these threats have a moral responsibility to take action to prepare for them.

It will not be possible to survive (or survive well without cataclysm) without a sustainable human population. Experts do not agree what that sustainable population number is, but stresses in the environment would suggest that fewer people result in a lighter burden on our world. Taming population growth is perhaps the most difficult task humankind has ever faced, because it involves looking at large, abstract by-products of the most personal of individual decisions. This dilemma epitomizes the tension between our innate tendency toward the short-term and personal and our emerging need to take the long view into account. As living beings, we are hardwired to procreate; sex is a biological imperative, and no amount of legislation, preaching or policy making will change the fact that people will have it. As tribes, we are soft wired to expand and protect our own. As spiritual beings, some of us sense that the imperative to be fruitful and multiply is our covenant with God. Whatever the reason, it seems that without the constraints that keep all other animal populations in check, answering the questions of human population growth is the possible solution to every dilemma of our age.

It is unrealistic to think that humanity would willingly choose to revert to a more tribal state where famine is allowed to take its course, food is not stockpiled or even grown domestically in any great quantity, advances in medicine are slowed, and issues of public health are not addressed. It is equally unlikely that individuals will begin to make decisions about their sexual practices based purely on worries of overpopulation. Our short-term, immediate hopes and dreams with regard to offspring will far outweigh our concerns about world population growth. Our best hopes for population growth, then lie in culturally evolved solutions based foremost in education.

Delight thyself also in the Lord; and he shall give thee the desires of thine heart. (Psalms 37:4)

14

On Environment and Energy

Of all the adverse effects population growth has had on our world, the most significant has been the stress caused by increased human demands on the land itself. Since the agricultural revolution, whose centerpiece was our emerging ability to alter Earth's natural processes to serve our specific needs (to the exclusion of the rest of the community of life), humans have handily annexed most of Earth's natural resources and are in the process of laying claim to the rest. To some extent the facts detailed in this chapter will be the most familiar to readers.

In the past 10,000 years, and in particular the past 100 years, we have very successfully wrung as much out of our planet as we could. We have converted Earth's stores of energy to forms that can directly support human life and, as a result, supported the exponential rate of human population growth we are experiencing. We have been enormously successful in our endeavors in this regard; the human species, through its social collaborations and cultural inventions, has been able to achieve dominion over its environment. The end result of this is an ability to manipulate and control the natural world to the point where we are able to squeeze resources from it almost at will. This ability has given us a security of survival unparalleled in the community of life, and enabled us to increase our numbers well beyond what naturally occurring resources would be able to support.

Humans have inhabited almost every environment on the planet, from the tropics to the Antarctic, from thousands of feet beneath the ocean's surface to miles above Earth's troposphere. We don't simply inhabit these places; we change them significantly. We dig into the Earth to tap sources of energy to fuel our lifestyles and do so as if such sources of energy were never going to run out. At present, humans have altered about 50% of the land in the world from its natural state (Vitousek,

Mooney, Lubchenco, & Melillo, 1997), and Earth's atmosphere and oceans have also been irrevocably damaged by human activity. Animals and plants have also suffered. To serve our specific needs, humans have bred, tamed, and controlled the species with which we share our world, and we have done so at their expense. We have made it common practice to eliminate plants that are not useful to us and cultivate those that are, and we commonly think of animal populations in terms of their viability as human food instead of life forms with their own intrinsic worth. In fact, over the past century, human dominance over the environment appears to have played a significant role in the extinction of many species, including 25% of bird species (Vitousek, Mooney, Lubchenco, & Melillo, 1997). Because the presence of human civilization has been only a moment when taken in the context of evolutionary time, it remains to be seen how this will unfold in the long term: Either it will lead to a steady pattern of diminishing diversity and increasing entropy, or it will be a strange fluctuation within larger trends on Earth that will eventually give way to greater biodiversity after the slate is wiped somewhat clean of humans. Time will tell which of these outcomes is to be, but in either case, we can only hope that humanity will be around in some form to observe the consequences of our actions.

Ain't Nobody Gonna Break My Stride (Matthew Wilder)

How has nature not been able to keep humanity in check? How has such gratuitous consumption not been curbed? We consume energy and natural resources with a rabid hunger, and we are not held accountable by the checks and balances the rest of the natural world must abide by. We have found ways to make vast energy stores and resources available, and it is these energy stores and resources that propel the human enterprise forward. Like any other organism, we will do what we can to give ourselves the best chance at survival, but unlike other organisms, our culturally enhanced ability to literally change the face of the planet takes our fate out of the hands of our environment and puts it squarely in our own hands. While we may benefit immensely from such ability, we are beginning to see that our short-term species-specific success is having disastrous long-term consequences for all life (which, of course, includes us). The by-product of our consumption (exacerbated by exponential population growth) is that we, as a species, are depleting Earth's usable stores of energy faster than they can be regenerated, are polluting the very resources we depend on for survival, and are producing an incredible amount of waste that cannot easily be reused by other living beings.

Most of us have very recently been made more aware that all these actions, as well as our belief systems that support them, are unsustainable. That is, we have realized that the way we have been treating Earth cannot continue indefinitely, and more important, without consequence. It seems, though, that we had to push matters to the brink of cataclysm before waking up to the fact that our ways of life are incredibly destructive to the natural order. Why has it taken us so long to figure this out?

Part of the answer is that our (First World) civilization has been constructed in such a way that we often do not have to directly confront and experience the production or by-products of our most caustic decisions. Our food, itself once alive, appears under cellophane and in brightly colored plastic packaging. Produce grown all over the world is stacked high in the supermarket just down the road from us, and supplies never seem to waver. There does not seem to be a shortage of consumer goods, clothing, or even gasoline for our cars. The waste that we make, even as individuals, is carted away on a weekly basis to be dumped somewhere we never have been and never will go. Even the waste our bodies make, which is not waste as much as fertilizer for plants and food for microbes, magically disappears at the pull of a lever. We biological beings have, in effect, isolated ourselves from the sources and effects of our very existence.

Many of us take this for granted. We are outraged when our luxuries are not immediately available, or when we are forced to actually confront the waste we make. This is nothing new. Humans, for thousands of years, have adapted to a certain cultural standard of living. However, never before in human history has such a standard been as unsustainable as it is now. Humans have always made waste and impacted the environment around them, but for most of human history the population was small enough that the majority of the waste could be reused or recycled by nature. Even if a culture proved itself wasteful or damaging to its local environment, there was plenty of room to dispose of the waste, or to pick up and move if they needed a fresh start.

More recently, though, as population levels have grown exponentially and humans have inhabited every conceivable corner of the globe, we have become increasingly aware that there are limits to which our consumption and wastefulness can go before we are forced to confront them directly. For one, we are running out of physical space. Virtually all the land on Earth has been explored, mapped, accounted for, and inhabited. There is not the great unknown land on the horizon like there was even a hundred years ago; we are increasingly forced to make do with what land we have. For another, our once vast supply of natural resources is shrinking. We can thank our vastly complex cultural systems for insulating us from this tough reality for so long, but the time is upon us when not even that can save us from confronting the nature of our unsustainable lifestyles.

Nature/Culture Interactions

It is common to think of humanity as separate from the rest of the natural world. We humans, despite our biological heritage, often prefer not to acknowledge our close cousins on the phylogenetic family tree as genetic relatives, but no one can deny that a human and a chimpanzee have 96% of their DNA in common (National Institutes of Health, 2005). All this is to say that we need to think of humanity as a subset—albeit a very unique and special subset—of the animal kingdom as opposed to an entity that somehow exists outside the natural order.

It is true that humans have certain unique characteristics, most notably our highly developed and incredibly complex cultural systems, but we have more in common with the biological world than most of us are aware of or would like to admit. And moreover, the things about us that make us uniquely human share many similarities with properties found elsewhere in nature. If anything, systems of memes created by the human mind bear an uncanny resemblance to processes and relationships that have evolved in nature over millions and billions of years. This can be as simple as using the wings of birds as inspiration for designing human flying machines, as Leonardo da Vinci famously did, or as complex as fitting economic models to ecological phenomena, such as charting the flow and stock of forest resources to determine sustainability (Leefers & Castillo, 1998). E. O. Wilson has drawn many parallels between ant colonies and human society (as well as several important differences) (Margulis & Punset, 2007), and Jane Goodall can attest to elements of human culture that can be found in chimpanzee society (Margulis & Punset, 2007). That we see so many parallels between human culture and the rest of the natural world should only reinforce the fact that we are not as separate from the rest of creation as we often believe.

We have overlaid our own cultural systems on Earth's natural systems, and the interplay of the two has positioned our culture to act as a parasite to the larger host organism of our planet. What many of us have ignored, forgotten, or never properly understood, is that human survival depends completely on our environment and its health, and this is true no matter how much we try to insulate ourselves from the ecological truths to which we are subject. Again, humanity needs to be thought of as a part of the living world and all its interconnected systems, instead of some foreign entity that does not belong in the natural order.

Save the Humans (Thought Riot)

Scarcity of natural resources and harmful human impact on those that remain is indeed a dilemma of our age. What can be done to save the world? The world, in the long run, will be fine. Even if humanity causes what we consider to be irreparable damage to our natural environment, our judgments of such damage sprout from a human scale of perspective, and given a couple million years (itself a very short amount of time in the grand timeline of natural history), Earth, its natural process, and the life forms adapted enough to survive will begin to heal and even flourish. Humans do present a special and acute case in the 4.6-billion-year history of our planet, but when taken in the larger perspective, all of humanity may just be a footnote in the story of Earth. According to some, the rest of the community of life could even be better off without humans around to impede their evolutionary course (Weisman, 2007).

The world does not need saving; it is the humans that need saving. Even as the human parasite grows exponentially as population accelerates, even as scientists and experts prognosticate that we have moved well beyond certain critical points (Hansen et al., 2008) and are causing irreparable damage to that which sustains us, we still feel the urge to "save the world" so we can save ourselves. Like any other successful life form, our instinct for survival is strong. Until recently, it was precisely this instinct for immediate short-term survival that drove us to take more than we were able to give back, and to engage in practices that have damaged the life sustaining ability of Earth. With everything we are learning about the interaction of human culture and the natural world, we need to change our tactics. In our shorter human scale of perspective, we need to alter how we interact with the rest of the world, not to save it, but to save us. We need to base our efforts at survival on a fresh understanding of our deep connection to and place in the natural order.

Energy: The Currency of Nature

Before we involve ourselves with what we consider our impact on the natural world, how nature's balance has been thrown out of whack, and what we are able to do to correct that imbalance, it is important to understand how nature's processes work. It is our hope that a small (but crucial) bit of knowledge about how the world works will tell us why things are out of balance, and maybe even what we can do about it. There are no doubt many well-trained scientists, engineers, environmentalists, policy makers, and community leaders who have cultivated comprehensive understandings of how our world works and are hard at work on the issues caused by human impact on the environment. None of these efforts has been as important and informative as former U.S. Vice President Al Gore's *Inconvenient Truth* (2006). We believe that a foundational knowledge of how the world works will go a long way toward helping us to reframe our individual actions, choices, and beliefs when it comes to our relationship with the environment.

Energy: A Few More Scientific Facts

A fundamental law of nature is that energy cannot be created or destroyed, only transferred from form to form. At no point does energy magically appear, and at no point does energy magically disappear. It simply

332

changes forms. The Earth (and everything on it) holds a lot of energy, much more than we could easily imagine, and ostensibly more than we will ever need in all 6.7 billion of our lifetimes. The ultimate source of almost all usable energy on Earth comes from the Sun, in the form of light[18] and electromagnetic radiation. Of the radiation that reaches Earth (about 1,370 watts per square meter of the Earth's atmosphere) (NASA, 2009), only 40% of that makes it to the Earth's surface. And of the light that reaches the Earth's surface, only about 1% is converted into biological energy (Raven, Evert, & Eichhorn, 1992). This includes all the energy stored in fossil fuels, as well as the energy in every living thing on the planet. Other than through photovoltaic cells (a very recent invention), the only way that this small fraction of energy is transferred into something usable to humans is by the process of photosynthesis in green plants and photosynthetic aquatic creatures such as phytoplankton. Even though the percentage of sunlight that is transferred to biological energy via photosynthesis is minuscule, it is enough to power the entire community of life on Earth and all its varied enterprises, humanity included.

Thus, plants that convert sunlight into chemical energy via photosynthesis in turn serve as the energy source for the rest of life on the planet. We can trace the energy we use for our daily activities to photosynthesis. This can be a very direct transfer (we grow spinach in our garden and then eat it to obtain energy for ourselves), or there may be several intermediary steps: A dinosaur eats a plant millions of years ago, and when it dies that unused energy is stored as a chemical bond in the matter that made up its body. Over time, the dinosaur's body is converted into a "fossil fuel" like coal or petroleum. Millions of years later that stored chemical energy is unearthed, refined, and used to power the electrical grid in your hometown.

---

[18]   This, incidentally, is why the energy available to us is finite: the sun only has so much fuel. While we expect the sun to continue to burn for the next several billion years, at some point the sun will explode like any other star. When this happens, the earth will lose its energy source (and be incinerated in the process). Similarly, the energy available to the universe is finite. There are a lot of stars, but there are not an infinite number of them.

Not all forms of energy are beneficial for all things. For example, humans can't drink gasoline to obtain energy, and we can't put green bean casseroles in ours gas tank to make our cars go (although it does give some of us gas). To make energy usable to us, we actually need to spend what energy we have to convert certain sources of stored energy into a usable form. Nature will do this for us if our concern is to obtain energy for ourselves (wild plants and animals we use for food), or if we have a couple million years to wait around for fossil fuel deposits to form. If we are not content to depend entirely on wild plants and animals for sustenance (which includes almost all of us), and cannot stand to wait around for a couple million years for more fossil fuels to form (which includes all of us), we have to invest some of the limited energy available to us to access more energy in usable forms.

If the "spend energy to get energy" paradox weren't enough, the principle of entropy confounds the problem. We remember from Chapter 2 that entropy is the tendency toward chaos and disorder, but in terms of energy, entropy has a more specific meaning. The principle of entropy allows us to infer that the amount of available energy has been dissipating since the Big Bang and will continue to do so. In other words, when energy changes forms, some is inevitably lost to forms generally unusable or unintended. In the specific case of energy on Earth, entropy explains why energy transfers from one form to another are never 100% efficient; while a percentage of energy will become transferred into another usable form, the remainder of energy will be transferred to an unusable (or at the very least an unintended) form, which is most often heat. Think again of the tiny light bulb in the flashlight in your basement. The energy stored in batteries is intended to be converted to light energy, and a lot of it is, but there is also some energy that is converted to heat. It matters very little to us whether our light bulbs are hot—only that they give off light. Therefore, heat is considered to be an unusable form of energy, and the energy from the battery that is converted to heat is said to be lost. Another excruciating example of this is the internal combustion engine found in our cars: Stored chemical energy contained in gasoline is converted to mechanical energy (the wheels on our cars go around, propelling us down the road), but the process also creates a great deal of heat, which is considered to be an unusable by-product of the energy conversion. Surprisingly, car engines are highly entropic, converting less than 40% of the energy stored in gasoline to mechanical energy ("Energy Lost," 2007).

Thus, between having to spend some of our energy to quickly access more usable energy and the principle of entropy, we find ourselves in a considerable energy debt to the universe. And like the current economic crisis created from overextending monetary debt, we may find that our cultural investments that depend so much on available and usable energy will not be backed indefinitely by the currency of the universe.

Our energy needs operate on two simple levels. Because we are living things, our personal physiological energy needs demand stored energy that is found in other living things, namely food. On a cultural level, other stores of potential energy must feed our energy needs. Currently, the source of these other stores is most often deposits of decaying organic matter that have been converted to fossil fuels, but they also can include stores of energy that our technology has only recently been able to access. In 2007, 37.5% of all energy consumption in the United States came from petroleum, 23.3% came from natural gas, 22.5% came from coal, 8.3% came from uranium (nuclear energy), and 1.7% came from propane. All these sources are nonrenewable (within the time period where we will demand more). The remaining 6.7% of energy consumption was fed by renewable sources, which include biomass (3.6%), hydropower (2.4%), geothermal (0.3%), wind (0.3%), and solar power (0.1%) (U.S. Energy Information, 2008). Whatever the source, this potential energy is later translated to electricity, heat, and mechanical energy, as well as a few other forms.

We have made it our business to take full advantage of Earth's available energy stores, and we have done so quite selfishly. We feel entitled to them and often use them for our own personal short-term benefit, regardless of what adverse consequence it may have on other species or even Earth itself. The entirety of the modern human enterprise can be thought of as an attempt to maximize the amount of usable energy available to us and to improve the processes we use to convert energy to usable forms with as little effort as possible. To our credit, we have been extremely successful. We have been in constant pursuit of more efficient and effective ways to grow and raise food and of developing technology that allows us to do more with less energy expenditure. We have altered the very functioning of the planet's ecosystems to better accomplish this goal. We are the first among living things to have constructed our own biome: the urban biome. This is what we have called progress. In mathematical calculations of progress, and by casual observation of everything humans have created, it seems as though we have been extremely successful in our enterprise. However, it is becoming clear that our so-called progress has far reaching consequences that on every level may be adversely affecting the sources of the energy we need.

Recharging Our Batteries

In terms of energy, humans (along with all other living things) can be thought of as rechargeable batteries.[19] Like actual batteries, to get recharged living things need for energy to be in a specific form. The energy currency of life takes the form of energy stored in chemicals, most commonly the chemical adenosine triphosphate (ATP). This is the chemical formed by the process of cellular respiration, where glucose and oxygen are processed to assemble ATP, and water and carbon dioxide are given off.[20] To obtain the raw materials and stored energy necessary to recharge our batteries, we need to eat food. And food, of course, is organic material, which at one time had battery-recharging needs of its own. If we trace the chain of energy back, we will find that almost any form of energy usable to us was originally sunlight converted into ATP via photosynthesis. Sometimes, the chain of energy transfer passes through many steps and organisms. With each step, entropy will cause more energy to be lost to heat or other unusable forms. Confounding this

---

[19]   It is a peculiar way to think about humans, but the concept shouldn't be so strange, considering that we hopefully now are also accustomed to thinking of humans as gene and meme containers.

[20]   It is a commonly thought that plants only perform photosynthesis. This is not true. Plants also undergo cellular respiration. The difference between plants and animals, then, is that plants are able to form their own glucose from sunlight, water, and CO_2, while animals must draw glucose from other living things in their environment. Interestingly, through untold ages of evolution, it just so happens that the by-products of cellular respiration are exactly the same molecules that plants need to photosynthesize light energy into glucose. This happy symbiosis between plants and animals should never be overlooked.

process is the fact that energy transfer between each stage in the food chain is at best 10% efficient, which is why it is most efficient and in our best interest to recharge our personal batteries with foods that use as few steps between sunlight and our dinner plates as possible. Again, we see ample reason to embrace a vegetable-heavy diet. This is largely the reason why author Michael Pollan (2008) stresses that we eat "mostly plants."

Plants, then, are nature's solar panels. The more plants there are, the more energy is available for use by living things; the fewer plants, the less energy. It's really as simple as that. Therefore, every square foot of plant life we kill and replace with concrete or steel is that much less energy ultimately available. In a fairly cruel irony, then, every plant we cut down to make more space for human civilization decreases the amount of energy available to that civilization. We are not going to willfully stop building cities and towns, so we must build with the knowledge of what concrete does to our available biological energy.

While all plants will contribute to the pool of energy available to us in the big picture, some plants suit our energy needs better than others. Avocado trees, for example, are much more useful to people as an energy source than poison ivy. Likewise, cabbage and carrots are of far greater use to us than dandelions, which is why we promote the growth of carrots and pull out the dandelions in our gardens. Because of agricultural innovations, we have the ability, to some extent, to dictate which plants will grow and which will not. This has afforded us a large store of battery-recharging fuel in the short term, but it has also upset the stability that the plants themselves need to grow. While we have purposely replaced certain plants not immediately useful to us with plants that are, as has been the practice of agriculture for 10,000 years, this upsets the natural balance of ecosystems. An excellent example of this is the effects of monoculture (the growing of a single crop over a large area). The practice of monoculture can increase plant yield by eliminating competitive plants, but the long-term effects of monoculture renders soil much more infertile than it would be otherwise. Additionally, in the event that disease or blight is spread throughout a plant population, plants that are grown under the practice of monoculture are much more susceptible to harm. Introducing diversity to a field increases the hardiness of the system. It is no coincidence that nature uses this exact strategy.

Plants are the sources from which we recharge our batteries. Therefore, the fate of plants, which depends on certain environmental conditions and the presence of other living things, will ultimately become our fate. If we continue to tamper with systems and interactions that nature has honed and refined over millennia via the evolution of plants and other energy-generating life forms, then we are, in the long run, pulling the plug on our own energy sources, no matter what short-term gains in our stores of usable energy we might enjoy.

Recall that human energy needs operate on two levels: food (for physiological survival) and fuel (for cultural survival). In the case of food, we see a comparatively quick turnaround between our investment in an energy source and its ability to recharge our batteries. Living things that we consider food can grow and yield their energy to us many times over in our lifetimes. However, for processes integral to the continued success of our culture that involves more steps than simply growing food and eating it, the natural means by which energy is converted and stored into usable forms of energy takes hundreds of thousands of years, at minimum, to accumulate to any significant amount. For example, the process by which decaying organic matter is converted into fossil fuel demands precise geological conditions and lots of time, which is why coal, petroleum, natural gas, and similar fuels are precious and rare resources indeed, resources that we must consider nonrenewable.

In the history of Earth, our planet has yielded a very limited amount of fossil fuel. It is difficult to think of fossil fuel as finite when the United States currently consumes 20 million barrels of oil, 60 billion cubic feet of natural gas, and 3 million short tons of coal every day (Energy Information Administration, 2007), but given the comparative size of Earth and the time fossil fuels have had to accumulate, the quantity available to us is really not very large. We discovered the usefulness of coal during the industrial revolution, learned how to refine liquid fuel from coal in the 1840s, and developed technology that allowed us to use natural gas in the 1860s; our access to vast stores of untapped energy ignited a cultural acceleration the likes of which the world had not seen. With these innovations, the seemingly useless form of stored energy immediately became a commodity, and moreover, the amount of fuel that had become available almost overnight was staggering to us. Thus, humanity built its postindustrial civilization upon the seemingly inexhaustible stores of fossil fuels. We are finding out now that this staggering amount can be consumed with an equally staggering speed and with damaging effects to the life-supporting environment.

We once again see the consequences that our exponentially accelerating culture has imposed on our far slower biological selves. In *An Essay on the Principle of Population,* Malthus (1798) postulated that increasing population (a phenomenon whose acceleration is attributable to culturalevolution) would far outpace food production (still very much under the constraints of biology), and in a similar fashion, we are beginning to realize just how much our consumption of usable forms of energy has outpaced the ability to convert energy to such forms.

Having realized such problems, we are, with varying success,in the midst of trying to reconcile the dilemma with cultural solutions. We are attempting to harness processes that do not ultimately depend on plant photosynthesis for energy, such as the kinetic energy created by wind, waves, and tides, or the chemical energy found inside the nuclei of radioactive atoms. In parts of the world, the heat generated by Earth's core is being harnessed to generate usable forms of energy. Alternatively, we are attempting to circumvent plants entirely by using photovoltaic cells to generate electrical energy directly from solar power. All these process are currently employed somewhere in the world, and to some extent all are successfully generating usable forms of energy for humanity, but, for various reasons, they are currently too inefficient, too costly to implement, too limited in availability, too dangerous, or too tied to business and political interests to completely replace consumption of fossil fuels. Nevertheless, alternative energy sources represent the most viable cultural solution to the energy demand that humanity poses to its environment.

Alternative energy sources are meant to produce culturally usable energy, such as electricity. However, this does not mean that alternative energy sources cannot directly help us with food energy.[21] Electricity will not make crops grow on its own, but when we consider just how much cultural energy is needed to grow, harvest, transport, disinfect, package, market, and prepare food for us, we see that alternative energy sources

---

[21]   Here we speak of food on a personal scale, not of the industrial agriculture that produces such food, which is a cultural invention.

can positively impact our individual physiological needs as well as our cultural ones. While solar or wind power can be employed to increase the productivity of the agricultural industry, plants grown

Botswana fire 2005

for energy are still subject to a different set of operating parameters according to the laws of nature. Similarly, our biological requirements from our cultural world, and a corresponding different set of problems.

In terms of keeping our personal batteries recharged, we require a daily input of other formerly living things to eat. As the human population increases, this demand also increases, which causes insult to the rest of the living world. The community of life is fluid and cyclical, and if population levels are kept mutually accountable to one another, the system is sustainable. However, because humanity has developed agriculture to the point where it overwhelms indigenous plant and animal life, those checks and safeguards are no longer there. Our energy concerns are not just a problem of economics or scientific advancement; our energy concerns are problems of ecology and environmental science.

We Are Causing Damage to the Earth: Things Are Heating Up

It is clear now that because of our advanced technology and highly developed civilization, coupled with ever-increasing numbers of people, our activities and energy needs place a demand on the environment that is not sustainable and is causing damage.[22] There are literally thousands of smaller trends and practices we can track that serve as testament to the damage humans have caused to Earth: air pollutants billowing out of smokestacks, smog covering cities, the changing pH of the ocean's waters, the depletion of topsoil in the most fertile parts of the world, melting glaciers and ice sheets, and so on. These small-scale examples are useful to us; they personalize much larger abstract trends and serve as tangible evidence that human culture and Earth's natural processes are not getting along. These smaller examples might give us a sliver of the larger picture on a more personal, human scale, but it is also important to not lose sight of the forest when examining the trees.

While naturally occurring temperature fluctuations are scientific reality, it is also an indisputable reality that the changes in climate we are seeing today are not attributable to these natural processes. Instead, they are directly attributable to human activity, most specifically the by-products of our ever-accelerating culture and technology. It is true that there are naturally occurring phenomena that cause temperatures to fluctuate on our planet. Some of these changes operate on scales larger than our own Earth, such as slight variations in the Earth's distance from the Sun, changes in the Sun's energy output, and chance collisions between the Earth and other celestial bodies such as meteorites. Other naturally occurring phenomena on Earth have caused a cyclical change in temperature that is responsible for "ice ages." Ice ages ebb and flow

---

[22]   More correctly, it is not our activities that have changed, but the scale to which we are able to carry out our activities thanks to our accelerating technology. One farmer who grows enough food to feed his family and works the land with handheld tools is engaged in the same activity as an industrial farm with fleets of diesel-powered threshers and harvesters, but the single farmer causes far less insult to the earth than the industrial farm does.

rhythmically in geological time and according to geological phenomena, such as the movement of continents to and from the poles and equator; changes in greenhouse gas composition due to volcanic activity, fire, and relative rates of photosynthesis; changes in wind and ocean currents (sometimes, due to plate tectonics); and the amount of light energy that is reflected back out to space by already present ice sheets. The proximate cause of climate change is fluctuation to the content of Earth's atmosphere. Human activity has caused buildup of greenhouse gases (the four most significant of which are carbon dioxide, methane, ozone, and water). The two primary sources of this buildup are burning of fossil fuels and killing of plants through deforestation. Burning a fossil fuel uses oxygen and releases carbon dioxide and water, both greenhouse gases. Photosynthesizing plants of the world are able to keep the buildup of carbon dioxide and water due to animal cellular respiration in check, but plants cannot photosynthesize fast enough to counterbalance the amount of greenhouse gases being pumped out of our fossil fuel–burning factories, power plants, vehicles, machines, and homes.

It is estimated that the burning of fossil fuels accounts for 80% to 85% of all greenhouse gases in the atmosphere today ("What Human Activities Contribute," 1997). If we wished to work toward offsetting such greenhouse gas emissions, it would make sense to promote plant growth, but as it turns out, that is the exact opposite of what we are doing. It is estimated that 32.1 million acres of forest are lost every year, and that number is steadily increasing (Global Forests Resources Assessment, 2005). Forgetting for a minute about the other terrible effects of deforestation, such as loss of biodiversity (which provides for ecological stability), soil erosion (which renders land unfit for farming), disruptions in the water cycle (which decrease the amount of available water for us), and loss of resources valuable for human civilization, cutting down so many trees can only keep increasing the amount of atmospheric carbon dioxide, which continues to trap heat here on Earth via the greenhouse effect.

Figure 14.1 Temperatures increase when carbon dioxide levels rise.

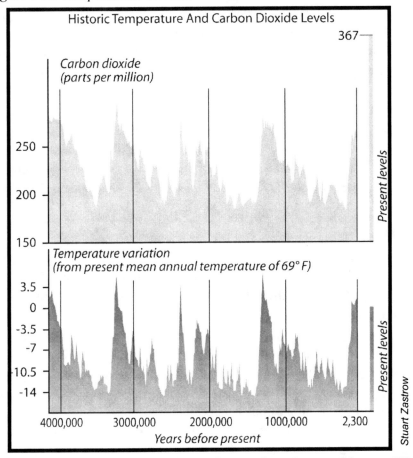

Source: Retit, J.R., et al. 1998. Climate and atmospheric history of the past 420,000 years from the Vostok Ice core in Antarctica, Nature 339 (3 June), pp 429-436.

The connection between increased levels of greenhouse gases and temperature increase is not a tenuous leap; it is a direct and undeniable correlation. This is as true over long-term historical trends on Earth as it is in the shorter term. The graph in Figure 14.1 demonstrates that in the past 400,000 years, every time carbon dioxide levels increased so did temperature.

In more recent history, this relationship is more pronounced. Since 1880, data of CO_2 content in the atmosphere and average atmospheric temperature show a coincident upward trend as well. The graph in Figure 14.1 is particularly instructive because not only does it directly demonstrate the relationship between increase in CO_2 and temperature, it also shows that the increases in both carbon dioxide and global temperature are following an exponential trend. That is, they are two more examples of acceleration. One of the reasons this exponential trend is seen is because increasing atmospheric CO_2 and temperature interrelate and operate in a positive feedback model. More specifically, when temperatures increase because of elevated levels of greenhouse gases, more ice melts. Less ice means less reflective material that bounces solar energy back out to space, leading to more solar energy that is absorbed and stored as heat in the world's liquid water.

The cumulative effect of this process is that the average global temperature is expected to increase one-half degree Celsius by the year 2030 (Handwerk, 2005). This seems quite benign at first glance, but as the world's oceans heat up, even in such small amounts, more and more phytoplankton die. Phytoplanktons—microscopic one-celled plants that live in the ocean—are responsible for about half the carbon-fixing photosynthesis on the planet (Roach, 2004). That means that if phytoplankton were to die off, we could count on up to double the amount of CO_2 in our atmosphere. It goes without saying that the effect an event like this would have on the positive feedback loop of temperature increase would be appalling. Additionally, buildup of carbon dioxide in the atmosphere increases the acidity of oceans (Caldeira & Wickett, 2003), which further kills off phytoplankton (as well as other sea life, some of which humans use for food). Therefore, the further we spiral upward in terms of CO_2 levels and temperature, the less likely it is that phytoplankton will recover. Less phytoplankton causes more buildup of carbon dioxide, which increases ocean acidity, traps solar energy, and raises the planet's temperature, which causes even more glacial ice to melt . . . and so on. Some believe that we have passed the point of no return in this positive feedback system and the best we can hope to do is slow the increases in both CO_2 and temperature (McCarthy, 2006).

Not only does the melting of ice further increase temperatures, it also represents the loss of an enormous source of fresh water upon which humans depend completely for survival. Additionally, the loss of fresh water into the oceans—specifically, the fresh water held in ice sheets in

Greenland and the Arctic—will slow ocean currents such as the Gulf Stream, which will in turn have dramatic effects on the climate in places such as Europe and North Africa (Gore, 2006). Even though London and Calgary lie at approximately the same latitude, London's (and all of Europe's) winters are not as prohibitively cold as Canada's winters, thanks to the warm air that comes off the Gulf Stream currents. A slowing of the Gulf Stream current could plunge temperatures in Europe (Kerr, 1997), although the intensity of the effects of such a potential event has been disputed (Seager et al., 2002). Whether or not European winters grow less mild, this cascading effect could potentially change the nature of seasonal cycles, which, as will be discussed, has surprisingly serious consequences for plant, animal, and cultural life.

Effects of Climate Change

One of the most direct consequences of temperature increases, even in such small amounts, is disruption in precipitation rates and changes in water cycles. Recent studies tell us that ocean levels are rising twice as fast as they were 150 years ago ("Global Warming Doubles," 2005), the melting of sea ice and the ice in Greenland was at record levels in 2008 ("Annual Arctic Report Card," 2008), flooding has increased significantly in recent years, and extreme weather events such as hurricanes, tsunamis, tornadoes, and even droughts are happening with greater and greater frequency (Sawin, 2003). These changes in environmental water cycles have a dramatic impact on civilization, ranging from loss of crops (as was seen, for example, in the Midwestern United States in the spring and summer of 2008) to widespread destruction (as was seen in New Orleans in 2005). We would like to think that our civilization could withstand the weather. In some ways it can, but our ability to bounce back from natural disasters comes at a great cost, and the costs rise with every disaster. The 2008 flooding in the Midwest, an event that incited looting and hospital evacuations, and required the presence of the National Guard, cost the state of Indiana an estimated $126 million in damages ("Flooding Damage Estimate," 2008), required the complete evacuation of cities in Iowa, and caused six tornadoes to touch down in the same day in Wisconsin (National Weather Service, 2008). The economic costs of Hurricane Katrina for the states of Louisiana and Mississippi topped

345

$150 billion (Burton & Hicks, 2005). The storm, which left more than four fifths of the city of New Orleans submerged in water; displaced more than 1 million people; begat riots, looting, rape, and murder; and resulted in 1,836 deaths (Beven, Avila, Blake, Brown, Franklin, et al., 2008). Even something as tragic as Hurricane Katrina does not compare in sheer numbers to the 118,000 lives lost to the 2004 tsunami in the Indian Ocean (CNN.com, 2004). To be sure, we can insulate our civilizations from the weather only so much. In the end, we must confront nature.

Temperature increases will also have deleterious effects on animal life. Most animals have adapted to specific temperature ranges, and variations from such ranges would mean the end of those animals. The animals most affected would be the smallest and simplest animals on the planet, the ones that make up the foundation of the world's food chains. Additionally, the changing of seasonal cycles will mean that formerly successful reproductive cycles may prove less so, predator-prey relationships that hold populations in check might be thrown off, and ecological niches that once were stable might become unstable. Thus, even if macrofauna (such as the animals we generally consider to be food sources) are able to withstand certain amounts of temperature changes, the animals that they eat might not. Reducing populations of animals early in the food chain will have dramatic effects on animals (such as us) further up the food chain. Namely, if the things we eat have nothing to eat themselves, then after a while we will be left with nothing to eat.

Longer ranging effects of changing temperatures include the proliferation of some species and the extinction of others. It has been estimated that given current accelerating rates of human activity and resultant habitat destruction and climate change, a million land-dwelling species could be "committed to extinction" by the year 2050 (Thomas et al., 2004), and that half of all bird and mammal species will be extinct within 200 to 300 years ("Extinction Rate Across the Globe, 2002). We already are experiencing a rate of species extinction 100 to 1,000 times greater than pre-human rates of extinction (Pimm et al., 1995), and like everything else, this number is accelerating. While some species may find themselves on a steady path to extinction, others may thrive, and those that thrive tend to be vectors for human pathogens, such as malaria-carrying mosquitoes. We have seen an emergence of pathogenic microbes and their resultant diseases such as SARS, West Nile virus, and avian flu in the last few years. The vectors for such diseases, most commonly insects, may be experiencing an increased viability due to climate conditions, both in an increase in the range of places in which they are able to live and a decrease in their natural predators.

It would be bad enough if the effects of climate change were limited to the realm of hard science. However, because our culture is so intertwined with the workings of the planet, climate change also has drastic consequences on government, politics, and economics. Climate change and deforestation put already-stretched resources in even shorter supply. Unfortunately, with increased population and acceleration of our culture and its products, demand for these limited resources and the energy they produce is going up, and consumption of these resources is doing more damage to the environment on which we are completely depending. Because there are shortages in supply and increases in demand, and because countries are not self-sufficient in terms of the resources they consume, questions of how to access these resources and distribute them fall to policy makers and governments. It is no surprise and no mere coincidence, then, that the countries that are most politically troubled in the world right now, countries like Afghanistan, Bangladesh, Haiti, Iraq, Madagascar, Pakistan, Rwanda, Somalia, the Philippines, and Nepal, are also the countries with the most severe environmental problems. In *Collapse: How Societies Choose to Fail or Succeed* (2005), Jared Diamond points out that the two are completely connected:

> Today, just as in the past, countries that are environmentally stressed, overpopulated, or both become at risk of getting politically stressed, and of their governments collapsing. When people are desperate, undernourished, and without hope, they blame their governments, which they see as responsible for or unable to solve their problems. They try to emigrate at any cost. They fight each other over land. They kill each other. They start civil wars. They figure that they have nothing to lose, so they become terrorists, or they support or tolerate terrorism. (p. 516)

Government and economics are, in many ways, cultural attempts to mitigate the unavoidable (or as Al Gore calls them, "inconvenient") truths to which we human animals are bound. Government tries to manage the tension between the one and the many, but often favors solutions that benefit its constituents in the short term. Economics, especially hands-off free-market systems, employ the "can implies should" mentality, which leaves the environment at a disadvantage from the human perspective. Things are heating up, and this is not just a problem for scientists and academics. Government and economics are severely impacted as well, and as such, government and economic systems should have an obligation to address the increasingly hot issue of climate change.

Biting The Hand That Feeds Us

In the context of energy and resources, we need to realize that Earth is our caregiver. This is not meant metaphorically: Earth provides everything we need to survive. Why, then, are we biting the hand that feeds us? Part of the answer is that we began to do so inadvertently, initially unaware that extracting energy and resources for immediate, personal, short-term benefit eventually would put our chances for long-term sustainable survival in jeopardy. We cannot go so far as to say that we have done such things unintentionally; the people who build factories and raze swaths of jungle are fully aware of what they are doing. Behind such an intention is a sincere hope to make one's life better, but this hope is grounded in short-term, personal decision-making. What is unintended in these actions, and what we have been unaware of for most of our history, is the long-term dangers that have sprung from such well-intended actions.

Again we see how the perspective that has worked wonderfully for hundreds of thousands of years has backfired on us in the age of our rapidly accelerating culture. We now have more knowledge about the consequences of our advancement, and hopefully a very real responsibility for our actions comes with this knowledge. Even though we cannot fault ourselves for thinking of our short-term interests first, we now realize that we must begin to think of our own personal short-term survival as something that is directly tied to the long-term viability of the entire planet. Instead of thinking of humanity as a species that resides somewhere outside the natural order, we must begin to think of ourselves as a crucial and integral part of that order, understand that our actions and decisions have a direct impact on our environment, and recognize that our fates are tied to nature's fate. Field theorists tell us that separation and independence are an illusion, that the only reality that we can believe in is formed by our relationships. It is therefore of the hoped that each of us becomes aware and establishes a personal relationship with the natural world to not just know, but to understand on a very deep level, just how interconnected everything really is, admittedly a very hard lesson for most of the world.

Because we do have a place in the natural order, because we belong here on Earth and are not just occupying space, we should consider it our duty to become acquainted with our neighbors and treat them with respect. That is, we should not feel that it is okay to do whatever we want to the planet at the expense of the other living things that share its resources. In our endlessly interconnected world, we should now be aware that destruction of distant forests and extinction of species we have never encountered would cast very palpable ripples into our lives. We should be aware that pollutants we dump back into the environment will render land unusable for agriculture, will make water unfit for drinking, and will ultimately change the climate of the entire planet such that Earth will be an increasingly harsh place for human life. Our relationship with the natural world has health and even psychotherapeutic benefits (White & Heerwagen, 1998), but we really do see such a relationship as vital to our very survival.

Environmental destruction cycles back and puts strain and pressure on humanity's most important cultural creations: government and economic systems. As a very salient and relevant case in point, issues of U.S. national security and the West's relationship with the Middle East hinge almost completely on the fact that countries in the Middle East possess vast stores of petroleum, upon which the United States depends. Economic organizations with amazing political power (such as OPEC) have been organized around the availability of fossil fuels within the borders of their member countries, and such organizations have enormous power at the world bargaining table. This is true even though many oil-producing countries are headed by totalitarian and fundamentalist regimes that democratic nations would probably not otherwise engage in diplomatic relations with. Dependence on Middle Eastern oil has corrupted worldwide politics and has provided fodder for Islamic fundamentalists to attack the infidels for their duplicitous policies.

To be sure, the global market for oil has co-opted much in the way of international policy, making strange bedfellows of seemingly ideological enemies. It is in the world's best diplomatic interest, as well as in everyone's best environmental interest, to wean ourselves from fossil fuels as much as possible. The big picture for human survival (on both ecological and diplomatic fronts) is to create a carbon-neutral economy that is not based on oil, and to do this on a global scale.

The amount of energy and resources that Earth can provide are more directly tied to the establishment of economic systems. In fact, the limited nature of our natural resources is exactly why economic systems developed in the first place. The whole of economics is based on the premise that there is not enough to go around, and the practice of economics is to determine how to best distribute what we do have as fairly and equitably as possible. Indeed, as population (demand) increases and the quantity of available natural resources (supply) decreases, we are seeing very clearly that resources are limited, and they become that much more precious as more of them are used up. As discussed earlier in this chapter, two of our world's most pressing economic issues involve food and fossil fuel, and it is no coincidence that these two represent the major energy sources we pull from Earth, which human physiology and culture need to survive.

Realizing Our Place in Nature

Thus, it is vitally important that we reframe our thinking about our place and role on Earth to include ourselves as an integral part of the natural order, and further realize the deep connections our cultural paths have made with the overconsumption of natural resources. Such a cognitive restructuring should be challenging in some ways, but should not in any way be beyond anyone's capability. This is because such realizations represent a return to our most basic biological operating premises, not a further stretch toward increasingly unsustainable cultural practices. We believe that the first and best thing anyone can do is to re-establish a personal connection with the natural world. In 1984, E. O. Wilson wrote that each of us has a "biophilia," an innate attraction to the natural world, and as such, a connection with our natural environment is just that: natural.

We believe that people would be more likely to understand the impact their actions have on the world if they were directly confronted with the consequences of their lifestyle choices. In other words, we encourage people to deal personally with the waste they make and the impact they personally have on the environment. Much of the damage done by our consumptive lifestyles could be avoided if we were made more aware of and held accountable for the extent to which our actions and choices are destructive.

People of course know that the waste they make does not just disappear, and that the by-products of their lifestyles are environmentally damaging, but it would be understood on a much more meaningful level if it were presented to them, very concretely, in their own personal reality. It is a basic principle of behaviorism that the consequence of an action needs to be closely associated with that action for it to have an effect on behavior (Skinner, 1965). People who have abided by the "Leave No Trace" ethic, which includes carrying all waste out of wilderness areas, understand this much more clearly because they have had to directly confront the waste that they have made.

Beyond establishing a personal connection with the natural world and requiring people to confront directly their impact on Earth's resources, we need to begin to proactively understand how our choices and lifestyles impact the world around us, and how that will, in turn, affect our lives. We need to take such ideas out of the abstract and make them very real and immediate to our present states. To that end, many organizations around the world have encouraged initiatives aimed at education, awareness, and action with regard to environmental issues.

Environmental Politics: The Green Movement

More people have recently tuned in to the dilemma of energy and environment. Al Gore earned a Nobel Prize for his work on climate change, and issues of the environment (along with the environment's inseparable ties to economics and international diplomacy) have taken center stage in politics. Some First World people today are slowly changing their perspective with regard to how we treat the environment and how we consume. Hybrid cars have replaced SUVs in terms of popularity among consumers, organic and locally grown produce has become increasingly prevalent in urban centers, and people are in general much more conscious about their consumption of finite resources. The Green movement, a meme in and of itself that is quickly picking up momentum, is an attempt to break away from practices that promote short-term personal benefits at the expense of the environment and to usher humans into a more sustainable long-term lifestyle.

We live in an age, for the first time in human history, where there is no real frontier. In previous centuries, people had the option of picking up and moving off into the wilderness if they needed to escape their current predicament, or if they caused enough destruction to their environment to render it unlivable. This has happened often throughout human history, from the time of tribal nomadism.

While we would like to believe in the "noble savage," that the indigenous peoples of the planet always lived in harmony with nature, that was not always the case. Some Native American cultures thought of as constructors of great civilizations, actually perished because of environmental degradation. The Anasazi, who lived in the modern-day Four Corners region of the American Southwest, and the Maya, who lived in what is now the Yucatan Peninsula, Guatemala, and Belize, experienced cultural collapses largely because of unintended and unforeseen consequences related to how they interacted with their environments, specifically the unsustainability of farming practices. Likewise, tribal inhabitants of the South Pacific sealed their inevitable fates by overfishing and overharvesting island resources (Jared, 2005). Humanity has always done whatever it needed to promote its own short-term survival, even when it meant harming the environment upon which its survival depended. The difference between us and civilizations that have come and gone before us is that because of our accelerated culture and technological capability, we are able to achieve these terrible fates much more efficiently.

In this century, we do not have the option to pick up and move to unexplored regions. We humans have done quite a thorough job of not only exploring but also populating every imaginable corner of the planet. Very few pieces of dry land have been unexplored by humans, and all land on the planet falls under the jurisdiction of some form of government. As a result, we do not have the option of moving off into unexplored and wild places if we ruin our present homes, as our ancestors did. Instead, for the first time in human history, we are being forced to directly confront our culture's effects on our local environments. Some of this is ameliorated by globalization and international trade, but reshuffling our cards does not ultimately change the hand we have dealt ourselves when it comes to total human impact on the planet's finite resources.

Climate change is a very immediate and tangible concern, and many among us believe, as Noah did, that we are on the brink of something terrible. Some of us believe, given certain data, that we have passed the point of no return, and the best we can hope for is to slow humanity's decline. Where do you fall as a reader of this book: into Noah's camp or his neighbors? Like the solutions to population, our culture can open avenues that may lead toward solutions in the environmental arena before Earth self-corrects with little regard for its parasitic residents.

One of the most promising cultural solutions to the problems of human-environment interaction is incorporating environmental principles into the recovery of the world economy. In a lecture titled "Green is the New Red, White, and Blue," presented to the Aspen Institute on July 5, 2007, author Tom Friedman said:

> The world is on the rate to double the CO_2 emission by the year 2050. Twenty-six terawatts of energy will be needed just to provide for the growth in the economies of India and China. What we are really talking about is a project of an enormous scale—changing the weather. The Green movement needs political scale, needs to be capitalist

pro-growth. . . . Green is the new red, white, and blue. Green or what I call GEO-GREEN is the new ideology that can provide THE answers to jobs, temperature, and terrorism. How stupid are we—we fund both sides of the war on terror, military in Afghanistan and Iraq, and by buying oil from unstable fundamentalist regimes. The first law of petro politics and the freedom house index provide a direct and inverse relationship to the price of oil. The higher the price of oil the less freedoms in the oil-producing nations including not only the Arab Middle East but also Venezuela and Russia.

Green is a competitive edge in a flat world. It is the foundation to the next great industrial revolution. Green products need technology that makes them smarter; this creates knowledge jobs. Green revolution needs government policy to allow for scale. The new oil that needs to be drilled for is in Washington DC. Unfortunately in the United States, legacy industries and their lobbyists dominate policy. We find ourselves in the unprecedented position of being stewards for those yet to be born. If we act, this will be the act of the greatest generation—the greatest act of stewardship.

Hurt not Earth, neither the sea, nor the trees. (Revelation 7:3)

But the nations became wrathful, and your own wrath came, and the appointed time for the dead to be judged, and to give their reward to your slaves the prophets and to the holy ones and to those fearing your name, the small and the great, and to bring to ruin those ruining Earth. (Revelation 11:18)

Conclusion:
Approach to Solutions

There is nothing more difficult to take in hand, more perilous to conduct, or more uncertain in its success, than to take the lead in the introduction of a new order of things. (Niccolo Machiavelli, Il Principe, 1532)

Three central concepts have emerged in the pages of this book that are foundational to its understanding. They are the understanding of our common humanity, the tension between short-term individual interest and long-term group interest, and the impact of accelerated population pressures and technology.

Understanding Our Common Humanity

Evolution is a proven fact: We are products of biological evolution. All of our adaptations, both physical and psychological have been refined and honed over millennia via natural selection. Like any other animal, we occupy a niche in our environment, even if our niche takes up more space because of our culture. Regardless of where we fit into the bigger picture, our current place in the universe is revealed to us through the lens of evolution. We can start rebuilding our understanding of ourselves and our relationship with our world with a solid understanding of evolutionary fact and how and why it applies to us. That is the reason for detailing our physical, biological, and cultural evolutionary past in the pages of this book. Let us emphasize; it really doesn't matter whether you, the reader, recognize the facts that science has brought us and history teaches us. It only matters that we recognize we are all governed by morals and ethics that should prevent us from pushing our beliefs as *The Truth*. It matters greatly that the spirit for life is dedicated to the life on this Earth and not reserved exclusively for a better hereafter.

We are connected to each other: Evolution has endowed the human species with diversity yet we share very similar genetic adaptations. We are most often drawn to the biological and particularly the cultural differences between us because variations are what we use to create distinctions to build our schemata. This is no small point; it has astounding implications as to why we have evolved and how we can cultivate a better understanding of our place on Earth. If we can all agree that each of us perceives ourselves as unique, then we can also all agree that our perceptions of reality will be unique and, therefore, subjective. One person's perspective cannot be the final word. No one holds the answer for the whole world, and it is only in collaboration with others that we can reach consensus and choose a path.

Our place in creation: Beyond a new understanding and acceptance of our connections with our fellow humans, it is basic that we cultivate a realistic and practical understanding of our species as it relates to the rest of creation. Where we are from is traceable to the very origins of not only our planet, but also the universe itself: In a very literal way, we are built from the same matter that was formed billions of years ago. When this universe was created, the stars coalesced, the Earth formed, and self-replicating packets of matters and energy evolved. So we are not unique in this regard; all the atoms and molecules that make up our planet and everything in it were formed by the same divine cosmic phenomena. We are a part of creation and have a special place in it, but that place is not one in which we are somehow granted power over everything else in creation. If we have assumed such power, we have taken it for ourselves. This common beginning should instill a sense of awe and connection.

We are more alike than we are different. From our beginning, we shared similar genetics, and a common frame of reference. Until the voyages of Magellan and Columbus, people didn't really know there wasa global anything: the world was their village, their parish, or their province. So not only was there no mechanism for communicating with the outside world, there was not much of a sense that an outside world even existed (early maps showed *terra incognito*, unknown land, and the edge of the sea was often marked with *"this way, monsters lie"*). This isolation has all but physically vanished from the globe, but culturally it is still here. Recent history, and the fractional nature of cultural and religious affiliations, has taught us, in some cases even convinced us, that we share very little with our fellow man across the globe. What we need to present is a larger view of humanity as a human race.

Tension Between Perceived Short-term Individual Interest And Long-term Group Interest

Humans have evolved biologically to promote individual survival in the short term over even our own long-term survival. This preference for short-term individual survival held a vital place in history. For most of human history, people lived hand-to-mouth, moment-to-moment; however, humanity has been so successful at promoting its own individual short-term survival through cultural adaptations that we now face a looming failure of extinction. In other words we, as a species, have gotten so good at living for today that our once adaptive survival strategy has begun to thwart our chances at survival in the long term. The point of hope is that our adaptability, which made possible our incredible, yet now damaging, success, is, of course, the only thing that can help us recover from the actual and looming dire straits we find ourselves in. There is no known historical precedent for a species that evolved to the point where its progress so threatened the physical environment that it faced the dilemma we now see: continue the course and make ourselves extinct, or shift our short-term interests.

We will not be able to overcome our predisposition to act in our own short-term interest any time soon; it has been pressed too deeply into our neurological circuit boards through millennia of biological evolution. The question that is presented is: How do we tailor our individual actions, beliefs, and choices to have them support a vision of long-term sustainable survival for everyone, while still appeasing a simple short-term survival need for us as individuals?

The ultimate end game of accelerated human evolution is to find the path to sustainability and thus, peace. Sustainable long-term survival of the group has the potential to take precedence over the strongest primal urges of individual short-term survival. This is a double-edged sword— memes powerful enough to override genetic programming have given us leaders like Ghandi, but they have also given us suicide bombers and schools that teach young children absolutes and hate. The great bibles explained how we came to be and how we should conduct our lives in order to prosper. Those documents applied only locally or tribally; our future blueprints need to be global, inclusive, and sustainable.

We need to be clever and help our culture to evolve a vision of long-term sustainable survival that is all-inclusive. A global "curriculum" is necessary to have widespread sufficient and clear education. The path of hope will have to lead through the education of children to change the mindset of future generations. The most effective way to start is through the empowering of Third World and religiously repressed women to take control of their lives and hence, their families. Examples of effective pilot programs include: providing very inexpensive internet access to Third World children, education for girls in Muslim countries, and secular elementary schooling in Afghanistan. It is these children who will have a chance to choose a sustainable family size and develop lives to push back fundamentalism. The highly educated will need to continue to push the clean green sustainable technology and push governments to demand them.

Our species has evolved the tools of communication that make these ideals possible. Web-based high quality learning opportunities are plentiful. If the goal to foster communication and education with a global curriculum is met, other questions persist.Can we harness the power of religion in terms of its ability to move people's hearts? What about the power of science in terms of its ability to move people's minds and offer technological innovation? Can we use the power of economics to connect policy with self-interest; the power of philosophical, psychological, and moral precepts to harmonize divergent thoughts and passions regarding what is good; and the power of government to incent behavior for the public's benefit? What if the above varies from your individual religious, scientific, or economic short-term viewpoint?

Bruce Gendelman

"The odds are against me." Galapagos Islands 2006

Acceleration of Population Pressures And Technology

With an exploding world population, depleted natural resources, destruction of natural environments on an unprecedented scale, prevalence of extremely poor and biased educational systems, and over 3 billion people earning less than $2 per day, there is enormous suffering. We need a better way. We can either continue with the widespread daily struggle of individual survival performed in each of our private fishbowls, or we can choose to plan our mutual escape and become part of a greater community. We propose a renewed approach to formulating those solutions, grounded in a new understanding of ourselves and our world, and how the two are related. Our old ways, ways of tribalism and

359

short-term survival, that have served us well for hundreds of thousands of years, are no longer sufficient. The newer ways are also not the answer; the failed movements of socialism and communism denigrated the role of the individual and destroyed the spirit, religious fundamentalism is close-minded and exclusionary because it ignores the facts that scientific rigor has produced, and the hybrid capitalistic systems too often don't produce an optimal balance between individual responsibilities and greed.

Our accelerating culture itself is not problematic, but the growth of certain elements of our culture is proving to be: Our population growth is itself accelerating, and we have spread ourselves into every conceivable corner of the globe, including places we did not previously think were habitable, presenting a demand for Earth's resources that is unsustainable. To compound the problems of just the sheer number of humans isour ability to produce and use technology (such as nuclear weapons, poisonous chemicals, polluting and warming machines) that renders us more able to cause significant and lasting damage to Earth and to ourselves. Our culture and its various elements are on a fragile, unsustainable course and at some point in the near future will reach the Earth's carrying capacity and cross the "tipping point," causing widespread calamity.

We have engineered our lives so that the fortunate among us are not forced to confront the means of our own survival and can still reap the benefits. And moreover, we humans are simply not wired to react intensely to threats that are not immediate challenges to our survival. We say that we need to change our course, but the motivation to really and truly do so will only register in our Stone Age brains if one day we turn on our water taps or gas pumps and nothing comes out. By then, of course, it will be too late.

To counter the negative aspects of acceleration, the population growth must be brought to a sustainable level. Overpopulation compounds all other problems, from the lack of education, depletion of natural resources, and corresponding destruction of the natural environment to religious conflict and war. This task is enormous. Again, the seed of the answer lies in educating children, providing opportunity for young women, and slowly changing religious taboos on family roles. To a significant degree, First World women who are educated and not religiously marginalized demonstrate what is humanly possible. There are ample small-scale successful programs in the Third World, but globally there is no consensus.

Summary

The path we have outlined, and the history we have presented in this book, is intended to reveal the common ground we all share, and is meant to demonstrate that Web-based tools can provide information and networking to solve varied and interrelated problems for a more peaceful future. The Ark that we urge you to help us build is designed to discover methods for the safe passage through storms ahead. It is constructed in the midst of the rapidly accelerating age of information, and is a collection of ideas that can positively impact the goal of a peaceful and sustainable future. These ideas of individual and group actions, beliefs, decisions, attitudes, and policies are the blueprints for constructing our global Ark.

We have the ability and the tools to evolve and avoid drowning in the great flood. This starts with the recognition of common basic human ground. Your challenge is to create or join projects that promote this collaboration and will start to build a society that is forever self-sustaining and peaceful, not just for you, but for all of our children and for all beings.

Swimming in tight circles, near those who think like we do, may give us the perception of safety and control, but perception is all it is. Leaving a narrow, myopic standpoint behind for a new, broader perspective is not as simple as slipping into a larger body of water. We need to understand and even visualize the complex cultural connections and adapt to modify those cultural systems. We need to broadly teach, particularly to the world's children, scientific facts, the lessons of history, and basic human morality. This seems so simple and so right, but creates a struggle against entrenched powerful institutions that see knowledge as a threat to their existence. We challenge you to jot down the rights you believe all humans are entitled to and you will see that in so many parts of the world there are cultural systems that would be threatened by this list.

Very few of us work with Noah's feverish resolve, and even fewer of us are in direct contact with the work that promises to sustain us through the flood. Our individual survival in the age of acceleration amounts to, in many cases, a narrow set of skills many degrees removed from what our ancestors would recognize, or see as worthwhile. Perhaps, then, we find it hard to empathize with Noah's hardships because we are—in design and in practice—more similar to his neighbors than to the Ark builder himself. And as long as we give ourselves permission and the ability to avoid having to confront the problems we have created for ourselves, our fate will be that of Noah's drowned contemporaries. We seek the feverish resolve for survival that we see in Noah, but unlike Noah, whose neighbors were judged not righteous enough for salvation, and who was commanded to save only his immediate family, the task is to save all of humanity.

The obstacles appear overwhelming; fear and greed are the emotions that govern economic behavior and are at the core of these obstacles. These fears are played out, to some degree, in every human's heart and mind and often used by those in positions of power to control groups. If you dig down and examine your own motivations you cannot escape this. Your neighbors, your friends, and your enemies are governed by these human traits, just the same as you. This is a common ground we can build on. Do not ignore, deny, or despair the path we are all on. Our ancestors throughout the epochs have struggled too hard for us to fail. We are, if anything, resilient and very adaptable and intelligent animals. Humanity depends on us.

Many mortals believe they can have sway over the future of humanity. Many even believe that life on Earth doesn't matter much, that the only truly important existence is the everlasting life with God in eternity. Many gods have been prayed to for safe passage. At the core, it doesn't matter what you believe governs the fate of man and Earth, but what does matter is that humans, as a global society, build a future that is sustainable and peaceful. This is the ultimate human evolutionary development. This is our challenge.

Seek peace, and pursue it. (Proverbs 34:14)

Bruce Gendelman

"Baobab – Tree of Life," South Africa 2004

Afterword

We welcome and encourage readers to help us evolve and construct an improved Fishbowl Principle—version 2.0. We have placed the entire contents of this book on the Web site. Each paragraph has a bulletin board feature in which we invite comments, criticisms, suggestions, references, and new ideas, which will be reviewed and possibly incorporated into the next edition of this "living document." Unlike most written works, this book is meant to be just the start of an organic developing effort, based on the collaboration of as many people over time as possible. This is an attempt at establishing the Wikimedia story of the history of our existence and cultural reality, along with a path for a better future.

At www.fishbowlprinciple.org we invite you to expand our small fishbowls into global common understanding with the goal of reaching a sustainable and peaceful future. There you will find an animation of Earl, meant to be an "everyman." Earl's story covers the gamut of time and culture that has been presented in the earlier chapters of this book. You will be invited into the ARKNODE. This social networking tool will allow everyone to construct and visually see the connections and common ground on any project, thought, entity, and individual. As connections are established you will be able to see that all actions and people are connected, be able to join others in projects of mutual interest, and be part of the action that takes small spheres and enlarges them.

About The Authors

Bruce Gendelman has had a lifelong fascination with the topics presented in this book. He received his undergraduate honors degree in economics and law degree from the University of Wisconsin in five years. Bruce founded and is chairman of a national property and casualty insurance brokerage. He has also founded a community bookstore, a natural bread bakery, and developed several real estate projects. He has invested in startup companies involved in agricultural genetics, medical research, and public safety fields. Bruce has also been an active board trustee in an N-12 school, a science museum with a mission to educate children, and various charitable organizations. He is a member of the Wisconsin and Florida Bars, and of the Society of Fellows at the Aspen Institute. His hobbies include mineral collecting, yoga, oil painting, photography, and alpine hiking. Bruce lives in Florida and Colorado with his wife of 33 years, Lori. They have four children.

Monk Balancing on Rock
Bruce Gendelman photo, 2005

Robert B. Miller decided at a young age to be a professional poet, but ended up taking his parents' advice. He skipped his senior year of high school and rushed through college and law school at Emory University. Bob returned to his home in Miami where he developed a winning track record as a trial and appellate lawyer. While he still considers himself a poet, he works in his day job as a partner in a law firm. Bob's passion is in unraveling and litigating complex cases of financial fraud. Prior to joining his present firm, he served as vice president and general counsel to an international cruise line. Bob heads his firm's pro bono program, in which legal services are provided to those who cannot afford them. Bob lives in Miami, Florida with his wife of 24 years, Debbie. They have two children.

In Another's Eyes

You're but a space in time my friend,
Whose life feeds on my glance.
You're here because I say you are;
It's not mere circumstance.

Live on! Under my ghostly gaze,
Perhaps you'll take the care
To listen to your whispered truth;
Fear not my knowing stare.

No God am I – I judge you not
For I am but your soul,
Reflected in another's eyes
I make your spirit whole.

(Robert Miller)

David Taus holds a degree in psychology from Brown University and a master's degree in education from Harvard University. He grew up in Milwaukee, WI, where he spent the school year asking many impertinent questions, and the summer leading children on camping trips with the YMCA. David has worked in biochemical genetic research at Children's Hospital in Boston, as well as in several clinical psychiatric settings. He has taught biology, psychology, chemistry, and environmental science in urban public high schools in Boston and San Francisco. David's current day job is as an educator with an innovative tutoring firm developing mentoring programs for teachers and parents. His night job is playing guitar, composing, and singing with his fusion rock group Guella. He has otherwise kept busy by creating, producing, and hosting an original weekly radio program on a noncommercial community station. He risks life and limb daily by commuting on his bicycle, where the wind always seems to blow directly into his face. David lives in San Francisco.

Bottom of the Hill

This city of currents and waves
At the end of the line
We arrive in this beautiful world
Unprepared and alive
We may dream of crossing a bridge
We may go far away
Sometimes we sit at the top of the hill
And sometimes we stay

Moving too fast, fearing the change
Shifting down, but a little too late

369

It's not time
 to lie in the dirt
It's not time
 for the pain

See the lights Under your feet
See the sun rushing by
This is not the life we would seek
It's alright

There's a road under a hill
There's a home in the fog
And you can go there to hide from this world
You can live there if you want

Your journey may lead you astray
You may roll with the waves
You may find that you can't return home
'Cause you're the one that's changed

And if you fall   Scared and alone
In the still of the night
Love will lead you safely home
It's alright
                    (David Taus)

References

Abelson, P. (1966). Chemical Events on The Primitive Earth.*Proceedings of the National Academy of Sciences*55(6), 1365–1372.

Allen, W. (1980). "My Speech to the Graduates." *Side Effects*. Boston: Ballantine Books.

Alvarez, L. (1983). Experimental Evidence That an Asteroid Impact Led to The Extinction of Many Species 65 Million Years Ago.*Proceedings of the National Academy of Sciences*80(2) 627–642.

American Federation of Teachers. (2009). Hot Topics—Standards-based Reform. Online: www.aft.org/topics/sbr/index.htm (Retrieved on February 8, 2009).

American Society for Microbiology. (2008). Humans Have Ten Times More Bacteria Than Human Cells: How Do Microbial Communities Affect Human Health? *Science Daily,* June 5. www.sciencedaily.com/releases/2008/06/080603085914.htm (Retrieved on August 5, 2008).

Anatomy of a Black Hole.archive.ncsa.uiuc.edu/Cyberia/NumRel/BlackHoleAnat.html (Retrieved on January 15, 2009).

Annual Arctic Report Card Shows Stronger Effects of Warming. 2008. www.research.noaa.gov/news/2008/effectsofwarming.html (Retrieved on December 18, 2008).

Applebaum, H. (1992). *The Concept of Work: Ancient, Medieval, and Modern.* New York: SUNY Press.

Archer, C. & Vance, D. (2006). Coupled Fe and S Isotope Evidence for Archean Microbial Fe (III) and Sulfate Reduction. *Geology* 34(3), 153–156.

Armstrong, K. (2006). *The Great Transformation: The Beginning of Our Religious Traditions*. New York: Knopf.

Asra: The Axial Peoples. Online: www.enotalone.com/article/18981.html (Retrieved on January 30, 2009).

Astington, J. (1993). *The Child's Discovery of the Mind.* Cambridge: Harvard University Press.

Australian Government Bureau of Meteorology. (2009). Drought Statement.www.bom.gov.au/climate/drought/drought.shtml (Retrieved on February 12, 2009).

Barrow, J. (2002). *The Constants of Nature.*London: Jonathan Cape.

Batson, C. D., Schoenrade, P., & Ventis, W. L. (1993). *Religion and the Individual.* New York: Oxford University Press.

Bauer, B. & Standish, C. (2001). *Ritual and Pilgrimage in the Ancient Andes.* Austin: University of Texas Press.

BBC News (December 15, 1999). World's Drinking Water Running Out. news.bbc.co.uk/1/hi/world/americas/566809.stm(Retrieved on February 12, 2009).

Bear, M., Connors, B., & Paradiso, M. (2001).*Neuroscience: Exploring the Brain.* (2nd ed.). Baltimore: Lippincott, Williams, & Wilkins.

Beilby, J. (2002). The Relationship Between Faith and Evidence in St. Augustine.*Sophia* 41(1) 19–32.

Benokraitis, A. T. (1997). The First Microprocessor and Beyond.www. acm.vt.edu/~andrius/work/microproc (Retrieved on February 9, 2009).

Berkner, L. V. & Marshall, L. C. (1965). N.A.S. Symposium on the Evolution of the Earth's Atmosphere: History of Major Atmospheric Components. *Proceedings of the National Academy of Sciences* 53,1215–1226.

Beven II, J., Avila, L., Blake, E., Brown, D., Franklin, J., Knabb, R., Pasch, R., Rhome, F., & Stewart, S. (2008). Annual Summary: Atlantic Hurricane Season of 2005 (PDF). *Monthly Weather Review* (American Meteorological Society) 136(3) 1131–1141. www.aoml. noaa.gov/general/lib/lib1/nhclib/mwreviews/2005.pdf (Retrieved on December 19, 2008).

Big Bang and WMAP Primer. (2003). *www.nasa.gov/centers/goddard/ pdf/97765main_MAPprimer.pdf (*Retrieved on *January 16, 2009).*

Biological Sciences Curriculum Study. (2003). *Biology: A Human Approach.* (2nd ed.). Dubuque, IA: Kendall Hunt.

Bittman, M. (2008). Rethinking the Meat Guzzler.*New York Times,*January 27. Online: www.nytimes.com/2008/01/27/weekinreview/27bittman. html (Retrieved on February 11, 2009).

Bjorklund, D. (2007). *Why Youth Is Not Wasted on the Young: Immaturity in Human Development.* New York: Wiley-Blackwell.

Blakeslee, S. (2006). Ancient Crash, Epic Wave. *New York Times*, November 14.

Blakeslee, Sandra. (1985). After 11,700 Years, World's Oldest Known Plant Gains Refuge. *New York Times*, February 24.

Boserup, E. (1981). *Population and Technological Change: A Study of Long-Term Trends*. Chicago: University of Chicago Press.

Boyd, R. & Silk, J. (2000). *How Humans Evolved.*(2nd ed.). New York: W.W. Norton.

Brabin, B. J. (1991). The Risks and Severity of Malaria in Pregnant Women. World Health Organization. Online: whqlibdoc.who.int/hq/1991/TDR_FIELDMAL_1.pdf (Retrieved on February 14, 2009.

Brahmins. *Mana Sanskriti (Our Culture)*. Online: www.vedah.net/manasanskriti/Brahmins.html#Brahmin_Population (Retrieved on January 31, 2009).

Bruer, J. (1997). Education and the Brain: A Bridge Too Far. *Educational Researcher*26(8) 4–16.

Bruer, J. (1999). Neural Connections: Some You Use, Some You Lose. *Phi Delta Kappan* 81(4) 264–277.

Bryan, C. P. & Smith, G. E. (1974).*Ancient Egyptian Medicine: The Papyrus Ebers*. Chicago: Ares.

Buick, R. (2008). When Did Oxygenic Photosynthesis Evolve? *Philosophical Transactions of the Royal Society London B: Biological Sciences.* 363(1504) 2731–2743.

Burton, M. & Hicks, M. (September 2005).*Hurricane Katrina: Preliminary Estimates of Commercial and Public Sector Damages*. Marshall University: Center for Business and Economic Research. www.marshall.edu/cber/research/katrina/Katrina-Estimates.pdf (Retrieved on December 19, 2008).

Bush Urges Congress To Double U.S. Aid to Africa. February 26, 2008. www.america.gov/st/peacesec-english/2008/February/200802261 41909idybeekcm4.999942e-02.html (Retrieved on November 23, 2008).

Caldeira, K. & Wickett, M. E. (2003). Anthropogenic Carbon and Ocean pH.*Nature* 425(6956) 365–378.

Campbell, N. & Reece, J. (2005). *Biology.* (7th ed.). San Francisco: Pearson.

Caro, R. (1990). *The Path to Power: The Years of Lyndon B. Johnson, Volume 1.* New York: Vintage.

Carroll, S. (2001). The Cosmological Constant. *Living Reviews in Relativity* 4(1).doi:10.1038/nphys815-<span (inactive 26 June 2008). relativity. livingreviews.org/Articles/lrr-2001-1/index.html (Retrieved on January 16, 2009).

Carter, J. http://www.wisdomquotes.com/000154.html (Retrieved on October 4, 2009).

Cattaneo, A. et al. (2007). The Apple Falls Increasingly Far: Parent-Child Correlation in Schooling and the Growth of Post-Secondary Education in Switzerland. Online: www.sts.uzh.ch/static/research/publications/pdf/apple.pdf *(Retrievedon* February 6, 2009).

Cereal Offenders. (2008). *The Economist,* March 27. Online: www. economist.com/finance/displaystory.cfm?story_id=10926502 (Retrieved on February 12, 2009).

Cha, A. (2008). Rising Grain Prices Panic Developing World.*The Washington Post*, April 4.

Chaisson, E. & McMillan, S. (1993). *Astronomy Today.* New Jersey: McMillan.

Chavez: Bush "Devil"; U.S. On the Way Down. CNN, September 21, 2006. Online: www.cnn.com/2006/WORLD/americas/09/20/chavez. un/index.html (Retrieved on February 1, 2009).

Chomsky, N. (1975). *Reflections on Language.* New York: Pantheon Books.

Clough, W. (1964). *The Necessary Earth: Nature and Solitude in American Literature.* Austin: University of Texas Press.

Clemson University. (2007). Energy Lost from Hot Engines Could Save Billions if Converted into Electricity. *Science Daily*, October 7.www.sciencedaily.com/releases/2007/10/071003154956.htm (Retrieved on February 14, 2009).

CNN.com. (December 30, 2004).Tsunami Death Toll Tops 118,000. www.cnn.com/2004/WORLD/asiapcf/12/30/asia.quake/index.html (Retrieved on December 19, 2008).

Cobo, B. (1990). *Inca Religion and Customs.* Austin: University of Texas Press.

Cohen, J. E. (1995). Population Growth and Earth's Human Carrying Capacity. *Science* 269(5222) 341–346.

Cooley, T. F., & Soares, J. (1996). Will Social Security Survive the Baby Boom? *Carnegie-Rochester Conference Series on Public Policy*. 45, December, 89–121.

Costa, A. & Kallick, B. (No date). Describing 16 Habits of Mind. www. habitsofmind.org/resources/OTHER/16HOM2.pdf (Retrieved on October 16, 2008).

Coulmas, F. (1989). *Writing Systems of the World.* Oxford: Blackwell.

Cowie, E. Meat, Bones and Marsh Plants: Could You Live Off Prehistoric Food? (July 10, 2006). Online: www.redorbit.com/news/ health/565170/meat_bones_and_marsh_plants_could_you_live_ off_prehistoric/index.html (Retrieved on February 9, 2009).

Cuban, L. (2003) *Why Is It So Hard To Get Good Schools?* New York: Teachers College Press.

Currid, J. & Navon, A. (1989). Iron Age Pits and the Lahav (Tell Halif) Grain Storage Project. *Bulletin of the American Schools of Oriental Research* 273, February, 67–78.

Cushman, H. (1918). *A Beginner's History of Philosophy.* Boston: Houghton-Mifflin.

Daly, M. & Wilson, M. (1999). An Evolutionary Psychological Perspective on Homicide. In D. Smith & M. Zahn (eds.), *Homicide Studies: A Sourcebook of Social Research* (p. 59). New York: Springer.

Dawkins, R. (1989). *The Selfish Gene.* New edition. Oxford: Oxford University Press, p. 12.

deMenocal, P. (2004). African Climate Change and Faunal Evolution During the Pliocene–Pleistocene. *Earth and Planetary Science Letters* 220(1–2) March 30, 3–24.

Diamond, J. (1993). *The Third Chimpanzee.* New York: Harper.

Diamond, J. (1997). *Guns, Germs, and Steel: The Fates of Human Societies.* New York: W.W. Norton.

Diamond, Jared, (2005).*Collapse: How Societies Choose to Fail or Succeed.* New York: Penguin.

Duangkamon Chotikapanich, D. S., Rao, P., Griffiths, W., & Valencia, V. (January 2007). Global Inequality: Recent Evidence and Trends. Online: www.wider.unu.edu/publications/working-papers/research-papers/2007/en_GB/rp2007-01 (Retrieved November 13, 2008).

Duke, D. (1998).Scientists Identify Strong Genetic Link to Allergies. record.wustl.edu/archive/1998/01-15-98/4477.html (Retrieved on February 9, 2009).

Dunbar, R. (1992). Why Gossip Is Good for You: Humans Live in Much Larger Groups than Other Primates. Language May Have Evolved as a Form of Grooming To Allow Us to Live with So Many People. *New Scientist* 1848, November 21, 28.

Elephant and the Blind Men. Jain Stories. JainWorld.com (Retrieved on August 29, 2006).

Ellis, E. & Ramankutty, N. (2008). Putting People on the Map: Anthropogenic Biomes of the World. *Frontiers in Ecology and the Environment.* 6(8) 439–447.

Energy Information Administration.A Primer on Gasoline Prices.www. eia.doe.gov/pub/oil_gas/petroleum/analysis_publications/primer_ on_gasoline_prices/html/petbro.html (Retrieved on December 19, 2008).

Energy Information Administration. (2007). Primary Energy Consumption by Source, 1949–2007. www.eia.doe.gov/emeu/aer/ txt/ptb0103.html (Retrieved on February 14, 2009).

Epstein, H. Evolution of the Reasoning Hominid Brain. Online: www. brainstages.net/evolution.html (Retrieved on January 23, 2009).

Erlich, P. (1968). *The Population Bomb.* New York: Random House.

European Space Agency. (2004). How Many Stars Are There in the Universe? www.esa.int/esaSC/SEM75BS1VED_index_0.html (Retrieved on January 16, 2009).

Evolution: Humans: Origin of Humankind. www.pbs.org/wgbh/ evolution/humans/humankind/j.html (Retrieved on January 20, 2009).

Extinction Rate Across the Globe Reaches Historical Proportions. (2002). *ScienceDaily*, January 10. www.sciencedaily.com/ releases/2002/01/020109074801.htm (Retrieved on December 18, 2008).

Fathi, N. (2005).Text of Mahmoud Ahmadinejad's Speech. *Week in Review.* New York Times, October 30. www.nytimes.com/2005/10/30/ weekinreview/30iran.html?ex=1161230400&en=26f07fc5b7543417&ei=5070 (Retrieved on February 1, 2009).

Figgis, J. (1896). *The Theory of the Divine Right of Kings.* Cambridge: Harvard University Press.

Findley, C. V. & Rothney, J. A. (2006).*Twentieth-Century World.*(6th ed.). Boston: Houghton Mifflin Harcourt.

Flooding Damage Estimate at $126 Million. Newsroom: Inside Indiana Business with Gerry Dick. www.insideindianabusiness.com/newsitem.asp?ID=29796 (Retrieved on December 19, 2008).

Food and Agriculture Organization of the United Nations. (2006). Spotlight: Livestock Impacts on the Environment. Online: www.fao.org/ag/magazine/0612sp1.htm (Retrieved on February 12, 2009).

Food and Agriculture Organization, International Fund for Agricultural Development, World Food Program. (2002). Reducing Poverty and Hunger, the Critical Role of Financing for Food, Agriculture, and Rural Development.www.fao.org/docrep/003/Y6265e/y6265e00.htm (Retrieved on February 12, 2009).

Fraser, A., Molinoff, P., & Winokur, A. (Eds.). (1994). *Biological Bases of Brain Function and Disease.* New York: Raven Press.

Freire, Paolo. (1970). *Pedagogy of the Oppressed.*New York: Continuum International.

Friedman, T.(2005). *The World Is Flat:A Brief History of the Twenty-First Century.* New York: Farrar, Straus and Giroux.

Fuller, C. J. (2001). Orality, Literacy and Memorization: Priestly Education in Contemporary South India. *Modern Asian Studies35*(1) 1–31.

Garber, D. (1998/2003). René Descartes. In E. Craig (Ed.), *Routledge Encyclopedia of Philosophy.* London: Routledge. Online: www.rep.routledge.com/article/DA026SECT5 (Retrieved on January 27, 2009).

Gardiner, L. (2007). Elements in the Earth's Crust.www.windows.ucar.edu/tour/link=/earth/geology/crust_elements.html (Retrieved on January 16, 2009).

Gardner, Howard. (2006). *Multiple Intelligences: New Horizons.* Basic Books.

Gazzaniga, M. & Heatherton, T. (2003).*Psychological Science: Mind, Brain, and Behavior.* New York: W.W. Norton.

George, Linda. (2005). Better in the Long Run. *Science & Spirit,* March–April, 62.

Giberson, Karl. (2005). The Evolving Debate*Science & Spirit,* July–August, 6.

Ginsburg, H. & Opper, S. (1988). *Piaget's Theory of Intellectual Development.* Englewood Cliffs, NJ: Prentice-Hall.

Gleitman, H. et al. (2000). *Basic Psychology.* (5th ed.). New York: W.W. Norton.

Global Forest Resources Assessment. (2005). Food and Agriculture Organization of the United Nations. Rome, Italy.

Global Warming Doubles Rate of Ocean Rise. (2005). *Science Daily,* November 25. www.sciencedaily.com/releases/2005/11/051124220656.htm (Retrieved on December 18, 2008).

Goldsmith, D. (1995). *Einstein's Greatest Blunder? The Cosmological Constant and Other Fudge Factors in the Physics of the Universe.* Cambridge: Harvard University Press.

Gore, A. (2006).*An Inconvenient Truth.* Chicago: Rodale Books.

Gore, A. (2007).*The Assault on Reason.* New York: Penguin.

Goudie, A. (2000). *The Human Impact on the Natural Environment.*(5th ed.). Cambridge, MA: MIT Press.

Greene, Brian. (2005). *The Fabric of the Cosmos.* New York: Vintage.

Greenpeace. (2008). *Amazon Cattle Footprint—Mato Grasso: State of Destruction.* Online: www.greenpeace.org/raw/content/international/press/reports/amazon-cattle-footprint-mato.pdf (Retrieved on February 12, 2009).

Handwerk, B. (2005). Global Warming: How Hot? How Soon? *National Geographic News,* July 27. news.nationalgeographic.com/news/2005/07/0727_050727_globalwarming.html (Retrieved on December 18, 2008).

Hansen, J. et al. (2008). Target Atmospheric CO_2: Where Should Humanity Aim? *Open Atmospheric Science Journal.*2, 217–231.

Harcourt-Smith, W. & Aiello, L. (2004).Fossils, Feet, and the Evolution of Human Bipedal Locomotion. *Journal of Anatomy.*204(5) 403–416.

Harmful Environmental Effects of Livestock Production on the Planet 'Increasingly Serious,' Says Panel.*Science Daily,* February 22. www.sciencedaily.com/releases/2007/02/070220145244.htm (Retrieved on February 12, 2009).

Haseltine, E. What Makes You Unique: The Neuroscience of Individual Differences. Aspen Institute, *Greenwald Auditorium*, July 8 2007.

Haught, J. (2005). For the Love of God.*Science & Spirit,* March/April, 45.

Hayman, R. (2002). *A Life of Jung.* New York: W.W. Norton.

Heller, S. (2006).*The Absence of Myth.* New York: SUNY Press.

Hill, R. D. (1992). An Efficient Lightning Energy Source on the Early Earth.*Origins of Life and Evolution of the Biosphere,* 22, 277–285.

Hinshaw, G. et al. (2008). Five-Year Wilkinson Microwave Anisotropy Probe (WMAP) Observations: Data Processing, Sky Maps, and Basic Results (PDF). *The Astrophysical Journal.*180, 225-245.

Hobbes, T. (1651). *Leviathan, Or the matter, forme, & power of a common-weath ecclesiastical and civill.* Online: publicliterature. org/books/leviathan/xaa.php (Retrieved on February 17, 2009).

Hollis, J. (2001). *Creating a Life: Finding Your Own Individual Path.* Toronto: Inner City Books.

Hollis, J. (2007). *Why Good People Do Bad Things: Understanding Our Darker Selves.* New York: Gotham.

Homo erectus. www.wsu.edu/gened/learn-modules/top_longfor/ timeline/24_h_erectus.html (Retrieved on January 20, 2009).

Hopfenberg, R. & Pimentel, D. (2001). Human Population Numbers as a Function of Food Supply.*Environment, Development and Sustainability* 3, 1–15.

Hunter, D. (1943) *Papermaking: The History and Technique of an Ancient Craft.* New York: Dover Publications.

Huntington, S. (1996). *The Clash of Civilizations and the Remaking of World Order.* New York: Simon & Schuster.

Jennings, M. K. & Niemi, R. G. (1968). The Transmission of Political Values from Parent to Child.*The American Political Science Review* 62(1) March, 169–184.

Johnson, M. (1997). *Developmental Cognitive Neuroscience.*(1st ed.). Malden, MA: Blackwell.

Jones, S. (October 29, 2008). www.timesonline.co.uk/tol/news/uk/ science/article4894696.ece

Jung, C. G. (1938).Psychology and Religion. In CW 11: *Psychology and Religion: West and East.* p. 131.

Jung, C.G. (1977 reprint). *Symbols of Transformation*. Princeton University Press.

Jungers, W.L. (1988). Lucy's Length: Stature Reconstruction in Australopithecus afarensis (A.L. 288-1) with Implications for Other Small-Bodied Hominids. *American Journal of Physical Anthropology* 76(2) 227–231.

Kaku, M. (2006). *Parallel Worlds: A Journey Through Creation, Higher Dimensions, and the Future of the Cosmos*. New York: Random House.

Kent, S. A. (2006). "A Matter of Principle: Fundamentalist Mormon Polygamy, Children, and Human Rights Debates." *Nova Religio* 10(1) August, 7–29.

Kerr, R. (1997). Climate: A New Driver for the Atlantic's Moods and European Weather? *Science* 275(5301), February 7, 754–755.

Kirby, D., Short, L., Collins, J., Rugg, D., Kolbe, L., Howard, M., Miller, B., Sonenstein, F., & Zabin, L. S. (1994). "School-Based Programs to Reduce Sexual Risk Behaviors: A Review of Effectiveness." *Public Health Reports.* 109(3), May–June, 339–360.

Kohn, Alfie. (1997). Students Don't 'Work'—They Learn. *Education Week*. www.alfiekohn.org/teaching/edweek/sdwtl.htm (Retrieved on October 8, 2008).

Kolmer, J. (2005). Tracking Wheat Rust on a Continental Scale. *Current Opinion in Plant Biology* 8(4) 441–449.

Kozol, J. (1992) *Savage Inequalities: Children in America's Schools*. New York: HarperPerennial.

Krakauer, J. (2004). *Under the Banner of Heaven: A Story of Violent Faith*. New York: Anchor Books.

Kramer, S. (1988). *History Begins at Sumer:Thirty-Nine Firsts In Recorded History*. Philadelphia: University of Pennsylvania Press.

Kuhn, T. (1996). *The Structure of Scientific Revolutions.* (3rd ed.). Chicago: University of Chicago Press.

Kunzig, R. (2003). Burnout: New images from Hubble Preview the Death of Our Sun: Swift, Colorful, and Surprisingly Tempestuous. *Discover*. Online: discovermagazine.com/2003/nov/Burnout (Retrieved on January 16, 2009).

Kvenvolden, K. A., Lawless, J., Pering, K., Peterson, E., Flores, J., Ponnamperuma, C., Kaplan, I. R., and Moore, C. (1970). Evidence for Extraterrestrial Amino-Acids and Hydrocarbons in the Murchison Meteorite. *Nature* 228(5275) 923–926.

Larson, E. (2004).Evolutionary Dissent. *Science & Spirit.*Online: www.science-spirit.org/article_detail.php?article_id=479 (Retrieved on January 27, 2009).

Leakey, R. & Lewin, R. (1996). *The Sixth Extinction: Patterns of Life and the Future of Humankind.* New York: Anchor.

Leefers, L. A., & Castillo, G. B. (1998). Bridging the Gap Between Economics and Ecology. *Conservation Ecology* 2(2) 19.www.consecol.org/vol2/iss2/art19/ (Retrieved on February 17, 2009).

Lehechka, R. & Delblanco, A. (2008). Ivy League Letdown. *New York Times*, January 22. Online: www.nytimes.com/2008/01/22/opinion/22lehecka.html (Retrieved on February 8, 2009).

Lenneberg, E. H. (1967). *Biological Foundations of Language.* New York: Wiley.

Lewis, S. (1994).An Opinion on the Global Impact of Meat Consumption. *American Journal of Clinical Nutrition* 59 (suppl.), 1099S–10102S.

Lieberman, P. (1991). *Uniquely Human: The Evolution of Speech, Thought, and Selfless Behavior.* Cambridge: Harvard University Press.

Lin, D. (2008). The Genesis of Planets. *Scientific American* 298(5) May, 50–59.

Lohr, S. (2009). The Crowd is Wise (When It's Focused), *New York Times*, July 19.

Long, B. & Rielly, E. (2007). Financial Aid: A Broken Bridge to College Access? *Harvard Educational Review* 77(1) 40.

Long Foreground–Species Timeline: Australopithecus afarensis. www.wsu.edu:8001/vwsu/gened/learn-modules/top_longfor/timeline/afarensis/afarensis-a.html (Retrieved on January 20, 2009).

Lorenz, E. (1995). *The Essence of Chaos.* Seattle: University of Washington Press.

Malthus, T. (1798). *An Essay on the Principle of Population.* New York: Oxford University Press.

Margulis, L. & Punset, E. (Eds.). (2007). *Mind, Life, and Universe: Conversations with Great Scientists of Our Time.* White River Junction, VT: Chelsea Green Publishing.

Marmot, M. (2005). Social Determinants of Health Inequalities. *The Lancet* 365, 1099–1104.

Martin, N. G. et al. (1986). Transmission of Social Attitudes. *Proceedings of the National Academy of Sciences* 83(12) 4364–4368.

Marx, K. (1843). Critique of Hegel's Philosophy of Right. Online: www.marxists.org/archive/marx/works/1843/critique-hpr/index.htm (Retrieved on February 1, 2009).

Maslow, A. H. (1943). A Theory of Human Motivation. *Psychological Review* 50(4) 370–396.

Matthews, T. J., & Ventura, S. (1997). Birth and Fertility Rates by Educational Attainment: United States, 1994. *Monthly Vital Statistics Report*, National Center for Health Statistics, 45(10) supplement.

May, R. (1992). How Many Species Inhabit the Earth? *Scientific American* October, 20.

McBrearty, S. (1990). The Origin of Modern Humans. *Man, New Series*, 25(1) March, 129–143.

McCarthy, M. (January 16, 2006). Environment In Crisis: We Are Past the Point of No Return. Online: www.terranature.org/environmentalCrisis.htm (Retrieved on February 14, 2009).

Menninger, K. (1945). *The Human Mind.* (3rd ed.). New York: Knopf.

Merton, *T. (*1966/1989). *Conjectures of a Guilty Bystander.* (Image ed.). Garden City, NY: Doubleday.

Millennium Ecosystem Assessment. (2005). Living Beyond Our Means: Natural Assets and Human Well-Being. Online: www.millenniumassessment.org/en/BoardStatement.aspx (Retrieved on November 13, 2008).

Miller, G. F. (1999). Sexual Selection for Cultural Displays. In Dunbar, R. I. et al. (Eds.). *The Evolution of Culture: An Interdisciplinary View.* New Brunswick, NJ: Rutgers University Press.

Miller, K. (2008). *Only a Theory: Evolution and the Battle for America's Soul.* New York: Viking.

Miller, S. (1953). A Production of Amino Acids Under Possible Primitive Earth Conditions. *Science* 117, 528–529.

Miracle Month—The Invention of the First Transistor. www.pbs.org/transistor/background1/events/miraclemo.html (Retrieved on February 9, 2009).

Moeller-Gorman, R. (2007). Cooking Up Bigger Brains. *Scientific American* December. Online: www.sciam.com/article.cfm?id=cooking-up-bigger-brains (Retrieved January 20, 2009).

Moyers, B. (2008). *Moyers on Democracy.* New York: Doubleday.

NASA. (2009). "NASA: Sun." www.nasa.gov/worldbook/sun_worldbook.html (Retrieved on February 14, 2009).

National Institutes of Health. (August 31, 2005). New Genome Comparison Finds Chimps, Humans Very Similar at the DNA Level. www.genome.gov/15515096 (Retrieved on January 21, 2009).

National Research Council, Commission on Behavioral and Social Sciences and Education. (2000). *How People Learn: Brain, Mind, Experience, and School.* Washington, DC: National Academy Press.

National Virtual Translation Center. (2007). World Languages. Online: www.nvtc.gov/lotw/months/november/worldlanguages.htm (Retrieved November 13, 2008).

National Weather Service Forecast Office. (June 7, 2008). Tornadoes of June 7, 2008. www.crh.noaa.gov/arx/?n=jun0708 (Retrieved on December 19, 2008).

Orwell, G. (1949). *Nineteen Eighty-Four. A Novel.* New York: Harcourt, Brace.

Pearson, M. & Rossingh, D. (September 12, 2007). Wheat Price Rises to Record $9 a Bushel on Global Crop Concerns. www.bloomberg.com/apps/news?pid=20601087&sid=ajqXR5gYqsak&refer=home (Retrieved on February 12, 2009).

Perlmutter, S. & Linder, E. (1999). Overview of Supernova Cosmology to Date.supernova.lbl.gov/~evlinder/SNcosmology.pdf (Retrieved on January 16, 2009).

Perry, E. J. (2001). *Challenging the Mandate of Heaven: Social Protest and State Power in China.* New York: M.E. Sharpe.

Pierazzo, E. & Chyba, C. F. (1999). Amino Acid Survival in Large Cometary Impacts.*Meteoritics & Planetary Science* 34(6) 909–918.

Pimentel, D. et al. (1995). Environmental and Economic Costs of Soil Erosion and Conservation Benefits. *Science* New Series, 267(5201), 1117–1123.

Pimm, S. et al. (1995).The Future of Biodiversity.*Science* 269(5222) July 21, 347–350.

Pinker, S. (1994).*The Language Instinct.* New York: Morrow.

Pinker, S. (2002).*The Blank Slate: The Modern Denial of Human Nature.* New York: Penguin Putnam.

Plodowski, A. et al. (2003). Mental Representation of Number in Different Numerical Forms. *Current Biology* 13(23) 2045–2050.

Plomin, R. et al. (1997). *Behavioral Genetics.* (3rd ed.). New York: W.H. Freeman.

Plomin, R. et al. (2006). Nature, Nurture, and Cognitive Development from 1–16 Years. *Psychological Science* 8(6) 442–447.

Pollan, M. (2006). *Omnivore's Dilemma.* New York: Penguin.

Pollan, M. (2008). *In Defense of Food: An Eater's Manifesto.* New York: Penguin.

Post, S. (1988). History, Infanticide, and Imperiled Newborns. *The Hastings Center Report* 18(4) 14–17.

Premack, D. G. & Woodruff, G. (1978). Does the Chimpanzee Have a Theory of Mind? *Behavioral and Brain Sciences* 1, 515–526.

Quinn, D. (1999). The Human Future: A Problem in Design. Address given at EnvironDesign 3, Baltimore, MD, April 30. www.ishmael.com/Education/Writings/environdesign

Quinn, D. M. (1998). Plural Marriage and Mormon Fundamentalism. *Dialogue: A Journal of Mormon Thought* 31(2) Summer.

Quinn, D. (1996). *The Story of B.* New York: Bantam.

Quinn, D. (1997). *My Ishmael.* New York: Bantam.

Raikes, H., Pan, B. A., Luze, G., Tamis-LeMonda, C. S., Brooks-Gunn, J., Constantine, J., Tarullo, L. B., Raikes, H. A., & Rodriguez, E. T. (2006). Mother-Child Bookreading in Low-Income Families: Correlates and Outcomes during the First Three Years of Life. *Child Development* 77(4) 924–953.

Raven, P., Evert, R., & Eichhorn, S. (1992). *Biology of Plants.* (5th ed.). New York: Worth Publishers.

Reader, S. & LaLand, K. (2001).Social Intelligence, Innovation, and Enhanced Brain Size in Primates.*Proceedings of the National Academy of Sciences* 99(7) 4436–4441.

Reagan, R. (March 8, 1983). Speech to National Association of Evangelicals. Online: www.hbci.com/~tgort/empire.htm (Retrieved on February 1, 2009).

Reed, K. (1997). Early Hominid Evolution and Ecological Change Through The African Plio-Pleistocene. *Journal of Human Evolution* 32(2–3) February, 289–322.

Rees, M. S., quoted in Kaku, M. (2006). *Parallel Worlds: A Journey Through Creation, Higher Dimensions, and the Future of the Cosmos.* New York: Random House.

Reisner, M. (1986). *Cadillac Desert: The American West and Its Disappearing Water.* New York: Penguin.

ReVelle, P., & ReVelle, C. (1992). *The Global Environment: Securing a Sustainable Future.* Sudbury, MA: Jones & Bartlett.

Roach, J. (2004). Source of Half Earth's Oxygen Gets Little Credit. *National Geographic News*, June 7. news.nationalgeographic.com/news/2004/06/0607_040607_phytoplankton.html (Retrieved on December 18, 2008).

Rosenzweig, M. et al. (1996). *Biological Psychology.* Sunderland, MA: Sinauer.

Russell, M. J., Daniel, R. M., Hall, A. J., & Sherringham, J. A. (1994). A Hydrothermally Precipitated Catalytic Iron Sulphide Membrane as a First Step Toward Life. *Journal of Molecular Evolution*, 39, 231–243.

Sagan, C. (1994). *Pale Blue Dot: A Vision of the Human Future in Space.* (1st ed.). New York: Random House.

Sagan, Carl. (1994). The Pale Blue Dot Speech to the University School of Milwaukee, River Hills, Wisconsin.

Sagan, C. (2007). *The Varieties of Scientific Experience.* New York: Penguin Press.

Sanchez, P. & Leakey, R. (1997). Land Use Transformation in Africa: Three Determinants for Balancing Food Security with Natural Resource Utilization. *European Journal of Agronomy* 7(1–3) September, 15–23.

Santelli, J., Ott, M., Lyon, M., Rogers, J., Summers, D., & Schleifer, R. (2006). Abstinence and Abstinence-Only Education: A Review of U.S. Policies and Programs. *Journal of Adolescent Health* 8(1) 72–81.

Sawin, J. (2003). Severe Weather Events on the Rise. Online: www.worldwatch.org/brain/media/pdf/pubs/vs/2003_weather.pdf (Retrieved on February 14, 2009).

Schonborn, C., Horn, S. O., & Wiedenhofer, S. (2006). *Creation and Evolution: A Conference with Pope Benedict XVI in Castel Gondolfo.* Fort Collins, CO: Ignatius Press.

Schopf, J. (2006). Fossil Evidence of Archaean Life. *Philosophical Transactions of the Royal Society London B: Biological Sciences,* 361(1470) 869–85.

Seager, R. et al. (2002). Is the Gulf Stream Responsible for Europe's Mild Winters? *Quarterly Journal of the Royal Meteorological Society,* 128(526) 2563–2586.

Section II: Hominid Evolution. serpentfd.org/section2hominidevolution. html (Retrieved on January 20, 2009).

Shelburne, E. (2008). The Great Disruption.*The Atlantic,* September.

Singer, H. W. (1975). Population Growth, International Economic Relationships, and Aid to the Third World. In Tabah L. (Ed.), *Population Growth and Economic Development in the Third World (Volume 2).* (pp. 741–782). Dolhain, Belgium: Ordina Editions.

Skinner, B. F. (1965). *Science and Human Behavior.* Free Press.

Soaring Food Prices Spark Unrest. (2008). *Philadelphia Trumpet,* October 11. www.thetrumpet.com/index.php?q=5021.3306.0.0 (Retrieved on February 12, 2009).

Soll, I. (2001). *World Book Multimedia Encyclopedia.* Madison, WI: World Book.

Soon, C. S. et al. (2008).Unconscious Determinants of Free Decisions in the Human Brain.*Nature Neuroscience,11*(5) May, 543–545.

Spencer, Herbert quotes Nature Neuroscience 11, 543 - 545 (2008) Published online: 13 April 2008 | doi :10.1038/nn.2112 Stanford University. (2007).

Stecker, F. W. & Puget, J. L. (1974). The Origin of the Diffuse Background Radiation. In *ESRO The Context and Status of Gamma Ray Astronomy,* 147–156

Stiglitz, J. (2003). *Globalization and Its Discontents.* New York: W.W. Norton.

Summers, L. (2008). The Economic Agenda: Challenges Facing the Next President. *Harvard Magazine,* September/October, 29.

Tagliabue, J. (1996). The Pope Pronounces Evolution Fit. *New York Times,* October 27.

Tarnoff, C. & Nowels, L. (2004). *Foreign Aid: An Introductory Overview of U.S. Programs and Policy. State Department, pp. 12–13, 98–916.* fpc.state.gov/documents/organization/31987.pdf *(Retrieved on February 3, 2009).*

Thomas, C. et al. (2004). Extinction Risk from Climate Change.*Nature* 427, 145–147.

Tuttle, R. H. (1981, May 8). Evolution of Hominid Bipedalism and Prehensile Capabilities.*Philosophical Transactions of the Royal Society London B: Biological Sciences,* 292(1057), May 8, 89–94.

U. S. Census Bureau. (2009). International Data Base.www.census.gov/ipc/www/idb/worldpopinfo.html (Retrieved on February 11, 2009).

U. S. Central Intelligence Agency. (2009). The World Fact Book.www.cia.gov/library/publications/the-world-factbook/rankorder/2054rank.html (Retrieved on February 11, 2009).

U. S. Department of Agriculture (1997). Agricultural Statistics 1997. Table 1-71, p. 8.

U. S. Energy Information Administration Annual Energy Review. (2008). www.eia.doe.gov/kids/energyfacts/science/formsofenergy.html (Retrieved on December 16, 2008).

United Nations Department of Economic and Social Affairs, Population Division. (April 25, 2003). Fertility, Contraception, and Population Policies. New York: United Nations. www.un.org/esa/population/publications/contraception2003/Web-final-text.PDF (Retrieved on February 14, 2009).

United Nations Department of Economic and Social Affairs, Population Division. (2007). World Population Prospects—The 2006 Revision (Highlights). New York: United Nations. www.un.org/esa/population/publications/wpp2006/WPP2006_Highlights_rev.pdf (Retrieved on February 14, 2009).

United Nations. (2008). State of World Population 2007. www.unfpa.org/swp/2007/english/introduction.html (Retrieved on February 12, 2009).

Unwanted Pregnancy: Fact Sheet-Overview. www.thenationalcampaign.org/resources/pdf/FactSheet-Overview.pdf (Retrieved on December 4, 2008).

Urbanization and Global Change. (2002). www.globalchange.umich.edu/globalchange2/current/lectures/urban_gc (Retrieved on February

12, 2009).US Department of State, Independent States in the World, Bureau of Intelligence and Research, July 29, 2009

USAID Africa Humanitarian Crisis.www.usaid.gov/locations/sub-saharan_africa/africa_humanitarian_crisis (Retrieved on November 23, 2008).

Vallely, A. (2002). *Guardians of the Transcendant.* Toronto: University of Toronto Press.

Vallely, P. (2006). How Islamic Inventors Changed the World. *The Independent*, March 11. Online: findarticles.com/p/articles/mi_qn4158/is_20060311/ai_n16147544 (Retrieved on February 9, 2009).

Valley, J. et al. (2002).A Cool Early Earth.*Geology* 30, 351–354.

Verhaegen, M., Puech, P.F.,& Munro, S. (2002). Aquarboreal Ancestors? *Trends in Ecology & Evolution* 17(5) 212–217.

Vitousek, P. M., Mooney, H. A., Lubchenco, J., and Melillo, J. M. (1997). Human Domination of Earth's Ecosystems. *Science* 277(5325) July 25, 494.

Warrick, J. (2006). White House Got Early Warning on Katrina. *Washington Post*, January 24.

Weisenberger, D. How Many Atoms Are There in the World? education. jlab.org/qa/mathatom_05.html (Retrieved January 18, 2009).

Weisman, A. (2007). *The World Without Us.* New York: St. Martin's Press.

Weisman, S. & Bradsher, K. (2008). A Plea for Aid to Avert Starvation. *New York Times*, July 2. Online: www.nytimes.com/2008/07/02/world/02zoellick.html (Retrieved on February 12, 2009).

Weiss, R. A. & McMichael, A. J. (2004). Social and Environmental Risk Factors in the Emergence of Infectious Diseases.*Nature Medicine* 10(12), December, suppl., S70–S76.

Westover, J. (2008). The Record of Microfinance: The Effectiveness/Ineffectiveness of Microfinance Programs as a Means of Alleviating Poverty. *The Electronic Journal of Sociology*.www.sociology.org/content/2008/_westover_finance.pdf (Retrieved on November 23, 2008).

White, R. & Heerwagen, J. (1998). Nature and Mental Health: Biophilia and Biophobia. In A. Lundberg (Ed.), *The Environment and Mental Health.* New Jersey: Lawrence Erlbaum Associates.

Wilber, K. (1985). John D. Barrow, The Constants of Nature. *Quantum Questions: Mystical Writings of the World's Great Physicists.* Boston: New Science Library.

Wilde, S. A., Valley, J. W., Peck, W. H., & Graham, C. M. (January 2001). Evidence from Detrital Zircons for the Existence of Continental Crust and Oceans on the Earth 4.4 Gyr Ago.*Nature* 409(6817) 175–178.

Wilford, J. N. (2007). Fossils in Kenya Challenge Linear Evolution. *New York Times,* August 9. Online: www.nytimes.com/2007/08/09/science/08cnd-fossil.html (Retrieved on January 20, 2009).

Wilford, J. N. (2009). Fossil Skeleton From Africa Predates Lucy.*New York Times,* October 2.

Williams, B., Sawyer, S. C., & Wahlstrom, C. (2005). *Marriages, Families & Intimate Relationships.*Boston: Pearson.

Wilson, E. O. (1984). *Biophilia: The Human Bond with Other Species.* Cambridge: Harvard University Press.

Wilson, E. O. & Hölldobler, B. (2008). *The Superorganism: The Beauty, Elegance and Strangeness of Insect Societies.* New York: W.W. Norton.

Wilson, E. O. & Perlman, D. (2000). *Conserving Earth's Biodiversity.* Washington, DC: Island Press.

WMAP Inflation Theory.map.gsfc.nasa.gov/universe/bb_cosmo_infl. html (Retrieved on January 15, 2009).

Wood, B. & Collard, M. (1999). The Human Genus.*Science* 284, April 2, 65–71.

Woolfolk, A. E. (1987). *Educational Psychology.* (3rd ed.). Englewood Cliffs, NJ: Prentice-Hall.

World Health Organization. (November 2004). Water, Sanitation and Hygiene Links to Health.www.who.int/water_sanitation_health/publications/facts2004/en/index.html (Retrieved on February 12, 2009).

World Meteorological Association. (1997). What Human Activities Contribute to Climate Change? www.gcrio.org/ipcc/qa/04.html (Retrieved on December 18, 2008).

World Wildlife Fund. (2008). Living Planet Report, 2008. Online: assets. panda.org/downloads/living_planet_report_2008.pdf (Retrieved on November 13, 2008).

World's Oldest Bacteria Found Living in Permafrost. (2007). *Science Daily*, August 28. Retrieved on January 21, 2009.

Wright, R. (2009). *The Evolution of God*, New York; Little Brown & Company

Zeilik, M. A. & Gregory, S. A. (1998). *Introductory Astronomy & Astrophysics,* (4th ed.). New York: Saunders College Publishing.

Zimmer, Carl. (2007). Keys to Long Life.*New York Times*, June 17.

Music References

Anastasio,T., Gordon, M., Marshall, T. & McConnell, P. (1996) Talk [Recorded by Phish] On *Billy Breathes*. [CD] Elektra.

Anderson, A., Carnes, K. & Johnson, C.D. (2001).Little Bit of This, Little Bit of That. (Carolyn Dawn Johnson). On *Room With A View*. [CS, CD]. Arista.

Bono, Clayton, A., The Edge, & Mullen, L. Jr. (1991). One. (U2). On *Achtung Baby*. [CD, CS]. Island.

Bono. (1987). God Part 2 (U2 and Bono). On *Rattle and Hum*. [LP, CD]. Island.

Burke, J. & Van Heusen, J. (1944) Swing On A Star. (Recorded by Bing Crosby) On Live Radio Broadcast, Recorded WWII, April 15 and June 15, 1944, Laserlight.

Carter, S., Ellis, L., Jones, N., & Wilson E.(2007) Success. (Recorded by Jay-Z) On *American Gangster* [CD] Roc-A-Fella.

Collins, A. & Van Zant, R. (1973) Free Bird.On *Pronounced Leh-Nerd Skin-Nerd*, [CD] MCA.

Cooper, A., Scott, E. & Steele, B. (1982) Adaptable (Anything for You). On *Zipper Catches Skin* (Alice Cooper). [LP] Warner Bros.

Crosby, D. & Kantner, P. (1999). Have You Seen The Stars Tonight. [Recorded by Jefferson Starship]. *On Across the Sea of Suns* [CD] Zebra (2001).

Culture, S. (2009) Conscious. On *Top Class*. [CD] King Step Recording.

DioGuardi, K., Gerrard, M., & Villalon, J. (2007) Human. (Recorded by The Cheetah Girls). On *TCG*. [CD] Disney.

Dylan, B. (1962). A Hard Rain's Gonna Fall. On *The Freewheelin' Bob Dylan* [Album]. Columbia Records.

Geddy, L., Lifeson, A., & Peart, N. (1979). Freewill. (Recorded by Al Rush). On *Permanent Waves*. Mercury.

Gossard, S. & Vedder, E. (1998) Do The Evolution. (Recorded by Pearl Jam). On *Yield*. [LP, CD] Epic.

Halligan, S., Railton, M., Shashani, K. & Torres, R. (2006).The Mating Game. (Recorded by Bitter:Sweet) on *The Mating Game* [CD], Quango Music Group.

Hendrix, J. (1966). Third Stone From the Sun. [Recorded by The Jimi Hendrix Experience] On *Are You Experienced*. [LP,CD] MCA.

Hill, B., Kinchla, C., & Popper, J. (1997) Business as Usual (Recorded by The Blues Travelers) On *Straight On Till Morning* [CD] A&M.

Hunter, R. & Garcia, J. (1976), Lady with a Fan on *Terrapin Station* (Recorded by Grateful Dead) Arista.

Hunter, R., Garcia, J., Lesh, P., & Weir, B. (1970). Truckin. (Recorded by The Grateful Dead). On *Workingman's Dead*. [LP, CD] Warner Brothers.

Islam, Y. (1970). Where Do The Children Play? Recorded by Dolly Parton and Yusuf Islam on *Those Were the Days*. Nashville, Tennessee: Sugar Hill Records.

Jackson, M. (1995) Earth Song. On *History: Past, Present and Future, Book 1*. [LP, CD] Epic.

Jagger, M. & Richards, K. (1968). Just Trying To Do This Jigsaw Puzzle. On *Beggars Banquet* [Album]. London: Olympic Sound Studios.

Jagger, M. & Richards, K. (1969). You Don't Always Get What You Want. On *Let It Bleed*. [LP] London: ABKCO.

Kravitz, L. & Ross, C. (2004) Where Are We Running? (Lenny Kravitz) On *Baptism (Bonus Track)*. [CD]Toshiba.

Lake, G. (1972). From The Beginning. (Recorded by Emerson Lake and Palmer). On *Trilogy* (Cassette). Atlantic.

Lennon, J. & McCartney, P. (1968). Revolution. (The Beatles).On the single *Hey Jude*. [LP] Apple.

LL Cool J. (1995) Doin' It.On *Mr. Smith* [CD] Def Jam.

M.I.A. (2007). Paper Planes. On *Kala*. [CD] XL.

Macmanus, D. (1994) This Is Hell. [Recorded by Elvis Costello]. On *Brutal Youth*. [CD] Warner Brothers.

Marley, B.(1979). Survivor. [Recorded by Bob Marley and the Wailers] On *Survivor* [Album] Tuff Gong.

Mayer, J. (2005) Gravity. (Recorded by John Mayer Trio) On *Trio! John Mayer Trio Live in Concert*. [CD, LP] Aware/Columbia.

McCartney, P. & Lennon, J. (1967) I Am The Walrus. [Recorded by The Beatles]. On *Magical Mystery Tour*. [Soundtrack, EP] Parlophone.

Mike (2002). Save The Humans. (Thought Riot). On *A-F Record Sampler*. [CD] AF.

Mitchell, J. (1969) Woodstock. On *First Family of New Rock*. [LP] Warner Bros.

Mitchell, J. (1970) Back to the Garden. [LP] Reprise.

Morrison, V. (1970). Domino. On *His Band and the Street Choir* [LP] Warner Bros.

Period, J. (2007). The Next Movement.On *The Best of the Roots* [CD] Truelements.

Prestopino, G. & Wilder, M. (1990) Break My Stride (Matthew Wilder). On *A Kick Up the Eighties, Vol.3: Love and Pride*. [CD] UK: Old Gold.

Simon, P. (1966). I Am A Rock. (Recorded by Simon and Garfunkel). On *Sounds of Silence*. [LP, CD] Columbia.

Taj Mahal (1969). Farther On Down The Road.On *Giant Step*. [LP] Columbia.

Toddy, E. & Toddy, H. (2007) Photosynthesis. (Recorded by The Hot Toddies). On *Smell the Mitten*. [CD] Asian Man Records.

Townshend, P. (1967). I Can See For Miles. (Recorded by The Who). On *The Who Sell Out*. [LP] Decca.

Townshend, P. (1969). Amazing Journey [Recorded by The Who]. On *Tommy* (LP), Germany: Decca.

Walsh, J. (1970). Tend My Garden. [Recorded by James Gang] On *Rides Again*. [LP, Cassette) MCA.

Waters, R. (1983) Sexual Revolution. On *The Pros and Cons of Hitch Hiking*. [CD] Columbia Records.

Waters, Roger. (1979) Another Brick in the Wall Part 2 (Pink Floyd).On *The Wall*. [CS] Columbia Records.

Wheeler, C., Simon, L., Hopper, N. & Jazzie B. (1989) Back to Life (However Do You Want Me)[Recorded by Soul II Soul].On *Club Classics Vol. 1* [7" Single, 12" Maxi Single, Cassette, CD Single] UK: Virgin Records.

Winwood, S. & Capaldi, J. (1971). Empty Pages. On *Winwood*. [LP] United Artists.

Writer Unknown, (2000). Portraits Hung in Empty Halls. [Recorded by A Long Winter]. On *Breathing Underwater* [EP] Tribunal (2003).

Your Head, Your Mind, Your Brain (Jack Black) Soundtrack to "School of Rock" (2003) Atlantic Records.

Zawinul, J. (1966) Mercy, Mercy, Mercy. On *Mercy, Mercy, Mercy! Live At The Club*. (Cannonball Adderly Quartet), EMI.

Index

LaVergne, TN USA
29 December 2009

168405LV00004B/2/P